R E A D I N G S for Social Studies in Elementary Education

READINGS for Social Studies in Elementary Education

THIRD EDITION

EDITED BY

John Jarolimek
UNIVERSITY OF WASHINGTON, SEATTLE

Huber M. Walsh
UNIVERSITY OF MISSOURI, ST. LOUIS

MACMILLAN PUBLISHING CO., INC.

NEW YORK

COLLIER MACMILLAN PUBLISHERS

LONDON

Macmillan Publishing Co., Inc.
866 Third Avenue, New York, New York 10022

Collier-Macmillan Canada, Ltd.

Library of Congress Cataloging in Publication Data
Jarolimek, John, ed.
   Readings for social studies in elementary education.

   Includes bibliographies.
   1. Social sciences—Study and teaching (Elementary)
I. Walsh, Huber M., joint ed. II. Title.
LB1584.J29   1974   372.8'3'08   73–3889
ISBN 0–02–360420–4

Printing: 1 2 3 4 5 6 7 8   Year: 4 5 6 7 8 9

Preface

This collection of professional articles dealing with elementary school social studies will be a useful resource for instructors and students in social studies courses as well as for in-service teachers and curriculum workers. For the most part, it includes articles published between 1969 and 1973, with a few articles of special significance selected from the early 1960s. There is little duplication of articles that were included in the first and second editions of this title. Therefore, the three editions present the reader with a sizable portion of the best periodical literature speaking to elementary school social studies published since 1960.

The articles in the three editions of *Readings for Social Studies in Elementary Education* were written and published during a time when social studies education was undergoing extensive study and reform. In reading these selections one can get a feeling for the changing concerns of social studies educators through the early 1960s and up to the present time. In examining the nature of the articles, the editors have concluded that the professional literature today deals with social realities much more profoundly than it did even a decade ago. The literature has become more people-oriented as opposed to being heavily discipline-oriented, as it may have been characterized earlier. There flows through the articles a concern for human values, a quality of humaneness, an attitude of care and concern for the human condition that was not so apparent to the editors in preparing the earlier editions.

The editors have grouped the articles in seven sections. An attempt has been made to arrange the articles to follow one another logically; but, of course, each one can stand alone and no particular sequence needs to be followed in reading them. As in the two earlier editions, entire articles are reprinted rather than what, in the judgment of the editors, would be only significant excerpts. The articles are presented just as they appeared originally in the journals in which they were published. The introductions to the sections were written by the editors and provide the reader with the broad framework within which the selections are to be considered.

The editors wish to express sincere appreciation to the many authors and publishers who kindly consented to have their articles included in the collection. The authors are identified by name in the Contents with their articles. Their present positions and the names of the journals in which the articles appeared are published on the first page of each article. For the convenience of the reader, an Author Index is provided.

J. J.
H. M. W.

Contents

Section Four
Values and the Valuing Process 233

Section ONE

The Social Studies Curriculum in a Decade of Unrest

The events of the past few years have presented Americans with some of their greatest challenges. Since the early 1960s, this society has experienced unprecedented social unrest, characterized by the assassination of high-ranking public figures, campus disturbances, riots in cities, and massive public demonstrations to protest social injustice. Either as a result of or coincidental with this unrest a number of significant social changes have occurred. Clearly the nation has made gains in surfacing and dealing with the evils of racism, even though it still has a long way to go. Progress is being made in ensuring equality of the sexes. The eighteen-year-old vote is now a reality. Great strides have been made in protecting the environment from continued damage through pollution. No one would claim that all of the nation's social ills have been attended to properly. Nonetheless, it is important to note that these problems have at least been brought into the social consciousness of large numbers of Americans for the first time during the past ten years.

Thus, in contemplating the nature, purposes, and organization of elementary social studies, one cannot be unmindful of the sociological, technological, and cultural forces that are at work in the contemporary world, both domestically and internationally. Curriculum models that were adequate for the 1960s are not good enough for pupils in schools of the 1980s. The social forces at work even in local government are so complex that the citizen must be sophisticated in his political knowledge and skill if he is to participate in local civic affairs. Descriptive information about geography, history, and government is not sufficient to equip the citizen to exercise his civic and civil rights—and responsibilities.

The social studies curriculum has come under a considerable amount of study during the decade of 1960–1970. Some of the nation's most prestigious scholars from the social science disciplines, as well as social studies educators, have addressed themselves to problems surrounding the nature, purposes, and organization of the social studies curriculum. Out of their work are evolving some well-defined trends, many of which are discussed in the articles in the first section of this book. Profiting from the thinking of these authors, the reader may himself proceed to formulate his own conception of the nature, purpose, and organization of elementary social studies education.

Perhaps the greatest discontent with social studies programs in recent years has been with those that are largely descriptive and lacking in opportunities for analysis and application of knowledge. What the newer programs seek to do, at least in theory, is to select content and utilize teaching methods that enhance the pupil's thinking abilities. Concern for the thought processes and their development is a major thrust of most of the modern social studies programs. These curriculums therefore incorporate valuing and decision making that lead to responsible social action. The viable programs in social studies education of the present and future will need to provide the learner with knowledge, abilities, attitudes, and skills that equip him to participate intelligently in the social and civic events that surround him in and outside of school. The reader will detect this emphasis in one way or another throughout the articles in this section and in others throughout the volume.

In Pursuit of the Elusive New Social Studies

JOHN JAROLIMEK

There can be little doubt that an impressive amount of innovative effort has been invested in the revision of the social studies curriculum in the past decade. A hundred or more major curriculum development projects were funded at extraordinarily high levels. Twenty-six of those are reviewed and evaluated in the November 1972 issue of *Social Education*. If one adds to this list the several hundred school districts that revised their social studies programs in recent years, the activity in this one area of the curriculum has been very substantial, indeed.

Reform Efforts

Yet in surveying these efforts and evaluating their impact on school practices, one is forced to conclude that they have not, by any stretch of the imagination, revolutionized social studies education. A social studies teacher of the early 1950s who kept abreast of contemporary affairs and current in his scholarly reading could return to many social studies classrooms in the 1970s and feel quite at home. The curriculum projects of the 1960s, whatever their individual merits, have simply not had a profound effect on the social studies curriculums of this nation.

The social studies programs that predated the reform efforts of the 1960s were generally of two types. First there were those that were highly pupil-centered and activity-oriented. They were direct descendants of ideas growing out of the Progressive Movement. At the elementary school level, these programs were characterized by their use of the comprehensive unit of work as an organizing framework. Social studies units were to serve as unifying centers of the total elementary school curriculum. At the secondary school level these programs took the form of the core curriculum, life adjustment, and so-called block programs that combined elements of social studies, language arts, and the humanities. The programs at both the elementary and

John Jarolimek is Professor of Education at the University of Washington, Seattle.

Reprinted from *Educational Leadership 30* (7): 596–599, April 1973, with permission of the Association for Supervision and Curriculum Development and John Jarolimek. Copyright © 1973 by the Association for Supervision and Curriculum Development.

secondary levels emphasized *process* outcomes; subject matter played an essential, but subordinate, role.

The second type of program common in the 1950s was the fact-oriented, history-geography centered traditional approach to social studies. In its worst form it was and is often caricatured to represent all of the unfortunate practices associated with lecture-textbook teaching—reading, reciting, memorizing, answering questions. In its better form, and in the hands of an imaginative and inspiring teacher, this approach helped learners develop a deep and abiding love for the substance of social studies—history, geography, government. Undoubtedly many of the curriculum reformers of the 1960s were first inspired to a lifetime commitment to the study of history or one of the social sciences by some teacher or teachers using approaches of this second type. Certainly the subject-centered, traditional programs were much more numerous throughout the country than were the pupil-centered, activity type.

It is significant that both of these approaches to social studies education came under criticism from the reformers of the early 1960s. The activity-type programs were found wanting because of their substantive thinness. Moreover, the nature of pupil involvement in them gave the impression that such classrooms were "play schools," thereby associating them with the late Progressive Movement, the latter always a target for criticism and ridicule. With Sputnik orbiting the earth, the nation was in no mood for play schools. It wanted work schools.

The traditional programs also drew fire. They were criticized because they (a) placed too much emphasis on memorization of facts, (b) were often inaccurate in subject matter or in emphasis, (c) ignored large portions of the world, (d) were dominated by history and geography, (e) developed little depth of understanding, (f) did not develop independent methods of inquiry, (g) relied too heavily on expository teaching procedures. Other criticisms could be added to this list. Suffice it to say there was little problem in making a case for the need of a major overhaul of the social studies curriculum. But who was to lead social studies out of the wilderness?

The Decision Makers

A fact of profound importance to an understanding of social studies reform of the early 1960s period is the extent to which important decision makers (that is, those who controlled funds for curriculum reform, namely the USOE, the NSF, and the foundations) and the shapers of public opinion were influenced by scholars from the various disciplines. This was true, of course, not only for social studies but for other curriculum areas as well.

Teachers and most particularly what the scholars called "educationists" had little or no role to play in these efforts. As a result, the proposals and projects designed to reform the social studies curriculum reflected a strong discipline bias. The reform model used in developing the "new math" and the "new science" was applied to social studies as well. Accordingly, curriculum projects focusing on economics, anthropology, geography, history, and sociology began to emerge. There was talk at that time of the development of "teacher-proof" curriculums to be prepared presumably by historians and social scientists in order that teachers and educationists could not mess things up. These early reform efforts stressed these ideas:

1. The structure of the disciplines.
2. A focus on basic concepts from the disciplines.
3. The methods of inquiry of the disciplines, especially what was called (probably incorrectly) *inductive* procedures.

Quite naturally, the reformers were critical of teachers for their lack of knowledge of history and the social sciences. Thus, an attempt was made on a massive scale to retrain (or less kindly, retread) practicing teachers. Thousands of teachers attended summer and year-long institutes sponsored and paid for by the USOE, the NSF, or by one of the private foundations. In these institutes teachers were to become familiarized with the latest ideas from history, geography, economics, sociology, or anthropology.[1] Presumably this new knowledge would be needed by the teacher as he began implementing one of the hundred or more new social studies curriculums then under development.

By the late 1960s, certainly by the end of 1968, it was clear that these approaches to the reform of the social studies curriculum were not productive, and the direction of change shifted significantly. The reasons for this shift were in part these:

1. A growing militancy on the part of minority groups and an increased sensitivity to racism.
2. Increased concern for relevancy.
3. Widespread questioning of many values embraced by this society, particularly the nation's involvement in the Vietnam War.
4. Demands for participatory democracy and involvement, with a corresponding questioning of the credibility of the authority in a field.
5. Introduction and legitimization of varying life styles.
6. Rise in strength of the counterculture.
7. A serious breakdown in society's capacity to cope with citizen dis-

---

[1] Regrettably these same institute directors and instructors were doing little, if anything, to change their regular campus courses in these subjects, nor were they doing much to change the teacher education programs on their campuses that produced teachers who immediately needed a retraining program to bring them up-to-date.

satisfaction as evidenced by rioting, burning of cities, assassinations, culminating in the shootings at Kent State and Jackson State.

In view of these developments, the academic approaches being advocated by the reformers made little sense. Looking back, even after this short a time, it does seem strange, indeed, that while the reformers were searching for basic concepts from the disciplines, society was desperately searching for its soul.

The Important Questions

As we moved into the 1970s, therefore, those on the forefront of social studies reform were concerning themselves with quite different matters than their colleagues were a few years earlier. The search for basic concepts was behind, as were shopworn arguments about whether programs should be single subject or interdisciplinary, whether there should be social science or social studies education. Gone, too, were the illusions or dreams of a packaged K–12 social studies program that would work well anywhere if teachers were trained how to use it. Today anyone who is concerned with social studies curriculum development *must* address himself to such questions as these:

1. How can social studies programs be made more meaningful, more highly individualized, and, most important, more *personal* for learners?
2. How can the in-school social studies program be related to the out-of-school lives of pupils?
3. How can the concepts and content of the social sciences, history, and humanities be *used* to provide pupils with insights about the world in which they live?
4. How can social studies programs realistically and truthfully depict the diversity of racial, ethnic, and national backgrounds of the people of this country?
5. How can social studies education become a vital force in combating the evils of racism that flow through the bloodstream of this society?
6. How can social studies programs help pupils build values consistent with the democratic traditions of this society?
7. How can social studies programs help pupils build skills that will enable them to learn how to learn and keep on learning about their social world for a lifetime?
8. How can the social studies program help the learner become a more effective decision maker?

9. How can the social studies program help learners grasp the reality of our international involvements—socially, economically, militarily?

Although the project approaches to curriculum revision have been disappointing in their results, the past 10–12 years have not been without their lessons for us. Actually, much of value has come from these efforts. The use of basic ideas as organizing frameworks for the substantive components of social studies seems to be firmly established, as is the increasing attention being given to inquiry, valuing, reflective thinking, and active social participation by students. There is continued search for ways to represent social reality accurately, to extend the content base of social studies education beyond the conventional disciplines, even beyond the social sciences to include the humanities. Innovative use of various teaching procedures and the use of multimedia are growing. Most important, *some* of the better social studies teachers seem to be helping *some* of the students come to grips with *some* of the great social issues of our times. All of these represent positive gains.

Our experiences with the projects should have taught us that when it comes to curriculums, the home-grown variety is the one that is most likely to survive. Curriculums do not transplant well in a highly decentralized system of education such as ours.

It is to the credit of the major publishers that they have incorporated the best of the ideas generated by reform efforts of the past decade into their programs. Instructional resources are much more in tune with emerging ideas than they were a decade ago. Today a teacher will have no problem finding materials that are conceptually based, inquiry oriented, interdisciplinary, and honestly present the social reality that surrounds young people.

A hopeful sign for the continued revision of social studies education is the work now under way in revising preservice teacher education. With the blending of preservice and in-service education of teachers into one continuous program of professional development, the time lag between development and implementation should be greatly reduced. The closer linkages between and among historians and social scientists, social studies educators, and practicing teachers in the schools should certainly contribute to constructive work in social studies curriculum development, as well as improved teacher education.

The great challenge facing social studies and, indeed, all of education in the years ahead is to teach young human beings how to live with each other peacefully, compassionately, and, above all, charitably. Perhaps the curriculum efforts of the 1960s were necessary in order that social studies programs might, at long last, begin moving in those directions in the 1970s.

Social Studies Curriculum Guidelines

THE NCSS TASK FORCE ON CURRICULUM GUIDELINES

GARY MANSON   ANNA OCHOA

GERALD MARKER   JAN TUCKER

Foreword

One of the important responsibilities of professional organizations is that of articulating and clarifying precisely what constitutes soundly-based professional practice. Consequently, various professional groups have issued formal statements concerning ethical practices, the preparation of practitioners, requirements for licensure, and standards of practice that are acceptable to the profession. The National Council for the Social Studies is issuing two such statements at this time, the statement on teacher standards and this one, a statement on guidelines for the social studies curriculum.

The publication of this document is particularly timely in light of the massive efforts to revise the Social Studies Curriculum that have taken place in the last decade. How is one to evaluate the various approaches to social studies education that have been proposed in recent years? How are school authorities to judge the soundness of the social studies program in their schools? Is a newly proposed curriculum design in accord with the best in recent thinking concerning social studies education? These and many similar questions are being asked by curriculum committees, social studies teachers, supervisors, curriculum directors, and parents in hundreds of school districts across the land. This document should be helpful in responding to these and other questions and issues surrounding the social studies curriculum.

There will doubtless be many questions raised concerning this document. Some will feel that it is too strong in the positions it takes on certain issues. Others may feel that the document is too bland and not sufficiently forceful. Perhaps some will take the position that not enough is known about social studies education to justify a statement of guidelines. The leadership of the National Council recognizes that these are legitimate concerns. The document is not perceived as a statement of standards that will be appropriate for all time, nor even appropriate for all schools at this time. The National Council is saying that after careful examination of recent developments in

Reprinted from *Social Education 35* (8):854–866, December 1971, with permission of the National Council for the Social Studies.

social studies education, and in light of current developments in the larger society, the guidelines presented in this document need to be carefully considered in building a social studies program in the years immediately ahead. If the document is controversial and results in a thoughtful consideration of what a social studies program ought really to be, it will have achieved one of the purposes the National Council had in mind in publishing it.

Whatever disagreements there may be within the profession on certain specific items in the Guidelines Statement, these should not be construed to mean that the entire document lacks validity. It should be stressed that the present document represents the official position of the National Council for the Social Studies on the social studies curriculum. As such, it should be used by teachers, supervisors, boards of education, and other school officials in making decisions concerning social studies curriculum development and evaluation. The National Council is urging its membership to promote the widest possible distribution of this document and to use it as the basis for the evaluation and development of programs in social studies education.

In order to insure that this statement of guidelines will remain under study, the President of the National Council is immediately naming a three-member Review Committee that will be charged with the responsibility of studying curriculum developments and for making recommendations for the revision of the document three years hence. During the next three years it is hoped and expected that the present document will be used, discussed, criticized, and thoroughly critiqued at the local, state, and national levels. Feedback from these deliberations can be used by the Review Committee to prepare a revised set of curriculum guidelines for the latter half of the 1970s.

The preparation of this statement has been an arduous and time-consuming assignment. A great number of individuals have contributed generously of their time and talent to the project. The National Council wishes to express sincere thanks to all who have worked on the document, especially to Gerald Marker, Gary Manson, Anna Ochoa, and Jan Tucker who prepared the original working draft; to members of the Advisory Committee on Curriculum, particularly James Eckenrod, Peter Dow, Paul Flaum, Karen Fox, Helen Greene, Carol Hahn, Howard Mehlinger, Charles B. Myers, Jane W. Mounts, Anthony Petrillo, Ethel Oyan, Patricia L. Johnson, James Ylvisaker, and Frederick Tuttle for their thoughtful and constructive criticisms; to the Advisory Committee on Racism and Social Justice, James A. Banks, Carol Evans, Geneva Gay, Andre Guerrero, Dan Honahni, Peter Martorella, Isadore Starr, and Robert Watanabe for their review of the document; and to Jean Fair, James P. Shaver, and Richard E. Gross for their final review for the Board of Directors.

John Jarolimek, *President*
National Council for the Social Studies

Preface

In November, 1969, the National Council for the Social Studies Board of Directors charged a task force with formulating Curriculum Guidelines useful for setting *standards for social studies programs, K–12*.

These Guidelines, which stem from the Board's charge, purport to serve two somewhat different curriculum development needs.

1. They can function *as a guide for schools and communities, teachers, departments, and school districts interested in updating their programs* especially by incorporating the more promising, recent, and visible developments in the social studies.
2. They can serve *as a baseline from which to move in even more creative directions beyond what most regard as modern and innovative.* For instance, drawing from what is generally known as the "new" social studies, many schools are seeking to develop a systematic curricular scope, sequence, and balance for several grade levels. Other schools, however, have abandoned these customary curriculum-building concepts in favor of a wide-open approach in which teachers and students operate in some variation of the "free-school" movement. This document seeks to serve and encourage both of these trends.

Given the beliefs that no one school of thought can adequately formulate the whole of social studies education; that diversity in social studies education is healthy and productive; that the rate of change in our culture and our profession leads to rapid obsolescence; and that the particulars of curriculum building are most properly a function of individual schools, the Guidelines avoid prescribing a single or uniform K–12 social studies program. They attempt to steer a middle course between suffocating detail and meaningless abstraction, and yet point out legitimate means to worthwhile purposes.

The Guidelines do take positions. Some will arouse little opposition; others may provoke anger. Hopefully, a few will excite.

The National Council for the Social Studies believes that assumptions underlying the development of social studies programs for the 1970s will differ substantially from those of the past decade. The highly cognitive, "structure of a discipline" approach of the 1960s, for example, was a much needed intellectual stimulus for the social studies, and programs of the future will no doubt be more vigorous and powerful as a result of this infusion of research scholarship. But this infusion of scholarly knowledge is at best a very necessary but certainly not a sufficient condition for developing social studies programs in the foreseeable future. *The National Council urges the profession to come to grips more directly with the social problems at hand and the personal concerns troubling young people and adults in every corner of this land.* We should at least entertain the thought expressed by many of these young people that they may be the last generation with a chance to avoid destruction of democratic ideals and perhaps civilization itself.

It is difficult and probably even foolish for anyone to construct a particular social studies program based upon some prediction of the nature of future society. However, it is likely that the future will differ from the present and the past. Consequently, any set of guidelines must argue for greater flexibility and responsiveness to change. Furthermore, schools in general—and social studies education in particular—need to provide better ways for continuous self-renewal. Social studies educators should become good observers and listeners, aware and receptive to the sights and sounds of our growing culture. Nearly a decade ago, Charles Frankel urged that this was a time in the social studies "which calls for self-interrogation, a disciplined dialogue with oneself and others, and effort to find out what the principles are to which we are willing to commit ourselves." [1] The need is even more urgent now. The commitment of social studies education is defined by the kind of social studies programs we are willing to provide for our students.

The task force has had the help of many persons in formulating the Curriculum Guidelines. Members of the Committee on Racism and Social Justice reviewed the document; members of the Curriculum Committee offered helpful suggestions; and a committee of three members of the Board of Directors contributed the suggestions of the Board.

Gary Manson
Michigan State University

Gerald Marker
Indiana University

Anna Ochoa
Florida State University

Jan Tucker
Stanford University

Organization

A "Basic Rationale for Social Studies Education" is the first section of this document. It identifies the theoretical assumptions basic to the guidelines which follow. The Rationale assumes that knowledge, thinking, valuing, and social participation are all essential components of the social studies program and that commitment to human dignity is a major purpose of social studies education.

"Guidelines for Social Studies Education" follow in the second section.

[1] "Needed Research on Social Attitudes, Beliefs, and Values in the Teaching of the Social Studies," in *Needed Research in the Teaching of the Social Studies,* edited by Roy A. Price, Research Bulletin No. 1, The National Council for the Social Studies, Washington, D.C., 1963, p. 28.

They represent characteristics to be found in social studies programs predicated on the Rationale. With each General Guideline is a set of Specific Guidelines intended to clarify the meaning of the General Guideline. A "Social Studies Program Evaluation Checklist" is provided in the third and final section.* Its purpose is to encourage assessment of specific social studies programs seeking to implement the Rationale. If those persons responsible for programs and instruction in the social studies can agree with the Rationale and the Guidelines, then they may find this checklist useful in examining the strengths and weaknesses of their own programs.

I. A BASIC RATIONALE FOR SOCIAL STUDIES EDUCATION

Social studies education has a twofold purpose: enhancement of human dignity through learning and commitment to rational processes as principal means of attaining that end. Although this dual purpose is shared with other curricular areas, it clearly directs the particular purposes and the guidelines for social studies education.

Human dignity means equal access to the rights and responsibilities associated with membership in a culture. In American culture human dignity has long included ideas such as due process of law, social and economic justice, democratic decision making, free speech, and religious freedom. Today that meaning has been extended beyond its political and economic connotations and now includes self-respect and group identity. The idea of human dignity is clearly dynamic and complex, and its definition likely to vary according to time and place. The essential meaning, however, remains unchanged: each person should have opportunity to know, to choose, and to act.

Rational processes refer to any systematic intellectual efforts to generate, validate, or apply knowledge. They subsume both the logical and empirical modes of knowing as well as strategies for evaluating and decision making. Rationality denotes a critical and questioning approach to knowledge but also implies a need for discovering, proposing, and creating; the rational man doubts but he also believes. The ultimate power of rational processes resides in the explicit recognition of each person's opportunity to decide for himself in accord with the evidence available, the values he chooses, and the rules of logic. Therein lies the link between human dignity and the rational processes.

But without action, neither knowledge nor rational processes are of much consequence. This century has witnessed countless blatant violations of human dignity in the presence of supposedly well-educated populaces. It has been frequently asserted that knowledge is power; however, the evidence that people who know what is true will do what is right is scarcely overwhelming. Commitment to human dignity must put the power of knowledge

* This last section has been omitted in this reprinting. [Editors' note.]

to use in the service of mankind. Whatever students of the social studies learn should impel them to apply their knowledge, abilities, and commitments toward the improvement of the human condition.

As knowledge without action is impotent, so action without knowledge is reprehensible. Those who seek to resolve social issues without concomitant understanding tend not only to behave irresponsibly and erratically but in ways that damage their own future and the human condition. Therefore, knowledge, reason, commitment to human dignity, and action are to be regarded as complementary and inseparable.

KNOWLEDGE

From its inception the school has been viewed as the social institution charged with transmitting knowledge to the young. Yet, despite this long-standing responsibility, it would be difficult to demonstrate that the school has handled this task well or that standards of accuracy and validity have been systematically applied to the information presented in the classroom. Nor can many schools assert that their curricula deal effectively with significant and powerful ideas.

Furthermore, the knowledge utilized by the school has reflected the biases of the white middle class and has distorted the role of minority groups. Such distortions have prevented white people as well as members of minority groups from fully knowing themselves and their culture. Such practices are clearly inconsistent with the requirements of individuals in an increasingly complex, pluralistic society.

Knowledge about the real world and knowledge about the worthiness of personal and social judgments are basic objectives of social studies instruction. Reliable beliefs are achieved by following the accepted canons of empirical inquiry, logical reasoning, and humanistic valuing, procedures clearly rooted in the twin values of rational process and human dignity. It would be naive, however, for social studies educators to disregard the fact that many people consider other ways of knowing such as revelation, common sense, and intuition as entirely legitimate and even desirable. A major task of social studies education is to demonstrate the power of rationally-based knowledge to facilitate human survival and progress, while at the same time demonstrating that the means of persuasion to this point of view are quite as important as the ends.

The traditional and obvious sources of knowledge for social studies are the social science disciplines.[2] They are and should remain important sources. However, the reasons for deriving social studies knowledge from the social sciences are not self-evident. Careful thought ultimately justifies such knowledge on arguments revolving around the "needs" of individual students and of society for powerful ideas, dependable information, and reliable methods

---

[2] We include history here, of course, under the social science rubric.

of inquiry. The question about appropriate sources of knowledge for social studies is indeed well-phrased in terms of the "needs" of students and society rather than the arbitrary and limiting assumption that social studies and the social sciences are identical.

Broadly based social issues do not respect the boundaries of the academic disciplines. The notion that the disciplines must always be studied in their pure form or that social studies content should be drawn only from the social sciences is insufficient for a curriculum intended to demonstrate the relationship between knowledge and rationally-based social participation. It is true that the social sciences can make marked contribution to clarifying the basic issues which continue to require social attention. But the efforts of social scientists to develop an understanding of human behavior through research are not necessarily related to society's persistent problems and are seldom intended to arrive at the resolution of value conflicts or the formulation of public policy. In short, one can "do" social science outside the context of the social problems which constitute the major concern of the social studies curriculum. Thus, while there could be no social studies without the social sciences, social studies is something more than the sum of the social sciences.

Other types of knowledge are also important contenders for inclusion in social studies. For instance, an additional and important source may be the growing tip of the culture which has hardly made its way into the research disciplines, but which is diffused through the mass media, sometimes in offbeat sources, and reflected in the arts. Such a growing tip is often found in the interests and values of students. In a rapidly changing society it is often young people who have greatest access to this emergent knowledge. If for no other reason, and there are other reasons, the rate of change alone makes it urgent that the social studies gives serious consideration to the interests and values that students hold about themselves and society. Ideally, then, various sources of knowledge, namely the social sciences, the humanities, the natural sciences, the communication media, and the perceptions of students would all contribute to the social studies program.

The knowledge component of the curriculum envisioned in these guidelines serves three more particular functions. First, it provides historical perspective. A sense of the past serves as a buffer against detachment and presentism—living just for today—and thereby enables an individual to establish a cultural identity. Second, knowledge helps a person perceive patterns and systems in his environment. It is this ordering function which makes the social universe, even with its increasing complexity, more nearly manageable. Recently developed social studies programs utilizing fundamental concepts and generalization from the social sciences represent a current effort to provide such structure. Third is the function of knowledge as the foundation for social participation. Without valid knowledge, participation in the affairs of society will be ineffectual and irresponsible.

In summary, the broad function of knowledge, whatever its source, is to provide the reservoir of data, ideas, concepts, generalizations, and theories which, in combination with thinking, valuing, and social participation, can be used by the student to function rationally and humanely.

ABILITIES

Abilities provide the means of achieving objectives, and one who is able and skillful reaches his objective efficiently. Included in the ability concept are intellectual, data processing, and human relations competencies.

Intellectual skills, usually called thinking, have received widespread attention in the social studies curriculum only recently. The school continues to be largely ineffective in this dimension. Lower-level intellectual operations such as memory often characterize assignments to pupils, questioning, and examinations. Inadequate attention is given to more complex cognitive processes such as analyzing, synthesizing, and evaluating. Inquiry-oriented approaches, which represent one effort to alleviate this situation, are receiving considerable attention in current educational literature, but extensive practice and support are not yet evident.

Thinking competencies serve several functions. In the first place, they provide the prime path to knowledge. They also enable an individual to ask significant questions; they permit him to analyze conflicts; they enable him to solve problems in both convergent and divergent ways; they enhance his decision-making power; and they support his efforts to form and clarify values. Such intellectual skills are of paramount importance in resolving social issues. In democratic societies which place a high premium on responsible flexibility, well-developed thinking processes act as a buffer against intellectual rigidity and represent a vital link between knowledge and social participation.

Although thinking entails a great variety of intellectual operations, two facets, divergent thinking and valuing, require special comment, for they are not only central to social studies education but are also among the more puzzling terms which are employed in the field.

Divergent thinking (defined in terms of flexibility, spontaneity, and originality) seeks uncommon answers to difficult questions. Individuals make the most of their potential powers not by staying with what is common, regular, already known, but by encountering the challenge of the open-ended and unsolved and by attempting to cope with perplexing and sometimes frustrating situations. What is needed is a climate which encourages fresh insights. But the need for divergence is not to be confused with irresponsible deviance or "just being different for its own sake." Divergent thinking is a necessary though not sufficient condition for creativity. Original thinking is highly demanding: (1) it relies on extensive knowledge, ideational fluency, and the ability to formulate and restructure questions; and

(2) it requires the courage to risk uncertainty and error, and to express minority points of view.

Valuing must be considered, in part, as an intellectual operation. Social studies confronts complex questions rooted in conflicting attitudes and values. Therefore it is neither desirable nor possible for social studies teachers to attempt to establish a "value-free" situation in the classroom; student behavior, teacher behavior, subject matter, and instructional materials all are the products of value-laden judgments. Any study of values should be conducted in a free and open atmosphere. Students must become experienced in discerning fact from opinion, objectivity from bias. Students need to learn to identify their own value assumptions along with those of others, to project and evaluate consequences of one value stance or another. When valuing is thought of as a rational process, students can be helped to clarify and strengthen their own commitments.

Data processing skills are often and rightly given considerable attention at the elementary school level. These skills include competence to locate and compile information, to present and interpret data, and to organize and assess source material. Social studies teachers should assume special responsibility for instruction in reading materials directly related to the social studies and in the use of the tools of the social scientists. However, higher levels of proficiency in data processing skills—for example, identifying hypotheses, making warranted inferences, and reading critically—cannot be attained unless they are incorporated in the curriculum of all grades, K–12. If provision is not made at all grade levels for the sequential development of these competencies, growth will be arrested at a needlessly low level, and students will be hampered in employing the more powerful extensions of these abilities.

A third aspect of ability development concerns the competencies associated with social behavior. Effective interpersonal relations seem to depend on a sensitivity to the needs and interests of others, adequately developed communication skills, and the ability to cope with conflict and authority. In the classroom and in the school at large students should have abundant opportunities to work out social relationships at the face-to-face level. Students should have experience in dealing with highly charged emotional conflicts in the social arena as well as with calm, rational inquiry. They should undergo the demands placed on them both as leaders and followers and should learn to make contributions in both roles. When students hold minority views, they can learn to function as thoughtful critics, seeking to bring about needed reform through legitimate processes. Neither aloofness from obligation to other individuals nor the chaos created by anarchy is acceptable.

Abilities are not developed as a result of accumulating information, isolated drill sessions, or exhortations. Instead, these proficiences are acquired only through real opportunities for constant practice and use, systematically planned for by curriculum workers and teachers. Equally important, however, is the recognition of skills as the critical bond between knowledge, valuing, and social participation.

VALUING

Social studies education neither can nor should evade questions of value. Value orientations are the foundations of social institutions, and the value positions of individuals and groups have consequences for action. Moreover, turmoil, discontent, and struggle for change characterize our times. Concern over a host of problems is heard on every hand and markedly so among those who are young. War, racism, environmental pollution, poverty, deteriorating cities, impersonal organizations, alienation, and an unfulfilled quality in living—society can contend with none of these without searching consideration of values.

Social studies education can, however, avoid mere indoctrination. Neither young people nor society will deal constructively with present social realities through blind acceptance of specified ways of behaving, or of particular positions on public issues, or even of basic cultural values. Substantial proportions of young people and their communities are objecting—and overtly—to the rigid requirements of uniformity. Limiting the school's role to indoctrination is not only ineffectual, but incompatible with the principles of a free society.

Still perplexing is the role of the school as an agent for inculcating in the young widely held societal norms, standards of behavior, and ideological preferences. The issue is clouded with conflicting attitudes held by various groups. Cultural pluralism in America rightly hinders the school from seeking or producing uniform values among its students. It is well to remember that the school is properly only one force influencing the values of the young.

However, what the school can contribute is impressive. It can help young people recognize that among men there are many sets of values rooted in experience and legitimate in terms of culture. Such a realization is a force against ethnocentrism.

The school can provide opportunities for free examination of the value dilemmas underlying social issues and problematic situations in the everyday lives of students. Students need systematic and supportive help in examining differences among other persons and groups and in clarifying the value conflicts within themselves. Students must come to understand that for all the importance of evidence, facts alone do not determine decisions, that there are times to suspend judgment, and that many problematic situations have no set answers. The expectation that problematic situations are open to inquiry coupled with increasing ability in the clarification and weighing of values contribute to student's feeling of competence and sense of identity.

We may even have faith that thoughtful sensitivity to one's own values and those of others will foster decent and humane values.

Moreover, the school can make clear its own valuing of human dignity by practicing it in the school as a whole and in social studies classrooms. The school itself is a social institution, and the values embedded in its daily operation can exert a powerful influence. Young children especially must learn the core values in the course of daily living; the school can hardly escape its responsibilties to them. Fair play and justice, free speech, opportunity for decision making, support for self-respect, choice, acceptance of the life styles of the community, group identity, the right to privacy, all these ought to be expected for all students and teachers in every classroom. Racism ought to be denied in every classroom. Schools have been more successful in professing the values associated with human dignity than in making them the order of the day. Indeed, in many schools the practice of those values would mean drastic change. Avoiding blind indoctrination need not mean blandly ignoring basic cultural values.

Frank recognition that the school and its social studies programs cannot be value-free may foster the serious consideration of what the school's role ought properly to be.

SOCIAL PARTICIPATION

Social participation in a democracy calls for individual behavior guided by the values of human dignity and rationality and directed toward the resolution of problems confronting society. The practices of the school and particularly of social studies programs have not provided for active and systematic student participation. Because social studies educators have usually limited their thinking to what has been described as "two by four pedagogy—the two covers of the textbook and the four walls of the classroom"—the potential applications of knowledge and thought have not been fully realized. A commitment to democratic participation suggests that the school abandon futile efforts to insulate pupils from social reality and, instead, find ways to involve them.

Social participation should mean the application of knowledge, thinking, and commitment in the social arena. An avenue for interaction and identification with society can build an awareness of personal competency—awareness that one can make a contribution—an ingredient essential for a positive self-concept. Programs ought to develop young adults who will say: "I know what's going on, I'm part of it, and I'm doing something about it."

Extensive involvement by students of all ages in the activities of their community is, then, essential. Many of these activities may be in problem areas held, at least by some, to be controversial; many will not be. The involvement may take the form of observation or information-seeking such as field trips, attending meetings, and interviews. It may take the form of political campaigning, community service or improvement, or even responsible demonstrations. The school should not only provide channels for such activities, but build them into the design of its social studies program, kindergarten through grade twelve.

Education in a democratic framework clearly requires that such participation be consistent with human dignity and with the rational processes. Such participation must be voluntarily chosen; no student should be required to engage in what he has not defined as desirable. Nor should social participation be undertaken without systematic, thoughtful deliberation. To do so would be to violate the values of human dignity and rational process. Educational institutions can make a significant contribution to society by providing students with the knowledge and experience necessary to be effective, singly or as part of organized groups, in dealing with social problems.

It is essential that these four curriculum components be viewed as equally important; ignoring any of them weakens a social studies program. The relationship among knowledge, abilities, valuing, and social participation is tight and dynamic. Each interacts with the others. Each nourishes the others.

II. GUIDELINES FOR SOCIAL STUDIES EDUCATION

These Guidelines represent a set of standards for social studies programs. They are not intended to prescribe a uniform program or even to propose an ideal program. In a pluralistic and changing society no one such program could be prescribed even if more were known about the process of education than is presently available. Schools—their students, teachers, and communities—have basic responsibility for their own social studies programs. It is hoped that many will develop insights which go beyond the framework of standards set forth here.

1.0 The Social Studies Program Should Be Directly Related to the Concerns of Students.

1.1 Students should be involved in the formulation of goals, the selection of activities and instructional strategies, and the assessment of curricular outcomes.

1.2 The school and its teachers should make steady efforts, through regularized channels and practices, to identify areas of concern to students.

1.3 Students should have some choices, some options within programs fitted to their needs, their concerns, and their social world.

1.4 All students should have ample opportunity for social studies education at all grade levels, from K–12.

Students of all ages confront situations demanding knowledge and social skills. They are called upon constantly to identify, to interpret, to organize the vast quantities of social data everywhere around them. Students need to use this social knowledge perhaps as a person relating to neighbors and friends, a citizen of the school community, a consumer of goods and services, an active participant in an organization or movement. These situations are directly comparable to those confronted by adults. Students should rightfully expect that their social studies education will be helpful to them in coping with their social and political world.

Yet the need to know and understand may stem also from a basic curiosity, a desire to comprehend, and a quest for order and meaning in the universe. Therein lies a fundamental motivation for learning upon which any adequate program must build.

Consequently, opportunities for social studies education should be available to all students from the primary grades through high school, and not merely to some elite group, the intellectually able, perhaps, or the white, middle class, and not merely to those who accept conventional subject matter or are satisfied with their own social situations. Young people should not be expected to fit themselves into uniform or rigid programs, those sanctioned merely by tradition, or designed without consideration of what matters to them.

In schools committed to human dignity, students are entitled to a voice, by one means or another, in shaping their education. All students are entitled to expect that they, their concerns, and their social origins have a place in the social studies curriculum.

2.0 The Social Studies Program Should Deal with the Real Social World.

2.1 The program should focus on the social world as it is, its flaws, its ideals, its strengths, its dangers, and its promise.

2.2 The program should emphasize pervasive and enduring social issues.

2.3 The program should include analysis and attempts to formulate potential resolutions of present and controversial problems such as racism, poverty, war, and population.

2.4 The program should provide intensive and recurrent study of cultural, racial, religious, and ethnic groups, those to which students themselves belong and those to which they do not.

2.5 The program should offer opportunities for students to meet, discuss, study, and work with members of racial and ethnic groups other than their own.

2.6 The program should build upon the realities of the immediate school community.

2.7 Participation in the real social world both in school and out should be considered a part of the social studies program.

The social studies program should enable students to examine the social world as it is, neither "all good" nor "all bad," neither all past nor all present, and certainly not bland. In too many social studies classrooms the social world is idealized, mythologized, far from reality. Three points need emphasis here.

First, these guidelines take the position that enduring or pervasive social issues such as economic injustice, conflict, racism, social disorder, and environmental imbalance are appropriate content for the social studies curriculum for grades K–12. The primary purpose of a social studies program is neither to advance the frontiers of knowledge nor to produce social scientists. Rather its task is to engage students in analyzing and attempting to resolve the social issues confronting them. To do so young people must draw on the content and methods of the social science disciplines as well as their own beliefs and considered values and, whenever and wherever appropriate, on such fields as the humanities and the natural sciences.

Second, the "real" social world varies greatly among people and places, yet classroom experiences often create a misleading impression of cultural uniformity. Many students come to view the world with knowledge drawn almost entirely from Western and middle-class traditions. But the majority of people are not white; although they may be influenced by the West, their cultures are neither Western nor dominated by a middle class. Moreover, American society itself is pluralistic. The mores, roles, and expectations of cultural groups other than students' own should be identified and their implications and merits explored. To seek understanding of any culture without the perspective of its own set of values is to do an injustice to that culture.

The students of social studies classrooms are themselves of diverse subcultural groups, all too frequently not taken into account in developing programs. Family and community studies, for example, may unwittingly attempt to promote normative behavior characteristic primarily of white, middle-class society. Classroom experiences may fail to fit, as they should, the life styles, the values, the aspirations, the perspectives of many students and their communities. Social studies programs must contribute to students' acceptance of the legitimacy of their own cultural group identity as well as the ways of others. Social studies programs which even inadvertently conceal the diversity of the social world tend to reinforce cultural bias and ethnocentricity.

Third, no program can successfully educate students for the real world by separating them from it. The school social system is as much a part of the students' real world as what occurs outside the school. Such techniques as role-playing, simulation, observation, and investigation are all promising means of learning to participate. Actual involvement in school, community, and larger public affairs, either individually or as part of organized group efforts, can break down the artificial barriers of classroom walls.

3.0 The Social Studies Program Should Draw from Currently Valid Knowledge Representative of Man's Experience, Culture, and Beliefs.

3.1 The program should emphasize currently valid concepts, principles, and theories in the social sciences.

3.2 The program should develop proficiency in methods of inquiry in the the social sciences and in techniques for processing social data.

3.3 The program should develop students' ability to distinguish among empirical, logical, definitional, and normative propositions and problems.

3.4 The program should draw upon all of the social sciences such as anthropology, economics, geography, political science, sociology, the history of the United States, and the history of the Western and non-Western worlds.

3.5 The program should draw from what is appropriate in other related fields such as psychology, law, communications, and the humanities.

3.6 The program should represent some balance between the immediate social environment of students and the larger social world; between small group and public issues; among local, national, and world affairs; among past, present, and future directions; and among Western and non-Western cultures.

3.7 The program should include the study not only of man's achievements, but also of those events and policies which are commonly considered contrary to present national goals, for example, slavery and imperialism.

3.8 The program must include a careful selection from the disciplines of that knowledge which is of most worth.

Recent and intensive research has produced what is popularly called "a knowledge explosion." Hence, it will be difficult indeed to close the gap between what is known and what is taught. Yet incongruities between scholarly knowledge and the content of ordinary social studies curriculum cannot be allowed to persist.

Although efforts must be made to insure the accuracy of information used in classrooms, accurate information is not enough. Far more powerful are the concepts, principles, and theories of modern knowledge. It is these which students most need to understand.

Moreover, modern bodies of knowledge are not fixed. Methods of inquiry, such as formulating and testing hypotheses, and techniques for processing social data, such as mapping, case studies, and frequency distributions, should have a place in classrooms.

Since it is patently impossible to "cover" all of man's knowledge of the social world, what is included must be most meaningful. Students need knowledge of the world at large and the world at hand, the world present and the world past. They must see man's achievements and man's failures.

They must have for themselves what is of most worth out of the disciplines. Yet useful ideas from anthropology, economics, social psychology, and psychology are ordinarily underrepresented in social studies programs; ideas from political science and geography are often badly out-of-date. "School history" is often repetitive, bland, merely narrative, and inattentive to the non-Western world; it is distorted by ignoring the experiences of Blacks, Chicanos, native American Indians, Puerto Ricans, and Oriental Americans. Related fields such as law, biology, and the humanities are often omitted or not related to social affairs.

Focus on pervasive issues, problems which loom large in students' worlds, and basic questions which have meaning in students' lives can be helpful in deciding upon what to draw from the disciplines. Imaginative approaches to relating the power of scholarly fields and the issues of our times deserve staunch support.

4.0 Objectives Should Be Thoughtfully Selected and Clearly Stated in Such Form As to Furnish Direction to the Program.

4.1 Objectives should be carefully selected and formulated in the light of what is known about the students, their community, the real social world, and the fields of knowledge.

4.2 Knowledge, abilities, valuing, and social participation should all be represented in the stated objectives of social studies programs.

4.3 General statements of basic and long-range goals should be translated into more specific objectives conceived in terms of behavior and content.

4.4 Classroom instruction should rely upon statements which identify clearly what students are to learn; learning activities and instructional materials should be appropriate for achieving the stated objectives.

4.5 Classroom instruction should enable students to see their goals clearly in what is to be learned, whether in brief instructional sequences or lengthy units of study.

4.6 Objectives should be reconsidered and revised periodically.

Most curriculum guides and courses of study state what are termed objectives. Typical of such statements are these: "Students will come to appreciate their American heritage"; "Students will learn the differences between democratic and totalitarian forms of government." Such statements may serve as goals, but not as objectives. Although such goals may point to the general direction and intent of a program, they have limited utility in making instructional decisions. Worse yet, such conventional and general statements may get in the way of coming to grips with the crucial problem of what students ought to learn.

Probably no curricular decisions are more significant than those about basic purposes and their definition as stated objectives. What students are to learn must be carefully selected through searching and continuous consideration of what is known about the students themselves, the real social world, and the scholarly fields. Students themselves must participate in the process of selection. Students cannot learn everything. Some selection will be made with or without sufficient consideration. What is selected without consideration is not likely to be that which is of most worth.

Decisions about what is to be learned will have little influence until they are translated into statements of objectives formulated in terms of both behavior and content and at a level of specificity which permits recognition of student competencies when they have been attained. Knowledge, thinking and other abilities, valuing, and social participation can all be conceived in behavioral terms and in identified content situations even if their definitions are not universally agreed upon. Statements of objectives become the bases for setting up learning activities, choosing instructional strategies, selecting instructional materials, and finding the degree to which students have been successful in learning.

Special mention should be made here of performance objectives. Such an objective names concretely the behavior-in-identified-content which the student is to demonstrate as evidence of learning and states the minimum level of acceptable performance. Some knowledge and skill objectives in social studies can best be defined as concrete performance objectives, and instruction planned accordingly. Students and teachers alike can identify achievement or lack of it. Performance objectives are most readily developed for matters which have "a right answer" or "a most effective way of performing a task." That all kinds of objectives—indeed, many of the most important—cannot be translated into concrete performance terms need not deny the usefulness of translating some, nor justify vague generalities as substitutes for clear statements. Nonetheless, social studies education should not be limited to what can be defined in concrete performance terms.

5.0 Learning Activities Should Engage the Student Directly and Actively in the Learning Process.

5.1 Students should have a wide and rich range of learning activities appropriate to the objectives of their social studies program.

5.2 Activities should include formulating hypotheses and testing them by gathering and analyzing data.

5.3 Activities should include using knowledge, examining values, communicating with others, and making decisions about social and civic affairs.

5.4 Activities should include those which involve students in the real world of their communities.

5.5   Learning activities should be sufficiently varied and flexible to appeal to many kinds of students.

5.6   Activities should contribute to the students' perception of teachers as fellow inquirers.

5.7   Activities must be carried on in a climate which supports students' self-respect and opens opportunities to all.

Scholars, teachers, educational theorists, and serious critics of education agree, almost universally, that students must be actively involved in the learning process at every level of education from kindergarten on. Modern programs without exception call for more active participation. Greater emphasis is placed on ability to devise questions and the means for answering them, to analyze and integrate knowledge, to propose and evaluate decisions. Conducting a disciplined attack on his own ignorance should be the principal means of an individual's education. Creative inquiry is both a potent instructional strategy and an essential competency. Actual mastery of knowledge, a legitimate but not sufficient goal of education, can best be attained when the knowledge is actively used by the learner.

A social studies curriculum must employ direct as well as vicarious means for learning. This principle is all too often neglected. There are geography classes without any form of field work and history classes without primary source material. Government classes ignore the student council and the workings of local government; a study of occupations goes on without the associated sights and sounds of real jobs; and attempts to deal with racism and poverty occur without emotional involvement. Students study about free speech without practicing it; they read about opportunity for all in sources unsuitable for some of them.

Certainly classroom lecturing is less defensible today than it has ever been. Students now have extensive and reliable sources of knowledge from which they can find out for themselves. Education is more than a process of telling students what they need to know.

Social studies programs, then, must include a wide variety of learning activities with appeals to many sorts of students: making surveys; tabulating and interpreting data; acting out scripts; using reference tools; reading or writing poetry; role-playing; hearing and questioning classroom speakers; writing up a policy decision; using case studies; listening to music; making a collage; brainstorming; studying films; working in a community project; conducting an investigation; advocating a thought-out position; manipulating mock-ups; simulating and gaming; making field trips; comparing points of view; studying social science books and articles; participating in discussions patterned on explicit strategies for behaviors such as communicating and valuing; and more. The purpose of such activities is not to set up what is merely clever or novel, but to offer opportunities for satisfying experience in what will lead to the objectives of instruction.

6.0 Strategies of Instruction and Learning Activities Should Rely on a Broad Range of Learning Resources.

6.1 A social studies program requires a great wealth of appropriate instructional resources; no one textbook can be sufficient.

6.2 Printed materials must accommodate a wide range of reading abilities and interests, meet the requirements of learning activities, and include many sorts of material from primary as well as secondary sources, from social science and history as well as the humanities and related fields, from current as well as basic sources.

6.3 A variety of media should be available for learning through seeing, hearing, touching, and acting, and calling for thought and feeling.

6.4 Social studies classrooms should draw upon the potential contributions of many kinds of resource persons and organizations representing many points of view and a variety of abilities.

6.5 Classroom activities should use the school and community as a learning laboratory for gathering social data and for confronting knowledge and commitments in dealing with social problems.

6.6 The social studies program should have available many kinds of work space to facilitate variation in the size of groups, the use of several kinds of media, and a diversity of tasks.

Learning in the social studies requires rich resources. No single textbook will do, especially one set up with the simple purpose of imparting information. Accomplishing objectives which represent all of the components of social studies education depends upon more information, more points of view, more appeals, more suitability to individual students.

Printed materials must be available for differing abilities in reading, differing needs for concreteness and abstraction. Students must have books, periodicals, basic references, case studies, graphs, tables, maps, articles, and literary materials suitable for the subject at hand. Yet important as reading and, indeed, verbal learning may be, they ought not to be overused in instruction.

Multiple media offer many avenues to learning. Films and sound-film-strips; pictures; recordings of speeches, discussions, and music; mock-ups; artifacts; models; audiotapes; dramatic scripts or scripts for role-playing; diagrams; simulation exercises; programs on television—these and others call upon the use of many senses, thought and feeling, and so enrich learning.

Moreover, resources need not be thought of simply as those of classrooms themselves. The walls between classrooms and the outside world need not be so confining. Students must be "out there," and the resources of community persons and organizations must be "in the schools."

Although the need for multiple media is no excuse for a smorgasbord approach, there is reason to recognize multiple paths to learning. No one sort of material and no one kind of resource will be satisfactory for all students, nor indeed for any one student at all times and for all purposes. Instructional resources must be suitable for the learning tasks at hand and for the students who are learning.

7.0 The Social Studies Program Must Facilitate the Organization of Experience.

7.1 Structure in the social studies program must help students organize their experiences to promote growth.

7.2 Learning experiences should be organized in such fashion that students will learn how to continue to learn.

7.3 The program must enable students to relate their experiences in social studies to other areas of experience.

7.4 The formal pattern of the program should offer choice and flexibility.

Structure in the social studies program has to do with the basic questions to be asked, the problems hopefully to be resolved, the patterns of behavior appropriate to the ends in view. Although far too little is known to identify definitively the processes of growth in social competencies or to state with certainty the superiority of any one sort of organization over another, some sort of flexible structure for the organization of experience is possible and desirable. It is likely that students will profit from experiences with different structures.

Both the social sciences and social issues contain structural elements. Basic concepts, principles, and methods in the social sciences can offer direction in organizing a study of human behavior. A proper focus on social issues requires identification of their causes, consequences, and possible solutions. Social studies programs may at times use one or the other of these organizations. Certainly social studies programs must demonstrate a reciprocal relationship among the social sciences, social issues, and action. However, it is clearly inadequate to limit programs to courses in the individual disciplines. The study of social issues drawing upon more than one discipline is frequently more suitable for the purposes of students in school. An issue arising out of the interaction between technology and the structure and function of modern society, for example, may call for the contributions of history, economics, and sociology as well as the humanities, law, and the natural sciences. Social issues are embedded in complex social conditions.

At times student concerns or those of their community or the requisites of active and effective social participation may become the base for some line of inquiry. Whatever the starting point, whatever the direction, structure must mean the students' own organization of their learning experiences. Social studies programs must offer more than mere accumulation of added information, even that subsumed under scholarly topics or social "problems," activities chosen and pursued out of momentary whim.

On the other hand, disorder and lack of direction stand in the way of continuous reorganization of experience. Moreover, it is time for a fresh look at the conventional pattern of subjects and formal course offerings. Schools ought to encourage mini-courses, or independent study, small group interest sections, specially planned days or weeks focused on social problems, alternative courses of study proposed by students, or other innovative plans for unfreezing the rigid school year. Structure can be used to promote the development of the tools and satisfactions which enable students to continue to learn.

8.0 Evaluation Should Be Useful, Systematic, Comprehensive, and Valid for the Objectives of the Program.

8.1 Evaluation should be based primarily on the school's own statements of objectives as the criteria for effectiveness.

8.2 Included in the evaluation process should be assessment of progress not only in knowledge, but in skills and abilities including thinking, the process of valuing, and social participation—all the components of social studies education.

8.3 Evaluation data should come from many sources, not merely from paper-and-pencil tests, including observations of what students do outside as well as inside the classroom.

8.4 Regular, comprehensive, and continuous procedures should be developed for gathering evidence of significant growth in learning over time.

8.5 Evaluation data should be used for planning curricular improvement.

8.6 Evaluation data should offer students and teachers help in the course of learning and not merely as the conclusion of some marking period.

8.7 Both students and teachers should be involved in the process of evaluation.

8.8 Thoughtful and regular re-examination of the basic goals of the social studies curriculum should be an integral part of the evaluation program.

Social studies programs must be systematically and rigorously evaluated. As program objectives are revised and new practices introduced, the evaluation program must be changed to assess innovations in ways consistent with their purposes. The all too common paper-and-pencil tests of information do not yield data about problem-solving abilities, the valuing process, and social participation, or even, in many cases, that knowledge which is of most worth. Many sources of data, many evaluation techniques, in and out of classrooms, are needed. Evaluation should extend far beyond formal examinations to include, for example, anecdotal records, role-playing, interviews with samples of community people, and interaction schemes for analysis of classroom dialogue.

Occasional and sporadic attempts, and narrow and unreliable efforts in evaluation are insufficient since significant growth in learning is both cumulative and long-term.

Evaluation must include what is diagnostic, not only for groups of students but for individuals. It must be useful to students in the process of their learning—to all students and not merely to those who take to conventional schooling or who are college-bound. A helpful evaluation process ought to enable students to see what they can do as well as what they cannot yet do. The process must clarify for teachers and others concerned what needs to be done to improve instruction and learning.

Evaluation must become not only a means of more effective instruction and learning, but a foundation for thoughtful formulation of basic purposes of social studies education.

9.0 Social Studies Education Should Receive Vigorous Support As a Vital and Responsible Part of the School Program.

9.1 Appropriate instructional materials, time, and facilities must be provided for social studies education.

9.2 Teachers should be responsible for trying out and adapting for their own students promising innovations such as simulation, newer curricular plans, discovery, and actual social participation.

9.3 Decisions about the basic purposes of social studies education in any school should be as clearly related to the needs of its immediate community as to those of society at large.

9.4 Teachers should participate in active social studies curriculum committees with decision-making as well as advisory responsibilities.

9.5 Teachers should participate regularly in activities which foster their professional competence in social studies education: in workshops, or in-service classes, or community affairs, or in reading, study, and travel.

9.6 Teachers and others concerned with social studies education in the schools should have consultants with competence in social studies available for help.

9.7 Teachers and schools should have and be able to rely upon a district-wide policy statement on academic freedom and professional responsibility.

Social studies education cannot be successful without the conditions necessary for good instruction. One of the conditions is a supply of adequate resources. Social studies education needs far more than teachers with textbooks and blackboards. It requires maps, reference books, periodicals, audio and visual materials, field trips, guest lectures, and much more. The classroom should be conceived as a learning laboratory. Such a concept means not only quantities of materials and equipment but also additional demands on teachers' time and competence.

Teachers must have both opportunity and responsibility for active participation in the improvement of the curriculum. They must engage in activities contributing to their professional growth as social studies teachers if they are to offer their students and the community what is due them. Contemporary theories of learning and instruction necessitate breadth, depth, and much skill. The burden is especially heavy on elementary teachers who are expected to be competent in virtually all fields. The practice of assigning inadequately prepared teachers as social studies instructors persists and should be ended. In addition to social studies consultant help, the administration should provide the incentives, encouragement, and opportunities that will further professional and academic training.

School administrators should demonstrate a degree of support at least commensurate with the support given other segments of the curricular program and with the importance attached to the needs of society.

The nature of social studies education, especially in a pluralistic and free society, makes it peculiarly vulnerable to criticism from many sides. The right of responsible criticism is inherent in and invaluable to a democracy; this right must be protected. Demands that schools instill particular beliefs and practices or that they avoid the thoughtful consideration of controversial topics must be met with vigorous resistance.

The Role of the Social Studies

NATIONAL COUNCIL FOR THE SOCIAL STUDIES

The social studies are concerned with human relationships. Their content is derived principally from the scholarly disciplines of economics, geography, history, political science, and sociology, and includes elements from other social sciences, among them anthropology, archaeology, and social psychology. The term *social studies* implies no particular form of curricular organization. It is applicable to curricula in which each course is derived for the most part from a single discipline as well as to curricula in which courses combine materials from several disciplines.

The ultimate goal of education in the social studies is the development of desirable socio-civic and personal behavior. No society will prosper unless its members behave in ways which further its development. Man's behavior tends to reflect the values, ideals, beliefs, and attitudes which he accepts.

Reprinted from *Social Education* 26:315–318*ff*, 1962, with permission of the National Council for the Social Studies.

As used here, beliefs are convictions which tend to produce particular behavior in given circumstances. In authoritarian societies, the behavior desired by the rulers is brought about by fiat, threat of punishment, and manipulation of the emotions. In a free society, behavior must rest upon reasoned convictions as well as emotional acceptance. Knowledge and the ability to think should provide the basis on which American children and youth build the beliefs and behavior of free citizens.

Not all of the knowledge included in the social sciences can be used for instruction in the social studies. Indeed, the accumulation of knowledge in the social sciences is so vast that only a small fraction of it can be dealt with in a school program. Equally important, many of the concepts in the social sciences are too difficult to be grasped fully by children and youth. Since curriculum-makers must, therefore, decide what materials to include and what to omit, criteria for selection have to be adopted. The basic criterion put forward in this document is that those curricular materials should be included which will be most useful in developing desirable behavior patterns for a free society. Consequently, the knowledge included in the social studies will be related to important generalizations about human relationships, institutions, and problems, together with sufficient supporting facts to insure that these generalizations are understood. Instruction will also stress the methods used by social scientists in seeking truth. Some mastery of the methods of scholarly inquiry will enable citizens to make intelligent judgments on the important issues which confront them.

To use knowledge effectively, the student must develop a variety of skills and abilities. To obtain knowledge, one needs skill in locating and evaluating sources of information, in observing, in listening, and in reading. To make knowledge socially useful, one must be able to think reflectively about data and conclusions derived from them. One must also be able to express his views orally and in writing, and have the will and ability to take part in the work of organized groups.

A number of considerations grow out of the brief description of the social studies and what they are good for. Instruction in the social studies is part of the education which should be provided to everyone. The kinds of behavior, beliefs, knowledge, and abilities mentioned in this statement are needed by all members of a free society. To attain the goals suggested, a comprehensive program of instruction in the social studies is required throughout the elementary and secondary school. In addition to the required program, elective subjects in the social studies should be provided so that individuals may pursue and develop special interests. The effectiveness of the social studies program is impaired if it is assigned a host of extraneous responsibilities. Instruction related to home and family living, personal health, and driver education, for example, has been included in the school program by decision of the public. But it is generally accepted that this type of instruction can best be handled by teachers outside the field of the social studies.

The complex task of teaching the social studies involves a heavy responsibility. The effective teacher must have some understanding of all of the social sciences. A comprehensive program for the education of young citizens clearly cannot be limited to instruction in one social science. It is also clear that in a world of rapid and continual change it is impossible to prescribe a fixed and immutable content for the social studies. Even though most of the information currently taught will remain valid and useful, the total body of content will require frequent updating and sharpening as new problems arise and new ways of dealing with persistent problems are discovered.

In summary, this statement includes four major considerations: (1) The ultimate goal of education in the social studies is desirable socio-civic and personal behavior. (2) This behavior grows out of the values, ideals, beliefs, and attitudes which people hold. (3) In turn, these characteristics must be rooted in knowledge. (4) For the development and use of knowledge, people require appropriate abilities and skills. The perpetuation and improvement of our democratic way of life is dependent upon the development of individuals who achieve these goals.

The Behavioral Needs in a Free Society

Behavior is the reaction of an individual in any situation. Most behavior is learned in a variety of ways in the society in which the individual grows up. Some kinds of behavior are not acceptable in a democratic society at any time. It is also true that the process of historical change may demand new ways of acting.

In approaching the problem of behavior the school recognizes that in a democratic society responsibility for appropriate behavior must be assumed by individual members. A democratic society depends upon self-discipline and upon societal discipline approved by a majority. In any free society individuals must be willing and able to participate effectively in the solution of common problems. They must also be willing at times to arrive at decisions reflecting compromises among different points of view. Such compromises are acceptable when they help society to advance toward desirable goals, but the compromises must not result in the sacrifice of those inalienable rights, principles, and values without which democracy cannot survive. While it is true that other institutions share in the responsibility for the development of desirable behavior by members of society, it is also true that education has a great responsibility in shaping the behavior of individuals.

Among the behavioral patterns which may be identified as essential for the maintenance, strengthening, and improvement of a democratic society are the following:

1. Keeping well informed on issues which affect society, and of relating principles and knowledge derived from the social sciences to the study of contemporary problems.
2. Using democratic means in seeking agreement, reaching solutions, and taking group action on social problems.
3. Assuming individual responsibility for carrying out group decisions and accepting the consequences of group action.
4. Defending constitutional rights and freedoms for oneself and others.
5. Respecting and complying with the law, regardless of personal feelings, and using legal means to change laws deemed inimical or invalid.
6. Supporting persons and organizations working to improve society by desirable action.
7. Scrutinizing the actions of public officials.
8. Participating in elections at local, state, and national levels and preparing oneself for intelligent voting in these elections.
9. Opposing special privilege whenever it is incompatible with general welfare.
10. Being prepared and willing to render public service and to give full-time service in emergencies.
11. Engaging in continual re-examination of one's personal values as well as the value system of the nation.

The responsibility for the development of patterns of democratic behavior in pupils falls in large measure upon the social studies program. Behavior grows from the intellectual acceptance of new ideas, changes in attitudes, and the formation of a personal commitment to values which are basic to our society.

The Beliefs of a Free People

Values may be defined as the beliefs and ideas which a society esteems and seeks to achieve. They inspire its members to think and act in ways which are approved. To the extent that actual behavior is consistent with the values claimed, a society is meeting the standards it has set for itself.

A fundamental premise of American democracy is that men and women can be taught to think for themselves and to determine wise courses of action. In choosing a course of action they need to take into account the values which are basic to our society. These values are rooted in the democratic heritage and provide a stabilizing force of utmost importance.

In meeting new situations Americans not only must consider whether possible courses of action are consistent with democratic values but they may need to re-examine the values themselves. Although the basic values of American democracy are permanent, secondary values are subject to change. Furthermore, there is always need for adjustment whenever one value is in conflict with another, as, for example, liberty and authority.

Other agencies than the schools obviously have responsibility for the inculcation of basic values. Nevertheless, a primary objective of instruction must be the development of a better understanding of our value system. At all grade levels, instruction in the social studies should concern itself with the attainment of this objective. To the extent that Americans have a thorough understanding of the values underlying their way of life, and accept this code as their own, they will be able to do their part in achieving the great goals which they have set for themselves.

Among the values which instruction in the social studies should seek to engender in youth are:

1. Belief in the inherent worth of every individual—that each person should be judged on his merit.
2. Belief that all persons should possess equal rights and liberties which are, however, accompanied by responsibilities.
3. Belief that all persons should have maximum freedom and equality of opportunity to develop as they desire, consistent with their capacities and with the general welfare.
4. Belief that individual and group rights must be exercised in such a way that they do not interfere with the rights of others, endanger the general welfare, or threaten the national security.
5. Belief that citizens should place the common good before self-interest or group or class loyalty, when these are in conflict.
6. Belief that freedom of inquiry, expression, and discussion provide the best way for resolving issues; that the will of the majority should govern; that the rights and opinions of the minority should be respected and protected.
7. Belief that citizens should be willing to act on the basis of reasoned conclusions and judgments, even though personal sacrifice is involved.
8. Belief that government must be based on properly enacted law, not on the caprice of men holding office; that government has a responsibility for promoting the common welfare.
9. Belief that people are capable of governing themselves better than any self-appointed individual or group can govern them, that political power belongs to and comes from the people; and that the people have the right, by lawful means, to change their government.
10. Belief that the freest possible economic competition consistent with the general welfare is desirable; that government has the obligation to stabilize economic growth and reduce gross economic inequalities.

11. Belief that both competition and cooperation are essential to the democratic process and to our national well-being.
12. Belief that the separation of church and state is essential.
13. Belief that maximum individual freedom, under law, throughout the world is the best guarantee of world peace.
14. Belief that change in relations between nation states should be accomplished by peaceful means, and that collective security can best be achieved within an organization of nation states.
15. Belief that Americans should work to achieve a world in which justice and peace are assured to all mankind.
16. Belief that Americans should have reasoned devotion to the heritage of the past, and a commitment to perpetuate the ideals of American life.

The foregoing beliefs and values have been subjectively derived. Quite possibly other lists would provide a different sequence and use different language. But the important point is that there would be a high degree of agreement on the basic beliefs included in such lists. A major purpose of instruction in the social studies is to help children and youth understand basic American values and develop loyalties to them. To attain this goal it is necessary to take values into account in the selection of content for social studies courses.

The Role of Knowledge

The attainment of goals in the social studies depends upon the acquisition and utilization of information, facts, data. Each of the social sciences, in effect, is a reservoir of knowledge to be used. But the kind and amount of knowledge which can be used from one or more disciplines is necessarily determined by curriculum requirements associated with a particular stage in the educational process. In any event, one cannot be concerned with the goals of social studies instruction without being drawn immediately into considerations of content. The National Council for the Social Studies, consequently, has made frequent examinations of content areas, notably in its yearbooks to which distinguished social scientists have contributed.

In the last few years the National Council for the Social Studies has recognized the necessity for making a more comprehensive study of the social studies curriculum. One report, issued in 1957, carries the title: *A Guide to Content in the Social Studies*. This report listed 14 themes which were proposed as guidelines for the selection of content. A second report, published in 1958, is called *Curriculum Planning in American Schools: The Social Studies*. The group which prepared this report showed special interest in the advances made by social science research in recent decades and was concerned that these findings be reflected in school programs in the social studies. Beyond noting some limited illustrations of these advances, the report underscored the need for cooperative effort among social scientists, educators, and teachers in the planning of the social studies curriculum. In such planning a fundamental problem would be the development of agreement on principles to be used in the selection and grade placement of content. Teachers have long recognized that the reservoirs of social science knowledge hold an embarrassment of riches. Indeed, the study of any one of the social sciences alone might well require all the time available in grades 1 through 12.

The Role of Abilities and Skills

If young people are to command the knowledge and develop the behavior and beliefs enumerated above, they must develop a variety of skills for locating, gathering, interpreting, and applying social studies information. Stated in another way, the purpose of teaching skills in social studies is to enable the individual to gain knowledge concerning his society, to think reflectively about problems and issues, and to apply this thinking in constructive action.

The need for the systematic teaching of social studies has become increasingly urgent for a number of reasons. With the development of modern media of mass communications and the expansion in the amount of scholarly material, there has been an enormous increase in the quantity and variety of social data that the citizens must deal with in locating and selecting information that is pertinent to a given issue. With the refinement and increasingly pervasive use of persuasion techniques in many areas of daily living, there is a correspondingly greater need for skill in appraising information and evidence and the sources from which they come. With the complicated forms of social organization which develop in an urbanized society, new skills of group participation are essential for effective action.

The development of some of these skills is the special responsibility of the social studies, such as those involved in understanding time and chronology. Others are shared with other parts of the school program, but have special application in social studies. The list of proposed objectives centering on abilities and skills includes both types, for students need both to deal with social studies materials.

The acquisition of abilities and skills is a form of learning. Consequently, some principles to guide instruction in them are essential to their development. These abilities and skills must be identified with sufficient concreteness so that the description helps in planning instruction and in evaluating various degrees of mastery. It seems clear that these abilities and skills cannot be developed in a vacuum but must be acquired by pupils as they study content derived from the social sciences. The nature of these abilities and skills is such that they will not be learned—nor should they be taught—incidentally, but rather through planned and systematic treatment. Effective instruction will recognize that the maturity of the students will largely determine at what grade level given abilities and skills can be developed most effectively. Teachers must also take into account that these abilities and skills should be developed in situations as nearly like those in which they will be used as possible, and that repeated practice will be needed if students are to become skillful in their use. Even so, there will be large differences in the facility with which students use skills at any grade level, as well as in the competence achieved by the end of the secondary school. The nature of these abilities and the individual differences exhibited by students indicate that complete mastery of most of them is never achieved. But the goal is to help each student achieve the highest level of performance each year that his own potential will permit.

The objectives listed in this statement involve abilities and skills needed for effective behavior; the abilities peculiar to the social science disciplines must be developed further as the college student pursues his specialized studies.

I. Skills centering on *ways and means of handling social studies materials*

    A. Skills of locating and gathering information from a variety of sources, such as:

        using books and libraries effectively, taking notes, using the mechanics of footnoting and compiling bibliographies

        listening reflectively to oral presentations

        interviewing appropriate resource persons and observing and describing contemporary occurrences in school and community

    B. Skills of interpreting graphic materials, such as:

        using and interpreting maps, globes, atlases

        using and interpreting charts, graphs, cartoons, numerical data, and converting "raw data" into these graphic forms

    C. Skills needed to develop a sense of time and chronology, such as:

        developing a time vocabulary and understanding time systems

        tracing sequences of events

        perceiving time relationships, between periods or eras and between contemporaneous developments in various countries or parts of the world

D. Skills of presenting social studies materials, such as:
organizing material around an outline
writing a defensible paper and presenting an effective speech
participating in a discussion involving social problems

II. Skills of *reflective thinking as applied to social studies problems*
A. Skills of *comprehension,* such as:
identifying the central issues in a problem or argument
arriving at warranted conclusions and drawing valid inferences
providing specific illustrations of social studies generalizations
dealing with increasingly difficult and advanced materials

B. Skills of *analysis and evaluation* of social studies materials, such as:
applying given criteria, such as distinguishing between primary and secondary sources, in judging social studies materials
recognizing underlying and unstated assumptions or premises, attitudes, outlooks, motives, points of view, or bias
distinguishing facts from hypotheses, judgments, or opinions, and checking the consistency of hypotheses with given information and assumptions
distinguishing a conclusion from the evidence which supports it
separating relevant from irrelevant, essential from incidental information used to form a conclusion, judgment, or thesis
recognizing the techniques used in persuasive materials such as advertising, propaganda
assessing the adequacy of data used to support a given conclusion
weighing values and judgments involved in alternative courses of action, and in choosing alternative courses of action

C. Skills of *synthesis and application* of social studies materials, such as:
formulating valid hypotheses and generalizations, and marshalling main points, arguments, central issues
comparing and contrasting points of view, theories, generalizations, and facts
distinguishing cause-and-effect relationships from other types of relationships, such as means and ends
combining elements, drawing inferences and conclusions, and comparing with previous conclusions and inferences
identifying possible course of action
making tentative judgments as a basis for action, subject to

revision as new information or evidence becomes available
supplying and relating knowledge from the social studies as
background for understanding contemporary affairs

III. Skills of *effective group participation*
   A. Assuming different roles in the group, such as gadfly or sum-
      marizer, as these roles are needed for the group to progress
   B. Using parliamentary procedures effectively
   C. Helping resolve differences within the group
   D. Suggesting and using means of evaluating group progress

Certainly a major purpose of social studies instruction is to place emphasis on the development of those abilities which encourage the accurate
and intelligent utilization of social science data and which make habitual
the orderly processes of mind necessary to carrying on reflective thought
and to taking action based on such thinking.

Looking Ahead

This preliminary statement of goals for the social studies is but a first
step in a process that looks forward to making recommendations for the
social studies curriculum in our schools. There remains for the future the
major task of working out a logical sequence of grade placement that will
present a systematic overview for the social studies curriculum. Here, there
must be concern for a sequential development of the essential knowledge,
skills, and attitudes that should be acquired by pupils going through the
school program. Also consideration must be given to programs for pupils
of widely varying abilities. Some experimentation with programs seeking to
achieve all the objectives set forth will in all probability be called for in
order to evaluate their effectiveness. Finally, it should be recognized that
there is no single way in which the materials can be best organized in arriving at the goals, but that several alternative patterns might well be suggested.

. . . .

Wanted—Social Studies in the Primary Grades

WILLIAM L. WALKER

Among the tasks facing education none is of more importance, exacting or demanding than that of the school to assist the young to acquire the social learnings which will enable them to function as responsible, effective members of a democratic society. Today we live in a complex, ever-changing, unpredictable society that prevents us from establishing dogmas that can set forth what the citizen should know. It is obvious that within our democratic society there exist enormous social problems. More in evidence each day is the impact of social, industrial, and technological change upon the child's place in society and the necessary adaptations of the child and society to the enrichment of both. The child has ready-made demands of society confronting him at an early age.

Within our emergent and broader conceptualization of the function and role of the school and in the midst of all the change going on about us, social studies is designated as the curriculum area which can best help orient children into society. If we desire children to gain a knowledge of the basic concepts in this area of the curriculum, then they need early contact with these concepts and a substantial foundation laid for such learnings in the primary grades. Even though the social education of children in an elementary school is only a part of their general education, it is an important part. The school discharges a large part of its obligation for social education through its organized social studies program.

Listed among the objectives in any typical social studies program are those designed to develop understandings, skills, and attitudes. The frame of reference in which these terms are used inevitably refers to the achievement of knowledge which can be used to develop understandings, make generalizations, draw conclusions, and solve problems; the development of thinking skills for problem solving and the development of skills and abilities necessary to produce democratic behavior; and the organizing of academic and social skills into attitudes which permit the individual to become his own best self and effect a satisfactory relationship with his society.

If we believe that proficiency in human relations is important in achieving one's self-realization as well as maintaining a democratic society and that these learnings can and must be taught at an early age: Why do inade-

William L. Walker is an Associate Professor of Elementary Education at the Indiana State University, Terre Haute.

Reprinted from *Contemporary Education* 41:289–292, 1970, with permission of the Indiana State University and William L. Walker.

quate primary social studies programs still exist? What price are we paying as a democratic society for poor, inadequate, or unplanned social studies programs in the primary grades?

Why do inadequate primary social studies programs still exist? The teacher functioning in the practical realm of the classroom finds increased enrollments and thus increased class size not only causing certain aspects of classroom management to be more difficult, but, more importantly, creating problems in instruction. With more children we get more individual differences, making it increasingly difficult for the primary teacher, through her instructional program, to provide for these differences adequately. As class size increases instructional time per pupil obviously decreases. Frequently the student now getting less individual attention needs more time for learning.

The strong pressure from all curriculum areas upon the classroom teacher to improve the quality of instruction in particular areas and to increase the quantity of that area in the total program presents the teacher with some practical, operational problems. The emphasis placed upon the areas of reading and language arts in the primary grades, coupled now with increasing emphasis on modern mathematics and science, plus a high proficiency expectation or a new program implementation in these areas places the classroom teacher in a dilemma. Since social studies is not as clearly defined, particularly operationally, nor as immediately accountable in the education of primary children—in the sense of Johnny's being able to read or not read, knowing his numbers or not knowing, being able to shape his letters properly—it becomes a neglected area.

The school administrator caught in the same kind of spiraling, changing world and faced with many of the same problems and pressures as the classroom teacher, frequently does not rank social studies in the primary grades as important. Thus he often does not offer the same intensity of instructional leadership in this area, is less familiar with social studies materials than, say, science or modern mathematics where lists of materials acceptable under NDEA have been prepared, and feels justified in spending less money to support the social studies program at the primary level.

There is a lack of well-defined purpose for social studies. Inadequate social studies programs are often produced because objectives are so vague or broadly conceived that it is difficult to structure an adequate program around them, or objectives are viewed under a separate subject concept with history and geography traditionally leading the way. Frequently objectives from other disciplines such as economics, political science and sociology, which are more closely related to the child's firsthand experiences, are not present to provide clearer direction. Teaching democratic values is a basic concern of social studies, yet not all teachers have the capacity to work harmoniously with children in activities where such values are truly observed.

Social studies is a broad field of study consisting of a number of disciplines from the social sciences and the teacher may not be sufficiently acquainted with all the disciplines involved to understand what might be learned at the primary level. Since social studies is a combination, there exists controversy over what proportion of each discipline ought to go into the combination and what form or structure should result. The lack of definitiveness about what constitutes the social studies and about what proportion of content should be drawn from each discipline further complicates the primary teacher's job and sometimes leads to an inability to cope with the situation; hence a withdrawal from teaching social studies.

The use of methods that still make learning largely a matter of reading and verbalization, too much emphasis upon textbooks, compartmentalization of the subject matter of the social sciences, and poorly conceived methodological practices continue to contribute to inadequate programs. The frequent overemphasis upon memory and recitation of subject matter often deals the "death blow" to interest and the normal, curious inquiry young children possess. Too many teachers, being sensitive to subject matter, still adhere to mastery of this subject matter to the neglect of social learnings. This develops an attitude that social studies is of little value since it is composed of such meaningless, unrelated factual knowledge. Changes in what constitutes readiness and recent developments concerning how children learn are not considered by many teachers. For many and various reasons, teachers fail to remain abreast of current trends in methods, present problems of a social, economic and political nature, and research findings.

What price are we paying as a democratic society for poor, inadequate, or unplanned social studies programs in the primary grades? We have long recognized that social learnings and attitudes develop outside of school. Children not only arrive at school at age five or six with many well-defined attitudes and social learnings but they continue to live in an out-of-school environment filled with stimuli that help reinforce and refine these and develop new ones. The lack of a well-planned social studies program in the primary grades continues to permit social learnings to be formed outside the deliberately structured environment of the school and without the educative process playing its proper role, which means that the school is not properly serving one of the functions society expects. The deepening, broadening, correcting, developing aspects of children's social learnings are lost or become an incidental part of the instructional program. Failure to offer a program within which healthy attitudes can be developed blunts the school's deliberate influence on the growth, expansion, modification, and development of attitudes in each child during this formative period. This is particularly unfortunate when we realize from the field of child growth and development that early school years are a foundational period in a child's development and that the teacher often becomes a significant factor in this development.

The need to begin conceptual development in the content of social studies at an early age has become apparent. Our concept of learning has shifted from an emphasis on learning facts and knowledges to relating experiences, facts, and ideas in order to develop understandings that will be meaningful and significant to the child. Certainly one cannot derive understandings in a vacuum. Facts, data, information, knowledges are still necessary but the content to be learned depends upon the life of each child and the life of others around him. Inadequacy in the early social studies program leaves the child with a poor start in gaining a knowledge of man and his relationship with other men and the world, a serious deficiency when the socializing and democratizing function of the school is considered.

Educational objectives, and concurrently the objectives of social studies, are being conceived more in functional, operational, and behavioral terms centering on the idea of development of the rational powers of the human mind; yet without a well-planned social studies program in the primary grades, skill development is left to the less desirable area of incidental learning. The task of helping children to learn to think, to improve their problem solving and creative skills, and to develop their decision-making and social, democratic living skills must be carefully and deliberately planned if these skills are to be taught effectively. Since well-planned social studies programs include deliberate skill development, the importance of this area is lost to children who fail to have such programs in the primary grades.

Failure of the schools to provide meaningful, life-like experiences through their deliberately structured environments tends to widen the gulf between life in school and life outside. School experiences must relate to those outside the school in order to be meaningful. Social learning is achieved through such appropriate kinds of experiences and their depth. Experiences intended to create or modify attitudes, to provide learnings essential to effective living for each individual, to make school more significant and influential, to aid in more accurate comprehension, to stimulate interest, and to help children become thinkers who will be able to perform intelligently are all an important part of the learning program in social studies for primary grades. Inadequate experiences in this realm unfortunately lead to poor learning. Sound learning experiences are vital.

How can we help primary children to begin to arrive at an orderly view of their society?

Despite increased concern about social studies at all levels, new special projects, more research and literature in the field, and increased communication with classroom teachers, the behavior of many primary teachers has not been affected. One can readily see the humble and retarded status of social studies in numerous primary classrooms. Certainly by recognizing the previously noted realities with which the classroom teacher must live, it is somewhat more understandable why we have effected so little behavioral change toward social studies. Yet, the classroom teacher is the key person in conveying the contributions that the social studies have to make to the education of children in a democracy.

More primary teachers need to recognize the value of placing children in situations and activities that allow for experiencing the responsibilities of group living at an early age. Direct experience in social studies through a well-planned, well-taught program is essential. All primary children do not possess the same readiness for social studies, but all have a need and are ready for the opportunity to grow in this area. Direct experiencing through sampling actual processes of social and economic life and through doing real work or problem solving is necessary.

We have begun to realize that it is in the primary grades where the foundations for all future learnings are laid. Learning how to examine and organize whatever content is selected for study must begin early in the primary grades as a method of attack whereby the child can learn to make generalizations about social behavior and to revise these general ideas as he encounters new evidence or content in social studies. The role of social studies in the elementary school has plainly become one of preparing children to live effectively now as well as in the future. All children must be provided the opportunity to learn to understand the society in which they live and the demands it makes upon them. They must have opportunity to build within themselves the learnings necessary for effective participation in their society. A democratic society requires individuals to exercise judgment in one situation after another.

Ideal social learnings are only partly attainable at best. Yet, if a primary teacher does an unsatisfactory job of orienting her pupils into society because of the lack of an adequate social studies program, what price are we paying? In essence, without a good social studies foundation whereby primary children grow in understanding their social, economic, and political world we cannot hope to develop a program through which children will be prepared, better than in the past, to handle their problems and to accept and strive for improvement of this world in which they live. Let's start improving the foundation of social studies in the primary grades so that even the young acquire the social learnings which enable them to function as responsible and effective members of a democratic society.

Elementary Social Studies in Transition

LLOYD N. SMITH

The early elementary schools of this nation did not include in the curriculum the field of study which we now refer to as social studies. As a matter of fact it was not until the early and middle 1800s that such subjects as geography and history began to emerge. Even then instruction in these fields was a "hit and miss" sort of thing. Not until the end of the nineteenth century did definite patterns for the social studies, as known at that time, begin to appear. It was largely through the work of professional organizations and special committees and commissions that a formal program for the social studies in the elementary schools developed.

Out of this work came rather fixed instructional programs which had definite scope and sequence and included the traditional subjects of history, geography, and government as the main part of the program. This pattern was largely one of so-called expanding environment. The sequence was rather "fixed" as it was thought that a pupil needed to learn things in a definite sequential order. This period was also one of complete textbook domination.

In due time there came a revolt against a scope and sequence that were "set and congealed" like concrete and the pendulum then moved from the extreme right to the extreme left, a swing which resulted in many schools having the so-called "incidental" programs in which little or nothing was structured. Shortly, there came a reaction against the incidental programs and, more recently, several trends emerged. Among these some of the following are the most notable:

1. There is a return to greater emphasis on organization and structure.
2. The concept of social studies has broadened to include areas not formerly included such as sociology, economics, and anthropology.
3. Greater emphasis on inquiry and concept development, thinking, as well as problem solving and research, rather than rote memorization of facts is evident.
4. Because of the increasing complexity of knowledge in the social sciences help from scholars in the various disciplines is being used.

Lloyd N. Smith is a Professor of Education at the Indiana State University, Terre Haute.

Reprinted from *Contemporary Education* 42:241–243, 1971, with permission of the Indiana State University and Lloyd N. Smith.

5. Attention is being given to development of increasing breadth and depth of understandings in the field.
6. Efforts are being made to develop clear understandings of other cultures.
7. Topics originally reserved for older children are now being taught at much earlier ages.
8. Much less concern is being expressed over sequence than in earlier years.

In 1957 Russia gave us Sputnik. With that event there came a barrage of charges against education in this country crying out that our people were far behind Russia in science and mathematics. Immediately pressure was brought by a disturbed citizenry which resulted in legislative enactments providing federal funds for special programs in science, mathematics, and foreign languages. Numerous programs in these fields were funded, millions of dollars being spent on them. These programs were so much in the foreground that for several years other portions of educational programs could not be seen. It took some time to convince the leaders of this nation that many of the problems of the country stemmed as much from a lack of human relations "know-how" as from a lack of scientific "know-how," that much of our trouble today is the lack of ability to sit down with peoples of the world and solve our problems at the intellectual level rather than from the standpoint of a strong power structure. With the realization of this fact programs in the area of the social studies were funded federally starting in the early 1960s.

Over a period of time more than forty social studies curriculum projects were developed. Perhaps as many as a dozen of these projects will have a definite impact on the elementary social studies curriculum of the future. After a decade of experimentation with the various projects, printed materials have begun to move to the schools of the nation. The projects are quite varied in goals and procedures and will, without a doubt, be used by different teachers in a variety of ways. Some trends and characteristics of the projects might be noted as follows:

1. Some projects attempt to take an interdisciplinary approach, but others emphasize a single discipline such as economics or anthropology.
2. Most projects show concern for structure of knowledge and claim to use inquiry and/or discovery teaching strategies.
3. Some projects stress cross-cultural studies, while others take a single culture approach.
4. Depth studies seem to be stressed rather than general surveys.
5. Some projects have thrown overboard the idea of expanding horizons and sequential development.

6. Many projects have developed a wealth and variety of materials to accompany the project rather than having to depend on the school library for such.
7. Recognizing the need for teacher preparation and guidance, many projects have developed background materials for teachers.
8. Most project materials have been field tested in practical classroom teaching situations and many have been revised a number of times, ultimately being published commercially.

Having come to the end of the decade of the sixties, surely it is time to stop and take inventory to determine where we have been and perhaps where we are and should be going. A good, long, hard look needs to be taken at our objectives in terms of real life situations for the years 1970 to 2000 and beyond for the children in the elementary schools of today who live out a normal life span will live a good portion of their lives during the twenty-first century. It is of course impossible to anticipate what life will be like in the very near future much less fifty years hence, but nonetheless the schools of the immediate future are producing the citizens of that era. Added to that problem there is also the much-discussed "explosion of knowledge" which has been taking place at a terrific speed during the past quarter of a century and which at the present time shows no sign of diminishing even in the future—much of this explosion is in the area of the social studies. These two considerations alone should cause us to take stock of our objectives for the social studies programs of the elementary schools.

It is hoped that out of the ferment of recent years and from the recent experimentation there will come programs which will meet the needs of future generations. Teachers, supervisors, and administrators will have to work together in deciding on suitable objectives for social studies programs of the future. Once the objectives have been decided upon they will then have to develop the best possible programs designed to meet these objectives. Ultimately the new programs will have to be evaluated in terms of their effectiveness—the ability of children and adults to function adequately in modern society.

Knowledge is presently so extensive that any one person can master only a very small portion of it within a lifetime, so it makes sense that the portion learned should consist of truly significant information. This means that social studies programs of the future will have to help children learn how to think, how to locate needed information, and how to solve problems. Equipped with such tools the citizen of the future would then be prepared to set about finding solutions to problems, of whatever nature, which must be solved in order that all peoples of the world may live together in peace and harmony.

In order for this dream to be fully realized it will be necessary for children to be treated as individuals. This will require adequate school staffs and a wide variety of instructional materials. It means that the best principles of child psychology and of learning will have to be applied.

Although much has been accomplished in elementary social studies in recent years, there are still many problems that need consideration. We must continue to search for more effective programs, experiment with the programs, and ultimately incorporate them into the elementary school curriculum.

Elementary Social Studies: Content Plus!

HUBER M. WALSH

In response to the widely recognized need for broader content emphasis in elementary social studies, teachers, curriculum workers and professors are effecting searching analyses and extensive revisions of existing programs. A result of this activity has been the emergence of a "new look" in elementary social studies in which programs are based (more distinctly than before) upon content drawn from the social sciences. In general this approach focuses upon major understandings or generalizations which are widely applicable key ideas taken from academic disciplines such as geography, history, sociology, anthropology, political science and economics.

Many persons welcome this approach for it promises to advance elementary social studies in several significant ways. *First,* this plan permits a more direct relationship between elementary social studies instruction and the parent social sciences—a relationship long in coming. *Second,* instruction built upon major understandings from the social sciences holds the promise of generally upgrading content coverage in the elementary school. *Third,* instruction in key ideas, according to authorities, can promote deeper comprehension, result in better transfer of knowledge and facilitate subsequent learning (2,4). Perhaps the greatest value of such instruction is that it prepares the learner for independent study (1).

Worthwhile though it is, this instructional plan may not be the panacea which many persons are seeking. Indeed, if made the sole basis for teaching, it could produce an undesirable imbalance in the social studies program. Present society demands that the schools of today equip future citizens with two essential ingredients for successful living: *knowledge* and *skill in work-*

Huber M. Walsh is Professor of Education at the University of Missouri, St. Louis.

Reprinted from *Childhood Education* 43:124–126, 1966, with permission of the Association for Childhood Education International and Huber M. Walsh.

ing effectively with others. Bringing youngsters into contact with big ideas from the disciplines will expose them to basic knowledge about man and his interrelationships. But, the acquisition of such information does not *ipso facto* insure the pupil will then apply appropriate aspects of this knowledge to improve *his own* human relationships. Teachers know that sometimes the child most able to verbalize eloquently about desirable behavior (*e.g.,* feelings of tolerance, patience with others) proves to be most inept in practicing what he preaches; obviously he has not learned beyond the level of sheer verbalism. If children are to extend knowledge beyond verbalism they must put it to work in deeds. This requires systematically planned learning experiences in which the pupil has the opportunity to *apply* what he has learned about desirable human behavior. These kinds of learning activities are the essence of what is commonly referred to as *social education.* Content alone, without provisions for social education, is not enough.

Content Plus

The child needs content *plus* social education. Content alone cannot constitute the whole social studies program any more than social education alone—both are essential and complementary, both must be in sensible proportion in a sound program designed for society's needs.

The present emphasis on subject matter does not automatically imperil acquisition and practice of important social learnings; but in some situations this stress on subject matter has been accompanied by a devaluation of social education. One reason is that educational respectability attaches more to the teaching of content than to the development and practice of social education. The danger is that social learnings in the elementary school will continue to receive diminished attention. If certain critics have their way, social education will be abandoned despite society's needs to the contrary (6). In some classrooms acquisition of information is regarded as an end in itself. Comprehension of key ideas and concepts is seen as the principal and exclusive instructional outcome. Little or no attention is given to providing social settings which give children opportunity to apply some of this knowledge in their day-to-day relationships under the guidance and direction of the classroom teacher. When this happens, teachers can miss determinate kinds of learning contacts in which the child's skill in human relations can be appraised, diagnosed and improved.

Overemphasis on content could now weaken the effectiveness of social studies programs in much the same way as overemphasis on social education did in the past. The former cry of critics was that the elementary child was being "socialized to death." Unless we avoid rushing to the opposite extreme, their future criticism may well be that the child is being "intellectualized to death." Why should we sacrifice either when we can have both? There is no reason to make it an "either/or" case. A sensible middle course can be maintained—*both* subject-matter and social learnings can be developed simultaneously without sacrificing either. They are compatible and complementary. Many social learnings taught and practiced in the elementary schools are predicated upon human relations skills closely allied to the funded knowledge in the social and behavioral sciences. Consider, for example, the major idea in political science: every known society has made rules on how its members should get along together and instituted coercive sanctions to help insure that rules are obeyed (3,5). This idea is germane to the classroom social context in which teacher and pupils together formulate guidelines and sanctions essential to their getting along together.

Specific social learnings in the classroom depend upon a variety of considerations. Examples for developing behaviors are: being a worthy group member (participating in discussion and resolution of questions and issues); practicing social amenities; communicating effectively (listening and speaking); respecting one's own rights and responsibilities and those of others.

These objectives can be served simultaneously through learning experiences in *both* subject-matter and social learnings. Illustrations of both follow.

Teacher-Led Group Discussions: Discussions with the entire class afford the teacher the opportunity to present new human relations ideas. For the pupil, such teacher-guided activities give practice in some of the social skills.

John's group is of the opinion that the class has gathered sufficient information on the way of life in India, but Virginia's group believes further research is necessary. The teacher might ask: How shall we decide? What do we need to know in order to make a reasonable decision?

This activity can be a confluence of *both* content and social learnings. Social learnings deal with group processes in sound decision making, while content learnings involve subject matter which is the essence of the discussion. Exchange of ideas can be instrumental in developing skills associated with precise transmission and reception of ideas.

Study Sessions: Study sessions can be settings for social education while children investigate content—especially when the class is divided into study groups of four or five. These small groups give opportunity to practice sound *leadership* and *followership* skills.

Paul, as group leader, determines with the others how the day's work shall be carried on. Each person may contribute ideas during the planning phase. Following that, each has an opportunity to practice directing his individual efforts toward reaching the mark. Through combined effort a team can work together to achieve the common goal.

Reporting: Groups of children can report to others the results of their studies. Usually reporting deals with content; but since it involves people working with people, it can function as settings for social learning. A group must decide what data and information will be presented and how this knowledge can be communicated clearly to the audience. During reporting time youngsters in the audience can practice what they have learned about courteous listening, respect and tolerance for the persons in the spotlight.

Each content experience need not unfailingly have a social dimension any more than every social learning must have content. As indicated above, there are worthwhile learning activities in which the two can be combined in a mutually beneficial way. Surely both are compatible in the same social studies program.

Most of today's pupils are destined to spend the rest of their lives dealing with others. Ideally, youngsters should begin learning and practicing good human relations during the formative elementary years. Teaching content and developing social learnings are not antithetical. Neither need be neglected if social studies programs are to be effective in preparing our future citizens. Wise educators responsible for improving social studies programs will be successful in finding the middle course which sacrifices neither content nor social education.

References

1. Jerome S. Bruner, *The Process of Education.* Cambridge: Harvard University Press, 1960.
2. E. R. Keislar and J. D. McNeil, "Teaching Science and Mathematics by Auto-Instruction in the Primary Grades: An Experimental Strategy in Curriculum Development." Los Angeles: the authors, October, 1961 (mimeographed).
3. K. N. Llewellyn, "Law and Civilization," in *People, Power and Politics,* L. J. Gould and E. W. Steele, eds. New York: Random House, 1961, pp. 321–329.
4. Philip H. Phenix, "Key Concepts and the Crisis in Learning," *Teachers College Record, 58:* 137–143, 1956.
5. Robert Rienow, *Introduction to Government.* New York: Knopf, 1956.
6. Mortimer Smith, "Social Studies Challenged," *The Toledo Blade Sunday Magazine,* July 26, 1964, pp. 4–5 ff.

Standards for Social Studies Teachers: Position Statement of the National Council for the Social Studies

DEVELOPED BY
NCSS ADVISORY COMMITTEE ON TEACHER EDUCATION AND
CERTIFICATION AND NCSS AD HOC COMMITTEE ON
TEACHER STANDARDS

Foreword

For at least a decade or more the National Council for the Social Studies has struggled with the problem of publishing a comprehensive statement dealing with standards for social studies teachers. Several committees have prepared such statements and from time to time the reports of those committees have appeared in *Social Education.* Although these were sound statements, they did not seem to meet the needs of teachers and others in the field who were faced with day-to-day decision making concerning teacher preparation and teacher assignment. In 1969, therefore, the Board of Directors appointed a special *ad hoc* committee consisting entirely of teachers, chaired by Helen M. Garrett, and charged it with the responsibility of drafting a comprehensive statement on teacher standards. It was out of the work of this committee, along with contributions from the Advisory Committees on Teacher Education, chaired by Richard F. W. Whittemore (1969), and by Theodore Kaltsounis (1970), that the present document evolved. Harris L. Dante, Jean Tilford, and John D. McAulay edited and prepared the final draft for the Board of Directors.

The preparation of a comprehensive statement on teacher standards is a particularly difficult assignment. Because there is little solid and convincing research to guide thinking, opinions vary greatly as to how social studies teachers should be prepared and what constitutes a proper job assignment for a social studies teacher. The matter is further compounded because the statement has to speak not only to standards for secondary teachers covering a broad range of teaching specialities, but also to standards for elementary teachers, including those in self-contained classrooms, as well as those in other organizational arrangements. Because there is not general consensus on many matters surrounding teacher preparation and assignment, any statement issued by the National Council would arouse some controversy.

This is as it should be, because controversy should lead to public discussion of this important professional problem. The alternative is to issue no statement at all, with the expectation that the problem will somehow ultimately resolve itself or simply go away.

Whatever disagreements there may be within the profession on certain specific items in the standards statement, these should not be construed to mean that the entire document lacks validity. It should be stressed that the present document represents the official position of the National Council for the Social Studies on teacher standards. As such it should be used by teachers, supervisors, boards of education, and other school officials in making decisions concerning teacher preparation and teacher assignment. The National Council is urging the membership to promote the widest possible distribution of this document and to use it as the basis for negotiating issues relating to teacher preparation and teacher assignment.

In preparing this document, the National Council has relied on the professional judgment of many of its members representing a full range of professional roles—elementary and secondary school teachers, supervisors, department chairmen, professors from teacher education, professors from history and the social sciences, and others. The Steering Committee of the House of Delegates reviewed the statement at its meeting in St. Louis in March 1971 and enthusiastically endorsed and approved it.

We believe that the statement represents the best current thinking on this matter at this time. Nonetheless, standards are subject to change, and therefore should be under constant study. In order to insure continued careful attention to teacher standards, the President of the National Council is immediately appointing a three-member Review Committee that will be charged with the responsibility of studying developments in teachers standards and for making recommendations for revision of this document three years hence. It is hoped and expected that the present statement will be used, discussed, criticized, and thoroughly critiqued at the local, state, and national levels. Feedback from these deliberations can be used by the Review Committee to prepare a revised set of standards for the latter half of the 1970s.

The National Council for the Social Studies wishes to express sincere thanks to the many individuals who contributed to the preparation of this and earlier statements on teacher standards: *ad hoc* Committee on Teacher Load and Assignment (1964), John Yee, *Chairman,* Harris L. Dante, John Jarolimek; Committee on Teacher Education and Certification (1966), Harris L. Dante, *Chairman,* Jack Sutherland, *Associate Chairman,* William W. Crowder, Frances Ferrell, Harriette Kuhlman, Howard Lawrence, Raymond H. Muessig, Helen Storen, Kenneth B. Thurston, Richard F. W. Whittemore; *ad hoc* Committee on Teacher Standards (1969), Helen M. Garrett, *Chairman,* Donald Anctil, Richard Cole, John R. Drain, William R. Pirone, Ethel Thorn, June Tyler; Advisory Committees on Teacher

Education and Certification, Richard F. W. Whittemore, *Chairman* (1969), and Theodore Kaltsounis, *Chairman* (1970); and the final editing committee for the Board of Directors, Harris L. Dante, John D. McAulay, and Jean Tilford.

John Jarolimek, *President*
National Council for the Social Studies

I. Introduction

The social studies teacher faces a complex task in a field that is becoming pedagogically unmanageable, and yet has become increasingly important in the preparation of future citizens who must address themselves to the challenge and responsibilities of modern society.

The teacher must secure some mastery of the various social science disciplines,[1] including an understanding of their interdisciplinary relationships, in order to know what issues are worthy objects of study. Knowledge and sophistication in regard to contemporary affairs and the ability to develop inquiry skills in regard to social values and decision making related to crucial social issues are also necessary.

The selection of these goals emerges from a mass of content in which there is no established pattern of continuity or sequence. Moreover, in meeting the needs and interests of students it is necessary to help them gain meaning and understanding from concepts which are often more abstract than concrete. It is to this difficult and insightful task that the social studies teacher is dedicated.

The following Statement on Standards for Social Studies Teachers has the classroom teacher as its primary focus. The teaching-learning act should be the center and the most important element in the entire educational enterprise. The teacher is the key figure in creating and sustaining the intellectual and emotional climate needed in the classroom to achieve the goals of effective learning.

The Statement deals with the teacher's qualifications, responsibilities, and the conditions necessary for successful teaching and learning. It is intended to assist teachers, administrators, and all those engaged in the pre-service and in-service education of teachers to improve existing programs or for the development of new ones. The goal is to give the teacher the psychological and professional support and the personal remuneration needed to reach the level of competence, effectiveness, and respect to be recognized as a true professional.

---

[1] The terms "social sciences" and "social studies" as used throughout this Statement will be assumed to include history.

II. Professional Preparation

There should be diversity and an open-endedness in teacher education and certification programs which would have responsible institutions free to develop experimental programs in response to the rapidly changing requirements of society, scholarship, and students.

However, each elementary and secondary social studies teacher should have a well-planned undergraduate program, including preparation in the areas of liberal general studies, an in-depth knowledge in areas of academic specialization, and professional education. The NCSS "Guidelines for the Preparation of Social Studies Teachers, 1966" suggests the following distribution of course work indicating a proposed minimum and a range extending to a possible maximum given as a percentage of total credit hours; general education 25–30 percent; academic teaching fields 50–60 percent (including professionalized subject matter for elementary teachers); professional education 15–25 percent.[2]

A. GENERAL STUDIES

All teachers need a liberal education as a basis for the intellectual independence that, in every great age, has animated the quest for understanding of those enduring principles and values that have helped to make man less of a brute and more of a civilized human being. There can be no uniform prescription for a liberal education but a beginning can be made with a rigorous introduction to the humanities and the social sciences, the physical sciences, the biological sciences. The prospective social studies teacher should immerse himself in a culture different from his own and should especially become sensitive to the contrasting styles and world views of the Western world and the non-Western world. The teacher should, of course, develop competent communication skills and should become knowledgeable in at least one discipline outside the social sciences.

B. ACADEMIC SPECIALIZATION

Elementary Teachers. All elementary teachers should have a minimum of 18 semester hours in the social sciences. Interdisciplinary courses involving content from the social sciences should be included in the prospective teacher's program.

Prospective elementary teachers should also have some advanced study in one or more of the social sciences or history relevant to the curricular

---

[2] "Guidelines for the Preparation of Social Studies Teachers" may be found in the October, 1967 issue of *Social Education.*

areas in which they plan to teach. This should require intensive studies in the literature of the field and the ability to do independent research.

Secondary Teachers. Beyond the basic introduction to all of the social sciences, the prospective secondary social studies teacher should have a close acquaintance with three social sciences including specialization with research experience in one. The insistent demands for urban studies, ethnic studies, area studies, and studies in social conflict require their inclusion in the program of preparation for social studies teachers.

Both *elementary and secondary* social studies teachers should have at least an introduction to the subject matters and modes of inquiry of one or more disciplines from each of the three general categories of social science: the synoptic (history and geography); the systematic (economics and political science); and the holistic (anthropology, sociology, and social psychology).

C. PROFESSIONAL EDUCATION

Studies in the professional sequence should introduce the prospective teacher to the theory and practice of modern social studies education.

Course work should include emphases on educational psychology and learning theory, teaching strategies, the use of various instructional media and other resources, testing and evaluation, and student teaching and/or internship. The prospective teacher should also develop competencies in creating a democratic classroom atmosphere, in communication skills, and in skills in interpersonal relationships.

A laboratory course in teaching methods should form the bridge between theory and practice. The prospective teacher should enter the classroom almost at once.

Professional coursework should involve field experience as well as work experience, including participation in community service organizations, in recreational activities or tutoring, or in similar employment.

Broad knowledge through coursework or experience which makes the individual sensitive to the problems of living in a pluralistic society, aware of the manifestations of racism in education, and informed as to approaches for minimizing or eliminating these conditions should be included.

The second major phase of professional preparation should consist of a year or more of paid teaching experience, comparable to a medical residency. The new teacher should have regular teaching responsibilities under the tutelage of experienced social studies teachers, the department chairman, and, if possible, a social studies supervisor.

III. The Professional Education Staff

State Departments of Education should not approve any institution for teacher education unless it can adequately staff the necessary courses and programs for both academic and professional instruction. College supervisors of social studies teachers and public school and State Departments of Education supervisory personnel should be subject matter specialists rather than generalists. They should also be experts in the teaching of the social studies. A full-time load of the college supervisor would normally be no more than 15 student teachers. The cooperating teacher should be a master teacher and a subject matter specialist who also meets the standards set forth in this statement. Generally, a master's degree and at least three years of successful teaching experience would be expected of the cooperating teacher, who should also be voluntarily willing to accept the professional responsibility of guiding the student teacher.

IV. Screening Candidates for Social Studies Teaching

The college student who is preparing to be a social studies teacher should be expected to meet various quality standards. The goals of this program should be clearly adequate general intelligence, strong record in any sequences which will be used in later teaching fields, desirable personality characteristics, absence of defects fatal to good teaching, and strong professional competencies.

Generally, the student would be admitted to the Social Studies teaching program at the beginning of the junior year. At this point the candidate should have above-average academic achievement and meet acceptable levels of competency in reading, writing, speaking, and listening skills. He should be free of any speech and hearing deficiencies.

The second screening would occur at the time of admission to student teaching. At this point the student should maintain all previous standards and should have at least a 2.00 cumulative grade average with 2.25 in his teaching fields and in the professional sequence.

The third screening would come at the conclusion of student teaching and if successful the candidate would be recommended for graduation and certification. The student teaching experience should represent a gradual induction into classroom responsibility and ultimately the assumption of a full day's teaching load. The student teacher should be assigned to a qualified cooperating teacher in the area of social studies for which he is prepared. Evaluation would involve the University supervisor, the cooperating teacher, and the student teacher. Before graduation the student would be expected to meet all standards with careful staff scrutiny of the student's physical, psychological, and other personal-professional characteristics.

V. Certification

State Departments of Education should reduce certification procedures to two simple steps: first, one-year probationary certification for the prospective teacher awarded on recommendation of an accredited educational institution; second, regular certification awarded after at least one year of appropriate teaching experience and on recommendation of a local or regional committee of social studies teachers and supervisors representing the profession. The State Departments of Education might have to retain supervisory jurisdiction over these procedures; the initiative must, however, lie with appropriate professional organizations.

VI. Recruitment and Assignment of Teachers

A. EMPLOYMENT OF THE TEACHER

No teacher should be employed or permitted to teach social studies at the secondary level or departmentalized elementary level unless he has completed a social science degree program leading to certification. Elementary teachers with multifield responsibilities should have an interdisciplinary social science background.

The person employed to teach social studies should be primarily interested in and dedicated to the teaching of the social studies. This dedication can be determined by ascertaining the individual's ultimate professional goals. No one teaching any social studies class should be employed just to accommodate the special needs of other departments or facets of the school programs.

B. TEACHER ASSIGNMENT

The teacher should be prepared for the level assigned. The level of the teacher's assignment should be changed only after appropriate preparation.

The teacher should teach only in the area or areas for which the teacher was prepared. The teacher's assignments should reflect the field of the teacher's greatest competency.

Teachers should be encouraged to develop and teach new courses in their own particular areas of interest and preparation rather than to be expected to teach existing courses outside their areas of interest and preparation.

Teachers should not accept responsibilities (administrative, curricular, co-curricular, or extracurricular) that interfere with their effectiveness as social studies teachers.

VII. Guiding and Directing the Learning Process

The social studies teacher as a facilitator of learning exhibits behavior harmonious with the nature of the learning process, the nature of social studies as revealed in recent trends, and contemporary social realities.

A. RELATIONSHIPS WITH STUDENTS

The teacher equally values each and every student as worthy human beings regardless of race, sex, religion, ethnic origin, socioeconomic level, or level of achievement.

Teachers should make every effort to understand each of their students and their strengths, weaknesses, and problems.

Teachers should heed the solicited and unsolicited views and comments of their students and their relationships with them, and consider such views in their self-improvement efforts.

The teacher analyzes student behavior—especially hostile behavior—on the basis of its causes.

The teacher recognizes that children are capable of learning by themselves as well as from each other and acts as a director of learning experiences, rather than as an authoritarian source of knowledge.

B. THE TEACHER AS PLANNER

The teacher develops significantly relevant objectives cooperatively with the students. Initiatory activities are planned which will help the students become aware of the basic problem, clarify the issues, and motivate them toward achievement of the objectives.

In order to plan meaningful learning experiences the teacher is aware of the basic contemporary social issues at the local, regional, national, and international levels.

The teacher understands the subject matter involved in terms of its basic concepts, generalizations, and unresolved questions.

The teacher knows the background of his students and utilizes knowledge of their previous experiences to make the teaching-learning relevant to them and to their social environment.

The teacher knows the investigative methods of the social sciences and utilizes them as guides in planning investigation-oriented learning experiences at the student's level.

The teacher is cognizant of individual differences and plans a variety of learning activities in order to reach all students.

C. THE TEACHER IN THE CLASSROOM

The teacher maintains an open and questioning atmosphere in the classroom in which students are free to develop a questioning attitude and are guided to learn in a variety of ways. Teaching strategies and materials would be varied rather than following a routine pattern.

The teacher is skillful in the use of various questioning techniques and is capable of leading the students in discussion involving higher levels of thinking, including analyzing, synthesizing, hypothesizing, testing of hypotheses, inferring, and evaluating.

The teacher utilizes the local environment, the experiences of the class, and a variety of other resources in motivating and directing the students in understanding various social situations and phenomena.

The teacher recognizes that academic freedom and responsibility to demonstrate a high commitment to the students' right to deal with controversial issues, including the establishment of criteria for choosing between alternative values in an intellectually honest way, are both necessary and important.

The teacher maintains an atmosphere of intellectual integrity by allowing and encouraging the consideration of all possible points of view in treating various topics and issues.

The teacher should not impose his views on the students but by teaching and allowing them to be critical of all sources of information he may state his own conclusions when appropriate.

The teacher considers the process of rational decision making to be the basic method of learning for the social studies and encourages students to apply it to contemporary issues.

The teacher views pupil progress and achievement in terms of understandings (concepts and generalizations), intellectual skills, and affective behavior. Evaluation is regarded as a continuous process and the teacher devises a variety of instruments making use of formal and informal techniques, including self-evaluation, in order to assess student growth.

VIII. The Teacher in the School Community

The teacher understands the community in which the students live and makes every effort to see that the school serves the interests of the community and the larger society.

The teacher heeds the solicited and unsolicited views and comments of those in the school community relative to teaching and the teacher's relations with them. These judgments are considered in the teacher's self-improvement efforts.

The teacher should exercise his political rights and participate in the political process as a voter, party worker, or candidate as he wishes.

IX. Basic Conditions for Teaching and Learning

Teachers, however competent they may be, cannot function to the best of their capabilities unless certain basic conditions of employment are secured. It is imperative that the proper educational climate be created and maintained for the teaching-learning experience to be effective.

A. ACADEMIC FREEDOM

The school administration should recognize the right and responsibility of social studies teachers to deal with controversial issues in a way which presents all possible points of view.

The school administration should publish guidelines and a clear policy statement regarding the right and responsibility of social studies teachers to deal with controversy.

Teachers and students should be able to utilize published materials, journals and other media, and resource persons that they deem necessary. The school library should subscribe to critical unpopular journals appropriate for given grade levels, and students should have the opportunity to get acquainted with them.

The school administration should make every effort to enlighten the public and various governmental agencies and bodies about the importance of this policy and resist any pressure to suppress academic freedom.

When a teacher's academic freedom is jeopardized, the administration should ask the teacher's organizations to help investigate and should consider their judgment in shaping further action to protect academic freedom rather than the narrow interests of pressure groups.

The teacher should teach in a school situation which encourages students to learn in the community and society at large, outside as well as inside the school building.

B. THE TEACHER'S CLASS LOAD AND CLASS SIZE

The secondary social studies teacher should teach no more than five periods per day in a school which is organized in the traditional 40–50 minute periods. Four periods per day, or their equivalent in a reorganized and more flexible school day schedule, would be an even more desirable goal.

The teacher should be given one period for preparation and one duty-free lunch period per day regardless of his teaching level. In schools in which team teaching is used, all teachers in a particular team must be given the same period for preparation.

The teacher's program should consist of no more than two basic preparations. The assignment of a course requiring an additional preparation is possible only on a voluntary basis.

The teacher should be responsible for no more than 25 students in schools that are traditionally graded and organized in self-contained classrooms.

The teacher should be responsible for no more than 125 students per day exclusive of homeroom assignments in schools in which teachers have different groups and classes of students.

C. THE TEACHER'S RELATED DUTIES

The teacher should be assigned no more than one extracurricular activity at a time during the school year.

The teacher should be relieved of many related routine duties by paraprofessionals and/or student assistants.

The teacher should be given assistance in the preparation of audiovisual aids and in the procurement and maintenance of audiovisual equipment.

D. THE TEACHER'S INSTRUCTIONAL ENVIRONMENT

Teachers should be provided with a specially equipped social studies laboratory for their classes.

A variety of instructional resources and audiovisual equipment should be readily accessible.

A social studies staff workroom equipped with desks, typewriters, duplicating equipment, and a professional library should be provided.

A staffed resource center in which students can engage in independent study should be available.

Social studies teachers should be consulted in the design of new school buildings to insure facilities necessary for an effective social studies program.

X. The Teacher As a Professional Person

As a professional person, the social studies teacher has an obligation to fulfill responsibilities which result in strengthening his profession. He should exhibit a commitment toward self-improvement both in professional and civic matters. He should belong to organized professional groups and actively work for the improvement of the teaching and learning of social studies.

A. THE TEACHER'S SELF-IMPROVEMENT

The teacher should continue his formal education through coursework in the areas of his concern and by keeping abreast of current related literature.

A fifth year of study, ordinarily completed within the first five years of teaching, is essential. Graduate programs should be planned that relate to the subject areas being taught, and appropriate work in professional education or other cognate areas should be designed to improve instruction, such as reading, instructional materials, and modern educational technology.

The teacher should voluntarily participate in special in-service programs and should attend or organize professional meetings that assess and seek improvement of the teaching and learning of the social studies and the school program as a whole.

The teacher utilizes every opportunity to improve himself professionally, through participation in volunteer organizations and through temporary service or employment in industries and agencies that meet social needs.

The teacher has the right to expect support and encouragement from his district and school administration in his professional growth efforts. This should be in ways such as funded in-service programs, well-supplied professional libraries, paid leaves and travel expenses for professional meetings and workshops, reimbursement for educational costs, and sabbatical leaves for long-term professional growth activities.

The teacher must continuously examine his views and beliefs and his social behavior in order to reflect and act on the need to eliminate possible inconsistencies.

The teacher has a responsibility to refuse assignments and employment both in and out of school that are detrimental to his teaching performance and to his self-improvement.

The teacher has a responsibility to act in ways which demonstrate his commitment to the elimination of discriminatory practices.

B. THE TEACHER AND THE ORGANIZED PROFESSION

Both the elementary and secondary teachers of social studies must join and participate in the activities of the local, state, and national councils for the social studies as well as in other appropriate professional organizations and learned societies.

As a member of local and regional social studies teachers' organizations, the teacher must encourage them to act in the following ways:

Bring about the necessary basic conditions for teaching and learning social studies.

Assess and revise existing local social studies curricula and programs.

Initiate, execute, and evaluate social studies experimental programs at the local level.

Discuss and evaluate research findings and new developments in social studies education.

Evaluate and recommend commercially produced instructional social studies materials.

Recommend and supervise the production of materials at the local level to supplement or replace inadequate commercially produced instructional materials.

Educate the public in new social studies programs.

The teacher should belong to and participate in the National Council for the Social Studies and support its actions which include:

Inspiration and support to the local organizations as they seek to carry out their professional responsibilities.

Evaluation of new developments in the social studies and assistance in the dissemination of these developments.

Stimulation of research in social studies education and the dissemination of research findings.

Encouragement of publishers and manufacturers of instructional aids to produce materials that deal critically with social issues and that are consistent with new developments in the social studies.

Secondary social studies teachers or elementary school teachers having a social science major should also belong to a learned society in the discipline of their specialization.

Teachers should have the right to engage in responsible social actions to gain and safeguard the basic civil and professional rights of teachers and students.

XI. Conclusion

This Statement has attempted to establish standards for the selection, preparation, and assignment of social studies teachers. It has indicated the responsibilities of the teacher in guiding the teaching-learning process, and in the relationships which the teacher has with students, the community, and the profession. It sets forth the facilities needed to aid effective instruction, the conditions necessary for teaching and learning, and the provisions that a school should make for the competency and continuous professional growth of its social studies staff.

The National Council for the Social Studies will keep this Statement under continuous review and revision as knowledge grows and as more comprehensive and sophisticated theory and practice related to social studies teaching emerge in the future.

The Problem of Evaluation in the Social Studies

ROBERT L. EBEL

Your approaches to the teaching problem, and to the evaluation problem, are basically sound. Both the maintenance of good educational programs and the improvement of educational procedures require good evaluation. Good evaluation, in turn, can only be made in relation to the goals of instruction. Too often when teachers make tests they forget their goals and remember only the subject matter they used in trying to achieve those goals.

I should warn you, however, that my answers to your question are going to be more complex and less satisfying than either you or I would wish them to be. The plain fact is that we do not have many evaluation instruments which will do the job you want done. What is even worse, our disappointing experience in trying to measure some of these outcomes is beginning to convince us that part of the job simply *cannot* be done. I even suspect that part of it *should* not be done. On the brighter side, there is much more we can do, and do better, than we are typically doing in evaluating student progress in the social studies.

Three broad categories of educational achievement are reflected in various degrees by the listed objectives:

I. Objectives primarily concerned with knowledge and understanding

    A. Transmit our cultural heritage

    B. Teach important historical facts and generalizations

    C. Teach time and space relationships

    D. Acquaint students with basic historical references

    E. Provide instruction and practice in locating information

Robert L. Ebel is Professor of Education at Michigan State University, East Lansing.

Reprinted from *Social Education* 24:6–10, 1960, with permission of the National Council for the Social Studies and Robert L. Ebel.

II. Objectives primarily concerned with attitudes, values, and feelings

    F. Promote moral and spiritual values
    G. Promote the attitude that history is interesting and useful
    H. Promote good mental health
    I. Promote aesthetic sensitivities
    J. Develop democratic citizenship

III. Objectives primarily concerned with instruction and practice in intellectual skills

    K. Writing notes from lectures and references
    L. Writing essay examinations
    M. Judging the validity of evidence
    N. Drawing sound conclusions from data
    O. Working in a group
    P. Facility in oral expression

The overlap among these three categories is substantial. Most of us have attitudes, feelings or values attached to much of the knowledge we possess. Conversely, most of our attitudes, feelings, and values have some basis in knowledge and understanding. Intellectual skills are heavily loaded with knowledge, and also have values attached to them. Thus some of the differences among the three categories are differences in the relative contributions of knowledge, feeling and practice to the attainment of the specific goals.

You may have noticed that my grouping omits entirely the second objective in your list, "Provide intellectual exercise for the discipline of the mind." The notion of mental discipline has been the target of considerable psychological criticism. Its most naive form, which assumes that the mind is analogous to a muscle that can be strengthened by exercise in learning anything, especially something difficult to learn, has been generally discredited. Even the notions of general mental *functions* such as memory, reasoning and will, which were supposed to be separate faculties independent of mental content, have been generally discarded. Modern studies of human and animal learning, and of brain function, suggest that the mind guides behavior by serving as a semi-automatic ready-reference storehouse of ideas derived from experience and reflection. The effectiveness of a mind seems to depend on how many of these ideas are stored in it, how accurately they represent the world outside the mind, and how easily they can be made available for recall and recombination when the occasion demands.

If by intellectual exercise is meant increasing the store of ideas, and if by discipline of the mind is meant improved accuracy and increased integration of these ideas, then this is indeed an important objective—so important, in fact, that it encompasses most of the others. If this is not what is meant, some further clarification may be required. In any case, I cannot suggest any tests which might be used to make a separate evaluation of it.

Knowledge and Understanding

For the measurement of knowledge and understanding in the social studies a number of excellent tests are available. The Cooperative Test Division of the Educational Testing Service offers social studies tests in its series of Sequential Tests of Educational Progress, and in its end-of-course achievement tests. The World Book Company offer tests in world history and in American history as parts of its Evaluation and Adjustment series. Science Research Associates distributes the test of Understanding of Basic Social Concepts from the Iowa Tests of Educational Development. Oscar Buros' *Fifth Mental Measurements Yearbook* [1] lists 60 tests in the social studies, with critical reviews of 23 of them. Not all of the tests listed are of high quality. The reviewers are rather critical of some. While the reader must occasionally discount the idiosyncrasies of particular reviewers, their comments are usually unbiased and always informative. This is the best available guide to educational tests of all kinds. It should be consulted by anyone who seeks better tests for specific goals.

You may have hoped for a more specific recommendation of a few tests exactly suited to measure achievement of the goals you listed. Unfortunately, this is not possible. In only a few cases have these particular goals been made the focus of specific test construction efforts. Even if tests of each goal were available, it is unlikely that the test author would conceive of these goals precisely as you do. So many facts and ideas are involved in our cultural heritage, and there are so many different value judgments that can be made of them that tests from different sources are almost certain to differ widely. Hence, even in this easiest area of educational measurement, you are not likely to find ready-made tests to meet your needs.

What, then, is to be done? One solution is to make tests of your own, based on a very specific definition of each goal in the area of knowledge and understanding. This is a difficult task. In the absence of substantial expert assistance (and liberal finances) it is not likely to be done very successfully.

Another solution is to get along with the published tests that come closest to covering the goals as you have defined them. This will be cheaper, and cost less effort, but may not be any more satisfactory in the end. What is really needed, it seems to me, is some nationwide effort by social studies teachers and other educators to agree on a definition of basic goals in this

[1] Highland Park, N.J.: Gryphon Press, 1959.

and other areas of common educational concern. Then the effort to build really good tests of the agreed-upon goals would be justified, and we would have a means for making sound evaluations of the achievement of our common goals. Unless a teacher foolishly devoted his whole teaching to the attainment of these common goals, completely suppressing his own special interests and disregarding local conditions and individual pupil needs, this would place no straitjacket on the curriculum. But if we are committed to the defense of the freedom of states, schools, teachers, or even pupils, to define all their own goals in whatever way they think best, then the task of getting meaningful measures of the degree of achievement of these diverse goals becomes almost impossible. The price we pay for what may be an excess of freedom seems rather high.

Attitudes, Values and Feelings

Adequate measurement of achievement toward goals in the realm of attitudes, values and feelings presents other, and still more difficult, problems. There is the problem of getting agreement on a clear definition of just what is meant by "democratic citizenship" or "aesthetic sensitivities." There is the problem of obtaining valid indications of the students' true attitudes, values and feelings. Direct questions in a test situation indicate mainly how the student thinks he *ought* to feel. Indirect, disguised tests are often low in relevance and reliability. The instability of pupil behavior from time to time and from situation to situation makes any single observation quite limited in significance. Finally, it is very difficult to create a test situation which is realistic enough to give valid indication of a student's probable behavior in a natural non-test situation.

For these reasons, good tests in the area of attitudes, values and feelings are quite rare. I know of none in the realm of moral and spiritual values. Remmers' multi-purpose instrument, *A Scale for Measuring Attitude Toward Any School Subject,* might be used to reflect general attitudes toward history, but probably would not indicate specifically the students' attitudes of interest in history and appreciation of its usefulness, and possibly not the students' genuine attitudes. Good mental health is a complex, poorly-defined concept. Clinical diagnosis is the best basis for estimating mental health, and even that leaves much to be desired. There are tests of specific kinds of aesthetic sensitivity in art, music, and literature. I wonder if these kinds of aesthetic sensitivity are commonly regarded as goals for a course in the social studies? If not, the concept of aesthetic sensitivity may require further definition. Even when so defined, I doubt that we could do more than measure knowledge of aesthetic principles. There are some tests of civic knowledge. There have been some attempts to predict good civic behavior, but there again the problems of trait definition and test validity have been so troublesome that no existing test can be recommended.

This lack of good, ready-made instruments is bad enough. What is even more discouraging is the lack of any promising techniques for the measurement of attitudes, feelings and values. It is gradually becoming apparent that the difficulties of measuring these traits with paper-and-pencil tests are inherent in the nature of the traits, and in the limitations of formal, written tests. Techniques of testing which are reasonably effective in measuring knowledge and understanding may never be even passably effective in measuring an individual person's attitudes, values and feelings simply because these are specific to situations which cannot be realistically reproduced by any test. Further, deficiencies in these traits can easily be hidden from the prying questions of the tester, behind a mask of conventionally correct responses.

Does this mean that teachers should abandon the pursuit of goals in this area? To some extent, yes. Many widely approved goals with respect to attitudes, values and feelings are generally acceptable only when they are left undefined. What consensus could we get in defining the activities of a good citizen, or the nature of ideal spiritual values? People in different localities, and of different political, religious, or philosophical persuasions would define them quite differently. Is tolerance a virtue or a fault? No teacher can avoid influencing pupils to adopt his own particular attitudes and values, but I doubt that these should become formal goals of teaching, or objects for testing, unless they are the predominant view of the culture, or unless they can be supported as rational consequences of valid knowledge about the world and man.

This suggests that some of our attitudes, values and feelings are determined by the knowledge we possess. I am persuaded that this cognitive basis for feelings is very influential, and that it constitutes a proper and productive focus for teaching and for testing. Consider the goal of good mental health. How can a teacher promote good mental health? One way is to understand mental hygiene and the causes of mental illness well enough so that most of his acts in dealing with students tend to improve rather than impair the student's (and the teacher's) mental health. Another is to teach a knowledge and an understanding of mental health to the students themselves. Good tests of this kind of knowledge can be built. But no paper-and-pencil test is likely to do an adequate job of assessing mental health or diagnosing mental illness. That is a task for the specialist who knows how to use complex clinical procedures.

Similarly, one could build good tests of knowledge about good citizenship, about aesthetics, about moral and spiritual values and about the uses of history. Imparting of relevant knowledge does not guarantee development of desired attitudes, values and feelings, but it surely must contribute substantially to their development.

The chief alternative to the development of desirable attitudes, values and feelings via knowledge is to develop them by indoctrination or conditioning. Many of our most cherished feelings were developed in this way. As children we learned acceptable social behavior largely through a complex system of rewards and punishments, and only secondarily on the basis of rational understanding of the *why* of the correct form (if indeed it was rational!). Indoctrination is almost the only way of teaching very young children, but it becomes progressively less necessary and less desirable as their minds develop. It is a more appropriate technique in the home than in the school. I seriously doubt that teachers, especially teachers of the social studies at the high school level and beyond, should intentionally have much to do with indoctrination or conditioning. Their attempts to develop desirable attitudes, values and feelings should have mainly a cognitive, rational base, depending on knowledge and understanding.

This emphasis on knowledge, rather than on attitudes, values and feelings, troubles some teachers greatly. Knowledge alone is not enough, they say. It is what a person does with his knowledge that counts. Arthur Guiterman said it this way:

> Theology, literature, languages, law
> Are peacock feathers to deck the daw
> If the lads that come from your splendid schools
> Are well-trained sharpers or flippant fools.[2]

He is right, of course, and so are the teachers. But they err, I think, if they assume that instances of misbehavior are caused mainly by deficiencies in attitudes, values and feelings which the school could correct if it only would try hard enough. Character traits are important determinants of behavior, but so are environmental circumstances. Teachers err if they assume that character is largely independent of knowledge, or that the same techniques of teaching and testing that have served for knowledge will serve also for attitudes, values and feelings. There is little in the experience of teachers or testers to support such assumptions. To evaluate individual achievement in these non-cognitive areas we may have to settle for measurement of relevant knowledge of how one ought to feel. We do not yet have good tests to do even this job, but we know how to make them.

For the rest of our evaluation of typical behavior, as influenced by attitudes, values and feelings, we may have to rely on systematic but informal observation of pupil behavior in real, non-test situations. This does not relieve us of defining clearly the traits we wish to observe. It does not promise to yield reliable measurements with little effort. But techniques for observing and recording typical behavior seem to offer more promise

[2] Arthur Guiterman, "Education," in *Death and General Putnam,* New York, Dutton, p. 74, 1935.

than any test-like instrument designed to probe a student's attitudes, values and feelings.

Nearly 30 years ago, Truman L. Kelley, writing on "Objective Measurement of the Outcomes of the Social Studies," stressed the importance of attitudes.[3] His emphasis on developing the basic determinants of behavior, rather than its superficial manifestations, seems eminently reasonable, and he said many true and wise things in supporting his thesis. Social studies teachers could profit much from re-reading his words today. He recognized the difficulties of measuring attitudes but was confident that these *could be* overcome, if only because they *had to be* overcome.

Today many of us are less sanguine. The experience of 30 years of generally unproductive efforts is beginning to convince us that we have set ourselves an impossible task, like squaring the circle or building a perpetual motion machine. Kelley himself later reported the unsuccessful outcome of an "Experimental Study of Three Character Traits Needed in a Democratic Social Order." [4] He commented, "This study emphasized the universal difficulty which has been experienced by those who have endeavored to obtain objective character measures of school children." But he did not lose faith in eventual success, ". . . for it still seemed practically axiomatic that traits of character and attitudes and interests are essential determiners of human conduct, independent of intellectual, sensory, and motor abilities and attainments."

Since 1942 an enormous amount of work has been done on personality testing. A great many tests have been developed. Some interesting findings have been reported, and some interesting theories proposed. But much of what goes on in the name of personality assessment is not much better than horoscope casting or tea leaf reading. We still have no personality test of demonstrated value that is practically useful in measuring the effectiveness of learning or teaching in the classroom. We may never have. It may be that our search for the "structure" of personality, and our attempts to "measure" its dimensions will be as fruitless as previous attempts to find the fountain of youth, or the philosopher's stone. Perhaps the problem needs to be reformulated. It may be that the really basic, stable determinants of behavior, so far as behavior is internally determined, are not attitudes, values and feelings, but ideas—rational, cognitive, teachable, testable.

Intellectual Skills

The third category of goals was concerned mainly with intellectual skills. Here again there are no good, ready-made tests that can be recommended.

[3] *Historical Outlook 21*:66–72, 1930.
[4] *Harvard Educational Review 12*:294–322, 1942.

To the extent that these skills rest on knowledge—and this is a considerable extent—they can be tested by conventional paper-and-pencil tests. To the extent that they rest on facility gained through practice, performance tests judged with the help of rating scales offer the most promise. The best solution may be a combination of knowledge and performance tests as a basis for evaluating skills in note taking, essay examination writing, effective group participation, and oral expression.

There are two objectives in this area—judging the validity of evidence and drawing conclusions from data—that may be so greatly conditioned by a student's background knowledge that the influence of generalized skill on his behavior may be relatively unimportant. I wonder if there are broadly applicable rules for judging the validity of evidence, principles which do not depend on the particular nature of the evidence under consideration. I wonder if the interpretation of data is an abstract procedure, like the diagraming of a sentence, that can be applied with reasonable uniformity to all kinds of data. If so, knowledge about these rules and procedures can be taught and tested *as abstract principles.* But I am persuaded that attempts to test these skills by asking a student to judge specific evidence or interpret specific data will reveal mainly how much he already knows about the source of the evidence or data, its meaning, and the problem to which it applies. In short, I wonder if these are important enough as abstract skills to deserve the status of goals of instruction.

Recommendations

What, then, would I recommend for the evaluation of student progress toward the goals of teaching in the social studies?

First, that goals be defined specifically enough so that one can judge how satisfactory a given test will be.

Second, that goals which cannot be defined specifically and with general acceptability, or which hypothesize traits of dubious independence from other more obvious and easily measurable traits, be eliminated or de-emphasized.

Third, that goals which have statewide or nationwide, not just local, validity be emphasized.

Fourth, that command over essential knowledge be emphasized as a primary goal of instruction, even in the areas of attitudes, values, feelings and intellectual skills.

Fifth, that social studies teachers continue to search for, or to construct, evaluation instruments of acceptable validity in terms of specifically defined goals.

Sixth, that the *Mental Measurements Yearbook* be consulted for guidance in judging the usefulness of available tests.

Seventh, that social studies teachers recognize and accept the necessity of building some new tests, whose quality will depend on how much effort and money they are prepared to spend on them, and on how much expert help they get and accept in creating them.

That I have completed this discussion without clearly recommending a single specific test for you to use is something I regret very much. It reflects the complexity of some problems of educational measurement. Even more, it reflects our failure to be realistic in setting our goals, and to be objective and precise in defining them. I am persuaded that the main reason why educational measurement sometimes seems inadequate is that we persist in setting impossible tasks for it to do. But I am also persuaded that if we concentrate on the right problems, and work on them energetically and intelligently, we can improve educational measurement substantially.

Section TWO

The Social Sciences, History, and the Humanities

*I*n most elementary school social studies programs one will detect elements of history, geography, economics, political science, sociology, and anthropology. These social sciences and others are ordinarily assumed to be the parent disciplines of the social studies. Tradition and legislative requirements have placed history and geography in favored positions as sources of content for the social studies curriculum. In recent years, however, the sources of content for social studies have broadened to include other social sciences and, indeed, have extended beyond the social sciences to the humanities as well.

There has always been a close kinship between the social studies and the humanities. Whether history belongs to the social sciences or to the humanities has never been resolved. Many historians allow that it can belong to either, depending on the approach and the style of inquiry applied. In a real sense the humanities represent some of the aesthetic products of human societies and their cultures—their art, music, literature, poetry, drama. With increasing emphasis on culture studies in the elementary school, it follows that the humanities take on added importance.

The humanities contribute to the enrichment of the social studies in a number of ways. Much of their value is inherent in their providing an additional dimension of meaning to social studies concepts. Much of social studies education has dealt with the study of people meeting their basic needs. Basic needs are often interpreted as food, clothing, and shelter. This formula of basic need satisfaction is applied to studies of the local community area as well as to the study of foreign groups. These are the simplest and most apparent needs that human beings have. But human beings have other needs as well, and it is through the satisfaction of these other needs that they acquire much of their "human-ness." These needs have to do with the expression of feelings and aesthetic impulses in a way that will endure throughout an individual's life span. Man creates poetry and stories that are passed on from one generation to the next. He paints or carves drawings on the walls of caves. Later in his development he composes music and invents sophisticated instruments through which he can express himself musically. He writes literary pieces that are printed. These, too, are important needs that in one way or another all human beings share. If social studies programs are designed to help pupils understand human societies, the aesthetic and cultural products of a society can provide important insights into the core values that guide the behavior of people. Perhaps this is the most important contribution of the humanities to social studies education.

When properly taught the humanities often carry delicate affective overtones that are long remembered by pupils. They sensitize pupils to man's efforts to create the beautiful and to his attempt to express his feelings through the arts and literature. In the humanities man reaches beyond himself, yet he himself is the creator. In the humanities we find man at his best.

Much of what the child learns in social studies will erode over a period of time. Battles and political campaigns won and lost will fade from memory. Dates and places will be lost to the retrieval system. Men who achieved great goals, with a few obvious exceptions, may or may not be remembered. But those experiences that precipitate deeply moving responses to art, beauty, drama, and literature become a permanent part of the individual's response to life itself. Decades later the individual will still recall that "I had a teacher once who loved. . . ."

Ultimately, of course, the curriculum organization and structure will determine the manner in which content is incorporated in the program. In any case, teacher judgment plays an important role in determining what is taught, what is emphasized, and what is omitted. In order to make such decisions in an intelligent way, the teacher will need to understand the rationale underlying the local program and have some knowledge of the broad range of options available. The articles that follow provide the teacher with background information concerning the substantive component of the curriculum and should prove useful in assisting him to select and organize social studies content in a meaningful way.

Changing Aspects of Geography and the Elementary Curriculum

PHILLIP BACON

In my mind's eye I see them yet, sweeping like a moving mirage over the silent emptiness of the Sahara. These were the nomads, the only true dwellers of this greatest of the world's deserts.

In time I came to know *les hommes blues au Maroc* well. I recall the father, irascible leader, his stern face bronzed and creased by the searing sun, continually moving his family and his herds like a lost seaman over the interminable ocean of sand. But most of all I remember young Ismail, faithful guardian of his father's flocks.

What a marvelous lad! It was Ismail who could find pasture when starvation seemed imminent. It was Ismail who swiftly warned of danger when the sky took on a yellowish cast, certain sign of the coming of the *chergui*— that devastating wind from the southwest that stirs up sand, withering and smothering everything in its path. And it was Ismail who knew that our only salvation at the time of the chergui was to throw the center post of the tent to the ground, where, crouched together beneath the heavy camel hair fabric of the flattened tent, we waited out the storm.

So it was that I came to understand how man has learned to respond to the challenges of the desert. I became confident that man in the desert, so well illuminated by Ismail, my friend, need not defend his liberty, for in the desert one is always free, nor need he defend visible treasures, for the desert is an empty place, but he defends a secret realm.

In the course of several years of travel, other landscapes and other people came into view. I know now that they should have helped me to differentiate the variety of patterns—physical-biotic-cultural—that one finds distributed over the surface of the earth.

There was, for example, a tiny farm overlooking a fiord that cut deeply into the Norwegian coast. It was summer when I was there, and the father was away from home with the fishing fleet from the nearby coastal village. It was young Olaf, I believe, who told me of the long winter nights, bitterly cold, when he took hay to the barn to bed down the cows. I remember still other cows, and a lovely flaxen-haired girl who followed the melting snow up into the alpine meadows of Switzerland. And there was that

Phillip Bacon is Professor of Geography at the University of Houston, Texas.

Reprinted from *Social Education* 31:609–611 ff., 1967, with permission of the National Council for the Social Studies and Phillip Bacon.

wonderful sampan family somewhere in Southeast Asia—I can no longer recall just where, but it was long ago and there were so many places and so many families. Next to Ismail, however, one I will never forget was the boy, Omak, who was learning to hunt the walrus and the seal. His fur clothing, his snow house, his stone lamp with its flickering wick floating in oil seemed, at the time, such perfect examples of man's adaptation to the difficult habitat of the Arctic coast.

From Dreams to Reality

Nostalgic memories of an extended world tour? Certainly—but a vicarious one, made as a child, traveling aboard a series of blue-covered geography textbooks, guided by some wonderfully dedicated elementary school teachers. Indeed, most of us who received our elementary school education during and since the 1920s trotted through similar adventures that are now recalled, depending on a whole variety of circumstances, with pleasure, indifference, or abject loathing. Rather anachronistically, too, a great many children attending elementary school today are still herding goats on the Sahara and building igloos along the shores of the Arctic Ocean. Might it not be appropriate, in this event, to paraphrase a popular television show and ask the real Ismail and the real Omak to stand up?

Unhappily, such characters drawn today would likely be no more true to life than the originals. It does seem fairly certain, however, that the real Ismail was never a nomad, unless one counts his fairly recent move from Algiers to Paris; and it may well be that good old Omak is actually a graduate of the University of Alaska who is now teaching his fourth graders in suburban Anchorage about a mysterious little nomad boy named Ismail!

Alas, then, that marvelous kaleidoscope of places and people that seemed so real as a child didn't belong to the real world at all. Or, at best, it was scarcely the representative portrait of the world that one ought to come to know after traveling about it for several years of social studies time. With this thought in mind, one certainly could, for example, ask why spend a month roaming with the nomads, when their numbers represent a terribly small percentage (less than five) of the world's people who occupy desert areas. Furthermore, even if the nomads could be made significant, why wade over the sand dunes when sandy deserts total less than ten per cent of desert surfaces? Why make those fur clothes and the oil lamp seem like such a burst of genius when they were developed by people living in other regions thousands of years before the Eskimos reached the Arctic? Indeed, no Eskimo had the time to sit around in a loin cloth in a sub-zero winter waiting to discover how helpful it would be to have a fur coat! And why, of all things, build igloos when today's Eskimo is more typically busy erecting the geodesic dome of a Distant Early Warning station for the Air Defense Command?

Reflections of Traditional Geography

Certainly Omak and Ismail were not, and are not, descriptive reflections of the sum total of elementary school geography. On the other hand, they are clearly linked to it; indeed, they are rather representative of geography as it has long been viewed by both common school and lay geographers. That this linkage has so long persisted is not difficult to understand. Geography as a field of study has, for centuries, been identified with exploration, and exploration has always focused on places and people located outside the realm of common experience. Further, there is little question but that a certain fascination with "strange lands and exotic people" continues to loom large in the popular mind. That nearly five million people are members of the National Geographic Society, whose magazine rather consistently includes descriptions and photographs of little known areas, is monumental testimony to the appeal of faraway places in geographical literature.

Several years ago, Professor William D. Pattison, in a most useful paper,[1] pointed up several traditions that have been, and continue to be, central to the field of geography. Exploration, both in a real sense and in the sense of the vicarious adventuring of children in elementary school classrooms, is centered in two of these traditions—the "man-land tradition" and the "area studies tradition."

Both of these traditions are clearly acknowledged even by those who have had little or no contact with geography as a scholarly discipline. "Man-land" refers to a search for interaction between man and his physical-biotic environment; "area studies" refers to the characterization of places, ranging in scale from the neighborhood in the primary grades to continents at the intermediate. Both traditions, unfortunately, have lent themselves to abuse in the elementary curriculum.

Out of the man-land tradition came a special bias, abandoned long ago by academic geography, but one that to this day continues to haunt school geography. This bias, known as environmentalism, is frequently confused with the entire man-land tradition in school geography. We can see its role in reflecting on our stories of Ismail and Omak. Hot and dry—nomadism; severe and prolonged cold—igloos! Of course this is wildly overstating the case. Yet a careful examination of the type study (area study) illustrations

---

[1] William D. Pattison, "The Four Traditions of Geography" *Journal of Geography* 63:211–216, 1964. Reprinted as Professional Paper No. 25. National Council for Geographic Education.

developed in so many curricula and texts prepared for the elementary level poignantly illustrates the impact of environmentalism.

Explaining man's behavior as a response to physical controls ignores the essential factor that people in similar physical-biotic environments simply do not make the same choices as to ways of life. What appears to one people as an ideal area for herding goats, appears to another as a marvelous setting for an intensively irrigated market garden, and to still another people as the perfect site for a desert resort replete with swimming pools, golf courses, and casinos. Academic geographers do not assume that man is the product of his physical environment. Neither do such theories have a place in modern school geography. Children, as young geographers, must be granted many opportunities to view the behavior of people in a given physical-biotic environment as a reflection of the attitudes, objectives, and technologies of the people themselves. In doing so they would be committing themselves to the study of environmental perception, a frontier area in modern academic geography.[2]

The man-land tradition, then, can and should continue to play an important role in school geography. It is most important to note, however, that it becomes truly meaningful only as it concerns itself with the real world, a dynamically changing setting as opposed to the static worlds of Ismail and Omak. This implies among a variety of other factors, intensified geographic analysis of urban areas as opposed to romanticized views of rural settings, and strong emphasis on where the people are as opposed to where they aren't.

If environmentalism is the curse of the man-land tradition, what has come to plague the house of geography from the area studies tradition? Out of this tradition sprang the inventory approach to school geography so unhappily recalled by generations of survivors of traditional geography programs. The inventory approach to area study simply refers to the all too prevalent lists of places and products that have so long dogged elementary school geography. While lip service to an avoidance of such drudgery has been given through the years by curriculum developers and textbook authors, the truth is too evident to be denied if one takes the trouble to examine their efforts. A preoccupation with factual detail—as opposed to a search for concepts, models, and principles—has traditionally been the lot of the young victims of an out-moded geography. A review of what Dean Lorrin Kennamer has called the "conceptual elements" of geography [3] is clear indication of a sharp move away from Gargantuan-like collections of miscellanea about places.

---

[2] David Lowenthal, ed. *Environmental Perception and Behavior* (Department of Geography Research Paper No. 109). Chicago: The University of Chicago, 1967.

[3] Lorrin Kennamer, Jr., "Geography in the Middle Grades." *Social Education* *31*:616, 1967.

The View Ahead

By combing current geographical literature, and by examining the contemporary curricula of leading departments of geography in this country, one could readily find satisfying documentation of the continued existence of each of Pattison's traditions.[4] Geography, regardless of the stance from which one views it, continues to find "its substance from man's sense of place and from his curiosity about the spatial attributes of the surface and atmospheric envelope of this planet." [5] The vast array of facts that might be used to fill out these spatial attributes are virtually limitless and as such lack a constant. Many of the geographical facts that one might learn in grade four, for example, may well be untrue or irrelevant by the time one reaches high school. Certainly, then, the goal for geography as a school subject, as with all fields of study, is to help the learner understand the conceptual structure of the discipline. Without this, as Professor Robert B. McNee has put it, geography would be "too abstract, too dry, too heaped with mountainous detail, too conceptually infertile, or too remote from the world as perceived by students to be attractive to them as an intellectual challenge." [6]

In counter-action to such unpleasant possibilities, much of the drive in contemporary American geography stems from the "spatial tradition." It is here that one finds concern for a whole gamut of generalizations related to spatial distributions, spatial associations, and spatial interactions. It is an understanding of these spatial relations and processes, along with an understanding of their significance to human activities, that encourages the student to analyze why things are where they are. Much of the work being done on the frontier of the discipline today falls into this tradition. Much of it is highly theoretical and much requires the utilization of sophisticated quantitative techniques. Needless to say, such studies lie well outside the reach of the elementary curriculum. Nonetheless, elementary school geographers can find a sustaining bond of fellowship with the research geographer in even the most rudimentary work that they might undertake in problems concerned with direction, distance, and location. These are spatial problems

[4] Pattison, *op. cit.* Two traditions, area studies and man-land, are discussed above. A third, the "earth science tradition," refers to a study "of the earth, the waters of the earth, the atmosphere surrounding the earth and the association between earth and sun. . . ." Brief discussion of the fourth, the "spatial tradition," follows.

[5] National Academy of Sciences-National Research Council. *The Science of Geography.* (Report of the *Ad Hoc* Committee on Geography, Earth Sciences Division, Publication 1277.) Washington, D.C.: National Academy of Sciences, National Research Council, 1965, p. 7.

[6] Robert B. McNee, "Toward Stressing Structure in Geographic Introduction, or Goodby to *Heavea Brazilliensis* and All That." Paper 4, in Commission on College Geography. *Introductory Geography, Viewpoints and Themes.* Washington, D.C.: Association of American Geographers, 1967, p. 31.

and, as such, are tied directly to the spatial tradition in the discipline of geography.

Geography is an exciting, dynamic, and wonderfully rewarding field of study. The elementary teacher and curriculum designer who will work toward establishing ties with this discipline cannot help but discover a wealth of ways in which he might link the frontiers of geographic research with geography as a school subject. Chorley and Haggett said it well in stating, "If we move with that frontier new horizons emerge into our view, and we find new territories to be explored as exciting and demanding as the dark continents that beckoned an earlier generation of geographers." [7] If it is time to say *adieu* to our old friends Ismail and Omak, we at least can take comfort in knowledge that we will gain lasting strength through our new grasp of the conceptual structure of the field.

The Dilemma of History in the Elementary School: Product or Process?

AMBROSE A. CLEGG, JR., AND
CARL E. SCHOMBURG

What is history? Why study it in the elementary school? This is the dilemma that faces anyone who examines the role of social studies in the elementary school curriculum.

History has been defined as an inquiry into the past with a view toward a better understanding of the present. While a historian may pursue his inquiry and investigation of the past solely for the development of scholarly knowledge, the role of history in the elementary school curriculum has often been quite different. Typically history has been looked on as an essential element in training for citizenship. A well-informed citizen, it has been argued, needs to know the background of his own cultural heritage, its myths and heroes, in order to make effective decisions about the present and future.

[7] Richard J. Chorley and Peter Haggett, *Frontiers in Geographical Teaching: The Madingley Lectures for 1963.* London: Methuen, 1965, p. 377.

Ambrose A. Clegg, Jr., is Chairman of the Department of Elementary Education at Kent State University, Ohio; Carl E. Schomburg is Coordinator of Elementary Education at the University of Houston, Texas.

Reprinted from *Social Education* 32:454–456 ff., 1968, with permission of the National Council for the Social Studies and Ambrose A. Clegg, Jr., and Carl E. Schomburg.

Traditionally, history has been the mainstay of the social studies curriculum in the elementary school. Such early books as Peter Parley's *History of the United States* (1828), helped to transmit the national heritage during the early years of our independence.[1] The McGuffey *Eclectic Readers* helped to build a background of legends, myths, and heroes of both the ancient and modern world as well as to give training in the 3 R's. As years passed during the middle of the nineteenth century, history began to share its place in the elementary school curriculum with geography, civics, and more recently with economics, sociology, and anthropology.

Lawmakers apparently believed that a knowledge of our history was necessary for elementary school children for effective citizenship. State legislatures, past and present, have mandated the teaching of state and national history and the celebration of a number of national holidays such as Washington's and Lincoln's birthdays, Memorial Day, Labor Day, Veterans' Day, as well as local holidays such as Independence Day in Texas, Patriot's Day in Massachusetts, Admission Day in California, and Huey P. Long's birthday in Louisiana. As early as 1827, Massachusetts required the teaching of American history in all towns of more than five hundred families,[2] and today every state requires that it be taught in the elementary and secondary schools.[3] While this legislative requirement has probably preserved the identity of immigrant groups and promoted sectional and class interests in some parts of the country, it has also helped to develop an awareness and pride in the national consciousness.

Today the history of one's state or region is often taught in the fourth grade, usually with strong emphasis on the state's early origins, first settlers, and the development of local institutions. American history is usually taught in the fifth grade as a chronological survey from the early explorers to the present. In some cases, this may be combined with geography of the various regions of the nation. The sixth grade usually combines a broadly based study of the ancient world as a background for Western civilization. These practices find their rationale and place in the curriculum as part of the familiar K-6 expanding environment approach to the study of man and his society.

It is interesting to note, however, that while the expanding environment approach proceeds on a sound logical and psychological basis from the familiar to the unknown, from the simple to the complex, there appears to be little justification, apaft from tradition or legislative mandate, for the

[1] Edgar Knight has noted that one history of the United States and three of New England had appeared by 1821, and that during the next decade eleven histories of the United States and three state histories had been published. *Education in the United States*, 2nd ed. Boston: Ginn, 1941.

[2] Richard E. Gross and W. V. Badger, "Social Studies," in *Encyclopedia of Educational Research*, 3rd ed., 1960, p. 1297.

[3] William H. Cartwright, "Selection, Organization, Presentation, and Placement of Subject Matter in American History." *Social Education* 29:435–444, 1965.

largely chronological organization or grade placement of the historical narrative of American history.

Indeed, there is considerable evidence to suggest that from the point of view of psychology of learning and child growth and development patterns, that the persistent emphasis on chronological order is misplaced. In that sense, history does not belong in the elementary school. But there are ways that history can focus on the "now and then" in the elementary school that are both psychologically and academically sound. We shall return to these later.

Some Basic Issues and Problems

The current ferment in the entire social studies field, K-12, has helped crystallize a number of major issues and problems regarding the role of history in the elementary school curriculum. These concern: (a) the relation between history and the social sciences, (b) curriculum goals, (c) methodology, (d) lack of a theoretical basis in learning theory, and (e) history as an inquiry process. Let us now turn to each of these and discuss them in some detail.

There has been much concern in recent years about the relation between history and the social sciences. Curriculum revision has focused on the identification of important concepts and generalizations from the various disciplines, and the nature of a fundamental structure presumed to underlie each. Yet historians are inclined to claim that history has no universal concepts, no underlying structure as do the social sciences; rather, there may be many competing structures. More often, historians tend to refer to history as one of the humanities and also a social science. Mark Krug,[4] for example, refers to it as a social science because it uses a carefully disciplined method of inquiry. But he also claimed it was a humanity because its final conclusions were intuitive and highly individual; they belong to the world of art.

When history is written in the grand tradition of a literary narrative, it becomes important not only as a scientific record of a segment of the past, but also as an artistic and aesthetic experience. Thus, history is also a branch of literature and belongs not only to the social sciences, but to the humanities.[5]

If this is true, it raises serious questions about history in a conceptually oriented curriculum modeled after the mode of inquiry of the social sciences.

A second basic issue is the relationship of history to major curriculum

[4] Mark Krug, "History and the Social Sciences: The Narrowing Gap." *Social Education 29*:515–520, 1965. See also Krug's address, "New Concepts and Approaches to Social Studies—Implications for Teacher Education," presented at the National Council for the Social Studies Convention, Seattle, Washington, November 22, 1967, in which he discussed this issue at some length.

[5] *Ibid.*

goals. Is the nature and intrinsic value of history and its subject matter of such importance that it should be studied primarily for itself in the sense of a separate scholarly discipline? Or is it in some way more directly related to the developmental needs of youth, to persistent social problems, to concepts of social change, or to the modern demands of citizenship? All of these have been posed at various times as appropriate philosophic criteria for the selection and organization of the curriculum. As we noted at the beginning of this article, the often professed purpose of history is its assumed relationship to the task of training for citizenship. Yet the teaching of it continues to be, for the most part, the recitation of the narrative of the American past with little or no connection with the current or the future tasks expected of the citizen. This is the essence of Professor Anthony's [6] objections to many of the new social studies programs. And similarly it is the lack of relevance that Shaver refers to when he calls for a redefinition of social studies.[7]

A third issue involves the methodology of teaching. Currently there is considerable interest in the use of inductive or inquiry teaching, the use of original source materials, and "the tools and methods of the historian." In contrast, the deductive method often depends on the synthesis of previous work of scholars, Professor Fenton's [8] recently developed material in the use of the inquiry method appears to give promise as a useful technique for study of history. So also does the current work by Kounslar and Frizzle [9] at the junior high school level. What is critically needed in addition are well-designed research programs that carefully test out the assumptions implied in those teaching methods that involve inductive or deductive modes of thinking.

Another major issue concerns the failure to relate learning theory more closely to the methods presently advocated in the teaching of social studies. The terms "problem solving" and "reflective thinking" have been too cosmic. They need to be defined much more precisely in behavioral terms and at the bits and pieces level of day-to-day operation so that clearly defined teaching strategies can be developed and managed by the classroom teacher. In this respect, Taba's [10] identification of three cognitive tasks gives

[6] Albert S. Anthony, "The Role of Objectives in the 'New History'." *Social Education 31*:574–580, 1967.

[7] James P. Shaver, "Social Studies: The Need for Redefinition." *Social Education 31*:588–592, 596, 1967.

[8] Edwin Fenton, general ed., *Holt Social Studies Curriculum.* New York: Holt, Rinehart & Winston, 1966. See also programs as *Comparative Political Systems, Comparative Economic Systems, Shaping Western Society, History of the United States,* all of which are based on an inductive approach.

[9] Allan O. Kounslar and Donald B. Frizzle, *Discovering American History.* New York: Holt, Rinehart & Winston, 1967.

[10] Hilda Taba, *Teaching Strategies and Cognitive Functioning in Elementary School Children.* U.S. Office of Education, Cooperative Research Project No. 2404. San Francisco State College, February, 1966.

much clearer direction to the classroom teacher than do many of the more classic statements on problem solving.

Neither Inquiry nor a Disciplined Study

The irony of all this is that what passes for history as taught in the elementary school is neither inquiry nor a disciplined study. What we may call "school-book history" tends to focus on the *product* of the historian, not the *process* of an inquiry into the past, disciplined by a rigorous method of investigation. What we also overlook is that the product of the historian's efforts is *an* interpretation of the material. We conveniently ignore the fact, too, that there may be varying and conflicting interpretations of the same data. Unfortunately, the historian's original scholarship and interpretive comment are often three or four times removed from the distillations that appear in the elementary school social studies texts. Somehow in the translation process we have lost sight of the assumptions, the biases, the perspective, and the tentativeness of the original in an effort to emphasize the narrative of the agreed upon facts. Thus we have clothed history with far more certitude than the historian ever intended. As a result, school-book history tends to be the approved recorded narrative of the past. In the terms of the anthropologist, history in the elementary school consists largely of passing down the myths and legends of our national heritage as part of the initiation of youth into the culture of the society.

The Process of "Historying"

As we have suggested above, history is not only a product, it is also a *process*. It implies the act of "inquiry" in the same way that "inquiry" is so much a part of modern curriculum developments in the natural sciences.[11] To express this in the sense of the verb, we have to resort to such awkward phrases as *doing* history, or *historying*. It is an activity, a process, not a passive absorption of someone else's account. Pupils are expected to work actively with the materials of history.

The relics or residue of the past constitute the materials of history. These may be such primary or original sources as artifacts, records, documents, diaries, newspapers, or pictures of past events. Other useful sources are the many available secondhand accounts of those who have talked to eyewitnesses, and the records of the remembered stories of others. Also

[11] J. Richard Suchman, *The Elementary School Training Program in Scientific Inquiry*. U.S. Office of Education Title VII, Project No. 216. University of Illinois, January, 1964.

included are the narratives of those who wrote the "history" of a contemporary period, for example Herodotus's account of Greece in his day, or a current figure such as Arthur Schlesinger, Jr., who has recently provided both an eyewitness account and an interpretation of the Kennedy administration.

"History Is What the Historians Do" [12]

The process of doing history or historying [13] involves both the activity of inquiring and the use of a carefully disciplined approach to the selection, analysis, and interpretation of evidence. Clements [14] has outlined a basic strategy or model [15] that is applicable to history as well as to any social inquiry. It includes such tasks as (1) identifying a heuristic or leading question, (2) selecting ideas or concepts that will be useful for analyzing the leading questions, (3) using the concepts to formulate propositions or hypotheses about the leading questions, (4) locating and collecting various sources of evidence, (5) cross-examining the evidence, and (6) preparing a report that presents the conclusions or interpretations of the study.

The tasks identified in Clement's model are not beyond the competency of elementary school children. Traditionally we have just not become involved in doing history as a process of inquiry in the elementary school. This is not to suggest, as some would advocate, that the schools train junior historians in the technical aspects of the craft. Rather, it is to argue as Henry Johnson [16] urged more than a quarter century ago, that children become critical students of how the historian produces his product, so that they can read and interpret history with an equally critical eye.

With some relatively minor changes in our procedures teachers could easily shift the focus from learning the product to engaging in the process of historying. For example, third or fourth graders traditionally study their local community. Because ready-made texts are seldom available, teachers (1) plan field trips to important sites, (2) help children find old records in

[12] Isaiah Berlin, "History and Theory, the Concept of Scientific History." *History and Theory* I, No. 1, 1960.

[13] We deliberately continue to use these concocted words to emphasize the sense of active engagement with materials of the past.

[14] Millard Clements, "The Disciplines and Social Study." *Effective Thinking in the Social Studies.* Thirty-seventh Yearbook of the National Council for the Social Studies. Washington, D.C., 1967, pp. 72–75.

[15] In an earlier work Clements referred to this as the "mystery model," comparing the process to that used by the detective in the fictional novel to solve the murder mystery. See M. Clements, W. Fielder, and R. Tabachnick, *Social Study: Inquiry in Elementary Classrooms.* Indianapolis: Bobbs-Merrill, 1966.

[16] See especially "School History and the Historical Method." *The Teaching of History,* Rev. ed. New York: Macmillan, Inc., 1940, Ch. XV.

the town hall or in early newspapers, (3) arrange for the visit and interview of a long-time resident, (4) collect and organize their findings on large charts, and (5) help the children prepare a book of stories, a series of oral reports, a mural, or perhaps present a play about some dramatic episode from the town's past. If these activities are not too heavily dominated by the teacher, then it can be said that the pupils are actively engaged in doing history at a relatively simple level.

Many suggestions have been made elsewhere for actively engaging pupils in the process of inquiring about times past. Vincent Rogers [17] has suggested some interesting uses of original documents in connection with the colonization of Jamestown, the stereotype of slavery, and the rush to settle new lands in the West. Clements *et al.*[18] have presented many examples of historical inquiry in a variety of settings: ancient and modern, local and national. And in a more specialized area, Clifford Lord [19] has edited an entire series of monographs on "localized history" with individual books on every state as well as major cities, important watersheds, and the principal ethnic groups that have immigrated to this country.

The Balance Between Product and Process

As noted above, the bulk of what passes as history in the elementary school consists largely of learning the accumulated traditions of the national heritage. While recognizing the value of this knowledge as a necessary part of the socialization process, the focus of this article has been to suggest that the balance be redressed to give the process of *doing history* its appropriate place in the curriculum. The issue is not an "either-or" proposition. Rather, an appropriate balance of history as both a product *and* a process needs to be established in the elementary social studies curriculum.

Summary

This article has examined the role of history in the elementary school in terms of the dilemma of product or process. The product of the historian's work was seen to be of value in that it served to acquaint the pupils with the past traditions of the nation, its legends, and its heroes. On the other

[17] Vincent Rogers, "Using Source Material with Children." *Social Education* 24:307–309, 1960.

[18] Clements, *op. cit.*

[19] Clifford Lord, ed., *Localized History Series.* New York: Teachers College Press, Columbia University, 1964.

hand, the pupil develops a false and misleading sense of certainty and truth in the highly distilled and antiseptically neutral account of the agreed upon facts that he reads in some school textbooks. To redress the balance between product and process and to nourish the spirit of intellectual inquiry, Clements's model was suggested as a useful strategy for actively engaging pupils in the process of doing history, using the materials and the methods of the historian at an elementary level.

The Humanities, the Social Studies, and the Process of Valuing

RAYMOND J. ENDRES

Once one owns one house, two cars, and three color TV sets—and a shriveled soul—what else is there to live for? And was it worth the effort? The question then that seems to lie at the heart of the problem is essentially a question regarding the meaning of life beyond affluence.[1]

—His Excellency Soedjatmoko
Ambassador of the Republic of Indonesia

Man throughout centuries of experience has developed social systems that have attempted to deal with these basic questions: What is real? What is true? What is good? The questions are short and sweet. How complex the answers! They are no more complex, however, than the systems built by a society to preserve "the truth" about the real and the good. Frequently organization and structure become ends in themselves, seemingly more important than the truth they are designed to protect. The basic questions lie forgotten in the dustbin of history.

Traditionally philosophers have dealt with these basic questions. They have developed whole ontological, epistemological, and ethical systems to answer them. Philosophers operate within cultures and it is a moot point whether their systems reflect cultural values or serve to help shape them. Most systems, furthermore, seem to have been built on the assumption that the questions were answered for all time. If there was a challenge to the

Raymond J. Endres is an Associate Professor of Social Studies Education at Bowling Green State University, Ohio.

Reprinted from *Social Education 34*:544–548 ff., 1970, with permission of the National Council for the Social Studies and Raymond J. Endres.

[1] Ambassador Soedjatmoko, "A Foreign Visitor's View of the United States: Stereotypes and Realities," *Social Education* (November, 1969), 33:791.

existing order, it often came from those who by disposition and training served as society's gadflies: its poets, artists, storytellers, and dramatists. It came from those humanistically inclined, from persons who insisted on asking questions about the human predicament. What is man? Does he have purpose? What is his relationship to man, to the world outside himself? Is there meaning in the world? Order? Comprehension?

The ways in which a society answers these questions about human experience are shaped by its value system and result in its continued evolution. A value system operates for us in at least three ways. First, it serves as a filtration mechanism. We are inundated with data. Our value system tells us what is important within that mountain of stimuli, that is, what things are real, true, and good. It says to us, "This perception makes sense; this one, nonsense." The result may be a xenophobia and an ethnocentrism, euphemisms for narrow-mindedness. They may, on the other hand, result in world-mindedness.

Second, a value system serves as a motivating force. In this sense it comes close to ideology. It provides us with a number of touch-points in the decision-making process, even to the extent of helping us decide what needs and demands will be met and the methodology of meeting those we deem most worthy. "Do not try to beat others at games," a Hopi mother warns. "That is not Hopi."

Third, a value system, as articulated in language, provides us a conceptual schema for interpreting our environment. It is, thereby, a product of culture. As the anthropological linguist might put it, "We start out speaking as we think and end up thinking as we speak." In other words, we come to believe and act upon those things we say.

The Humanities and Values

Art forms in the humanities may invite us to subscribe to new or modified values. Contemporary pop music does this. It invites its serious listeners to experiment with new or changed ways of operating, thus subscribing to a "new morality." Old forms, especially those that require us to wait in seeking pleasure and gratification, are passé. Changed attitudes about sex, war, peace, drugs, indeed, about the total range of human action and interaction are suggested in its lyrics and intensified by its variegated rhythms.

Art-forms also criticize existing values, a second function. Literature abounds with examples of social satire (*Alice in Wonderland*), of political satire (*Animal Farm*), and of social criticism (*David Copperfield*). In the last 40 years quantities of social prophecies, such as *Brave New World,* have been published that predict Armageddon if current policies and values are not reversed.

A third function, to reinforce existing values, prevails among those materials we tend to use with children. In infancy children are exposed to music, stories, and poetry by parents and publishers who have decided what is "good" for the little tykes. The good that emerges has passed through the filters of our value system. When children reach school, the process of socialization initiated at home is usually continued. By reinforcing traditional values we attempt to protect the young from the harsh realities of the world. This becomes important when we consider that a child's values become part of his total life style. "Recent research has abundantly reconfirmed a theory about learning expressed 2,400 years ago by Plato," John Gibson writes, "that the human being acquires values and attitudes of social significance very early in life." He continues:

> The socialization of the child is how he develops in a cognitive and affective manner by receiving messages from people near him, from media, and from his environment. Whether we refer to the political, economic, sexual, or whatever other category of socialization that has relevance to the social behavior of the individual, we may be assured that one's perception of man and society tends to develop while the person is very young.[2]

Two examples come to mind. Last summer we analyzed a number of film loops, among them one entitled "City and Country Life." The film showed alternating shots of city and country. The photography was excellent. Students supposedly analyzed the pictures and formed hypotheses based on this analysis. The film was silent. What spoke most loudly, however, was its editorial point of view: the country is a good place, the city a bad place. The country shots showed abundant fresh air, sunshine, open-spaces, natural beauty; in a word, country life was idyllic. It portrayed the city as crowded, dangerous, dirty, cluttered, filled with minorities; in short, city life was foreign, somehow less American than the country.

According to political scientists who have studied urban and rural political socialization, considerable evidence suggests that this film editor's values prevail among most Americans. "Give me the simple life," the song goes. This value on the bucolic has a long tradition in this country. It has been reinforced by rural-dominated state legislatures and Federal Congresses. One-man one-vote decisions have not so much shifted power to the city as to the suburbs.

How do the humanities reinforce existing values about rural and urban life? Look at how our suburban and country homes are furnished and what hangs on their walls. Pictures of landscapes portray the beauties of the country. Scenes from New England and Jackson Hole country prevail. These pictures have their historical setting in Colonial America or in the

---

[2] John S. Gibson, "Selecting and Developing Instructional Materials," *Social Studies Curriculum Development: Prospects and Problems.* 39th Yearbook, National Council for the Social Studies, 1969. p. 194.

Westward Movement. They fit in nicely with much of our Early American furniture. Contemporary abstract paintings, more likely to symbolize the complexity of modern urban life, are much less popular.

Pursue at leisure any children's anthology of poetry. Most of the poetry that has a geographic setting is pastoral and idyllic. That which is about city life is usually negative, often in the "let's get away from it all" vein. A personal favorite, Robert Frost, writes, "Whose woods these are I do not know. His house is in the village though." Beautiful, simple, and rustic.

Sandburg, less a romantic than many poets, pens the line: "Chicago: hog butcher of the world!" He states a fact and is not repulsed by it. Yet "butcher" strikes a harsh chord on our pastoral sensibilities. We may be a violent people, but we don't like to read about it, especially in poetry. Better to grow hogs in Iowa where there's much fresh air than to butcher them in the Windy City. Eleanor Farjeon sums it up in "City Streets and Country Roads": [3]

> The city has streets—
> But the country has roads.
> In the country one meets
> Blue carts with their loads
> Of sweet-smelling hay,
> And mangolds, and grain;
> Oh, take me away
> To the country again!
>
> In the city one sees,
> Big trams rattle by,
> And the breath of the chimneys
> That blot out the sky,
> And all down the pavements
> Still lamp-posts one sees—
> But the country has hedgerows,
> The country has trees.
>
> As sweet as the sun
> In the country is rain:
> Oh, take me away
> To the country again!

Television and advertising serve further to reinforce negative attitudes toward city life. The city is where the action is. Who is involved in the action? Pimps and panderers, juvenile delinquents and junkies, legal eagles and criminal types, people with strange sounding names and people who look different. These are the characters who hit the TV screen. Sandwiched in between episodes is the advertising which depicts the flight from the city in a powerful automobile that comes to rest in the green of suburbia, its

[3] From the book *Poems for Children* by Eleanor Farjeon. Copyright 1926, renewed 1954, by Eleanor Farjeon. Reprinted by permission of J. B. Lippincott Company.

serene setting, well-washed children, and beautiful wives. We are invited to get away from it all in a Pan Am jet. Fly the friendly skies of United to beautiful Hawaii, on credit, of course.

We conclude from this that the arts, whether pop or classic, do little to build a commitment to the humanization of life in urban settings. They do sing the praises of technology, a value orientation, paradoxically, somewhat in conflict with our negative view of urban life. Americans, pragmatists who love to tinker and experiment on a trial and error basis, have seen technology solve problems in the past. It has met our need for mobility by producing millions of automobiles each year. These in turn have created problems: pollutants spewed into the atmosphere; millions of acres gobbled up by superhighways. We desperately want to believe that technology will solve the problems of the city. We have practically given technology a life of its own, a personality, symbolized by the train in this poem of Emily Dickinson: *

> I like to see it lap the miles,
> And lick the valleys up,
> And stop to feed itself at tanks;
> And then, prodigious, step
>
> Around a pile of mountains,
> And, supercilious, peer
> In shanties by the sides of roads;
> And then a quarry pare
>
> To fit its sides, and crawl between,
> Complaining all the while
> In horrid, hooting stanza;
> Then chase itself down hill
>
> And neigh like Boanerges;
> Then, punctual as a star,
> Stop—docile and omnipotent—
> At its own stable door.

Technology is powerful! It has been our hand-maiden in controlling a recalcitrant environment. This desire for absolute control, coupled with the view that the natural environment is something hostile to be conquered, is an integral part of our value system. The results are positive—flood control, industrialization, development of energy resources—and negative—denuded forests and the pollution of air, field, and stream. Our view of environment is not symbiotic, where we live on an essentially friendly host which we preserve, protect, and enhance. Rather, our environmental *Weltansicht* is parasitic: man feeds on his host and ultimately destroys it. Perhaps we can retreat, at least mentally, to the country where we can escape our guilt for having raped the environment to feed our technology. The further this phantasy retreat into the country, the less we feel compelled to identify with the city's problems.

Today it is popular to set up a hue and cry about what we have done to pollute and exploit the environment. This rhetoric is not matched by a national commitment that says, "Money is no object. Let's get on with the job!" This commitment, in all its human and physical ramifications, will probably require us to alter some values we have held so dearly about individual freedom as related to private property. It will ask that we reinterpret the relationship of the individual to the community. It will require short term and long range planning. And it will demand of all citizens that they give just as serious consideration to action in the public as in the private sectors of their lives. Nothing will be more detrimental to our social order than the development of problems in the public sector that reach dimensions that seem to place them beyond the involvement of the citizen in the decision-making process. Perhaps we have reached that point already.

Values and the Schools

The foregoing should not suggest that teachers must inculcate values. It does suggest that we have failed to help children develop those critical and analytical abilities so necessary to the decision-making process, whether in childhood or adult life. Analysis, we contend, leads the child to perceive alternative models in solutions to a given problem. Certainly in the realm of values, schools have done little to help children perceive more clearly alternative structures. Yet we need look no farther for an alternative model than the Hopi Indian of the Southwest. In the *Desert Soliloquy* Nakima's father speaks:

The whole world must work in harmony, Nakima. Nature, the gods, the plants, the animals, and men need each other and must work together for the good of all. There is no place for selfish men or even for a selfish man among men. It would throw everything out of balance and endanger the whole universe. To be a good Hopi, Nakima, you will work for the good of your family, your clan, the village, and the whole world. Praise what others do. Belittle what you do yourself, Nakima. Keep a good heart.

Later Nakima speaks:

Man can, my people believe, exercise some control over the orderly rhythm of the world with his actions, thoughts, emotions, and will. Man must, to avoid failure, see the world whole and understand that relationship of all that goes to make up the harmonious ebb and flow, the decay and creation.[4]

[4] Walter Goldschmidt, editor. "Desert Soliloquy," *Ways of Mankind Records, Volume I*. National Association of Educational Broadcasters.

Whether real or the apocryphal incantations of a cultural anthropologist the validity of these comments as another modular view of man and environment remains. A child's education should include a consideration of the structures of various value systems. This should not take place, moreover, in a vacuum. Children can examine critical issues and how different cultural groups might respond to them. They can analyze the ways in which cultures meet such basic psychological needs as self-worth and individual adaptation to group needs. They can study the cultural means used to adapt to environmental conditions. The question, "Why these responses?", always takes the learner back to a consideration of values.

Values and Instructional Materials

Whether we like it or not, advertising has preëmpted many art symbols; it is a popular art form. Americans may laugh at or become frustrated by advertising but would find it difficult to deny that it helps develop such values as materialism and secularism. Its approaches have become more subtle, but advertising still promises the good life. In addition, it has a great influence over other art forms, especially those connected with mass media. As in poetry, its message is connotative, an appeal to the emotions. As an instructional resource related to value formation advertising has great potential.

Contemporary music offers much for analysis. Its lyrics are fraught with value implications. Clearly the message of protest comes across, sometimes directly, sometimes obliquely through advocacy of experimentation. Young children may or may not understand its nuances, but upper-elementary pupils could certainly form some valid hypotheses about values inherent in pop music.

Graffiti, a contemporary art form indigenous to our culture, can also be used by teachers of elementary youngsters. A recent graffito appearing in the *Toledo Blade* [5]—"Abominable snowmen dwell on Madison Avenue"— reveals on analysis a possible growing awareness of Americans to the limited function of advertising: to sell products and services. Graffiti have the added advantage of bringing humor to analysis. The cartoon also uses humor in its message. Children can, moreover, create their own graffiti and cartoons.

Awareness of values must extend beyond American culture. Children's analysis of alternative value systems need not be limited to contemporary societies. Haiku reveals the values of Japan in the 16th and 17th Centuries.

[5] Leary, "Graffiti," *The Toledo Blade* Peach Section. Wednesday, December 17, 1969. p.1.

In Haiku we analyze form—the attempt to link two disparate ideas around the central theme of season using an inflexible rhythmic system—and substance, which often becomes clear only on analysis. We are struck by the happy marriage of rigid form and fluid substance in such as:

> White chrysanthemum.
> Before that perfect flower
> Scissors hesitate.[6]

The cutting edge of this 17 syllable poem is its succinctness; so much is left to the reader. We are forced to draw inferences about the way the Japanese felt about natural beauty and its cultivation, about technology, and about the meeting of steel and stem. Are these a realistic people? What inferences can we draw from their use of "hesitate"? Or is this word merely a subscription to form?

By contrast look at a contemporary Japanese poem. The succinctness is still there. The values have changed. An incisive criticism prevails.

> Fujiyama—we sell.
> Miyajima—we sell.
> Nikko—we sell.
> Japan—we sell anywhere.
> Naruto, Aso—
> We sell it all.
> Prease, prease, come and view!
> Me rub hands,
> Put on smile.
> Money, money—that's the thing!
> We Japanese   all buy cars
> We Japanese   all like lighters
> We Japanese   all good gardeners
> We Japanese   all sing pops.
> All, all, are meek and mild. Yes! [7]

The secret in analyzing humanistic materials—whether artifacts, poetry, drama, stories, pictures, sculptures, or carving—is to take children beyond the superficial. So much of our study of other lands and people has centered on the material culture: what people wear, eat, and sleep in. A study of non-material values—whether dealing with family, politics, religion, or esthetics—is much more subtle; it is also much more exciting for teacher and pupil alike. When we look at an artifact, what does it tell us about the real, the true, and the good in a given culture? What might a picture of a family in India tell us about the relationships among persons in that family?

---

[6] Buson, "White Chrysanthemum . . ." *Japanese Haiku*. Peter Pauper Press, p.38.

[7] Takenaka Iku: "Tourist Japan," from *The Penguin Book of Japanese Verse*, edited and translated by Geoffrey Bownas and Anthony Thwaite (1964). Copyright © Geoffrey Bownas and Anthony Thwaite, 1964.

What inferences can we draw about the structure of the family, about the function of the family in the economic system?

Pictures are very useful in the study of cultural values. Good pictures, happily, are becoming more readily available. Teachers have themselves become avid picture-takers. On a recent field-study experience in Guadalajara, Mexico we took many pictures which we have already used to advantage with various groups. Most important in this process, however, is the analysis we bring to it. We recall one picture of a double column of children leaving a school yard in Refugio, a small *ejido* near Guadalajara. Among the children were two girls with rifles slung over their shoulders. We wondered why. On analysis, we found that they were still celebrating the November anniversary of the Revolution, were carrying forward the values inherent in that revolution and its relationship to the peasant population and to the land.

In Houston during the recent NCSS meeting we visited with Dr. and Mrs. Henry Furguson. Through Interculture Associates, Dr. Furguson has developed collections of materials from India that children can analyze in their attempts to understand India better. Clearly, teachers can use these materials to take learners beyond the material culture. The performing arts, so rich in Indian lore, will reveal on analysis many values important in this culture. Other materials, including books, will introduce children to values related to awareness of self in relation to others, decision-making, roles and statuses, mythology, religion, and cultural adaptation.

Although developed to introduce pupils to economic concepts, many of the materials compiled by Lawrence Senesh for use at the third-grade level have humanistic overtones. *Cities at Work* is obviously based on certain ontological and ethical assumptions.

The readings and the exercises recommended in this study of cities are intended to help children discover the many dimensions of a historical period. They are intended to help them feel the passage of time by counting the generations of people between the living person and the past event. The material tries to show that a historical period is characterized by many simultaneous developments—in standard of living, law, technology, science, art, architecture and literature and in ideas and the willingness of men to do something with those ideas.[8]

Other authors and publishers have produced materials that children can analyze and from which they can draw conclusions about the relationship between the things people do and their values, that is, their perception of reality, truth, and goodness. We can ourselves organize sets of materials for classroom analysis. We are limited only by imagination and will.

[8] Lawrence Senesh. *Our Working World* (a brochure). Science Research Associates, 1967. p. 5.

The Humanities and Emergent Values

Without doubt, the humanities function importantly in developing and reinforcing a value system. In the oral tradition of Sparta, stories of brave heroes bore directly on the training of Spartan youth. The plays of Aeschylus and Euripides certainly helped shape the way Athenians thought and acted. The life style of the Florentine was influenced by the art and architecture that surrounded him.

Contemporary humanistic art-forms are abstract, symbolic, and difficult to understand; the literature and drama of the past 25 years has emphasized nihilism, an attack on existing values rather than a delineation of emergent values. Consider the number of cacotopias which have appeared since Huxley wrote *Brave New World* in 1932. *Canticle for Leibowitz, Fahrenheit 451,* and *1984* certainly hold out little hope for man's future. They reflect, perhaps, the disillusionment of the age.

Dr. James Coke, director for the Center for Urban Regionalism at Kent State University, contends that tomorrow's hope rests with the dreamer, hopefully not a Dr. Strangelove, who can provide us with alternate utopian models on which to build a new society. Perhaps the utopian dreamer can build his model order on a set of postulates or values that enable man to use his creations, his machines, his technology for human ends.

Perhaps artists have been asking the wrong question: What is man's future? By current standards, it is bleak. Perhaps they should ask: What are man's potentialities? We really know so little of our capabilities, except that we seem disinclined to exercise them. Psychologists indicate that we may utilize as little as five percent of our intellectual potential.

Tomorrow's world will probably not be built on the established order but on a system of emergent values consistent with a new society's needs. We suspect that while the old order changeth, it will not change completely. Unless, of course, man's nature is significantly altered. The current state of art is either to support or to attack the established order. While these are valid and legitimate functions, we hope some artists will resume to function in those ways that portray the broad highway and alternative routes to human fulfillment. When this happens perhaps a New Renaissance will be upon us. We shall say then, with Oscar Wilde, "Life is an imitation of art."

Art in the Social Studies

THOMAS A. HAMIL

A picture is not *worth* a thousand words. It is different than a thousand words. A picture makes its own message, not a translation of a verbal message. Visual communication is direct, swift, and powerful.

Members of the literate culture are not often aware of the power of nonverbal communication.[1] But when we notice the reactions of the viewers to a show of avant-garde painting, of the trance compelled by the flickering television image, or the shudder when a flashing red light is seen in the rear-view mirror of our car, we may appreciate that all communication is not in words. The strong impact of vision is sensed in such expressions as "eye-sore," or "it delights my eyes."

Although many cognitive elements may be introduced in a picture, it is the emotional effect that is most noticed. Two pictures may show the appearance of a medieval village, for example, but the illustrator's use of color, technique, and the aspects of the scene he stresses may give the feeling of a romantic fictional past or the awareness of the squalor and poverty of the Dark Ages. Both pictures may give the same facts, but the reaction to them will be completely different. The viewer is reached on an affective level as well as through the information presented.

Children are often more comfortable with visual than verbal messages. They are constrained by vocabulary and grammar in their verbal communication, whereas visual communication seems more direct. Visual communication is natural to man. We have a 30,000-year heritage of visual art that seems as understandable now as when painted. Of course, our understanding may be different than the intentions of the painters, but we can appreciate the symbols on our own terms. Children also seem ready to accept art on their terms. Many works that are confusing to adults are accepted by children. I recall watching a little girl and her mother looking at a nonobjective painting. The mother looked perplexed; the little girl squealed delightedly, "Oh, isn't it noisy!"

This is not to say that understanding through vision is automatic. It takes

Thomas A. Hamil is an author and illustrator of children's books and an Associate Professor of Elementary Education at Wayne State University, Detroit.

Prepared especially for *Readings for Social Studies in Elementary Education,* Second Edition, and reprinted with Thomas A. Hamil's permission.

[1] J. Ruesch, *Nonverbal Communication.* Berkeley: University of California Press, 1956.

training to see as a hunter sees, or as a botanist sees, or as a painter sees. Work in visual expression has as one of its goals the development of visual acuity.[2] Children may develop their vision by looking at paintings and by working with the problems of visual expression. Some symbols in art require sophistication for full understanding, but some understanding, on a personal level, seems possible for everyone who is willing to look.

The Use of Art in the Social Studies

We expect to find the pages of type in our textbooks relieved by pictures. They are treated often as decoration to give the reader a pause in his study. But we expect illustrations to give information also. They may be considered supplementary, extending the ideas in the text, or they may contain their own body of facts that would be impossible to put into words. Some information must be shown. Imagine trying to describe the face of Lincoln.

As with all sources of fact, pictures must be carefully considered before the teacher uses them. Editors and illustrators try to be accurate. But illustrations have appeared with freshly attired pioneers, or Mongol warriors astride Western cow ponies! Obviously, teachers cannot go through the research necessary to certify each picture. But awareness of the importance of the information contained in the illustrations may help the teacher keep alert to errors. An accurate picture can be a research tool.

The teacher can ask questions that encourage careful looking by her students. The level of questioning can proceed from basic identification of things in the picture to conjecture of possible uses, outcomes, sources, and so forth.[3] Probing questions may bring out more from a picture than from the pages of type. The picture is open-ended; there are no limits to the suppositions that could be drawn from it.

Pictures not only show facts but they often reveal emotion. Scenes of historical events may show the setting and costumes and people involved and also show how the people felt on the occasion.

Paintings not only give information about an era, but the paintings may be a primary source. Scollon described the change in the attitudes of Americans shown in the sequence of portrait art. Early portraiture was done in imitation of European court paintings; later they became more and more indicative of individualism as men were portrayed in the gear of their

[2] G. S. Wright, Jr., "Elementary Art to Develop Visual Sensitivity." *School Arts* 2:19–21, 1963.

[3] B. S. Bloom, ed., *Taxonomy of Educational Objectives: The Classification of Educational Goals, Handbook I: The Cognitive Domain.* New York: McKay 1956.

trade.[4] A great deal can be learned from the subjects chosen by painters and how they dealt with those subjects. There are many examples: symbolic animals in many hunting cultures, the comparison of the idealized human in Greek art and the portraits of Rome, the absence of figures in Islamic art, and so on.

Art As a Means to Social Study

Art may be used by children as a means of study. In the social studies, we are concerned about the reading abilities of our pupils because so much of our material is verbal. But there is a great source of data that the reader and nonreader can share in the visual arts. Pictures may provide the means to find information and also the means to record information when it is found. The research skills can apply equally to gathering facts from illustrations as well as from texts. Many of the topics we study may be put directly into visual terms. Why write about the appearance of a California mission? Many topics are available in well-illustrated trade books that provide a research tool for all pupils. The illustrations may be used as a perfectly respectable method for learning, even for excellent readers.

Pictures can build a strong background for concept formation.

. . . for it was not so much by the knowledge of words that I came to the understanding of things, as by experience of things I was enabled to follow the meaning of words.

Plutarch [5]

A picture can come close to experience. The degree of the response to a picture depends on its quality. Pictures can be as dull as last year's memorandum if they present information without style. Or, the symbolism of a picture can be too obscure for the pupil to respond. But a painting that gives the information needed in an appealing form involves the child in a vicarious experience from which he can build his ideas.

There is one aspect of art that is used a great deal in elementary school social studies—that is the use of art as a presentational method. In most classrooms, the walls display maps, drawings, and murals that relate to the social studies content. Here is the place to add richness to the pupils' learning. These displays can be made artistically pleasing as well as factually accurate.

The first step toward good art in the social studies is to have the children

---

[4] Kenneth M. Scollon, "The Arts: Overlooked Witnesses of History." *Social Education 31*:29–32, 1967.

[5] Quoted in B. Bettelheim, *The Empty Fortress*. New York: Free Press, 1967, p. 89.

do their own drawings. Copies of illustrations are generally stilted and add no personal quality to the work. Details, the facts of the drawing, may be taken from paintings of the period or from illustrations, but the drawing should be the child's own expression. Only by taking the material of his study and putting it into his own expression can the child learn. As M. P. Follette commented:

Concepts can never be presented to me merely, they must be knitted into the structure of my being, and this can only be done through my own activity.[6]

Also by working with the problems of art, children can be made more aware of the artist's approach to those problems. The child then becomes a contributor to knowledge, not a mere recipient.

Develop the appreciation of the children in the works of children by showing the products of their peers from their own school, other schools in the area, and examples from around the world. The commonality of interests may present an important social lesson. Within the school district, schools of different social classes or with ethnic variations may trade pictures to build an appreciation of the views of others and to share their views. Diversity may be more apparent than real when we are made aware of the similarity of our arts. Children's art is an important facet of the world's art. When pupils see their work as a part of this art and not in competition with adult art, they may be more willing to display their work.

An awareness of the expressive quality of color can be encouraged. Descriptive color may contribute little to a drawing, especially if the color is stereotyped. Using colored paper as background for pastel or tempera paintings may bring more exciting effects than the usual manila paper. A huge combine roaring across a field may take on real drama if presented with brilliant colors.

The use of color can also be stimulated by short walks around the school-yard. Skies are not always blue, nor leaves green. Looking at a plant will show the wide variation of colors in its leaves. A word of caution in this regard, however. Children need to develop their own symbols before they can give them meaning.[7] Respect the child's symbol even while you bring him outside to look.

A variety of media will encourage the visual presentation of your social studies material. Crayons can be used dozens of ways. They can be broken and used for big, flat effects; they can be used with the paper placed on top of a textured surface, like wood or canvas, so the colored areas will have texture; they can be pressed hard against the paper so a deep layer of wax is left, then that wax polished with a paper towel to give a shiny, rich

[6] M. P. Follette, *Creative Experience.* New York: Longmans, Green & Co., 1924.

[7] R. Arnheim, *Art and Visual Perception.* Berkeley: University of California Press, 1954.

surface. There are many possibilities.[8] Paints, clay, papier maché could all be used for social studies reporting.[9] Murals might be made from torn paper, squares of paper cut from magazines, bits of cloth or other materials, as a change from tempera on butcher paper. There is no limit to the variety that can be introduced. Be willing to give new ideas a try, or better, be willing to let your class give new ideas a try.

Variety can be stimulated by bringing reproductions of art work into the class. They are available free, or for very little cost, through museums of art and other sources. Magazines carry pictures of architecture, sculpture, ceramics, dancers, and paintings that can be collected and used. How much better to have a reproduction of a work of art done *at* the time you are studying than to use an illustration *about* the time studied. Don't shy away from work that doesn't happen to be in your taste; give the children the chance to form their own opinions.

The child should be involved in choice. He should have as many opportunities as possible to decide and follow through on that decision. Art gives a chance for this social learning at a basic level. The child should choose his materials and techniques and see for himself the outcomes of that choice. The work should be an expression of the child, not an example of his ability to follow instructions. In this regard, the duplicated sheets of social studies material for coloring are a flagrant example of the misuse of visual media. The practice of providing those sheets robs both art and the social studies of any meaning.

There are activities used in the social studies that are related to art but that do not have the expressive quality. Those are the constructing activities. The object in construction is to replicate items for study. Maps, models, costumes, stage settings, or artifacts may be reproduced. The purpose in construction is to make the replication as accurate as possible. The details of construction should be checked from many sources. Someone's recollection of a Western movie is not enough research for constructing an Indian village. The children should be taught, for example, that the diverse cultures of the American Indians had many different ways of building homes and villages. Books and magazines, paintings and films can be used to check authenticity. A museum is an ideal place to seek an authority who can check the children's work or give some ideas for reference.

As nearly as possible, the construction should duplicate the materials and methods of building the original. There is no reason for making model pueblos out of cardboard when there is mud and clay available. There are limits to the practicality of using some materials, but the effort should be toward trying to find the closest substitute rather than duplicating the appearance only. The children will learn a great deal more in their attempt

[8] N. Laliberte, *Painting with Crayons*. New York: Reinhold, 1967.

[9] For example, F. Wachowiak, and T. Ramsay, *Emphasis: Art*. Scranton, Pa.: International Textbook, 1965.

to build as the original was built. In the construction of maps, accuracy again becomes important. The children will be limited in their ability to make an accurate map, but they can become aware of the care taken by cartographers in the process.

Work with the evidences of art and the materials of art can add richness to a social studies program. There is no facet of the social studies that could not benefit from the inclusion of art works or from the use of art materials as a reporting medium. The arts give us a strong bond with the qualities of people.

> The life of the arts, far from being an interruption, a distraction, in the life of a nation, is very close to the center of a nation's purpose—and a test of the quality of a nation's civilization.
>
> President John F. Kennedy [10]

Through the social studies, it is important that the life of the arts becomes a part of the life of the children.

Children's Books: Mirrors of Social Development

RICHARD L. MANDEL

How does our society inculcate its basic values?

To throw some light on this problem, we examined two sets of American children's books. Such books are a highly valuable source of information about the methods a society uses to instill its basic value system, because those methods are most clearly observable while a society is rearing its children.

The growing child has not yet learned how he should judge and act. He is in the process of acquiring his society's most fundamental system of values and motivations, which will make up his basic attitude and behavior orientation for the rest of his life. Thus, the society, unconsciously more than consciously, makes demands on the child for the fundamental kind of character its every socialized member must possess.

What is important for us is that these demands are being made in clear and simple terms so that the child can easily understand and fulfil them.

[10] Quoted on a poster by Art Education Inc., 1967.

Richard L. Mandel is Assistant Professor, Graduate School of Education, University of Pennsylvania, Philadelphia.

Reprinted from *The Elementary School Journal* 64:190–199, 1964, with permission of The University of Chicago Press and Richard L. Mandel. Copyright © 1964.

For our study, we have selected two sets of children's beginning readers from two periods of United States history: the mid-nineteenth century and the mid-twentieth century. We will analyze, compare, and contrast the books to discover differences in ways used to inculcate social character in the young reader.

Our essential assumption, then, is that widely read books written for and about children reveal the methods used to form the normative social character sought by the child's society. We can establish several concrete indications that the fictive world of the books does indeed reflect the world of their readers.

For each period we will rely on a series of books that have a fairly consistent set of characters. Such a series will give us a well-developed picture of the child's life during the period under consideration. Since we are dealing with social character as developed by the society in the upbringing of its children, we have selected two series that depict the activities of children. In the two series the storybook characters are the age of the intended reader, who was undoubtedly supposed to identify with them. By analyzing the characters, we can hope to understand what was expected of the child.

For the contemporary series, I have chosen the well-known Dick and Jane books for beginning readers up through the second grade (1). For the mid-nineteenth century series, I have chosen the Rollo series by Jacob Abbott (2–12). The tremendously popular Rollo books were published from about 1844 to 1860. Like the Dick and Jane books, the Rollo books under consideration are intended for beginning readers about six to eight years old.

Rollo and Dick

Rollo lives on a farm owned and run by his father. Mother spends her day doing housework. She is assisted by a servant girl who figures very little in the stories and by Rollo's older sister Mary. Father has an orphaned, teen-age boy Jonas to help manage the farm.

Mary and the kind, hard-working Jonas are depicted as "good" children who are respected by everyone. They, with their clear-cut characters, serve as foils for Rollo, whose character is not quite so simple.

Rollo's father is fairly well off, and he can afford to give his son a substantial number of toys, books, and treats of various kinds, including excursions and even the privilege of accompanying him on extended journeys.

Rollo's family is very religious by current standards. God as an authority and overseer constantly figures in conversations; and prayers are said every night.

Although life on the farm is fairly autonomous, visits by relatives who live nearby, occasional trips to a nearby town for supplies and farm business, and going to school all keep Rollo in contact with the world outside his father's farm.

Each of the Rollo books centers on some aspect of Rollo's life. Note the titles: *Rollo Learning To Talk, Rollo Learning To Read, Rollo at Play, Rollo at Work, Rollo at School.* These books try to follow the normal pattern of a child's development. Thus, Rollo and the young reader grow up together.

Dick, Rollo's contemporary counterpart, lives on Pleasant Street in the suburbs. Almost all his activities take place right in his neighborhood. Mother stays at home doing the housework, but occasionally she has time to go on a trip to the zoo or to join Father in games with Dick and his sisters, Jane, who is about Dick's age, and Baby Sally. Father works in the city and comes home in the evening. Unlike Rollo's parents, Dick's mother and father have a good deal of time for their children.

Dick and Jane have a great many toys and pets. They go to the country regularly to visit their grandparents, who own a farm.

Whereas Rollo walked some distance to school and met a whole new group of people there, Dick goes to school with the same neighbors he plays with every day.

Like Rollo, Dick and Jane and their friends grow up with the reader. The individual books, however, do not center on a single topic. Rather they concern themselves with the over-all life of the children and have such titles as *We Look and See, We Work and Play, Fun with Dick and Jane,* and *Friends and Neighbors.*

Natural Evil Versus Natural Good

Rollo's life on the farm is full of hard work and is not easy. Beneath all that is said and done in the Rollo books, there is an undercurrent that the world is indeed a serious place, fraught with sources of trouble. Learning to live properly in society is a job that requires constant attention and concentrated effort.

This idea is implied in the purpose of the Rollo series, as expressed by the author in his "Notice to Parents" in *Rollo at Work* and reaffirmed in all subsequent volumes. The purpose of the books is to help in "cultivating *the thinking powers* . . . promoting the progress of children *in reading* . . . cultivating the *amiable and gentle qualities of the heart*" (5:5).

Rollo must be trained to develop inner powers and qualities to protect himself against the evil prevalent in the world around him. This basic mistrust of the world is expressed in many ways. There are always "bad boys" Rollo must avoid playing with; he must never become familiar with strangers.

Even more important, however, is a feeling that while Rollo is potentially a good boy, he is filled with bad impulses and tendencies that he must be constantly on the watch for and that he must learn to suppress.

The Rollo series consists of experiences, most of them unpleasant, in which Rollo does something naughty or careless that has bad consequences. He interrupts his mother at her work, causing her to make a mistake; he leaves something that had been intrusted to him on a rock while he plays, and he loses it; he loses interest in a tedious job his father gave him, and he does not get it done on time. More often than not, if the evil in the world does not punish Rollo for letting down his guard, the evil within him, momentarily given rein, somehow gets him into a tight spot.

Often we see the two evils combining. When Rollo forgetfully goes into a field he has been told not to enter, a farmer leaving the field accidentally locks Rollo inside. When Rollo carelessly plays with a strange little boy, the boy accidentally breaks his knife.

But for Dick the world is certainly not dangerous and full of forebodings of evil. We get the impression that his world is waiting eagerly for any child who will walk in and introduce himself. Strangers excite interest; the children on the block eagerly await and welcome new neighbors.

Bobby, a new boy, is watching Jim and John dig for potatoes in their garden. He would like to join them, but he is shy and afraid to ask. When he finally summons up the courage and asks, the two boys unhesitatingly accept him, and some unknown force rewards him by enabling him to find the biggest potato.

Nature never conspires against the careless child; there are no "bad boys" to avoid. Everyone—from Big Bill the friendly policeman to Zeke the handyman—is ready to help a child out of a scrape, whether he has lost five pennies or has lost his way in a game.

Similarly, there is no indication that there is anything within the child that he must learn to control. Dick and his friends merely follow their impulses toward play and fun. They have a good time, approved and fostered by the adults around them.

This contrast between Rollo and Dick will be clarified and enlarged upon as we discuss other problems, but we may make our first generalization now:

I. In the first group of books, the world is full of dangers and evil temptations, and the child himself is full of evil impulses that he must learn to control. In the second group, the world is full of good possibilities, and the child himself has only good impulses which should be given rein and encouragement.

Precept Versus Experience

With all the potential for badness outside and inside Rollo, it is natural that he should be given some sort of mechanism to protect himself from danger. From the first, Rollo is being taught a code of Christian virtues, which he is to adopt in order to resist the evil around and within him.

The first step in inculcating such a set of rules for behavior is to impress the child with the wisdom and the sanctity of authority. Rollo, by negative example of what happens if he ignores authority, must be taught to obey his parents unquestioningly.

The following is typical of a story in the first Rollo book:

> Here is a picture about powder. Don't you see it flashing—blazing up? There are some boys; they have been playing with powder. They are bad boys; their mother told them they must not play with powder, for they would get hurt; but they did not obey her. They went away out into the woods;—do you see the trees there? Well, they went out into the woods, where their mother could not see them, and played with the powder. They were bad boys; they disobeyed their mother. The powder exploded; it flashed in their faces, and burnt their eyes. Do you see the smoke? and see! one of the boys has put his hands up to his face, because it has burnt him; and there is another boy lying upon the ground. Poor boy, I am afraid he is very much hurt; perhaps it has put his eyes out, so that he will never see again. Poor boys, if they had done as their mother told them, they would not have been burnt so. But they were bad boys, they disobeyed their mother, and now you see how they are punished [2:23].

Unquestioning obedience having been established, it remains for society to give the individual inner strengths and virtues so that he can confront new situations with his own established mechanisms. Rollo is constantly doing wrong things. His father must constantly point out the mistakes he has made so that he will not make them again.

Rollo has been eagerly looking forward to an excursion and has insisted all day, in spite of threatening clouds, that it will not rain. He persists in this conviction even after drops begin falling. His father reasons with him:

> "You are *self-conceited*—vainly imagining that you, a little boy of seven years old, can judge better than your father and mother, and obstinately persisting in your opinion that it is not going to rain, when the rain has actually commenced and is falling faster and faster. You are *ungrateful* to speak reproachfully of me, and give me pain, by your ill-will, when I have been planning this excursion, in a great degree, for your enjoyment, and only give it up because I am absolutely compelled to do it by a storm; *undutiful* in showing such a repining, unsubmissive spirit towards your father; *unjust* in making Lucy and all of us suffer, because you are unwilling to submit to these circumstances that we cannot control; *selfish* in being unwilling that it should rain and interfere with your ride, when you know that rain is so much wanted in all the fields, all over the country; and *impious,* in openly rebelling against God, and censuring

the arrangements of his providence, and pretending to think that they are made just to trouble you" [4: 80].

The excerpt is taken from the fourth book of the series, *Rollo at Play,* the subtitle of which is *Safe Amusements.* Notice that even playing means playing properly, at the right time, in the right way, with the right people and toys. Every situation and action has for Rollo a potentiality for wrong behavior.

From the world of simple obedience to outer authority, through the world of inner virtue, Rollo is led to the man's world of law. In a later volume, Rollo becomes involved in a situation in which a friend loses a knife that was lent to him by another boy. Rollo's father discusses the law of bailment with his son. This is the conclusion of their conversation:

"I want you to remember what I have said, and practice according to it. Boys bail things to one another very often, and a great many disputes arise among them, because they don't understand the law of bailment. It applies to boys as well as men. It is founded on principles of justice and common sense, and, of course, what is just and equitable among men, is just and equitable among boys.

"You must remember that whenever anything belonging to one boy is intrusted to another in any way, if it is for the benefit of the bailee, if any accident happens to it, he must make it good; unless it was some *inevitable* accident, which could not have been prevented by the utmost care. If it is for the benefit of the bailor, that is, the boy who intrusts it, then he can't require the other to pay for it, unless he was grossly negligent. And if it was for the common benefit of both, then if the bailee takes what may be called good care of it, he is not liable to pay; if he does not take good care, he is" [9: 74].

This is how the important moral and social values are presented to Rollo and inculcated into his thought and behavior.

Since Dick's world is seen in a different way, and since Dick himself does not have Rollo's tendencies, no such code needs to be impressed upon him.

Situations that would call for long talks by Rollo's parents turn out well for Dick and his friends. There is no need to be constantly on guard, no need to master a set of abstract moral principles.

Tom goes to the store and buys some cookies; on the way home he gives all of them away to the friends and neighbors he meets. No lecture ensues on being carelessly spendthrifty or too free with people. By coincidence, Mom has just finished baking a batch of cookies, and Tom can eat them.

Again, Bobby takes the biggest apple from a pile and puts it in his back pocket. The apple gets stuck there, and he cannot sit down in class, but no moral about greediness is forthcoming. The teacher merely cuts a slice out of the apple to remove it. It is no longer the biggest apple, and everyone has a good laugh.

Jane takes her sister Sally's toys and opens up a store; Dick takes his mother's food and opens up another store. Rollo's parents would have a field day in a situation like this, when toys and supper are found missing. Here is what happens in *Our New Friends:*

"I see," said Mother with a laugh. "You took many things, but you did not ask for them. Now Sally wants her toys, and I must take all the food."

So Dick and Jane helped take everything into the house again. Soon they did not have anything in the two stores. Not an apple or an egg or a cookie. Not a car or boat or ball or doll. Not anything for anyone to buy. But soon Dick and Jane were glad. Soon they had a very good dinner [1: 137].

Where does Dick find his source of moral and social value? The problem involves the very complex consideration of identity, which we will discuss later. But from what has already been said we may present our second generalization:

II. In the first group of books, social behavior is handed down with unshakable authority to the child in a complete set of established rules and virtues which he must live up to. In the contemporary books, no such abstract rules are instilled in the child, but he seems to get his ideas about right and wrong from everyday social experience.

Father Versus Peer Group

We have discussed the inculcation of Rollo's abstract code of moral behavior. What motivates Rollo to accept and follow this code? How does this motivation come about?

Besides the character of Rollo himself, Rollo's father is unquestionably the most important fact in the book and in Rollo's life. After Rollo's mother has taught him to talk, Father figures in every stage of Rollo's development and activity.

In every situation Father presents the problem to be solved or the goal to be achieved and explains in the detail we have observed why an action is right and should be done or why an attitude is good and should be held. Father doles out punishments and rewards; he corrects and encourages.

It is Father who introduces Rollo to society, giving him work to prepare him for the bigger and bigger jobs ahead, teaching him the correct forms of social behavior, taking him on trips to encounter the larger world around the farm.

Yet there is very little of what we would call sympathetic kindness on Father's part. He is willing to lead only if Rollo is willing to try and follow. His love is not given freely, but must be earned.

Two stories from *Rollo Learning To Read* will serve to illustrate. In the first, Father discusses with Rollo the boy's plans for the day and points out that what Rollo calls *mine* really does not belong to him at all, since Rollo neither produces nor earns any of the things he uses. They really belong to his father, who lends them to Rollo as long as his son deserves them:

"Well," said his father, "I shall let you wear these clothes of mine then. I am very glad I have got a house, and some breakfast, and some clothes for my little Rollo boy, since you have not got any of your own. But I think if I get a house for you to live in, and breakfast for you to eat, and clothes for you to wear, you ought to be a very careful, faithful, obedient, little boy" [3: 108].

Even more striking is the story called "Selling a Boy," in which a poor father tries to sell his own son to get bread to eat. He is offered first one, then ten, then a hundred dollars for his boy. Each time he rejects the money because it is not enough to compensate for his good companion who will be unable to share the bread and may be treated harshly. The father finally determines not to sell his son, but to find work to support them both. The conclusion:

This is a fictitious story. It is written to teach children that if they are good, and kind, and obedient, their fathers will love them, and work hard, if necessary, to get them bread, and will not sell them, even if any body should offer them a thousand dollars [3: 180].

Father then is the giver of gifts: reading, social code, material well-being. These gifts, however, are given only to the child he loves, and Rollo must earn Father's love and respect by becoming like Father. Only as Rollo masters the rules and achieves the goals established by Father, can he be sure of his love and the security derived from it; and it is Rollo's father himself who continually embodies all the moral, social, and material virtues toward which Rollo must strive. By identifying with Father, Rollo becomes like Father, is rewarded by Father, knows he has done right, and is secure and happy.

While Rollo had a definite system of rules to work with and a specific authority to hand them down and motivate him to accept them, Dick has no such obvious rules. It is thus more difficult to find his source of authority. By setting down general observations about the Dick and Jane books, however, some particularly striking and relevant aspects of Dick's life will become apparent.

The books consist almost exclusively of conversation among the children; there is very little narrative. The children seldom interact with their parents or other figures of adult authority. When this interaction does occur, it is the adults who react to a situation established by the children.

The children spend their time having fun while playing with one another, while going to school, or while participating in humorous little incidents described as *funny* or *silly*. An unbelievable amount of time is spent at parties they host for one another and in planning and attending social events, usually birthday parties, at which gifts are given. The children frequently visit relatives and neighbors and go in groups to places like zoos and construction sites.

Perhaps we should also note that while Dick has a sister his own age and a baby sister he plays with, Rollo, for all practical purposes, appears to be an only child. Mary is always inside the house helping Mother, and Jonas is in the field working with Father.

We arrive at the conclusion that Dick's behavior is distinctly gregarious and what we would call social in nature; he is continually and intensely involved with his peer group.

Bobby is rewarded for trying to make friends as recorded in the potato story. Tom is rewarded for generously sharing his cookies. Even Dick and Jane seem to be rewarded for playing store, although their game involved taking what did not belong to them.

As we have suggested, while Rollo is adopting precepts, Dick is adapting to social experience. These stories obviously demonstrate the value of experience that involves interaction with friends. We are dealing with a friendly world. The character of the good people who populate this world is molded by daily interaction with their peers, who become their authority for correct social behavior.

As would be expected from our first generalization, there is a noteworthy lack of negative examples in these stories. One can assume, however, that Bobby would have been "missing something" if he had not forced himself to make friends. His uneasiness about his hesitancy indicates this, and he is suitably rewarded for his friendly behavior by finding the biggest potato. We feel that all the children would feel uncomfortable at being removed from their group.

In *Friends and Neighbors* there is, in fact, the story of John Hill who visits Grandma Hill on Pleasant Street and is uneasy because he fears there will be no boys and girls to play with: "Oh Grandmother! I don't think I'll like the city. I don't see any children to play with me" [1: 57]. Of course his fears disappear as soon as he is happily welcomed by all the children of the neighborhood.

Here is our third generalization:

III. In the first group of books, the child finds his source of identity and motivation in his father. In the second group of books, the child's identity is confirmed and his social behavior is molded by his peer group.

We should recall that the explicit purpose of the Rollo primers included the cultivation of *"thinking powers"* and of *"amiable and gentle qualities of the heart"*—inner strengths to be instilled in the child. The only explicit purpose of the Dick and Jane books is to teach the child reading—a basic element of much contemporary social experience.

Thus our essential assumption, that the content of the books accurately reflects their societies' methods of inculcating basic social character, seems to be borne out in this case. The internal content of the books correlates closely with their external purpose in their respective societies.

One World Versus Two Worlds

We have of course been oversimplifying at every turn, but we must keep in mind that our materials themselves are purposely oversimplified for the benefit of their readers. Indeed, that is why we choose them. One more comparison can be made which will serve as our conclusion by incorporating the other three.

The dangerous nature of the world in which Rollo lives requires that a definite authority be established, the imitation of which will protect the child. There is only one world, one authority, one source of identification and motivation. Rollo must grow up to be like his father to satisfy the demands made upon him. The law of bailment "applies to boys as well as men . . . and, of course, what is just and equitable among men, is just and equitable among boys" [9: 74]. "The men's way is best," says Rollo [9: 91]. There is one ideal of social character, and Rollo's training serves to bring him ever closer to achieving that ideal as embodied in his ever present father.

Dick's world requires no constant watchfulness with confirmed inner virtues always on hand to protect him. His identity and motivation are found in the free and easy interaction readily available to him. His world is distinct from the world of adults. Indeed, adults foster the autonomy of Dick and his group. Each individual finds self-confirmation and a source of meaning in social interaction with his peers.

IV. In the first group of books, the child's social character is developed by his being brought into the world of adults. In the second group of books, the child finds acceptance and meaning from being a member of his peer group, and his social character seems to have its source there.

Our children's books mirror broad trends in methods of inculcating American social character. How these changing methods relate to different kinds of social character and what the social and historical reasons are for such changes are problems for further study. In these investigations, children's books undoubtedly will continue to provide a valuable and lively source of information.

References

1. William S. Gray, Marion Monroe, A. Sterl Artley, May Hill Arbuthnot, *We Look and See, We Work and Play, We Come and Go, Fun with Dick and Jane, Our New Friends, Friends and Neighbors, More Friends and Neighbors.* Chicago: Scott, Foresman, 1956.
2. Jacob Abbott, *Rollo Learning To Talk.* Boston: Phillips, Sampson, 1855.
3. Jacob Abbott, *Rollo Learning to Read.* Boston: Phillips, Sampson, 1855.
4. Jacob Abbott, *Rollo at Play.* Philadelphia: Hogan & Thompson, 1850.
5. Jacob Abbott, *Rollo at Work.* Boston: Phillips, Sampson, 1855.
6. Jacob Abbott, *Rollo at School.* Boston: Phillips, Sampson, 1855.
7. Jacob Abbott, *Rollo's Vacation.* Boston: Phillips, Sampson, 1855.
8. Jacob Abbott, *Rollo's Experiments.* Boston: Phillips, Sampson, 1855.
9. Jacob Abbott, *Rollo's Museum.* Philadelphia: Hogan & Thompson, 1850.
10. Jacob Abbott, *Rollo's Travels.* Boston: Phillips, Sampson, 1855.
11. Jacob Abbott, *Rollo's Correspondence.* Boston: Phillips, Sampson, 1855.
12. Jacob Abbott, *Rollo's Philosophy. Part I: Water.* Philadelphia: Hogan & Thompson [undated].

Literature Enlivens the Social Studies

MILDRED A. DAWSON

In discussing how literature enlivens the social studies, our immediate concern is with its contribution to the goals implicit in the social studies curriculum. We want the children to become familiar with the story of our country—the Westward Movement, the development and meaning of the Bill of Rights, the contributions of pioneers, inventors, industrialists, and labor to the greatness of the United States. Our pupils, too, should learn the course of world history, not only its contribution to our nation but also the background that makes each foreign land what it is in its ideals, religious status, current economic and social conditions, and its relations to the rest of the world.

Knowing the sweep of history, the children should normally and naturally gain some understanding and permanent interest in such current affairs of the "Atlantic Community," the rapid emergence of African nations into

Mildred A. Dawson was formerly Professor of Education at California State University, Sacramento, California.

From *Education 85*:294–297, 1965. Reprinted from the January, 1965, issue of *Education.* Copyright © 1965 by the Bobbs-Merrill Company, Inc., Indianapolis, Indiana.

independent members of a world-wide organization, the turmoil of Southeast Asia.

Along with history comes geography with its interplay between man and his environment, as well as sociology and economics as factors influencing the direction which citizens in every clime and at every time take. It is not only in relation to 1964–1965 that children should be concerned with the problems of the culturally deprived, but at every stage of history.

Currently our civilization is being transformed through space-age science; but the inventions such as the wheel, the printing press, the steam engine, the varied harnesses for electrical energy, and the modern agents of instantaneous communications have had their earth-shaking consequences. Children should learn about the progress of the human race.

Thus far we have been largely concerned with the social studies' goals of transmitting information in the form of history, anthropology, geography, and the like. But ultimately the goals are directed toward making good citizens, of developing in children the values that will develop interested, constructive citizenship locally, nationally, and world-wide. It is to such goals that literature can make a significant contribution.

The Role of Literature

We teachers of the social studies rely heavily on textbooks, reference books, and parallel readings of an informational nature as a foundation and organizer of the materials in our courses. True it is that the authors of these printed materials are generally persons of wide knowledge, good judgment, and vision in the area of the social studies. Yet, from the tremendous mass of available information, they must select rigorously and present a severely restricted set of facts presented in the most economical style.

These basic materials of the social studies tend to be skeletal, cold-bloodedly factual, pedestrian in style. They are unlikely to stir the reader's blood, to build strong pride in the character and acts of great men, to give insight, to develop ideals. If we are interested in developing patriotism, world citizenship, feelings of responsibility for making a contribution to humanity, we will have to look beyond textbooks, parallel readings, and encyclopedias.

It is in our best of juvenile literature that the men of history come alive with their problems, motivations, achievements, even failures and inherent weaknesses. It is a trade book, carefully authentic, that can reveal great men as persons and clearly indicate to its reader the ideals, goals, behavior that he himself may well emulate. The deeper goals of the social studies can be fully realized only as the life and conditions of the past or far-away become explicit through the pages of true-to-life fiction, biography, and books of travel.

Literature activates the past and the distant as it deals with living men, on-going events, localized current conditions—geographic, economic, sociological. Through perusing the pages of a well-written book, a pupil can gain insight, feel sympathy and empathy, sense the values of patriotism, formulate rules of conduct. In other words, literature causes the basic teachings of the social studies to be *absorbed* or *assimilated.*

In what may seem to be a lighter vein but actually is not, we might consider a major goal in the social studies to be encouraging children to read *just for fun.* With the shortened and shortening work-week, there is increased leisure, more time for recreation—and what better way to spend a few hours per week than to read significant articles in periodicals or a book of biography, travel, or insightful fiction? Let us help the teacher of reading to make lifetime readers of our girls and boys!

Some Examples

Let us consider a few of the books among many thousands to which we may turn in enlivening our lessons in the social studies. An understanding of early peoples will result as children read authentically historical fiction such as Haugaard's *Hakon of Rogen's Saga* (early Vikings) or books about early Americans like McNeer's *The American Indian Story* and Haig-Brown's *The Whale People .*

Colonial and pioneer times come to life as children admire the bravery of early colonists in Smith's *Pilgrim Courage,* see superstitions of witchcraft in Speare's *The Witch of Blackbird Pond,* fight Indians with Edmonds' *The Matchlock Gun,* go traveling in Coatsworth's *Away Goes Sally,* roam the fields with Mason's *Susannah, the Pioneer Cow,* live the pioneer life in Steele's *Westward Adventure* and Laura Ingalls Wilder's *Little House* books, colonize California in Politi's *The Mission Bell,* or see the sweep of history in Caudill's *Tree of Freedom.*

The stress and strain, the horrors of battle will become real as child-readers identify with the Civil-War teen-ager in Keith's *Rifles for Watie.* Or, civics of today become intriguing through books such as Johnson's *The Congress.*

Or let's turn to biography. Primary children will thoroughly enjoy the colorful and carefully authentic d'Aulaire biographies of great Americans of the past or Dalgliesh's *The Thanksgiving Story.* With older children, the past fairly glows as they read Daugherty's *Daniel Boone,* Sandburg's *Abe Lincoln Grows Up,* or the scholarly volumes by May McNeer, Genevieve Foster, and Clara Judson. There are remarkably fine series available, too, as for instance the *Landmark Books* or the *Childhood of Famous Americans*.

The early days of Poland and medieval England are vividly relived in Kelly's *Trumpeter of Krakow,* De Angeli's *The Door in the Wall,* and Gray's *Adam of the Road* (all beautifully literary in style). Or let the children turn to the old favorite, Pyle's *Otto of the Silver Hand* and to the recent book on Biblical times, Speare's *The Bronze Bow.*

The children may gain insight of modern times as they read Lattimore's *Little Pear,* Flack's *The Story of Ping,* or Bemelmans' *Madeline.* Older children may sympathetically "visit" Latin America through such books as Clark's *The Secret of the Andes* and *Magic Maize* or, instead, "see" Europe in such books as Dodge's *Hans Brinker* and Spyri's *Heidi.*

One of America's problems is the development of understanding among our own people for fellow citizens who manifest regional and cultural differences. Sympathetic understanding, even empathy, come as children read such books as Credle's *Down, Down the Mountain,* Justus' *Here Comes Mary Ellen,* Clark's *In My Mother's House,* Krumgold's *And Now Miguel,* De Angeli's *Thee, Hannah!* and Lois Lenski's regional series.

Insight, not only into the problems of others but into deep-down personal disturbances, may result from living with the characters in Estes' *One Hundred Dresses,* Beim's *The Smallest Boy in the Class* and *Two Is a Team,* De Angeli's *Bright April,* Enright's *Kintu,* Sperry's *Call It Courage,* Speare's *The Witch of Blackbird Pond* or De Angeli's *The Door in the Wall.* Here we have such problems as intolerance, economic, religious, or social; differences in size or dress; overpowering fear to be overcome; physical deficiency.

The books mentioned above are examples of the diverse, high-quality literature to which teachers of social studies in the elementary school can turn as they seek to achieve personalized learnings about the people, events and conditions of present and past, close at hand and far away. Children's books can indeed enliven the social studies for boys and girls who are growing toward responsible citizenship.

Bibliography

Jerrold Beim, *The Smallest Boy in the Class.* Morrow, 1949.
Jerrold Beim, *Two Is a Team.* Harcourt, 1945.
Ludwig Bemelmans, *Madeline.* Viking, 1939.
Rebecca Caudill, *Tree of Freedom.* Viking, 1949.
Ann Nolan Clark, *In My Mother's House,* Viking, 1951; *Secret of the Andes,* Viking, 1952.
Elizabeth Coatsworth, *Away Goes Sally.* Macmillan, Inc., 1934.
Ellis Credle, *Down, Down the Mountain.* Nelson, 1934.

Alice Dalgliesh, *The Thanksgiving Story*. Scribner, 1954.
James Daugherty, *Daniel Boone*. Viking, 1939.
Marguerite De Angeli, *Bright April*, Doubleday, 1946; *The Door in the Wall*, Doubleday, 1949; *Thee, Hannah!* Doubleday, 1940.
Mary Mapes Dodge, *Hans Brinker* (many editions).
Walter Edmonds, *The Matchlock Gun*. Dodd, 1941.
Elizabeth Enright, *Kintu*. Rinehart, 1935.
Eleanor Estes, *The Hundred Dresses*. Harcourt, 1944.
Marjorie Flack, *The Story of Ping*. Viking, 1933.
Elizabeth Gray, *Adam of the Road*. Viking, 1942.
Roderick Haig-Brown, *The Whale People*. Morrow, 1963.
Erik Haugaard, *Hakon of Rogen's Saga*. Houghton, 1963.
Gerald Johnson, *The Congress*. Morrow, 1963.
May Justus, *Here Comes Mary Ellen*. Lippincott, 1940.
Harold Keith, *Rifles for Watie*. Crowell, 1957.
Joseph Krumgold, *And Now Miguel*. Crowell, 1953.
Eleanor Lattimore, *Little Pear*. Harcourt, 1931.
Lois Lenski, *Cotton in My Sack*, Lippincott, 1949; *Corn-Farm Boy*, Lippincott, 1954.
May McNeer, *The American Indian Story*. Farrar, 1963.
Miriam Mason, *Susannah, the Pioneer Cow*. Macmillan, Inc., 1941.
Leo Politi, *The Mission Bell*. Scribner, 1953.
Howard Pyle, *Otto of the Silver Hand*. Scribner, 1957.
Carl Sandburg, *Abe Lincoln Grows Up*. Harcourt, 1928.
E. Brooks Smith, *et al., Pilgrim Courage*. Little, 1962.
Elizabeth Speare, *The Bronze Bow*, Houghton, 1961; *The Witch of Blackbird Pond*, Houghton, 1958.
William O. Steele, *Westward Adventure*. Harcourt, 1962.
Laura Wilder, *Little House* series. Harper, 1953.

Law and Order: The Policeman Is Our Friend—Off the "Pig"

A. GUY LARKINS

Cops Are "Pigs"

She's black and beautiful, has a dazzling smile, is quiet, and seldom speaks up in class. She's feminine, shy, looks great in a mini, boots, and Afro. She's seventeen and holds hands occasionally with the boy in the next seat—self-consciously. But when she says "I hate pigs!", her voice is pure venom. The image of feminine reserve, of softness and gentleness, shatters, and I believe her words. I feel her hate.

She's not alone.

The girl two seats up is a teacher's delight, a better student, more middle class. She obviously comes from a good home. Her language is more polite, but her point of view is similar—an attractive young black girl doesn't feel protected by or safe from the law.

The young man at the end of the row is her opposite in more ways than sex. Teachers won't be recommending him for academic scholarships. He has been offered football scholarships from junior colleges which he will probably never attend. He's powerful, stubborn, physically intimidating, and a damn good kid. He's not articulate, but he can communicate his feelings about cops well enough.

The star center of our basketball team sits three rows over. He's our clean-cut all-American boy—a good mind but not a scholar yet, polite but not subservient, self-confident but not cocky. He wants to know why the local police department allows bigoted officers—90% of them are racist, according to one department representative—to remain on the force.

These students differ in many ways, but are alike in at least two: each is black and each is down on cops. A few years back, each was taught that the policeman is our friend.

These are good kids, not trouble makers. Even the most militant believes that policemen are necessary and helpful. The young lady who "hates pigs" believes that police are needed to maintain order. But she and her classmates

A. Guy Larkins is Associate Professor of Social Science Education at the University of Georgia, Athens.

Reprinted from *Social Education* 35 (5) 503–506 ff., May 1971, with permission of the National Council for the Social Studies and A. Guy Larkins.

are angry. Eighteen of twenty-three strongly agreed with the statement, "A white cop is just another pig." Seventeen of twenty-three strongly agreed with, "A cop would shoot a Negro before he would a white man." All but one agreed or strongly agreed that policemen are too hard on black demonstrators. All but four thought Negroes should own guns to protect themselves from whites. Twenty of twenty-three agreed with, "Black men should have their freedom, even if they have to shoot white cops to get it." [1]

These students are also ignorant of certain facts. They voice support for the Black Panthers, but know little of them. They thought, for instance, that the Panthers are the black man's equivalent of the Ku Klux Klan, and were surprised to learn of the Panther's disavowal of riots and racism. Although these students are angry with the police, they know little of alternative policies proposed by black leaders for confronting and curbing misbehavior by the cops or for improving police protection for black people. The students seem also to have given little thought to the consequences of the policies they favor—partly, I think, because they haven't seriously considered following any policy.

The students are right about one point: the view given them of the police in elementary school social studies was incomplete, unrealistic, and lily-white. It did little to prepare them to deal rationally with issues related to the police and public policy.

Should it have done so?

More Than a Rosy View Needed

It is difficult to see how elementary students can be taught adequately about "Law and Order: Conflict and Dissent" without first teaching them a different view of the police than is usually presented in elementary school social studies curricula. A broader and more complete view is needed.

Nearly all serious dissenters sooner or later either confront or are confronted by the police. When violence is the reaction to dissent, when dissent borders on or embraces violence, or when the police are used to crush or discourage dissent, public controversy over the proper role of the police is nearly unavoidable. Students, therefore, cannot be properly taught about violence and dissent without raising serious questions about the working behavior of policemen, about the ways in which the state uses its police powers, and about how dissenters should respond.

There are objections, however, to presenting a broader and more com-

---

[1] There is no intention on my part to pass these results off as generalizable research. Nor do I claim that an unambiguous interpretation can be placed on the responses to each item. I would not be surprised, however, if a national sample of black high school students held strong negative views of police.

plete view of police work if it means telling elementary school children about the "bad side" of cops. A serious concern is for the student's sense of well-being. Some research in political socialization suggests that a young child's view of the police affects his feeling of personal security.[2] The policeman is a major authority figure; perhaps the first figure the child is aware of as having more power than his parents. An awareness of his "bad side" might threaten the child as it challenges his internalized belief that policemen help and support rather than harass or oppress.

Perhaps this concern is overdrawn, especially if we are talking about social studies for upper elementary grades, or for children in middle schools.

Another concern is social cohesion. Young children are impressionable. Some adults fear that a negative view of the police presented as part of the curriculum will have lasting and deleterious effects on the child's willingness to support the existing social-political order.

A sense of personal well-being and the need for social cohesion are important. Neither should be blatantly violated by the school. Neither should we assume, however, that a rosy view which is contradicted by experience outside the school will produce lasting positive effects in the child. It is quite possible that an unrealistically optimistic view of the police, when contradicted by the child's own experience or the experience of his friends and family, will produce just that sense of distrust and insecurity which the school seeks to avoid.

There are also political problems concerning the school in relationships with the community: Can the elementary school get away with presenting a controversial view of policemen? Will the community allow it? I think the community will, especially if the content of instruction is selected on the basis of a well thought-out rationale such as that advocated by Oliver and his students. Detailed discussions of the definition and rationale for social studies as the analysis of public issues are readily available elsewhere and will not be repeated here.[3] We should note, however, that the theme of this Supplement is particularly appropriate for the public issues view of social studies. Our business is to train future citizens for a pluralistic democratic society. Conflict and dissent are central to such a society; there would be little justification for democracy in a social order that neither contained nor valued opposing viewpoints. It is assumed that our political system works best when major issues are widely debated in an attempt to resolve important conflicts, and that the more rational the discussion the better the policy. If

---

[2] David Easton and Jack Dennis, *Children in the Political System: Origins of Political Legitimacy* (New York: McGraw-Hill Book Company, 1969), pp. 229–242.

[3] See: Donald W. Oliver and James P. Shaver, *Teaching Public Issues in the High School* (Boston: Houghton Mifflin Co., 1966); Fred M. Newmann and ·Donald W. Oliver, *Clarifying Public Controversy* (Boston: Little, Brown and Co., 1970); and James P. Shaver and Harold Berlak, *Democracy, Pluralism and the Social Studies* (Boston: Houghton Mifflin Co., 1968).

social studies is citizenship education, it ought to concentrate, then, on training students to analyze public issues rationally.

Selecting Issues

What public issues about policemen might be pursued under the topic "Law and Order: Conflict and Dissent"? One set could focus on controversial use of police power, another on support or violation by the police of basic American values, a third set could be about alternative responses to police misconduct.

Political-ethical questions similar to the following could be asked about the controversial use of police power: To what extent should the police be used to crush or discourage dissent? Were Southern policemen morally justified in enforcing segregation laws during the 1960s? Under what circumstances should the police be used against dissenting students on college campuses? What procedures should policemen use to control riots, arrest non-violent demonstrators, enforce curfews or regulations prohibiting unlawful assembly, and question suspects?

Political-ethical questions could also focus on how police power is related to basic values which protect dissent. For instance: Under what circumstance, if any, should the police be allowed to invade the privacy of dissenters by tapping their phones, reading their mail, or searching their quarters? Under what circumstances should the police power be used to limit dissenting speech, or to limit the association of dissenters? Should the power to arrest or detain suspects be used to harass organizations like the Black Panthers?

Another approach is to ask political-ethical questions about alternative responses to the misuse of police power. Suppose black citizens have good reason to believe that many policemen are bigots—that they enforce the law differently for blacks than for whites, for the rich and powerful than for the poor and weak. Questions like this might be appropriate: Are blacks justified in forming guerrilla units such as Medgar Evers once thought of organizing in Mississippi? [4] Should they bird-dog the police the way the Black Panthers did in Oakland? [5] Should they agitate for gradual change in the police department through better pay, better training, and the hiring of more black officers? Should they push for more community control over the hiring and firing of officers? Should their strategy stress non-violent confrontation with those in power, or should they consciously employ violence or the threat of violence?

[4] Mrs. Medgar Evers with William Peters, *For Us, the Living* (New York: Ace, 1970), p. 83.
[5] Bobby Seale, *Seize the Time* (New York: Vintage, 1970), pp. 85–89.

Selecting Content

A public issues unit on the police ought to include at least two types of content. The first furnishes information which is needed by the student to understand the issues chosen for study. The second type of content focuses on critical thinking concepts and discussion skills needed for analyzing the issue.

The first type of content will need to include information about the police —their tasks, duties and responsibilities, powers or authority, and limitations and restrictions placed on the exercise of that authority. This information can be labeled "the official view of police work." Information is also needed about the way policemen actually behave when on duty. They are like teachers and other workers; the way it is on paper and the way it is in reality sometimes differs. The official view could probably be explained quite well by a representative of the police department. In some cases, the second type of information could also be obtained directly from policemen. If not, selections from books such as *Cop!* [6] might help students empathize with the day-to-day life of policemen.

One reason for presenting the official view of police behavior, especially the responsibilities and restrictions, is that it provides at least an initial standard for judging alleged acts of police misconduct. On the local level, affidavits alleging police brutality are a source of information. Complaints are sometimes filed through official channels. Sometimes, community organizations also collect and store affidavits of misbehavior. These organizations are information sources when victims avoid official channels for fear of reprisals, or when officials will not cooperate in releasing information about complaints.

Popular books are a valuable source of information about dissenters' experiences with and attitudes towards the police. Mrs. Medgar Evers,[7] Coretta Scott King,[8] and Anne Moody [9] give powerful and mostly negative views of the Southern police officer. Bobby Seale,[10] Gene Marine,[11] and George Jackson [12] provide insight into the attitudes and beliefs of militant urban blacks about the police. Although too involved for most upper-

---

[6] L. H. Whittemore, *Cop!* (Greenwich, Conn.: Fawcett, 1970).

[7] Evers, *op. cit.*

[8] Coretta King, *My Life With Martin Luther King, Jr.* (New York: Avon, 1970).

[9] Anne Moody, *Coming of Age in Mississippi* (New York: Dell, 1970).

[10] Seale, *op. cit.*

[11] Gene Marine, *The Black Panthers* (New York: Signet New American Library, Inc.), 1969.

[12] George Jackson, *Soledad Brother: The Prison Letters of George Jackson* (New York: Bantam, 1970).

elementary school children, John Hersey's *The Algiers Motel Incident* [13] would be enlightening to many teachers.

From the other side of the fence, national magazines have given attention to the plight of the American policeman—the frustrations, tensions, and dangers of a job which offers few financial or social rewards.[14] Dick Gregory [15] presents a view of the policeman's dilemma which is both critical and sympathetic.

Teaching materials for the second type of content—critical thinking concepts and discussion skills—have been developed as part of the Shaver-Larkins social studies project.[16] Sample lessons are contained in the final report to USOE, available from ERIC.

In the Shaver-Larkins curriculum, concepts are divided into five major categories: The need for consistency in one's beliefs; the nature and importance of language; word disputes; factual disputes; and value disputes. Lessons on the first set of concepts are intended to help students understand how our experiences, needs, and desires affect our views of the world. These concepts should help students make more astute judgments about factual claims, understand how well-intentioned people can end up on different sides of an ethical issue, and understand why people with different viewpoints cling so tenaciously to the positions they take.

Lessons on the second set of concepts stress the importance and power of language. They are intended to improve the climate of discussion by reducing the emotive loading of words and clarifying meaning. At the least, a student who understands the ideas presented about language should be able to guard against being overly influenced by emotive language.

The last three sections are intended to help students resolve three types of disputes explicit or implied in nearly every public issue. These sections contain lessons designed to help students evaluate evidence, construct definitions, and improve communication in discussion of issues, and judge the relative importance of conflicting values.

The Shaver-Larkins curriculum was developed for use with secondary students, but the author of this article has used some of the teaching suggestions with sixth-grade children and found them effective when reasonable modifications are made. Lessons were not written specifically to be used with a unit on issues related to the police; nor were they developed to be used exclusively with any other set of issues. The authors' intent was that

---

[13] John Hersey, *The Algiers Motel Incident* (New York: Bantam, 1968).

[14] "Snipers in Ambush: Police Under the Gun," *Time*, 96 (11), pp. 13–15, Sept. 14, 1970.

[15] Dick Gregory, *The Shadow That Scares Me* (New York: Simon and Schuster, Inc. [Pocket Books, 1969]).

[16] James P. Shaver and A. Guy Larkins, *The Analysis of Public Issues: Concepts, Materials, Research* (Final Report on U.S.O.E. Project No. 62288. Logan, Utah. Bureau of Educational Research, Utah State University, ERIC No. ED 037075), Oct. 1969.

they be used either prior to, or concurrently with, the study of almost any public issue.

Teachers who want concrete examples of other curricula based on the public issues rationale should examine the Oliver-Newmann pamphlets.[17] Elementary teachers will be particularly interested in the units developed by the Metropolitan Saint Louis Elementary Social Studies Project, containing materials specifically developed by Berlak and Tomlinson for grades four to six.[18] The Oliver-Newmann pamphlets are usually marketed for use with secondary students, but they have been used with children at least as young as those in Grade Seven.

Summary

How should policemen behave? How should the state use its police power? How should dissenters respond to the police? These issues follow almost automatically from serious consideration of the topic, "Law and Order: Conflict and Dissent." They require, however, a different view of policemen than is usually contained in elementary school texts. We must be willing to present a more realistic picture of cops and how they are used by the state, if students are to come to grips with real issues. Students will also need considerable assistance in developing skills of analysis needed for handling questions like "Should we off the pig?".

[17] Donald W. Oliver and Fred M. Newmann. *Public Issues Series/Harvard Social Studies Project* (Columbus, Ohio: American Education Publications, 1967).

[18] Development of a model for the Metropolitan Saint Louis Social Studies Center. Feb. 1967. Available from ERIC Reprint ED #012390, Washington, D.C. GPO.

Folklore As a Mirror of Culture

ALAN DUNDES

The various forms of folklore: myths, folktales, legends, folksongs, proverbs, riddles, gestures, games, dances and many others can provide a vital resource for a teacher who seriously wishes to (1) *understand* his students better, and (2) *teach* those students more effectively about the world and about the human condition. For folklore is *autobiographical ethnography*—that is, it is a people's own description of themselves. This is in contrast to other descriptions of that people, descriptions made by social workers, sociologists, political scientists or anthropologists. It may be that there is distortion in a people's self-image as it is expressed in that people's songs, proverbs, and the like, but one must admit that there is often as much, if not more, distortion in the supposedly objective descriptions made by professional social scientists who in fact see the culture under study through the culturally relative and culturally determined categories of their own culture. Moreover, even the distortion in a people's self-image can tell the trained observer something about that people's values. Out of all the elements of culture, which ones are singled out for distortion, for special emphasis?

Folklore as a mirror of culture frequently reveals the areas of special concern. It is for this reason that analyses of collections of folklore can provide the individual who takes advantage of the opportunities afforded by the study of folklore a way of seeing another culture *from the inside out* instead of *from the outside in,* the usual position of a social scientist or teacher. Whether the "other culture" is far from the borders of our country or whether the "other culture" is lodged within these borders, a world shrunk by modern technological advances in transportation and communications demands that education keep pace. We need to know more about Vietnamese worldview; we need to know more about American Negro values.

One of the greatest obstacles impeding a better understanding of Vietnamese, American Negro or any other culture is what anthropologists term "ethnocentrism." This is the notion, apparently held in some form by all the peoples of the earth, that the way *we* do things is "natural" and "right"

Alan Dundes is Professor of Anthropology and Folklore at the University of California, Berkeley.

Reprinted from *Elementary English* 46:471–482, 1969. Copyright © 1969 by the National Council of Teachers of English. Reprinted by permission of the publisher and Alan Dundes.

whereas the way *others* do them is "strange," perhaps "unnatural" and maybe even "wrong." The Greek historian Herodotus described ethnocentrism, without of course using the term, as follows:

If one were to offer men to choose out of all the customs in the world such as seemed to them the best, they would examine the whole number, and end by preferring their own; so convinced are they that their own usages surpass those of all others.

One of the purposes of studying folklore is to realize the hypothetical premise. Man cannot choose out of all the customs in the world until he knows what these customs are. Traditional customs are part of folklore. Obviously the point in collecting, classifying, and analyzing the customs and other forms of folklore is not necessarily to allow the investigator to choose a way of life other than his own. Rather by identifying the similarities, the actual historical cognates such as hundreds of versions of Cinderella, a tale which folklorists label as Aarne-Thompson tale type 510 in the internationally known index of Indo-European folktales first published in 1910, or by identifying the near-similarities, the probably noncognate folkloristic parallels which seem to depend upon universal or quasi-universal human experiences (such as the introduction of death into the world because of some unthinking or foolish action on the part of a culture hero or trickster figure), one has convincing data which can effectively be used to promote international understanding. If only the Turks and Greeks realized that they had the same folktales and the same lovable wise fool of a Hodja figure in many of these tales. The same holds for the Arabs and the Jews. In this light, it is sad to think that folklore, instead of being used as a constructive force for internationalism, has all too frequently been the tool of excessive nationalism.

The history of folklore studies reveals that folklorists in many different countries have often been inspired by the desire to preserve their national heritage. The Grimms, for example, at the beginning of the nineteenth century, imbued with nationalism and romanticism, and armed with the fashionable methodology of historical reconstruction, collected folktales and legends with the hope of rescuing something ur-German, that is, something truly Teutonic, before it faded from the scene altogether. The Grimms were surprised and probably more than a little disappointed when they discovered that many of their "Teutonic" tales had almost exact analogues in other European countries. The Grimms incidentally, like most nineteenth century collectors, rewrote the folklore they collected. This retouching of oral tales continues today in the children's literature field where reconstructed, reconstituted stories written in accordance with *written not oral conventions* are palmed off as genuine folktales.

One can see that the basic mistrust of folk materials is part of a general ambivalence about the materials of oral tradition, the materials of the folk. On the one hand, the folk and their products were celebrated as a national treasure of the past; on the other hand, the folk were wrongly identified with the illiterate in a literate society and thus the folk as a concept was identified exclusively with the vulgar and the uneducated. (The folk to a modern folklorist is any group of people whatsoever who share at least one common linking factor, e.g., religion, occupation, ethnicity, geographical location, etc. which leads to Jewish folklore, lumberjack folklore, Negro folklore, and California folklore. As an American I know American folklore; as a professor I know campus folklore; as a member of a family, I know my own family folklore.) The equation of folklore with ignorance has continued. The word "folklore" itself considered as an item of folk speech means fallacy, untruth, error. Think of the phrase "That's folklore." It is similar to the meaning of "myth" in such phrases as "the myth of race." This is *not,* however, what folklore and myth mean to the professional folklorist. A myth is but one form or genre of folklore, a form which consists of a sacred narrative explaining how the world and man came to be in their present form. Folklore consists of a variety of genres most of which are found among all peoples of the earth. Nevertheless, the association of folklore with error (consider "folk" medicine as opposed to "scientific" medicine) has made it difficult for the study of folklore as a discipline to gain academic respectability and has generally discouraged the use and study of folklore by educators.

It is still mistakenly thought that the only people who study folklore are antiquarian types, devotees of ballads which are no longer sung and collectors of quaint customs which are no longer practiced. Folklore in this false view is equated with survivals from an age past, survivals which are doomed not to survive. Folklore is gradually dying out, we are told. Moreover, since folklore is defined as error, it is thought by some educators to be a good thing that folklore is dying out. In fact, it has been argued that one of the purposes of education is to help stamp out folklore. As man evolves, he leaves folklore behind such that the truly civilized man is conceived to be folkloreless. From this kind of thinking, one can understand why education and folklore have been on opposite sides and also why when well meaning educators move into other cultures, e.g., in Africa or in a ghetto school, they actually believe they are doing their students a service by helping to suppress local customs, superstitions, folk speech, and other folkloristic traditions. So it is that African students are taught Shakespeare and Chaucer as great literature while their own superb oral literature is not deemed worthy of classroom treatment, assuming that the western educated teacher even knows of its existence. How many teachers of literature, of the epic in particular, are aware of the fact that the epic is a living oral form and that epics up to 13,000 lines are now being sung in Yugoslavia, among other places? How many teachers of American Negro children have ever heard of the "dozens" (or "rapping and capping" or "sounding" etc.) or of the "toast," an important Negro folklore genre in rhyme reminiscent of epic form? Yet the technique of verbal dueling known as the "dozens" and the epic toast are extremely viable forms of American Negro folklore and they encapsulate the critical points and problems in Negro family structure and in Negro-white relations. One could teach both literature and social studies from such folkloristic texts (were they not "obscene" by *our* standards) with the advantage that these texts would be known by the students from their own lives and experience.

Why not teach children about the nature of poetry by examining their own folk poetry: nursery rhymes, jump rope rhymes, hand clap rhymes, ball bouncing rhymes, dandling rhymes, and autograph book verse among others. There is almost no method or approach found in the study of literature which could not also be applied to folk materials. One could discuss formal features such as metrics, rhyme, alliteration; one could discuss content features such as characterization, motivation, themes. By using the materials of folklore as a point of departure, the educational process may be comprehended as dealing with the real world rather than with a world apart from the world in which the students live. With folklore, the classroom becomes a laboratory or forum for a consideration of "real life" as it is experienced and perceived by those being educated. Let me briefly provide just a few examples of folklore and try to illustrate how they might be used to enliven and stimulate classroom discussions.

One technique which can immediately show children something important about the nature of oral tradition is to select one item of folklore and ask each child to tell the other members of the class his *version* of the item. It doesn't matter what the item is: when Christmas presents are opened (Christmas Eve, Christmas morning, one on Christmas Eve and the rest on Christmas day, etc.) or what one says near the end of *Hide and Seek* to summon all the other players: Olly, olly oxen free, Olly Olly Ocean free, (All ye, all ye "outs" in free?????), Home free all, etc. After a number of versions have been elicited, the students should be able to see that although there is considerable diversity, there is also considerable uniformity. If there are differences—such as how many candles are placed on the birthday cake (some have the number of candles equal to the number of years old while others have that number plus one with the extra to grow on, etc.), even these differences are traditional. How many children believe that the number of candles left burning after the attempt to blow them out signifies the number of children one will have? How many believe the number left burning signifies the number of years to pass before one's wish (made right before the blowing attempt) comes true? Through such devices, the children can learn that there are frequently subtraditions within traditions. Then the teacher may ask the children "Which version is correct?" "Which version is the right one?" Normally, there will be extended debate on this, individual students championing their own individual versions, perhaps pointing to the statistical evidence available within the classroom to support one version over another. Gradually, the children will come to realize that in folklore as in life, there is often no one correct or right version. One traditional version is just as traditional as another version. A's way of observing Christmas or birthday rituals is no better and no worse than B's. Isn't this a marvelous way of showing what ethnocentrism is: people insisting that the way they know is best and proper while the strange unfamiliar way is wrong? And isn't this a marvelous way of teaching tolerance? If children can learn that their fellows' ways are not "wrong" but "alternative, equally traditional" ways of doing things, this could be one of the most important lessons they are ever likely to learn.

Having illustrated the nature of variation in folklore, the teacher might wish to discuss why there is variation. Here the difference between oral and written (or printed) traditions is crucial. Folklore is passed on by means of person to person contact. And an item of folklore may be changed by different individuals in accordance with their own individual needs, the demands of a particular social context—the make-up of the audience—is it boys and girls, just boys, children and grown-ups, etc. or the requirements of a new age. So it is that each item of folklore is passed on through time, sometimes remaining the same, sometimes changing. This is why the task of collecting and analyzing folklore can never be completed. Tomorrow's version of a folksong may or may not be the same as the one we know today which in turn may or may not be the same as the one which was known in the past. This is in marked contrast to the products of written tradition. If one reads a play of Shakespeare or a novel of James Joyce today, one can be reasonably sure that one hundred years from now, the identical text will be read by others.

There is a tendency to underestimate the differences between a visual/written record and an aural/oral record. It has only recently been suggested that the mass media, radio, television, motion pictures, etc. have, by discouraging or impinging upon time formerly spent in reading, made us an oral rather than a written culture. Actually, one should say, has made us an oral culture *again*. In evolutionary terms, pre-literate society which was orally oriented became literate, but now we have "post-literate" man who is influenced by oral communication once more. Yet the education system has not always kept pace. The traditional emphasis has been upon "reading and writing." What about "speaking"? Oratory, valued so much by oral cultures around the world, has become almost a lost art in literate societies. Interestingly enough, in American Negro culture there is tremendous value placed upon rhetoric as one aspect of style. The "man of words" is highly esteemed and anyone who has heard American Negro preachers use their voices surely recognizes the eloquent power of that oral style.

It is a pity that our educational philosophy continues to worship the written word. Note that "literacy" is still thought by some to be a *sine qua non* for an individual to be able to vote. The fact that intelligent peoples all over the world are capable of reaching decisions without anything more than oral communication seems to be overlooked. We tend to trust what is "down in black and white." "Put it in writing," we say; we tend to distrust oral testimony, regarding it as unreliable. We forget that much of what is written down—in newspaper, in books, circulated as oral communication first. Even the Bible was in oral tradition before it was committed to written form! With such bias in favor of written tradition, it is easy to see why there has been relatively little interest in the study of oral tradition. But by failing to recognize the differences between oral and written traditions, we do a disservice to ourselves as well as our students. Who has never heard someone give orally an address which was written out in advance? Yet relatively few written works read well aloud. Similarly, students taking written notes from an instructor's free-flowing oral classroom delivery are often dismayed by the sentence fragments, the agreement errors, etc. There are major lexical and stylistic differences between oral and written tradition. "Indeed, Moreover, One cannot escape the conclusion . . ." are acceptable written conventions, when *seen* on a printed page, but they may *sound* stilted when heard in speech. A word or phrase may *look* right, but *sound* wrong. But by the same token, a word or phrase which sounds fine, may look terrible in print. In oral speech, one can use slang, folk similes (as cool as a cucumber) and folk metaphors (to fly off the handle). In written tradition, these are branded as "clichés" by diligent teachers of English composition. Such teachers are wont to warn their students to "avoid clichés." The folklorist would urge that children *not* be told never to use clichés but rather that they be taught the difference between oral and written traditions and *not* to confuse the conventions of each. In oral tradition, originality is neither desired or expected. The more traditional (=unoriginal) the better. However, in our written tradition, originality is essential. But children cannot avoid clichés. Do they not learn to speak before they learn to read and write? The point is simply that children should not be taught to write as they speak and they should not be taught to speak as they write. The unfortunate confusion of oral and written conventions is one reason why most printed collections of folklore are spurious. They have been edited and rewritten to conform to written rather than oral style. The expletives, meaningful pauses, the stammers, not to mention the eye expressions, the hand movements and all the other body gestural signals are totally lost in the translation from oral to written tradition. This is why it is impossible to learn what folklore is by *reading* books. If one is interested in learning about folklore, one must elicit oral tradition. A useful class exercise might be to have a child tell a joke or legend to his classmates whose task it becomes to write it down. One could then discuss at length just what was "left out" in the written version that had been in the oral version.

In order to more fully understand and utilize folklore, one must have some idea of the functions of folklore. Folklore reflects (and thereby reinforces) the value configurations of the folk, but at the same time folk-lore provides a sanctioned form of escape from these very same values. In fairy tales, the hero or heroine is inevitably told not to do something; don't look in the secret chamber, don't answer the door, etc. Of course, the protagonist violates the interdiction. He may be punished for his disobedi-ence, but usually he comes out ahead in the end. For example, the hero marries the princess. The escape mechanism is equally obvious in tradi-tional games. On the one hand, educators urge that games be played to teach "teamwork," "cooperation," and "fair play." On the other hand, once in the game, children can compete and they can compete aggressively. One can "steal" the bacon or "capture" the flag of the opposing team. In "King of the Mountain," boys can push rivals off the raft. In adolescent games such as "Spin the Bottle," "Post Office," or "Padiddle," the rules *require* the participants to do that which they would very much like to do but which they might not otherwise do. Folklore provides socially sanctioned forms of behavior in which a person may do what can't be done in "real life." One is not supposed to push anyone around in real life—at least if one believes the "Golden Rule," but in games one is supposed to take a chair and leave someone else without one to sit on (in "Musical Chairs"). As a young adolescent, one cannot kiss a casual acquaintance without feelings of guilt or hearing cries of derision. Yet in kissing games, one *must* do so. The folkloristic frame not only permits, but *requires* the taboo action and it also thereby relieves the individual from assuming the responsibility (and guilt) for his actions. The individual has no choice; it is a mere spin of the bottle or some other act of chance (such as seeing a car with only one headlight working) which dictates the sexual behavior. In children's games, the drama of real (adult) life is often enacted. Yet neither teacher nor student may be fully aware of just what is involved in a particular game. In much the same way, folk—and social—dances allow for hetero-sexual body contact in a society which true to its Puritan heritage has consistently condemned the body and its domain. The fact that boys can dance with girls, girls can dance with girls, but boys cannot dance with boys in American culture reflects our great fear of homosexuality. This is striking when one recalls that most societies even have men's dances from which women are excluded. Ameri-cans remain slaves to a tradition in which the body is seen as dirty, as something to be denied or repressed. Note that we still insist on *physical* (corporal) punishments for intellectual/mental lapses. The body is pun-ished, not the mind, every time a child is struck or spanked!

As a specific example of how folklore functions, let me cite one riddle text. A child comes home from school and at the dinner table asks his parents: "What is black and white and red all over?" The parent, if he's alert and has a good memory, replies: "A newspaper" which in fact is one of the older traditional answers to this riddle. But there are other modern traditional answers. Some of these are: a sunburned zebra, an embarrassed zebra, a zebra with measles, a wounded nun, a bloody integration march, and for the sophisticate: *Pravda,* the *Daily Worker,* or the *New York Times* which involves an interesting play on the original "newspaper" answer. Now what precisely is going on? What function, if any, does this riddle or the hundreds like it serve? I believe that this kind of riddle provides an effective mechanism for reversing the normal adult-child relationship in our society. In our society, it is the parent or teacher who knows all the answers and who insists upon proposing difficult if not "impossible" questions to children. However, in the riddle context, either the parent doesn't know the answer to the elephant or little moron joking question—in which case the child can have the great pleasure of telling him what the answer is *or* the parent gives the "wrong" answer (e.g., "newspaper" would be considered "wrong" by the child who has *another* answer in mind—and aren't there plenty of instances where the child answers an adult's question perfectly well but fails because his answer was not the particular answer the adult desired? This is also what happens whenever an unthinking adult asks the kind of questions which can be labelled as being "Guess what's in my mind" questions. In this instance where the parent has given the "wrong" answer, the child has the even more exquisite pleasure of *correcting* rather than merely informing the parent.) Children also use riddles with their peers where a similar function is evident. A child goes one up if he has a riddle which stumps a friend. I should perhaps mention that riddles or joking questions are by no means confined to children's usage. Many adults use such devices in daily interpersonal rituals. Some of these riddling questions provide serious reflections of our culture. Do you remember the "knock-knock" cycle? Well, have you heard the World War III knock-knock joke? No? Okay, "Knock-knock" (audience): "Who's there?"—(long silent pause—signifying that no one would be left to answer in the event of total nuclear world war.)

Literature for Children or Literature of Children

The analysis of the content of children's folklore could help anyone seriously interested in understanding children. I refer specifically to that portion of children's folklore which is performed *by children for other children.* This is distinct from that portion of children's folklore which consists of materials *imposed upon children by parents and teachers.* The analysis of the latter kind of children's folklore would probably give more of an insight into parents and teachers' worldview than the worldview of children. I suspect that in courses dealing with children's literature, it is this latter category which receives most of the attention. In other words, the emphasis is on "literature for children" rather than "literature of children!" (By "literature of children" I mean their oral literature, their folklore, their traditions, not their little *individual* written compositions or poems.) This is, in my opinion, the same kind of thinking that makes Peace Corps teachers teach Shakespeare and Chaucer to African students instead of utilizing African folktales and proverbs, that is, using some of the "native" literature as the basis for an understanding of the nature of prose and poetry. Educational, as well as foreign, policy is invariably made in accordance with the value system of us, the teacher or the American. Such decisions may be rational from our point of view; they may even prove to be "correct," but in the majority of cases, these decisions are probably all too often made without sufficient knowledge of the groups we honestly want to help. We tend to think of the "other" people be they inhabitants of villages in Asia or children in our classroom as poor little sponges who need to soak up as much of our material as they possibly can.

The phrase "culturally deprived" is a prime example of this faulty kind of thinking. From an anthropological perspective, of course, there can be no such thing as culturally deprived. Culture in anthropological usage refers to the total way of life of a people, and not to a very select group of elitist materials such as opera, the great books, etc. All human beings have culture in general; some people share one culture rather than another. Hopi culture is different from Vietnamese culture. So it is impossible in this sense for any individual to be "culturally deprived"; our minority groups have just as much culture as anybody else. The point is simply that it is another culture, a different culture. To call a minority group "culturally deprived" is a kind of survival of nineteenth century "white man's burden" thinking. The real question is: Do we want "them"—and "them" could be American Negroes, South Vietnamese, children in our classrooms, etc. to give up their culture and accept our culture in its place or do we not insist on a melting pot metaphor with the pot to take on the consistency of the dominant ethos? In my opinion, the "unmelting pot" might be a more apt metaphor. If so, then perhaps we should allow or better yet, encourage "them" to enjoy, understand, and take pride in their own culture. Obviously, the culture of our children is closer to our adult culture than the culture of a distinct ethnic minority or some foreign population to our culture in general. Nevertheless, the principle in terms of educational philosophy is the same.

What kinds of things do we see in our children's own folklore?

> Teacher, teacher, I declare
> I see *so and so's* underwear.

> Charlie Chaplin went to France
> To see the ladies' underpants . . .

> I see London; I see France
> I see *so and so's* underpants.

We see the child's curiosity about the body and the immediate body covering. The child finds it difficult to accept the adult's apparent rejection of the body and its natural functions. Consider the following jump rope rhyme:

Cinderella, dressed in yellow
Went downtown to see her fellow.
On the way her girdle busted
How many people were disgusted? 1, 2, 3, etc.

Clearly, children, in this instance little girls, are fascinated by a particular undergarment, the girdle. Note that the girdle busts while Cinderella is on the way to see, or in some versions to kiss, her fellow. Do children really know what they are saying?

Folklore and Sibling Rivalry

Less symbolic, but equally important are the sentiments underlying these familiar jump rope verses:

Fudge, fudge, tell the judge
Mama's got a new born baby.
It aint no girl, it ain't no boy
Just a newborn (or "common," or "plain ol,' " or "ordinary") baby
Wrap it up in tissue paper
Throw (send) it down the elevator.
First floor, miss
Second floor, miss, etc. (until the jumper misses)

This is really an extraordinarily revealing rhyme. First of all, why is the judge informed about the newborn baby? Is the judge the person who can take away children from parents or the person who has the power to punish parents for mistreating children? In any case, here is explicit sibling rivalry. What child does not resent the arrival upon the scene of the newborn child who threatens the previously existing relationship between the older children and the mother? Notice how the poor baby is demeaned. It is sexless. It's not a girl, not a boy, in other words, it's *nothing*. It's just—and that word "just" tells all—an ordinary baby, nothing exceptional, nothing to make a fuss about. And what does the jumper-reciter recommend should be done with the baby? *Throw* it down the elevator. The jumper then jumps as many floors as she can without missing. Thus by being a skillful jumper, a girl can send her baby sibling far away. The more jumps without misses, the further the baby is sent away. Thus through jumping rope, a young girl is able to do something "constructive" about getting rid of her inevitable aggression against the new sibling rival. This inter-sibling hostility, I submit, is an integral part of American children's worldview. Look at the following jump rope rhyme:

> I had a baby brother
> His name was Tiny Tim.
> I put him in the bathtub
> To teach him how to swim.
> He drank up all the water;
> He ate up all the soap.
> He tried to eat the bathtub
> But it wouldn't go down his throat.
> He died last night
> With a bubble in his throat.

This is an equally blatant example of an expression of sibling rivalry. Note the tense of the verb in the first line. I *"had"* a baby brother. Here is wishful thinking, a common element in all folklore. The baby rival is gone, and before the rhyme really gets started. What of the rest of the rhyme's content? Precisely where is it that the newborn baby gets so much obvious physical attention? In American culture, it is the bath. It is during and after bathing that the baby is fondled, powdered, played with, etc. So the older child takes things into his own hands. He puts the baby into the tub pretending to teach him how to swim. What does the baby do in the tub? He tries to eat everything. Babies are in fact orally inclined as it is this body zone which provides the initial point of contact with the world, a body zone which operates by incorporating what is needed, i.e., mother's milk. From the older child's point of view, the baby is always being fed—hence it appears to have an insatiable appetite. What then is more appropriate from the older child's perspective than to have his baby brother choke to death from eating something he shouldn't be eating, from trying to eat too much, that is, symbolically speaking, from trying to take too much, more than his share of their common parent's bounty. Of course, children hate their parents too:

> Step on a crack (line)
> Break your mother's back (spine)

Symbolism in Folklore

No doubt many people who are unsympathetic to psychology and symbolism may doubt the validity of the above interpretations of children's folklore. Such interpretations, they would argue, are *being read into* innocent folklore rather than being *read out* of the folklore. Yet the astonishing thing is that much the same symbolism is contained in the folklore *for* children as communicated by parents and teachers. It has long been wrongly assumed that folktales—e.g., Grimms' *Kinder und Hausmärchen* and *nursery* rhymes are strictly children's fare. This is not true. These materials were related by adults to other adults as well as children. If adult males have Oedipus complexes, then it is clear why it is they who relate the story of Jack and the Beanstalk. A boy lives alone with his mother, throws beans out of a window at his mother's request, climbs a tall magic beanstalk, hides from the threatening giant in the friendly giant's wife's oven, kills the giant by cutting the giant stalk with an axe which is often helpfully provided by his mother waiting at the foot of the stalk, and finally lives happily ever after with his mother! (Parents, of course, to the infant's eye view of the world appear to be giants!) For women with Electra complexes, it is normally a girl versus a wicked stepmother or witch. Whereas the donor figure in male folktales may be a female (cf. Jack's mother, the giant's wife); in female folktales, the helper may be a male (cf. the woodsman in "little Red Riding Hood"), although to be sure sometimes kind father figures help boys and kind mother figures (e.g., fairy god-mothers) help girls. In Hansel and Gretel, the children are tempted orally and they nibble at the witch's house. (The children were not given food by their parents.) The witch, like so many cannibalistic villains in fairy tales, intends to employ the infant's first weapon (eating, sucking, biting) by devouring the children. In this tale, the heroine, Gretel, succeeds in duping the witch into being burned up in her own oven. The female-oven symbolism is consistent. In Jack and the Beanstalk, the boy hides in the giant's wife's oven to escape the giant; in Hansel and Gretel, a tale featuring a girl's point of view, the heroine eliminates the female villain by making her enter her own hot oven! And what of Cinderella whom we noticed in jump rope rhymes? What is the significance of the story of a girl who marries a prince because of a perfect fit between a foot and a glass slipper? What has the ideal marriage to do with a foot fitting into a slipper? And why do we still tie old shoes on the bumpers of cars carrying newlyweds off on their honeymoon?

One clue to the symbolism of slippers and shoes comes right from Mother Goose. One of the rhymes which parents read to children is:

> There was an old woman who lived in a shoe
> She had so many children she didn't know what to do.

A literal, historical interpretation would have to locate a place where women once lived in actual shoes. But how would one explain the stated connection between "living in a shoe" and "having lots of children." Fortunately, another verse to this rhyme reported in the Ozarks in the 1890s makes the symbolism even more overt:

> There was another old woman who lived in a shoe.
> She didn't have any children; she knew what to do.

With symbolic systems, it is never a matter of one isolated instance. Within a given culture, there are whole consistent patterns of symbolism. The symbolism of a culture will be manifested in the folklore of that culture. So we should not be surprised to find other nursery rhymes:

> Cock a doodle doo
> My dame has lost her shoe
> Her master's lost his fiddling stick
> They don't know what to do.

Remember these are part of the children's folklore which is transmitted to children by parents and teachers. I do not necessarily believe that parents are aware of the symbolic content of folklore any more than I believe that children are consciously aware of all the symbolism. Clearly, folklore could not function successfully as an outlet if there were conscious awareness of its being so used. Folklore is collective fantasy and as fantasy, it depends upon the symbolic system of a given culture. I should be remiss if I did not state my conviction that the communication of collective fantasy and symbols is a healthy thing and I would strongly oppose those educators who advocate placing Mother Goose and fairy tales on a high shelf or locked case in the library. Folklore is one way for both adults and children to deal with the crucial problems in their lives. If our folklore sometimes deals with sexuality and the interrelationships between members of a family, then this is obviously something of a problem area in our daily lives. We know that folklore in all cultures tends to cluster around the critical points in the life cycle of the individual (e.g., birth, initiation, marriage, death) and the calendrical cycle of the community (e.g., sowing, harvesting, etc.). In fact, if one collects the folklore of a people and then does a content analysis of that folklore, one is very likely to be able to delineate the principal topics of crisis and anxiety among that people. So if American folklore, both adult and children's folklore has a sexual element, then we must face the problem which is reflected in the folklore. Squelching folklore as if such a thing were really possible—it is impossible to censor oral tradition as opposed to print—would not help in solving the original problems which generated the collective fantasies in the first place.

Folklore About Teachers

There can be no doubt that folklore reflects culture and as a final example, I will briefly mention teacher folklore. The folklore of and about teachers reflects both teachers' attitudes about themselves and students' attitudes about teachers. There is the resentment of administrators as illustrated in the numerous dean stories, e.g., "Old deans never die; they just lose their faculties." There are the parodies of teaching methods. An English teacher is explaining to her class how to write a short story: It should have religion, high society, sex, and mystery. Within a few moments, a little boy says, "OK., I'm finished." The teacher, surprised at the speed of the boy's composition, asks him to read his short story aloud to the class. "My God," said the duchess, "I'm pregnant! Who did it?" There are also commentaries on teachers who run their classes without any regard for what their students might like or think. A professor gives an advanced seminar in algebraic functions. Only one student shows up. However, he strides to the lectern and reads his hour-long lecture. Each day, the professor does the same thing. He sets up his notes and reads his lecture. One day, while at the blackboard writing a long series of equations and formulas, the professor sees the one student's hand raised. "Excuse me, professor, but I don't see why x cubed equals y cubed. Why wouldn't x cubed equal y cubed plus z cubed?" The professor replied, "That's a very interesting question but I don't want to take up valuable class time with it. See me at the end of the hour." In a variant of this joke, it is a professor of art history who offers a seminar in advanced Burmese vase painting. Again there is one student and again the professor reads his lecture. This time, the professor is at the faculty club talking to his colleagues. When they discover that he has only one student for the seminar, they ask him what he is doing in the class. He tells them that he reads his lecture just as he always has. "Good heavens," one colleague exclaims, "with just one student why don't you run the class as a discussion?" whereupon the professor replied, "What is there to discuss?" Of course, I don't have to say how distasteful modern students find this philosophy of education.

The folklore of teaching includes elementary school teachers too. For example, there's the story of the elementary school teacher who taught look-say reading. One day in backing her car out of a parking place on the street, she banged into the car parked behind her. She immediately got out to survey the possible damage and looking at her rear fender she said, "Oh, oh, oh, look, look, look, Damn, Damn, Damn!" Notice the threefold repetition in the punchline. There are three words each of which is repeated three times. Is this unusual? Certainly not. Three is the ritual number in American folklore. Whether it's three brothers in folktales, three wishes, a minister, a priest, and a rabbi, or the fact that there are frequently three action sequences in jokes and three repetitions of lines in folksongs: John Brown's body lies a moulderin' in the grave, Polly put the kettle on, Lost my partner what'll I do?, etc., the pattern is the same. This pattern is *not* universal; most American Indian peoples have the ritual number *four*. Here is yet another illustration of how by analyzing the folklore we gain insight into the culture which it mirrors. Three is a ritual number not just in American folklore, but in all aspects of American culture: time—past, present, future; space—length, width, depth; and language—good, better, best, etc. This is why we have the three R's (Reading, 'Riting and 'Rithmetic), Primary, Secondary, and Higher Education, the latter with its three degrees B.A., M.A. and Ph.D., the first of which can be cum laude, magna cum laude, and summa cum laude. This is why we have such pedagogical principles as: "Preview, Teach, and Review" which retains its tripartite form in the folk translation: tell 'em what you're going to tell 'em; tell 'em and tell 'em what you told 'em.

Folklore as a subject of study can be a most rewarding one. It does serve as a mirror of culture and it is a mirror well worth looking into. The teacher who encourages his class to examine their own folklore or better yet sends them out with collecting projects, such as collecting the folklore of a group from another "culture" can give his students as well as himself an educational experience of immeasurable value. We need to use every available means to better understand ourselves and our fellow men. Folklore is one such means, one available for the asking. We are all folk. All one needs to begin such work is people, people to ask and people to listen. Whether an individual asks about his own folklore or asks others about their folklore, if he listens, he will learn.

Suggested Readings

Those interested in general folklore theory should consult Alan Dundes (ed.), *The Study of Folklore* (Englewood Cliffs, N.J.: Prentice-Hall, Inc., 1965). For American folklore in particular, one may look at Jan Harold Brunvand, *The Study of American Folklore: An Introduction* (New York: W. W. Norton, 1968) and Richard M. Dorson, *American Folklore* (Chicago: University of Chicago Press, 1959). Those curious about the number three may enjoy Alan Dundes, "The Number Three in American Culture," in *Every Man His Way: Readings in Cultural Anthropology* (edited by Alan Dundes) (Englewood Cliffs, N.J.: Prentice-Hall, Inc., 1968), p. 401–424.

Section THREE

Inquiry and the Development of Intellectual Processes

*I*s the social studies teacher's *main* task to transmit knowledge about the culture and the social world of man, or is it to help the learner develop independent skills of inquiry in order that he can find out, on his own, what he needs to know? When put this way the question distorts the present emphasis that social studies educators are placing on inquiry procedures in teaching social studies. One cannot say that the *main* task of the teacher is to do one or the other of these for he must obviously do both and do them well. Neither can one say that inquiry strategies are in all cases to be preferred over expository strategies. Here again, the teacher needs to be skillful in using both in situations where one or the other would be the more appropriate.

Undoubtedly there has been overuse of expository strategies in teaching social studies in the past. The balance needs to be redressed in favor of a greater use of inquiry. Inquiry and discovery are not entirely new ideas, although recent developments have provided more sophisticated techniques, thus giving new impetus to this kind of teaching. Psychologists who advocate the use of investigation-oriented instruction often claim two distinct advantages for it: (1) children tend to retain the knowledge longer when they discover it for themselves; and (2) discovered knowledge has greater transfer value. Interest in inquiry and discovery teaching strategies has also been stimulated by the current emphasis on the development of thinking processes in children.

The intellectual operations involved in achieving the various types of social studies objectives are not identical, and therefore teaching and learning processes need to be varied. In forming and attaining concepts, for example, breadth of experience is important because the learner needs to

144

encounter the concepts in wide and varied settings. When such broad exposure is lacking, the pupil is likely to develop a limited knowledge of the concept. Similarly, there are basic principles of learning that need to be applied in teaching skills, values, and attitudes.

In practice, however, learnings do not fall into neat categories or packages that can be labeled as understandings, attitudes and values, and skills. More often than not, learnings contain elements of each of these categories. Skills, especially intellectual skills that are so important in social studies instruction, have a substantive or cognitive base. How can a child, for example, learn thinking skills without having something of substance to think about? Values and attitudes also have a relationship to cognitive components. Indeed, ignorance is often the source of undesirable and ill-founded attitudes and values. In teaching, therefore, the teacher must plan for both the cognitive and neocognitive elements in almost all social studies instruction.

In addition to considering variables that have to do with the nature of the learning task, effective teaching and learning is a highly individual matter. Specific teachers have styles of teaching that are particularly effective for them, yet these same styles of teaching may be less productive for someone else. Individual pupils may have styles of learning that are especially well suited to them. It is well known that not all pupils learn in the same way. Some are endowed with well-developed verbal and linguistic skills and prefer learning styles that rely on such abilities. Other pupils are more visually oriented. Still others need kinesthetic experiences in order to learn readily. In addition to these idiosyncracies in learning styles, pupil variation is such that the sequence of learning is often different for individual children.

The articles that follow address themselves to these and similar problems. They offer a wide range of thought concerning the development of social studies learnings. Men have taught each other and their young for thousands of years. As a result, there has been built up a substantial amount of what might be called "conventional wisdom" about teaching and learning. Much of it is common sense and soundly based. Yet much of what we do in teaching is based on myths, feelings, and beliefs that have no foundation in modern psychology. It is indeed surprising how little is actually known about the teaching and learning process considering how long man has been engaged in it. The research in education and psychology of the past fifty years has produced helpful guidelines for the development of psychologically sound teaching strategies. Nonetheless, a considerable amount of additional research is needed in many aspects of human learning. Our knowledge of this complex process is far from complete.

The Nature of Teaching

HILDA TABA

Teaching is much more complex than is generally assumed. The usual paradigm of teaching is a mixture of sets of scattered ideas and conceptual models and of simplistic assumptions. Neither a comprehensive theory of teaching nor a set of satisfactory conceptual models is available to describe individual teaching acts or teaching strategies and their effect on learning.

Assumptions About Teaching

Several assumptions prevail about the nature and function of teaching. Among the simplest and most obstinately held has been the idea that the chief, if not the only, function of teaching is to impart knowledge, i.e., to explain and tell. According to this assumption, effectiveness of teaching bears a direct relationship to teachers' knowledge of content areas. Evidence of this idea can be found in the practically self-teaching and presumably "teacher-safe" curriculum packages and in the emphasis on training teachers in the content backgrounds as the chief way of ensuring excellence of teaching and learning. While improvement and updating of the content of curriculum and of the content background of teachers no doubt improves teaching, it also involves the danger of a uniform curriculum uniformly and unimaginatively taught to all varieties of students and under all varieties of conditions.

Another widely accepted but equally inadequate assumption about teaching is that it consists of mastering certain special "methods," such as "methods for teaching history." Often the idea of method is narrowed still further, such as to a chronological or a topical "method" of teaching history. Acrimonious debates about the method of teaching reading consist largely of putting one method against another as the only right method of teaching a subject, such as reading. This assumption is the base of the prevailing scheme of separate methods courses in teacher training. This assumption takes for granted that there is *one* right method of teaching anything and that that

The late Hilda Taba was Professor of Education at California State University, San Francisco.

This selection is Chapter II of a research paper entitled *Teaching Strategies and Cognitive Functioning in Elementary School Children,* Cooperative Research Project No. 2404. U.S. Office of Education, 1966.

method is equally effective in the hands of all teachers for all kinds of students and under a variety of learning conditions (Medley and Mitzel, 1963, pp. 85–88). However, the chief weakness of teaching modeled on this assumption is that it would be determined solely by the unique characteristics of subjects and not also by the requirements of general educational objectives, such as the development of thinking and certain values.

Still another assumption is that good teachers are born, not made. Those operating on this assumption regard teaching as a sort of mystical art, the secrets of which a few "good" teachers grasp intuitively. Such an assumption denies the possibility that teaching involves techniques and skills that can be learned by a great range of individuals, provided we can identify those techniques and skills and help teachers to master them.

Perhaps the most basic recent criticism leveled against approaching teaching as a theoretical construct is that the concepts of methods have been inferred too directly from the various partial and inconsistent learning theories, each of which postulates a different basic mechanism of learning, such as conditioning, identification, and the organization of perception and cognition. Each of these leads to a different teaching model. The first suggests that teaching is conditioning of responses by controlling the stimuli; the second, by providing models; the third, by arranging stimulus conditions to induce reorganization of perception and cognition. The confusion is further compounded by the fact that many learning theories are derived from laboratory studies, often of lower animals, in which learning occurs in tightly controlled environments that have little or no resemblance to a classroom. Page (1962, pp. 74–75) suggests that there has been a gross misapplication of behavioral sciences, especially psychological theories, and has called attention to the "verbal magic" in which both psychologists and educators engage in translating laboratory findings into educational theory. He defines "verbal magic" as a process of over-generalizing laboratory findings, such as generalizing from the reactions of hooded white rats to electric shock, to the reactions of organisms in general, and then applying the generalization to human learning in a classroom. The resulting inference would be that, since hooded white rats learn less well from punishments than from rewards, the same can be said for organisms in general or third graders in particular.

Another difficulty in analyzing teaching is caused by lack of adequate differentiation among types of learning: among learning facts, developing skills, learning to think, and acquiring attitudes. Without such differentiation it is difficult to match teaching strategies to particular types of learning. Often, therefore, principles of learning relevant to one type of learning are applied indiscriminately to all types with understandably unsatisfactory results.

Past studies of teaching which have concentrated largely on the relationship of teacher characteristics to teaching effectiveness have been rather fruitless. Getzels and Jackson conclude that, despite the importance of the problem and a half-century of prodigious effort, very little is known about the relationship between teacher personality and teacher effectiveness:

> The regrettable fact is that many of the studies so far have not produced significant results. Many others have produced only pedestrian findings. For example, it is said after the usual inventory tabulations, that good teachers are friendly, cheerful, sympathetic, and morally virtuous rather than cruel, depressed, unsympathetic and morally depraved. But when this has been said, not very much that is especially useful has been revealed. For what conceivable human interaction—and teaching implies first and foremost a human interaction—is not better if the people involved are friendly, cheerful, sympathetic, and virtuous rather than the opposite? (Getzels and Jackson, 1963, p. 574)

The Nature of Teaching

Teaching is one of the most complex human activities. Even simple decisions, such as what questions to ask a third grader, require considering and integrating a multitude of factors as shown in the chart below (Taba and Hills, 1965, p. 48):

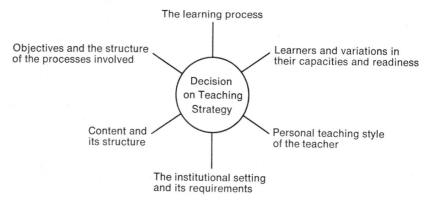

Considerations in Making Decisions About Teaching

Decisions regarding teaching strategies are affected first by the nature of the content taught and by one's view of that content. To the extent that there are differences in the structures of the various disciplines, there must also be variations in the strategies of teaching them.

In addition, if teaching is addressed to multiple behavioral objectives, the behaviors implied by these objectives must be differentiated and appropriate strategies differentiated and planned. For example, attitudes cannot be "taught" in the same sense one teaches geographic principles nor yet map-reading skills.

Further criteria for formulation of teaching strategies are supplied by knowledge about the learning process *qua* process. What do principles such as generalizing in an inductive sequence, such as focusing on manageable targets and such as pacing the learning appropriately, imply in deciding what questions to ask third graders about community organization, or what research assignment in history to give fifth graders? A particularly important principle for those concerned with autonomous learning is that of involving students actively in the business of their own learning.

Still more criteria and modifications are dictated by differences among learners' abilities, cultural backgrounds, and maturity levels. Such differences require the teacher to determine ways of motivating students, or the optimum size of the steps in a sequence of learning tasks. The latter is especially important when the tasks involve conceptualization, abstraction, and other forms of thinking.

Finally, there are the considerations of whether certain teaching techniques harmonize with the teacher's personal style of teaching and with the requirements and limitations of the institutional and community setting. Even techniques that are generally the best can be unproductive if they do not fit into a given style of teaching or are inappropriate to a given school setting.

Generally, however, the above diagram suggests that teaching is a way of synthesizing into one sequence two aspects of a logical model: the structure of the content and the behaviors to be attained by the students. Too often, in current considerations of teaching, these factors are separated.

Studies of Teaching

Recently, the previously mentioned limitations of directly modeling teaching from results of laboratory studies and of inferring teaching effectiveness from the personality characteristics of teachers, or from a general list of *a priori* competencies, have begun to be recognized, and a number of studies have been conducted of normal class situations. The model for assessing teaching effectiveness is also moving toward evaluating the effects of interaction between teacher and students.

In these studies of teaching the description of teaching acts and of teaching strategies has become one of the chief tools for securing data. However, the acts selected to be described differ, as do the systems of description, both apparently as functions of what the researcher considers important in teaching. The studies of teaching tend to differ, therefore, in several important respects.

One difference lies in the range of teaching behavior observed. Whereas one set of observations may be concerned with the logic of teaching, others may focus on classroom climate, on critical thinking, or on communication patterns.

A second source of variation is the setting and the population that is being studied. For example, certain studies observe classes while they are studying a specific subject, while others cut across subject areas. Some investigators are interested in observing teaching of gifted children; others study under-achievers. Some concentrate on high school classrooms only and others investigate elementary school classrooms.

A third difference is the observational procedure itself. In one study observations may be recorded in the classroom during the lesson while in others the analysis of teaching is made indirectly by examining tape recordings, kinescopes or tapescripts. As a rule, the observational procedures used tend to be a function of the kinds of behavior under study. For example, analysis of many dimensions of a particular unit of behavior precludes the direct coding of immediate observation as the sole method of coding and requires the availability of a permanent record (Kliebard, 1966, p. 47).

Finally, the studies differ according to whether they focus on teacher or on student behavior or on both simultaneously.

In one of his earlier statements, Smith (1950, pp. 229–41) maintained that, in order to develop an adequate theory of didactics, one must first describe the behavior of the teachers. The tactics of teaching could be described later. Smith believes that such a description should cut through the verbality which now obstructs intensive analysis of teaching behavior.

Because studies of teaching show progression in methodology of recording as well as in types of behavior analyzed, the major prototypes are presented in a semichronological sequence.

One of the earliest studies by Marie Hughes (1959) analyzed teaching acts. Her study examined the effects of control and freedom in the classroom. Among the categories describing teacher acts were the following:

1. *Controlling,* acts which tell children what to do, how to go about it, and who should do what;
2. *Facilitating,* acts such as those which check, demonstrate, and clarify;
3. *Content development,* acts such as those which elaborate the structure of the problem under consideration, or build data for generalizing;
4. *Personally responsive* acts, and
5. *Positively* and *negatively* affective acts.

Hughes inferred certain qualities of teaching and a certain impact upon what the students learn from frequencies in the categories of teaching acts. For example, a large percentage of controlling acts by the teacher is considered indicative of a tendency to limit students' intellectual activity to memory and recall. A large percentage of acts designated as content development is considered to imply that mental processes other than recall are being developed.

Flanders (1963; 1966) is interested in somewhat similar categories of behavior and their effects on the classroom climate and goals. He uses ten categories to describe the behavior of teachers and students. Seven of these ten describe teacher behavior: accepting feelings, praising and encouraging, using ideas of students, asking questions, lecturing, giving directions, criticizing, justifying authority. The first four represent indirect teacher influence and the last three direct influence. Flanders' thesis is that indirect influence expands the freedom of action for the student and makes him less dependent upon the teacher while the direct influence has the opposite effect. By combining these behaviors in interaction matrices, Flanders plots the concentration of direct and indirect influence and, from the ratio of the two, infers the impact of teaching acts on students (1962a, pp. 50–62). Both of these studies catalogued teacher behavior while observing in the classroom.

Smith (1962) made the transition to the use of tapescripts as a method of recording classroom transactions. His first study was mainly concerned with teaching acts apart from their effect on learning. He classified teaching acts according to certain categories of operation: logical ones, such as defining, classifying, comparing, contrasting, evaluating, or others, such as directing and admonishing. His second study (1964) is devoted to establishing a framework for studying teaching strategies.

In the latter, "ventures" and "moves" constitute the basic elements for describing various teaching strategies. The venture is defined as a "segment of discourse consisting of a set of utterances dealing with a single topic and having a single over-arching content objective." Usually five or six such self-contained units of discourse may be found in a lesson. This definition of ventures as self-contained units assures that the teaching strategies will not be fragmented as they would be if time units were used. But such large units also constitute a source of unreliability in identification. Nine types of ventures were identified according to their cognitive import, central meaning, or theme:

1. *Casual ventures* dealing with cause-and-effect relationships;
2. *Conceptual ventures,* or the over-arching criteria for determining what is a member of a class and what is not;
3. *Evaluative ventures,* namely, the rating of an action, object, or event as to its goodness, correctness or worth;
4. *Informatory ventures,* or clarifications and amplifications of specified topics;

5. *Interpretive ventures,* namely, those dealing with the meaning of words or symbols;
6. *Procedural ventures,* attempts to disclose a sequence of actions by which an end may be achieved;
7. *Reason ventures,* attempts to reveal the reasons for action, decision, policy or practice;
8. *Rule ventures,* namely, the conventional ways of doing things or analytical relationships which may be used to guide action, and
9. *System ventures,* that concentrate on functional relations of the parts of a mechanism that produce a given end.

The move is a verbal maneuver that relates the terms set forth in a proposition to events or things. Moves are multiple. For conceptual ventures alone, eighteen types of moves are identified. Moves and ventures, combined in certain ways, make up strategies which consist entirely of abstract moves or which combine abstract moves with "instancing" moves. Smith and his associates identified two basic dimensions of strategy, namely, the treatment dimension or that of structuring the information, and the control dimension or the devices that the teacher uses to guide and to control the students' operations on the content.

Arno Bellack (1963) and his associates perceive teaching as a form of rule-governed game. Their study is essentially a description of the roles that the teacher and students play when engaged in the game of teaching and learning. The game is verbal and it is assumed that the principal function of language is to communicate meaning. Therefore, the analysis of language in the classroom offers the most promising way of studying the communication of meaning.

In the game of teaching, Bellack distinguishes four basic verbal maneuvers which constitute the first dimension of meaning:

1. *Structuring,* the function of which is to focus attention on the subject matter or a classroom procedure in launching interaction;
2. *Soliciting,* designed to elicit a verbal response, to encourage the persons addressed to attempt something, or to elicit a physical response;
3. *Responding,* which is reciprocally related to soliciting; and
4. *Reacting,* occasioned by structuring, soliciting, or responding functions.

These latter moves serve to shape or mold classroom discussions by accepting, rejecting, modifying or expanding what has been said.

The content of what is said is subdivided into two categories: 1. *substantive meanings,* such as international trade, and 2. *instructional meanings,* such as managerial statements and those concerned with assignments and procedures.

Bellack's findings (1965) are as follows:

1. The chief cycle consisted of teacher soliciting → student responding → teacher reacting; this cycle made up more than three quarters of all verbal moves made.

2. Teachers were verbally more active than students. Teachers structured the lesson, solicited responses from pupils, reacted to pupils' responses and, to some extent, summarized the discourse. The pupils responded primarily to teachers' solicitations; they did not overtly evaluate teacher statements; they evaluated the responses of other pupils only at the infrequent times when the teacher asked them to.

3. In most classes, structuring accounted for about 10% of lines spoken. Soliciting, responding, and reacting each accounted for 20% to 30% of the lines. Summarizing was rather infrequent.

4. Regarding content, instructional meanings accounted for 25% of the discourse and approximately 75% of the discourse was specifically concerned with substantive meanings. The largest proportion of these utterances consisted of stating facts or explaining while, in contrast, analytic and evaluative meanings accounted for only a small portion of the total discourse in any class.

5. The most frequent activities were teachers' statements about procedures, assignments, and other instructional matters.

6. Teachers' behavior was characterized by a relatively stable emotional style.

The study described in this report as well as the study that preceded it (Taba, Levine and Elzey, 1964) differs from those described above in several respects:

1. This study was conducted in an experimental setting rather than a naturalistic one. This experimental setting included a newly organized curriculum plus training the teachers to develop cognitive processes in the students. (Note that Bellack did include some training.)

2. The study focused on a single target—the development of cognitive processes.

3. The study attempted simultaneously to analyze, in terms of cognitive processes, two poles of interaction: teacher behavior and the quality of student responses.

4. The study attempted to identify both the functions (in terms of behaviors sought) of the individual teacher acts and of the combinations of these acts defined as strategies, namely, the sequences, clusters, pacing, and flow.

5. The study attempted to examine a series of dependent variables. For instance, it examined the relationship of the target objective—the levels of cognitive process—to social sciences content achievement, to intelligence, to economic status, and to reading and language ability.

Perhaps the chief distinction between the studies described above and the current study is that they generally analyzed spontaneous teaching behavior of teachers who were not specially trained to promote the behavior being studied in the students. In this study, it was assumed that the teacher had certain techniques made available through training. The emphasis was on how the teacher managed these techniques and how he combined them into a personal style of teaching.

The Learning of Concepts

ROBERT M. GAGNÉ

For those interested in the design of effective instructional conditions in the school situation, the learning of concepts is a matter of central concern. School learning is preponderantly conceptual in nature. Nevertheless, there is great variation in the ways in which the term "concept" is used by educational writers and, accordingly, a variety of descriptions of the essential conditions for learning concepts by students. What *is* a concept, anyhow, in a generic sense? How is it related to a "fact" or a "principle" or a "generalization"? How is it related to methods of learning, such as repetition, or to discovery?

Being a psychologist, I naturally think that one should attempt to seek an answer to such basic definitional questions in that body of partially organized knowledge that has originated from controlled experimental research on behavior. For surely it is true that human learning of concepts can be studied in the framework of controlled laboratory experimentation. Whatever may be the variation in concepts of science, mathematics, language, art, or other content subjects, when people speak of concept-learning they must be referring to a kind of change in human performance that is independent of such content. And if it is independent, then it would seem possible to arrange a set of conditions under which the learning of a concept can be studied systematically.

When one examines the experimental literature on "concept formation" "concept-learning," and related matters, it appears that here too the word

Robert M. Gagne is a Professor at the Center for Educational Technology, Florida State University, Tallahassee.

Paper given as part of a symposium on "Concept-Learning and the Curriculum" at the annual meeting of the American Educational Research Association, Chicago, Illinois, February 12, 1965.

"concept" is not being used with great consistency. Under the heading of concepts, one can find experimental studies dealing with such things as the learning of nonsense words, the acquiring of a new category word by children, the inferring of common functions of a set of objects, the combining of object qualities to achieve new categories, and even the solving of mathematical puzzles. All of these kinds of experiments undoubtedly represent studies of learning. What is not entirely evident, however, is whether they reflect the learning of the same kinds of capabilities. It is truly difficult to describe what it is that these experimental studies have in common, or whether they are in fact devoted to the study of a common problem.

What does "learning a concept" mean? The approach I should like to take here is one that depends largely on observations of what happens in school learning. I do this, not to suggest that one can study the problem systematically in this way, but rather that perhaps one can begin to *define* the problem in such a manner. Perhaps if there can be agreement on what a concept is, and on how it is typically acquired in practice, then it will be possible to design experimental studies to find out the effects on its learning of various conditions of the learning situation.

An Initial Distinction

Some anticipation of my conclusions needs to be stated at the outset in order to spare you the details of a historical account. As a result of examining the kinds of situations that are said to represent concept-learning, I have arrived at the following propositions:

1. There are at least two different, important kinds of phenomena commonly referred to as concept-learning. One refers to the acquiring of a common response, often a name, to a class of objects varying in appearance. This may best be called *concept-learning*. The second refers to the combining of concepts into entities variously referred to as "ideas," "facts," "principles," or "rules." I prefer to call this *principle-learning*.

An example of these two different kinds of capabilities can perhaps be illustrated by *number*. First of all, there are such things as number concepts. When a young child is able to correctly assign the name "three" to collections of any three objects, and at the same time not assign it to collections of two or four objects, it may be said that the child has learned the concept "three." But as mathematics educators will be quick to point out, this is only the most elementary meaning of what they have in mind when they speak of the child "knowing the concept three." Obviously, they want the child to know that three is a set that may be formed by joining the sets two and one, by taking one member away from the set four, by subtracting zero from the set three, by dividing six into two equal parts, by taking the square root of nine, and so on. Perhaps all of these together could form what might be called the "meaning of three." But each of these is a separate *idea* or *principle*. Each of them is achieved by *combining* the concept three (in the simple sense previously described) with some other concept, perhaps equally simple. There is, then, the concept three, the correct choosing of objects to which the name three can be legitimately assigned. And in addition there is a set of principles of three, which are actually combinations of simpler concepts.

2. The basic reason for the distinction between *concept* and *principle* is that they represent two different kinds of learned capabilities. In the first case, the criterion performance is simply being able to answer such a question as "Which of these collections of objects is three?" In the second case, the criterion performance is being able to *use* the concept three in combination, as in the question "What number added to two will give three?" These are quite different performances. Obviously, a child who is able to do the first may not have learned to do the second. If the second question is asked in a way which excludes the possibility of verbal parroting (as it needs to be), then it seems very likely that a child who does it correctly *will* be able to answer the simpler question correctly.

3. If it is true that knowing a concept and knowing a principle are two different capabilities, then it is also quite possible that the conditions for learning them are also different. I shall have more to say about this presently.

Learning Concepts

How is a concept learned? What are the conditions that need to obtain in the instructional situation in order for a new concept to be acquired? It should not be too difficult to identify these conditions. For one thing, we know that animals can acquire concepts. The Harlows' monkeys acquired the concept "odd" when they had learned to choose the odd one of any three objects presented, two of which were nearly identical. If two identical cubes and a sphere were presented, they would choose the sphere; if two boxes and a stick were presented, they would choose the stick.[1] It is instructive to note that what the monkeys learned was the capability of choosing an "odd" one, regardless of the physical appearances of the objects presented. They learned to respond to a *class* of situations which the experimenter could classify as "odd."

How did the animals learn the concept "odd"? Actually, it required a lot of practice with a variety of specific situations each containing "an odd one"

[1] H. F. Harlow and M. K. Harlow, "Learning to Think." *Scientific American. 181:* 36–39, 1949.

which was correct and each differing from the preceding one in the actual objects it contained. Human beings, too, can learn concepts this same way. In fact, sometimes psychologists force them to learn concepts this way in order to analyze the phenomenon. But one should not be led to suppose that humans *have* to learn concepts this way. In one way or another, it is almost bound to be true that the process of concept-learning gets shortened by human beings. Language is one thing that operates to bring this about. For example, studies by the Kendlers indicate that four-year-olds learn a reversal problem by extended trial-and-error, whereas seven-year-olds learn to reverse a discrimination in virtually a single trial.[2] The strong suggestion is that seven-year-olds can say something like "opposite" to themselves, whereas four-year-olds do not yet have the language to do this.

Suppose the concepts "liquid" and "solid" are to be taught to a young child. It seems likely that the learning situation would be something like the following: [3]

1. Show the child a glass containing water and a glass containing a rock. Say "This is a solid" and "This is a liquid."

2. Using a different container, show the child some powdered substance in a pile in a container and some milk in another container. Say "This is a solid; this is a liquid."

3. Provide still a third example of solid and liquid, using different materials and containers.

4. Show the child a number of examples of liquids and solids which he has not seen before. Ask him to distinguish the liquids and the solids. (In this example, I assume the child has previously learned to repeat the words "liquid" and "solid" readily when he hears them; they are familiar in sound.)

The characteristics of this learning situation are, first, that several varieties of the class, themselves of varying physical appearance, were used to exemplify the class to be responded to. Second, words already familiar as responses were used to guide the learning. Under such circumstances, one might expect a child to learn a fairly adequate set of concepts of "liquid" and "solid." This is tested by asking the child to identify liquids and solids from a set that he has not seen before and that has not been used in the learning.

It is also important to note two things that were *not* present in this situation. First, this is not repeated trial-and-error learning. Only three examples are used, all different. The situation is not repeated identically over and over again. Second, although there is language here, it is by no means extensive. One has not tried to teach the concepts, for example, by making such verbal statements as "A liquid is a substance whose particles move

[2] H. H. Kendler and T. S. Kendler, "Effect of Verbalization on Reversal Shifts in Children." *Science.* 141:1619–1620, 1961.

[3] Robert M. Gagne, *The Conditions of Learning.* New York: Holt, Rinehart & Winston, 1965.

freely over each other so that its mass assumes the shape of the container in which it is placed." This characteristic of a liquid is directly exhibited, rather than being verbally described.

Presumably, much the same sort of conditions may obtain when an older student learns a new technical term. Something like this must have to be done when a student learns a concept like "point of inflection" in mathematics, or when he learns concepts such as "cell," "nucleus," or "mitochondrion" in biology, or when he learns what a "simile" is in English. Sometimes, it is true, even more extensive verbalization is used, and I shall return to this point in a moment.

Learning Principles

What is meant by learning a principle (or rule)? And how does this differ from learning a concept? It needs to be recalled here that a principle is a combination of concepts.

Principles, being combinations, can become very complex. But let us start with an extremely simple one, such as "liquids pour." What kind of learning situation would be set up to bring about the learning of such a principle? Actually, there are two possibilities, and this does not make my task easier.[4]

Possibility one is this: After determining that the concepts "liquid" and "pour" can be identified, make the statement that "liquids pour." To test the learning, give the student a liquid in a container, and say, in effect, "Show me." This technique is what is often called *reception learning,* and there is little doubt that a very large proportion of school learning is basically of this sort, as D. P. Ausubel says.[5]

Possibility two is this: First determine that the concepts "liquid" and "pour" can be identified. Then, give the student a number of different liquids in a number of different containers. Ask him to demonstrate ways in which the liquids are alike and different from solids. One thing he will do is pour them; he may also make the verbal statement, "Liquids pour." This learning technique is called *discovery learning,* and there is some evidence, though not much, that the principle learned this way is better retained and transferred than is the case with reception learning.

Regardless of the learning technique, however, the important thing to note is that what is learned is a combination of concepts, called a principle. There is no particular reason to think that there are any important formal differences between a simple principle of this sort and the great variety of more complex principles that are learned at later ages, such as principles of using adjectives, or of dividing quantities into fractional parts, or of

[4] *Ibid.*

[5] D. P. Ausubel, *The Psychology of Meaningful Verbal Learning.* New York: Grune & Stratton, 1963.

specifying the functions of a legislature, or of relating force and mass and acceleration.

The characteristics of the learning situation for principles are, first, that the concepts of which it is composed must be previously learned. Second, the principle is either stated verbally or discovered by the learner. The acquisition of the principle is tested by asking the student to demonstrate its application to a particular case which he has not encountered during the learning.

Note particularly that the conditions of learning for a principle are *not* the same as those for a concept. Perhaps the outstanding difference is that the concepts which make up the principle must already be learned; they are prerequisite to the learning. Second, there is no requirement to illustrate the principle by two or three examples (although of course this may be done *after* the learning, for other purposes). Third, it is possible to discover a principle, since the two or more concepts which make it up may be theoretically "combined" in a number of different ways. But pure discovery, without verbal guidance, does not usually occur as a process in the learning of concepts by human beings. One could more aptly describe what monkeys do in attaining concepts as "discovery." Since they cannot be guided by language, they must go through a rather lengthy trial-and-error procedure to get to the point where they can choose the odd one or go to the middle door. If human beings had to "discover" new concepts in this way, it would take them a very long time to learn all the things they have to learn. Using a familiar word accomplishes the instruction much more rapidly. But it also short-circuits the process of discovery.

Concept-Learning by Definition

While the distinction between concepts and principles in terms of conditions required for learning seems fairly clear, there is another source of confusion between them: When people are verbally sophisticated, they often learn concepts verbally, as pointed out by J. B. Carroll in a recent article.[6] That is to say, individuals learn concepts "by definition." If a person does not know the concept "caliche," he may learn what it is by reading or hearing the verbal statement, "a crust of calcium carbonate formed on stony soil in arid regions."

It is important to note that in this kind of learning situation, a *principle* is being used to provide instruction for the learning of a *concept*. The verbal statement itself is obviously a principle, because it contains several concepts: crust, calcium carbonate, stony soil, arid, region. And just as obviously, the learner will not be able to acquire "caliche" as a concept

[6] J. B. Carroll, "Words, Meanings and Concepts." *Harvard Educational Review,* *34:*178–202, 1964.

unless he does indeed know what each of these other concepts means, that is, unless he has previously learned each of them.

There can be little doubt that many new concepts are learned in this verbal manner by literate students and adults. Lest one think, however, that this method of learning concepts is a flawless one, a caution should be noted. A concept that is learned by way of verbally stated principles may have some inadequacies. For example, if an individual visits Texas for the first time in his life after hearing a verbal definition of caliche, will he make a certain identification of this material? Or will he be somewhat hesitant about it, and tend to confuse it with something else? Perhaps everyone would agree that for learning what caliche is, nothing can quite take the place of actually observing it.

This principle of "seeing is believing" is of more than passing importance to the problem of concept-learning. It is, for example, a fundamental reason why science educators are so firmly convinced of the value of the laboratory. If the student is to learn concepts like "power," "energy," "osmotic pressure," and many others, he can, to be sure, learn them in some sense by means of definitions. But there is a danger that the concepts he learns this way are inadequate in one way or another. Accordingly, most science educators would maintain that the performing of operations, including observation in the laboratory, is an essential part of the learning situation required for the learning of fully adequate, generalizable concepts. The role of the laboratory in school learning serves to remind us of the concrete basis for learning concepts and of the potential insufficiencies of concept-learning which is based solely upon verbally conveyed definitions. This is equally true in subjects other than science. The requirement for direct observation exists in all school subjects.

Summary

In summary, it appears to be of some importance for the design of curriculum content and instructional method to recognize a distinction between concepts and principles. Different conditions are applicable to the learning of concepts and the learning of principles. Two differences that I have mentioned are perhaps of greatest importance. The first is that concepts are prior to principles and, in this sense, are simpler than principles. To learn a principle, one must have previously learned the concepts of which it is composed. A second difference pertains to verbal guidance versus pure discovery as a learning method. Learning concepts by pure discovery would appear to be an inhumanly inefficient thing to do, given the existence of language. But principles can be learned by discovery. There is some slight evidence to suggest that such a method of learning principles may be advantageous for retention and transfer, although it is likely to be more time-consuming for initial learning. Additional soundly designed research could well be devoted to this latter question.

Conceptual Approaches: Their Meaning for Elementary Social Studies

JOHN JAROLIMEK

At some point in the remoteness of antiquity, man made a gigantic leap in his development that would forever separate him from all other living creatures. The similarities and differences between man and the universe of living things has been the source of some fascination through the centuries, and many explanations have been suggested for his uniqueness. Unquestionably, the unbridgeable gap between man and the rest of the animal kingdom lies precisely in his capacity to engage in high-order, abstract mental operations facilitated through the use of a complex symbol system. This is not to say that man thinks and animals do not. It is, rather, to suggest that the mental processes of animals and those of man are separated by several orders of magnitude.

Man has the amazing capacity to attach symbols to reality and thereby manipulate reality intellectually. Moreover, he can and does attach symbols to abstractions that do not exist physically at all (terms such as *tradition, colonialism, democracy*), and he can manipulate those mentally. Man's neurological system is such that it is able to classify, store, retrieve, and process a phenomenal amount of information. Because man has this capacity, he can accumulate and transmit a social heritage. He can also use his intelligence to create and invent new variations of that heritage. He can be taught to solve intensely complex social problems. He can, finally, develop and adapt a culture, something no other creature is able to do.

It is well known that lower animals can be taught or conditioned to respond to words. When trained, a dog, a horse, or a bird will react in a predictable way to a given command. Animals frequently behave in deceptively human-like ways. Because the response is often so well executed, it is sometimes mistakenly assumed that the animal engages in reflective thought, akin to that of human beings. When man responds to symbols, however, he is doing so in an altogether different way from that of a dog, baboon, or talking bird. He does something besides and beyond simply

John Jarolimek is Professor of Education at the University of Washington, Seattle.

Reprinted from *Social Education* 31(7):534–536, 1966, with permission of the National Council for the Social Studies and John Jarolimek.

reacting to a sign symbol. Man associates meaning with a symbol, a meaning that goes considerably beyond a sensory impression. When man hears or sees the symbol *concentration camp,* his memory system immediately scans and sorts a vast amount of information and selects the appropriate data to associate with this symbol, thus giving it meaning. This assumes, of course, that the individual has had some prior opportunity to become acquainted with the meaning of this term. But it is not necessary for him to have personally and directly experienced concentration camps in order for this symbol to have meaning for him. He may have read about them, seen pictures of them, heard accounts of persons who had been in them, seen a movie about concentration camps, and so on. When we refer to the meanings associated with words and symbols in this way, we are defining *concepts.* Concepts may be regarded as categories of meaning. Attaching meaning beyond sensory impression to abstract symbols is what is meant by conceptual thought. It is intellectual behavior that is distinctly and uniquely characteristic of human beings.

It is doubtful if anything but the most elementary conceptual thought would be possible without a highly developed symbol system. This is so because concepts are abstract ideas and are detached from specific experiences. In order to handle ideas in this way, it is necessary to have labels or symbols to attach to them. If ideas are to be communicated, there must be common agreement on the meanings of the labels or symbols. Words provide convenient labels for concepts, and, consequently, word-symbols are sometimes confused with the concepts they represent.

Using concepts as categories of meaning makes it possible for man to establish order in all of the many thousands of specific perceptions and unique experiences he has. Concepts provide an intellectual filing system for meanings. Concept development, then, calls for the placing of information in correct cognitive categories. In developing the concept *city,* as an example, pupils must learn to differentiate a city from other political and social entities. A city is not a county; neither is it a village, nor a town, nor a hamlet. Pupils could test the validity of a vast number of statements concerning the characteristics of a city, and in so doing their understanding of the concept would be enlarged, i.e., A city has more people living in it than a village; A city provides opportunities for many types of jobs; A city must have a good transportation system; and so forth. Suppose, however, pupils conclude that "Large cities are not located close to other large cities." A test of this statement would show that there are many exceptions to it. This is not a statement that would correctly apply to all or nearly all cities. It is incorrect information.

When one includes incorrect information in a category, he then forms a *mis*conception. Pupils who learn about the English *race* and the French *race* are associating incorrect information with the race concept and are therefore forming misconceptions. It is apparent that in developing concepts it is important for the learner to have a broad exposure to the idea, encountering it in a variety of settings, and experiencing both positive and negative instances and exemplars. Concept development is largely an information sorting, discriminating process, including in the category all associations and relationships that belong and excluding those that do not.

In social studies, concepts are often expressed in the following ways:

1. as *words*—river, mountain, city, urbanism, tradition, culture, democracy, colonialism, migration, import, export, cargo, trade.
2. as *phrases*—cultural diffusion, balance of power, trade agreement, balance of payments, income tax, polar regions, representative government.

In conceptual approaches to social studies curriculum development and teaching, a great deal is made of generalizations—as organizing ideas from the disciplines, main ideas, key ideas, and so on. Sometimes they are also labeled *concepts,* although such nomenclature is not altogether consistent with the conventional and widely accepted use of the term. A generalization is defined as a declarative statement expressing a relationship between concepts or other variables and has more or less universal applicability. The statements describing cities cited earlier are examples of generalizations. Other examples that have been widely used in the social studies are: Every society creates laws; Land is used for many and varied purposes; Change is a condition of human society; Culture is socially learned.

The following generalization from geography may be used to illustrate the relationship between generalizations, concepts, and facts:

Climate is determined by sunlight, temperature, humidity, precipitation, atmospheric pressure, winds, unequal rates of heating and cooling of land and water surfaces, irregular shape and distribution of land and sea, ocean currents, and mountain systems.

This generalization has imbedded within it a number of concepts that must be understood if the statement is to make sense: sunlight, temperature, humidity, precipitation, atmospheric pressure, winds, and so forth. Moreover, each of the concepts has many specific facts associated with it that give it meaning, as for example: *sunlight*—amount, intensity, composition; *temperature*—variation, change, effects; *winds*—direction, patterns, causes; *humidity*—degree of moisture, dampness, effect on comfort. Concepts and generalizations are transferable from one setting to another. Facts, on the other hand, have no transfer value—they are useful and applicable only in their specific settings: Columbus discovered America in 1492; The Chicago fire took place on October 8, 1871; The Great Depression followed the stock market crash of October 1929. Conceptual approaches are intended to provide a framework or design for the building up of meanings from facts to concepts to generalizations.

It has long been known that social studies programs typically include an overwhelming amount of specific information. Not only is the existing fact-load heavy but the problem is additionally confounded because (1) the amount of specific information is increasing at a rapid rate due to the discovery of new knowledge; (2) specific information is ephemeral and becomes obsolete quickly; (3) the rate of forgetting specific information is known to be high; and (4) unless specifics are tied to larger ideas, it is impossible to establish functional criteria for the selection of facts to be taught. In recent years, therefore, curriculum workers in the social studies have turned their attention to the use of concepts and generalizations as organizing schemes in an attempt to overcome the problems just cited. The basic idea is to focus instruction on a relatively few fundamental concepts that have high transfer value and that help to explain or predict social or natural phenomena. Specific subject matter is selected to illustrate particularly well the concepts under study and to permit the application of certain methods of inquiry.

In principle the use of organizing designs of the type under discussion have been received favorably by educators and social scientists alike. There is considerable agreement that the programs of the past have over-stressed learning goals dealing with the accumulation of information mostly of the descriptive type. Major curriculum revision projects of the past decade have, without exception, given some attention to an emphasis on basic concepts and generalizations. The usual procedure has been to turn to the various parent disciplines contributing to social studies and attempt to identify the core ideas from those disciplines. Numerous social scientists have been involved in the search for and identification of basic concepts from the social sciences, and several lists have been compiled. It is safe to say, however, that to date there are few very good models of social studies programs that incorporate basic concepts from the social science disciplines into functioning curriculums. Hardly any are markedly different from those of the past. Perhaps more will be available after programs now under development, such as those in Project Social Studies, are reported.

If conceptual approaches are to become the basis for elementary social studies curriculums, something more needs to be done besides simply over-laying a list of concepts from the social sciences on a traditional scope and sequence chart with some minor shifts of content allocations from one grade to another. Likewise, conceptual approaches will not contribute needed vitalization of elementary social studies if conventional methodology is employed. A substantial re-orientation to both content and method will be needed before the real values of conceptually based curriculums can be achieved.

The attention to and development of concepts necessarily suggests an instructional emphasis stressing inquiry and inductive teaching. This is not to suggest that a pupil has to discover everything he needs to know—to do so would mean that he could not profit from the accumulated wisdom of mankind. What is being suggested is that the total approach be investigation oriented—that teachers will *not* write generalizations on the chalkboard for pupils to learn or have them memorize dictionary definitions of concepts. If the emphasis on concept teaching results in practices such as these, our programs will be in a bad way, indeed. Pupils build meanings into concepts by what they themselves do and experience—through a range of encounters with concepts and through the use of a vast amount of supporting detail. Generalizations for the most part should be considered either (1) as tentative conclusions arrived at after lenghty and careful study or (2) as propositions, assumptions, or hypotheses to be tested by study and research.

It seems clear, too, that the role of the teacher in social studies instruction needs to shift from what it has traditionally been. In today's concept-based and inquiry-oriented programs, the teacher simply cannot remain the chief data source for the class. In many, perhaps most, elementary social studies classes, the teacher and the text continue to be the most important information sources, utilizing the conventional *transmitter* (teacher and text)– *receiver* (pupils) teaching model. It is obvious that there is little to be gained in re-writing curriculum documents in social studies if prevailing teaching strategies do not conform either to the philosophical base or the psychological orientation of the new program. The role of the teacher will need to shift to the extent that his behavior has to do *mainly* with stimulating, questioning, clarifying, supporting, providing feedback, guiding, and diagnosing. Because educational technology is making it possible for devices to do many tasks teachers have traditionally performed (providing information, giving assignments, correcting papers), increasingly it will be necessary for teachers to attend to those unique tasks that only human teachers can do.

In the present period of curriculum reform, it has become the accepted custom to insist that elementary teachers have a better knowledge of the subject matter relating to their teaching assignments. This assumed need is often accepted uncritically. Given the current educational climate, emphasis on knowledge of subject matter, however valid such an emphasis may be, tends to encourage traditional information-giving teaching roles.

There can be little question that the elementary teacher of today and tomorrow will need a better background in the social sciences than his counterpart did a generation ago—although not for the reasons ordinarily given. The teacher needs a strong background not to pass the information on to the pupils he teaches but to be able to know what possibilities for investigation inhere in a topic, to know what questions to ask, to know how to test hypotheses, and how to arrive at valid conclusions. The uninformed teacher may not know enough about a topic to be able to plan an extended and soundly-based investigation of it with today's informed and sophisticated pupils.

Additionally, teachers in concept-based programs need to know a great deal about the psychology of cognitive processes and the organization of knowledge itself. How do pupils learn concepts and generalizations? How can knowledge be organized to enhance learning? How can concepts be programed on a continuum of difficulty? What are the relevant concepts from the various disciplines? How does the teacher enhance and assist transfer of learnings? What concepts are particularly appropriate for slow-learning pupils? Are the same procedures for concept development equally valid for slow learners as for average and high-achieving pupils? Questions such as these must be answered before much headway can be made in developing concept-based programs that really work.

A generation ago a prevailing notion in elementary education was that process goals were more important than content goals. This was embodied in the cliché "What pupils learn is less important than how they learn it." Fortunately, we do not go around saying things like that anymore, for we have recognized that in addition to teaching pupils in ways that are educationally and psychologically sound, we also expect them to learn something of substance. There is a lesson in this for current thinking about social studies.

In the shift from traditional content-oriented, descriptive, fact-centered social studies programs to those that are concept based, there is the tendency again to assume that specific content is not especially important as long as it is representative and that it provides a good vehicle for the development of concepts. This may be a valid assumption from the standpoint of instruction. A child *can* develop such concepts relating to family life as role, status, and sanctions, for example, by studying a primitive Indian family of South America. Or a pupil *can* learn about social stratification by studying an Oriental society. But in making the selection of specific content to be used in developing concepts, it would seem important to bear in mind that there is a body of informational content that is necessary for ordinary civic and social literacy. It would be well to remember, too, that society has institutional expectations regarding social studies and elementary schools—there are some things pupils are expected to know when they complete the elementary school. Perhaps on a common-sense basis one might conclude that it is more relevant for American school children to learn something about the social forces operating in their own community than to engage in a depth study of a pre-literate society in a remote part of the world. To have social studies programs designed to build basic concepts does not mean that topics selected for study need to be unusual, unique, or esoteric. There is no reason why elementary social studies programs cannot combine the development of basic concepts *and* the building of backgrounds of functional information *and* appropriate processes of thought.

When man substitutes impulsive, emotional, and thoughtless action for behavior that has resulted from the exercise of rational, reflective, thoughtful processes, he is not behaving in accordance with those characteristics that set him apart from other animals. All of education, and particularly the social studies, should strive to enhance and promote in pupils those qualities from which man derives his humanness. This is a highly relevant concern for elementary teachers because of the nature of the child during the time he is in the elementary school. Pupils in the elementary school today will in a few years be adult citizens of their communities, holding offices, voting, serving on school boards, advising their elected officials, and making decisions individually and collectively on social and civic affairs. Conceptual approaches to social studies education, supported by compatible teaching procedures, tempered by the good sense and patience of an understanding and psychologically warm teacher, should assist pupils to learn how to come to grips with the realities of social and civic affairs in thoughtful, intelligent, and rational ways.

Cognitive Power Through the Social Studies: Upper Grades

THEODORE KALTSOUNIS

For a long time social studies in the upper grades were descriptive in nature. Whether the course was about the local state or a foreign country, the children were mostly memorizing the names of rivers, mountains, and cities, or they were making lists of imports and exports. Soon after they had passed an examination, youngsters in most cases were forgetting everything. If there was anything left in their minds, it was usually a bitter taste for social studies as a school subject.

With the spread of the conceptualization approach during the past ten years from the fields of science and mathematics into the social studies, the emphasis has been placed on the development of concepts and generalizations. A shift was effected from studying isolated facts to studying facts, events, and phenomena that could be clustered together in order to be simply labeled or used to explain various happenings and trends. No one would doubt that this new direction raised many hopes for a sound social studies program, but what has happened thus far should not be perceived as adequate in terms of developing the student's cognitive power to the extent possible or needed.

An illustration will probably make this point clear. Can anyone think of a bank that limits its function to collecting money, to classifying it into

Theodore Kaltsounis is Professor of Education at the University of Washington, Seattle.

Reprinted from *Educational Leadership* 27(7):665–667, 1970, with permission of the Association for Supervision and Curriculum Development and Theodore Kaltsounis. Copyright © 1970 by the Association for Supervision and Curriculum Development.

denominations, and to labeling each denomination? Of course not. In order for a bank to grow, or even exist, it must invest the money which it collects. The better the investment decisions are, the faster and stronger the bank will grow. Needless to say, decisions made by bankers are usually good when they are supported by relevant knowledge and by a capability to analyze and project on the basis of present economic trends.

Beyond Generalizations

The above analogy can apply to human beings as well. The main emphasis of this article is that the cognitive power of the individual grows faster and stronger when the individual goes beyond the development and accumulation of concepts and generalizations into their actual use through the application of a sound decision-making process.

The overemphasis on concepts and generalizations during the past decade was probably due to the rather strong influence that social scientists have had on the curriculum, but there is a difference between the orientation of a social scientist and that of an average citizen. The task of the social scientist is to analyze data and discover basic principles. The average citizen is primarily concerned with how to use this knowledge to resolve the dilemmas which he faces in his dealings with his social environment. As Shirley Engle pointed out,

In marked contrast to the meticulous research orientation of the social sciences, the social studies are centrally concerned with the education of citizens. The mark of a good citizen is the quality of decisions which he reaches on public and private matters of social concern.[1]

The Teacher and Decision Making

The power to make intelligent decisions is a very important commodity in our society today. The social crisis that prevails all around us can no longer tolerate citizens who decide and act solely on the basis of narrow interests and without careful consideration of the consequences of their decisions as far as their relationship to the dignity of other men and the general welfare is concerned. Our society needs active citizens whose actions must be controlled by a steady capability to make wise decisions. How can teachers in the upper grades, or any grades, help develop this capability through social studies?

[1] Shirley H. Engle. "Decision Making: The Heart of Social Studies Instruction." *Social Education* 24(7):301; November 1960.

The most important step is for the teacher to understand the decision-making process. One source describes this process in six phases as follows:

1. Identification of the problem
2. Obtaining necessary information
3. Production of possible solutions
4. Evaluation of such solutions
5. Selection of a strategy for performance
6. Actual performance of an action or actions, and subsequent learning and revision.[2]

In essence, decision making is the inquiry method or the problem-solving approach, taken a step beyond simply arriving at conclusions about the status of phenomena or situations. Decision making is more dynamic in nature than problem solving or inquiry in that it requires action as a result of and following each instance of systematic intellectualization.

One of the most fundamental aspects of decision making is that it involves, besides knowledge, the affective domain of the individual—what are commonly referred to as feelings, values, attitudes, and beliefs. Human beings usually establish an equilibrium between their knowledge, their beliefs, and their behavior; any decision for action tends to preserve and be influenced by this equilibrium. A segregationist clergyman, for example, most likely knows the Bible just as well as any other clergyman, but he uses his knowledge to justify his segregationist beliefs and behavior.

Decision making, then, requires that the teacher and the school be concerned about the affective domain of the child just as much as they have been and continue to be concerned about increasing his knowledge, whether it is in terms of factual information or in terms of generalizations and concepts. If the school is to emphasize intelligent choice and decisions, no longer can attitudes and beliefs continue to be considered private matters that should remain outside the classroom. This appears to be inconceivable when sociologists remind us that "Values and norms are the main sources of energy to individuals and society." [3]

Curriculum for Decisions

Turning to more practical matters, it should be emphasized that the social studies program should be structured in a way that would allow opportunities for exercise in decision making. Social studies should com-

[2] Orville G. Brim *et al. Personality and Decision Processes.* Stanford, California: Stanford University Press, 1962, p. 49.

[3] Lawrence Senesh. "Organizing Curriculum Around Social Science Concepts." In: John J. Gibson. *New Frontiers in the Social Studies: Action and Analysis.* New York: Citation Press, 1967, p. 82.

prise an active program, one that would require involvement. Whether one deals with the local state, the region, the nation, or the world, the field of social studies is probably more open-ended than any other school subject. An effort should be made to keep it open-ended. One way to do this would be to select topics that tend to bring out the major issues of our time. A traditional textbook approach to the study of the United States in the fifth grade, for instance, should be strengthened by more relevant topics such as the following:

1. The changing nature of family in the United States
2. The rise of the city, and resulting urban and suburban problems
3. Changing interpretations of Civil Rights and the growing responsibility of the federal government in their enforcement
4. United States and the world
5. Environmental pollution
6. The role of labor, management, and government in determining labor-management-consumer relations.

The topics listed and others like them have the potential of raising in the students' minds some very personal questions that will stimulate involvement. Some of these questions could be: Why can I not swim in the lake? Is there anything that can be done about it? What can I do? Is it right for my grandparents to live in a small apartment by themselves? Why can they not live with us? Should I talk to my dad about it? What should be done about poverty in the United States? What can we do to eliminate this problem from our own community? Questions of this type help to bring into the open the children's own values, and eventually their consideration usually leads to action.

Whatever decisions for action the children make, the teacher should be sure they are made after careful consideration of all possible alternatives. The merits of each alternative should be examined and debated in terms of its consequences.

Helpful New Teaching Strategies

Teaching strategies also changed along with the curriculum. Emphasis on decision making generated some rather stimulating teaching techniques. Role playing, games, and simulation are among these techniques. Children in a particular community, for example, were studying the local problem of bussing children from one neighborhood school to another. This was initiated to bring about integration, but some felt it was not as successful as originally expected. The school board had to decide whether or not to continue bussing children to different neighborhoods. While the community was waiting for the board's decision, the children were asked to play the role of the school board, and reach a decision on this problem by considering all points of view and by following exactly the same procedure that would be used by the board. In this way, the children not only learned the facts and became aware of reality, but they projected their feelings as well, and they were able to clarify them in view of the facts.

Ours are very difficult times. The society in which we live has many problems. Consequently, it needs not just knowledgeable citizens, but socially concerned and active knowledgeable citizens who would have the power to make the appropriate decisions at the appropriate times. To develop this special cognitive power in citizens, work must start early in their education. One of the most serious problems teachers in the upper grades have in their effort to develop in children the decision-making process is the fact that it is not emphasized enough in the lower grades. Unfortunately, there are too many people who still feel that the three R's should dominate the program.

Inquiry: Does It Teach How or What to Think?

GARY A. MANSON AND ELMER D. WILLIAMS

Numbers of social studies educators, including classroom teachers, curriculum developers and teacher educators, have come to regard inquiry as both a powerful means of instruction and an important competency to be learned by pupils.[1] Such acceptance of inquiry has been a reaction to the tremendous proliferation of knowledge—its sheer quantity rendering transmission to children virtually impossible—and a conviction that investigation-oriented learning is more durable. The advocates of inquiry maintain that existing curricula and instructional practices have overemphasized information, lecture, and memory while neglecting the key ideas, investigative methodologies, and thinking skills requisite to understanding the social sciences and resolving social problems. Although such views are neither wholly accurate reflections of the current status of knowledge nor the

Gary A. Manson is Assistant Professor of Geography at Michigan State University, East Lansing; Elmer D. Williams is Assistant Professor of Social Science Education at the University of Georgia, Athens.

Reprinted from *Social Education 34*:78–81, 1970, with permission of the National Council for the Social Studies and Gary A. Manson and Elmer D. Williams.

[1] Bernice Goldmark, *Social Studies: A Method of Inquiry.* Belmont, California: Wadsworth Publishing Company, Inc., 1968; H. Millard Clements, William R. Fielder, and B. Robert Tabachnick, *Social Study: Inquiry in Elementary Classrooms.* Indianapolis: The Bobbs-Merrill Company, 1966; Byron Massialas and Benjamin Cox, *Inquiry in Social Studies.* New York: McGraw-Hill Book Company, 1966.

events occurring in many social studies classrooms, it is fair to say that much social studies instruction does not adequately prepare students to cope with knowledge explosions, to direct technological revolutions, and to participate in cultural transformations. It is out of this context that a strong case for inquiry has been constructed.

The search for a capsule definition of inquiry is, and will continue to be, futile; the nature of the word itself suggests continual redefining. Some evidence for this proposition was provided at a recent conference of social studies educators [2] at which a group of inquiry's most responsible proponents was unable to establish a mutually acceptable meaning for the term. There is, nevertheless, widespread consensus that if inquiry were placed on a continuum of teaching methods ranging from expository-didactic to hypothetical-heuristic, it would certainly approximate the latter. If, on the other hand, inquiry is taken to imply intellectual activity by learners, then seeking and transforming knowledge is certainly more appropriate than accepting and reproducing it.

Instruction based on the pupil as a knowledge seeker is generally posed as the antithesis of expository teaching in which the learner is to be a knowledge recipient. Learning may occur in either situation, but proponents of inquiry maintain that the nature of the learning is likely to differ. This is to be expected since the purposes for which the methods were designed are quite different. Exposition may be better suited to transmitting knowledge while investigation may be more effective in developing thinking; however, the paucity of research does not permit a final conclusion about such a claim. What can be asserted is that learning resulting from expository teaching need not be meaningless, and that learning resulting from inquiry teaching need not be meaningful. Lecture is not inherently bad nor is inquiry necessarily good. "Problem solving can be just as deadening, just as formalistic, just as mechanical, just as passive, and just as rote as the worst form of exposition." [3] The instructional format should not be mistaken as adequate assurance of desirable learning.

Unfortunately, basic points of agreement concerning what inquiry is and is not are often obscured by the use of terms such as problem solving, the scientific method, techniques of the scholar, reflective thinking and discovery in a manner suggesting they are synonomous. These are not completely interchangeable concepts; some refer to teaching methods while others relate to intellectual processes. In fact, a problem central to the issues surrounding the meaning and implications of inquiry lies in a failure to distinguish ways in which a person learns from ways in which one individual causes another to learn. It is this distinction between inquiry as intellectual activity of the pupil, as it is inferred from what the pupil does, and inquiry

---

[2] The 48th Annual Convention of the National Council for the Social Studies at Washington, D.C., November 25 to 30, 1968.

[3] J. P. Guilford, *The Nature of Intelligence*. New York: McGraw-Hill Book Company, 1967.

as instructional conditions created by the teacher that provides the basis for the remainder of this article.

Inquiry and Student Responses

To investigate, to analyze, to validate, to reflect and to solve requires the generation of additional information beyond that which is given. During an inquiry session, for instance, a class may be confronted with situations incongruent with their previous experiences, *e.g.* agriculture without machines; eras without wars; families without fathers. In resolving such incongruities, the student is expected to ask questions, to formulate hypotheses, to search for additional data, to draw inferences and to reach tentative conclusions. But the amount and kind of responses produced by the student involves more than sheer ability to go beyond what is given. His statements and queries are also influenced by an interpretation of the learning task and a perception of the teacher's purposes, two critical variables often overlooked in the design and conduct of inquiry.

From the teacher's point of view, confrontations with problematic situations entail one of two basic instructional designs: *convergent* or *divergent*. A convergent model prevails when the quantity, kind and structure of information given the pupil are sufficient to determine his response. In other words, there is only one legitimate answer to the problem, and the relevant data is organized to guide the learner to the answer, the procedure to be used is clearly implied or even stated, and the task of the learner is to arrive at that answer. Programmed learning and the game "Twenty Questions" usually follow convergent formats. A divergent model prevails when information content and organization, while influencing student responses, permit and indeed encourage a range of legitimate alternatives. Multiple-answer questions, remote association tasks, and problem finding are usually of divergent quality. The differences between divergent and convergent tasks may be summarized thusly: "In the former case, restrictions are few; in the latter there are many. In the former, the search is broad, in the latter, it is narrow. In the former, output is in quantity; in the latter, it is limited. In the former, criteria for success are vague and somewhat lax and may, indeed, stress variety and quantity; in the latter, criteria are sharper, more rigorous and demanding. . . . The information produced (by the student) is more or less fitting in light of the search model." [4]

From the student's point of view, an inquiry task can be perceived as applying a known procedure in order to resolve an imposed problem with the objective of arriving at an answer already known to the teacher. Such a perception, while it may be quite accurate, should not be expected to con-

[4] *Ibid.,* pages 214–215.

tribute to intellectual flexibility, fluency, and originality, characteristics of much scholarly investigation. Inquiry, however, may also be perceived by the student as devising a means to resolve a discovered problem with the objective of arriving at one of several "correct" answers. In such a situation, a student is more willing to utilize hypotheses that deviate from the norm, information that initially appears to others as irrelevant, and solutions that are innovative, or at least so they seem to him.

It should not be assumed that the divergent model is to be preferred in all cases, since competency in convergent problem solving is also a legitimate instructional objective. While it is probably true that convergency pervades most learning, and therefore may suggest greater efforts in direction of divergency, it is more important that the teacher first become aware of the differences between the two and then select the model suitable to his objective.

Inquiry Teaching in the Convergent Model

The instructional conditions contributing to learning are largely determined by the classroom teacher. In the process of inquiry he may select and present the problems, provide the bulk of the resources utilized during the investigation, and respond to the ideas and questions of the pupils. During the process of pupil-teacher interaction, the instructor influences the kind and amount of thinking that his pupils display; that is, the instruction may lead to few or many ideas being forwarded and, in turn, may develop either convergent or divergent thinking strategies.

In the convergent model, the inquiry task is chosen and organized by the teacher. Pupils are expected to recall information or to seek additional data before posing answers or hypotheses. In all likelihood, the teacher has thought through the problem and anticipated possible student responses. He also knows which one of these responses is conventionally accepted, either by the populace at large or by social scientists. This becomes the answer that he tends to accept even though pupils may be able to substantiate, at least partially, other alternatives. Unanticipated or unusual pupil responses are usually acknowledged but quickly dismissed.

To illustrate use of a convergent inquiry model, consider the case of an elementary school class involved in a study of today's modern shopping centers. Derived from his own observations and reading, the teacher designs an inquiry task requiring pupils to determine the shopping center plan that will create maximum customer flow throughout the center. Perhaps this teacher's experience is limited to those shopping centers having the major department stores located in the center of the development acting as "traffic generators." Centralized placement of large stores, in this case, is the principal variable in customer movement. Should additional investigation suggest this same spatial arrangement, he may believe that it constitutes "the best solution," and that his pupils, through investigation and careful thinking, should arrive at this solution and only this solution.

Having been presented with the task, the pupils call upon their previous experiences with shopping centers and seek further information through observation, reading, or questioning. This data serves to direct student responses to the problem and to filter out inappropriate or unrealistic proposals. For example, if a pupil knows that a large number of customers frequent a center during peak hours, that centers are intended to concentrate business activity, or that the construction of a center requires huge outlays of capital, then he is less likely to propose moving the buildings to the people as a means of maximizing customer flow. While it may represent a creative effort, such a proposal is neither logical nor supported by the data. Legitimate criteria for a problem's solution is required in both the convergent and divergent models.

During the period of student inquiry the teacher interacts with the pupils by organizing research activities, providing information and focusing individual efforts on the task. If the convergent model prevails, the teacher's verbal as well as nonverbal behavior, deliberately or not, is employed to guide pupil efforts toward "the best answer." Reinforcement strategies are used by the teacher to support desired responses and to eliminate the undesired. The student soon perceives this intention and will structure his thinking to "match" that of the teacher or refrain from responding. This perception leads the student to believe that there is one correct answer; thus "reasonable" alternatives may not be pursued. In effect, the teacher serves as a filter or criterion for the student's proposed solution(s) in a manner similar to reason and information. While the pupil can accept reason and data as appropriate tests for his ideas, he may find it difficult to understand the teacher's seemingly arbitrary rejection of an answer he believes to be fairly well substantiated.

Inquiry Teaching in the Divergent Model

Inquiry as an instructional process may also facilitate the generation of divergent thinking, the situation where the desired behavior of pupils is production of a number of verifiable and defensible alternatives rather than one "best" answer. Although the criteria of knowledge and reason must still be fulfilled, the approach now is one of allowing for pupil responses that might be regarded as deviant or irrelevant in the convergent model.

How does the divergent model differ from that previously presented? The teacher's personal experience with shopping centers could point out layouts that do not place the traffic generators in the center of the complex. He may have seen successful shopping centers that positioned the large department stores at opposite ends of the center, and as customers walked from end to end for comparative shopping purposes they would be passing the multitude of establishments situated between these large business "magnets." Or, while preparing the unit of study, the teacher may encounter similar information leading him to the realization that various spatial arrangements exist and persist. The implication of these statements is clear; if the teacher does not have experience with numerous alternatives, and if his resource material does not adequately represent the range of reasonable choices, distortion, error and unwarranted convergent-type answers are equally likely outcomes.

As the teacher employs the divergent form of inquiry, his objective is neither arriving at "one" answer agreed upon by all nor the mastery of a prescribed procedure for investigating and solving. Instead, he is more concerned with the process of delineating an entire range of proposals meeting the criteria established for legitimate responses: "Does the data warrant the proposal?" and "Is the proposal reasonable?". He anticipates, desires, and supports a variety of viewpoints. His behavior, both verbal and nonverbal, communicates his wish to engage them in the process of determining and justifying a variety of alternatives. Although the teacher may have anticipated a number of pupil responses, he recognizes the possibility of more than one being correct. He is receptive to those answers that he did not anticipate and provides pupils with the opportunity to explain the reasoning that led to them. While the criteria of knowledge and reason continue, the preferences and preconceptions of the teacher no longer serve as a barrier or filter for pupil thinking.

Experience with divergent inquiry may be expected to influence the pupil's perception of his responsibility as a learner and reinforces those types of cognitive behavior that result in multiple and less conventional responses. The learner understands that his task is not the reproduction of known information but rather is the generation and verification of propositions. The teacher becomes less concerned with correctness and more concerned with the degree of appropriateness; in divergent inquiry truth is relative. If, on the other hand, the goal of the teacher is transmission of knowledge that the students are to accept whether that knowledge be factual or conceptual, then divergent inquiry may not be the most efficient or the most effective mode of instruction.

SUMMARY

Perhaps the most fitting way to summarize is to pose some questions suggested by this discussion:

1. Is inquiry the appropriate term when the person structuring the learning task knows the answer and delineates the procedure in such a way so that only this answer can be "discovered" by the learner?

2. Can the teacher provide for divergent inquiry and at the same time insure the mastery of facts, concepts, and generalizations?
3. Does training in the convergent model of inquiry have a deleterious effect on subsequent tasks requiring divergent responses?
4. Is inquiry simply a new means of teaching students "what to think"?

Swing Toward Decision Making

THEODORE KALTSOUNIS

1. Why Change Again?

Take a few minutes to look at the children in your class. Consider them in a very special way. Project their lives into the future. As the children pass in review, look at them as a concerned and responsible member of an older generation—not necessarily as a teacher. Try to see these young people as future teen-agers, as young men and women, and finally as mature adults. How are they reacting to their social environment? Are they fully prepared to meet its many problems and challenges?

Regardless of what standards of appraisal you may use, many of your present students will appear to be successful, happy, and content. But you will see others who are confronted with enormous problems. One of them, just an innocent kid, may be walking down a street, when a "pusher" approaches, perhaps reluctantly but with determination, and tries to get him "in tune with the younger generation." Another student had heard a great deal about pollution in high school and had participated enthusiastically in projects to clean up the shoreline of a nearby river. Yet, as you see him now, he lives in a filthy neighborhood where nobody is taking any action to improve conditions in the slightest degree. A third student has just married and wants to buy a house that he and his bride like very much. His neighbors to be don't want the couple because the color of their skin is different.

In this imaginary future, you may be old enough to retire. The war in Southeast Asia is over, but if it is true that history repeats itself, another war will be spreading death and destruction somewhere else in the world. Once more it will be showing man's inability to control his inhumanity.

Theodore Kaltsounis is Professor of Education at the University of Washington, Seattle.
From *Instructor* *80*(8):45–56, 1971. Reprinted from *Instructor,* © April 1971, The Instructor Publications, Inc., used by permission of the publisher and Theodore Kaltsounis.

There you see a group of your boys troubled because they must go to this new war, knowing quite well that several will not come back. Some are seriously considering refusing to go and die .in a foreign place, but the alternatives and consequences are just as bad.

Meanwhile, on the home front, riots still occur. Streets, parks, and neighborhoods are less and less safe to enjoy. The universities are misused or abused, or they are not what they used to be. Unemployment goes up and down while hunger and poverty are as prevalent and visible all over as wheat fields in Kansas and oil wells in Texas and Oklahoma. Health care is becoming an insurmountable financial burden on the taxpayer. Excessive materialism and narrow, selfish interests have continued to be the primary motives for the life style and behavior of many people.

Your students will be a part of all this. Will they be puzzled and frustrated by it? How many will say, "This is life," and just go on? Hopefully, others may be wondering what they can do to improve conditions, and will take the initiative to find workable solutions to social problems.

Now, as a teacher, ask yourself what role you want your children to play in a world like this. You know your students are going to be faced with problems. You know that the problems will force them to make important decisions affecting their own lives and the lives of others. What are you doing to prepare boys and girls to make such decisions?

Shift in Role of Social Studies

Teaching children how to make good decisions is becoming a very important, and most likely the ultimate, objective for the social studies. If social studies is to help children understand and find their place in society, and if the conditions in society continue to be as uncertain and threatening as they are at present, this new emphasis on decision making does make sense.

Decision making has come into prominence to fill a vacuum in social studies. It is important to realize the existence of the vacuum, prior to analyzing and defining this significant process that could be considered the backbone of a democratic society.

FOR A LONG TIME, SOCIAL STUDIES WAS MORE DESCRIPTIVE THAN ANALYTICAL IN NATURE. CHILDREN SIMPLY COVERED THE PRESCRIBED PAGES IN THE TEXTBOOK AND ACCEPTED WHAT THEY READ OR SAW WITHOUT RAISING CRITICAL QUESTIONS.

They were not learning to perceive conditions as they really were, but accepted whatever was presented in books. Even though there was poverty and unhappiness in society, everyone in the books appeared to be prosperous and happy. Though we have always had minority cultures in this country, few received adequate attention in the textbooks and stories being written at that time. Consequently and unfortunately, the children who belonged to these subcultures were made to feel that they were unwanted and worthless.

Furthermore, social studies, as taught in years past, failed to project the dynamic character of society. Society has been changing in a variety of ways and continues to change, but for a long time social studies had remained the same.

Children changed too. With advancements in transportation and the mass media, the experiential background of children expanded and their informational knowledge increased. As a result, social studies became too elementary and superficial. Educators at the university level, and classroom teachers, realized this and many became concerned. At the time, few received support for their opinions and there were no appropriate materials available to help them do a better job.

Then came Sputnik. The Russians were thought to be ahead of us in scientific developments, and the schools were the first to be blamed for it. As a result, schools were forced to turn their full attention to the sciences and the scientific method. First, it was the biological and physical sciences. Sophisticated mathematics followed almost immediately. Finally, social scientists started developing curricula for the elementary schools. The social sciences began to replace the social studies. The structure of the disciplines (geography, history, sociology, anthropology, political science, and economics), and fundamental concepts and generalizations drawn from the disciplines, became the ultimate objectives of what was formerly called social studies. Inquiry and social sciencing assumed importance as ends in themselves. A number of children's textbooks were published and the term "social sciences" gained prominence.

This entire movement was good to get social studies off the ground. No one would deny that it created excitement and raised many hopes. But there were some educators who felt that it did not go far enough. At least it did not go far enough in the right direction. People started having second thoughts about what was being called the new social studies. In their opinion, the great amount of emphasis placed on the scientific methods of social sciencing could be justified only if the purpose of the elementary school was to give children an early start on their way to graduate school. However, that is not the purpose of the elementary school and of the social studies in particular.

WHAT ALL CHILDREN NEED IS TO BE PREPARED TO FUNCTION NOW AS WELL AS LATER IN THIS COMPLICATED SOCIETY IN WHICH THEY ARE LIVING.

They need to be able to face their problems, and the dilemmas which confront them. They need the know-how and courage to make decisions, and to make them in a rational way. To accomplish this, social studies must look beyond concepts and generalizations. Children must have active practice in making decisions through a commitment to and involvement in appropriate social action.

Nature of Decision Making

It should be made clear that decision making does not minimize the value of concepts, generalizations, inquiry, social sciencing, and the like. It simply shifts their position from ends to means.

The student continues to analyze and explain social situations, and strives to discover and understand relationships, but he does not stop there. He uses them in order to be able to make rational decisions.

DECISION MAKING INVOLVES THREE BASIC ELEMENTS: KNOWLEDGE, VALUES, ACTION.

Values, which include the feelings, disposition, attitudes, and beliefs of the decision maker, are just as important as knowledge in making decisions. *At times, value factors can be more important than knowledge.* For example, a person may inquire into the unfair treatment of the minority groups. He may conclude and declare that discrimination is evil. Yet, when it actually comes down to supporting an open-housing policy for his neighborhood, he finds all kinds of excuses to oppose it. He might say, for instance, that he does not object to having a minority person move into his neighborhood, but he is concerned about what this might do to property values.

During the past, the school has done a great deal to increase children's knowledge. The more recent emphasis on concepts and generalizations has strengthened this function even more, but little has been done in the area of values. There is a need for the school to expand its role and to devote more time to designing ways which will stimulate children to discover their inner world of values, to analyze them, and to modify and perhaps reorganize them.

FINALLY, DECISION MAKING REQUIRES ACTION. IT IS THIS STEP THAT HAS THE POTENTIAL OF MAKING SOCIAL STUDIES EXCITING AND USEFUL TO THE INDIVIDUAL AS WELL AS TO SOCIETY. IT IS IN THE ACTION THAT THE CHILD WILL SEE THE RELEVANCY OF WHAT HE KNOWS AND IS LEARNING.

The anticipation of his role in action will be a self-test for the child to determine what he still needs to know. Taking action gives the child an opportunity and the stimulation to bring out his inner feelings and values.

He can test their validity in the light of related information, and the feelings and values of his classmates and other persons closely associated with him.

DECISION MAKING TAKES SOCIAL STUDIES BEYOND SIMPLE INTEL-LECTUALIZATION CONCERNING THE SOCIETY AND INTO THE REALM OF POSITIVE SOCIAL ACTION.

By placing greater emphasis on decision making, children become conscious of the problems of human interaction and are provided with the necessary skills to deal more promptly and effectively with these problems.

SUMMARY

1. By focusing on decision making, social studies is expanding its role beyond concepts and generalizations.
2. Knowledge becomes a means for facilitating decision making.
3. Children's values assume greater importance in social studies because they influence decisions.
4. Decision making is developed through and implies appropriate social action.
5. Children and their roles in society—not the social science disciplines —become again the center of social studies education.

2. Decision Making and the Curriculum

We have been hearing about the importance of the structure of the disciplines for more than ten years now. By structure, we mean the basic ideas (concepts and generalizations) that make up the body of knowledge for each of the social sciences—history, geography, sociology, anthropology, political science, and economics. Most of the national social studies curriculum projects of the 1960s and numerous locally developed programs were built strictly around concepts and generalizations. (Examples of the national projects: Educational Development Center's *Man: A Course of Study;* Taba Curriculum Development Project, Californa; Michigan Elementary Social Science Education Program; Greater Cleveland Social Science Program; Project Social Studies, University of Minnesota; and the Experiment in Economics Education, Purdue University.)

Now, the direction is toward developing rational decision makers. However, this does not mean that the techniques of the social scientist are being discarded altogether. Instead, teachers can help children take advantage of specific disciplines which would tend to clarify a problem. For example, history and geography could be useful when considering the growth or decline of a community. The techniques of the anthropologist would help students discover factors affecting the culture of an area. A study of unemployment would involve economics.

Let us follow a particular teacher as he has to face the task of having to decide what to teach. First, he would have to settle on the topic or setting. This is the general or specific area within which the children will operate. The traditional social studies framework could provide this setting. There is nothing wrong about studying the family in first grade, the neighborhood in second grade, the community in third grade, the United States in fifth grade, and other cultures in sixth grade.

Most of the new projects and textbooks follow this sequence. Some projects mentioned earlier in this article designed a new sequence but this does not necessarily mean abandoning the old entirely.

THE FRAMEWORK COULD REMAIN THE SAME BUT CONTENT MUST BE DIFFERENT.

In the primary grades, for instance, it is not enough simply to describe the various community helpers and what they do. The curriculum must be designed in a way that will bring the child face to face with the helpers (figuratively or literally) in situations in which the child will have to make decisions. The decisions may be based on his relationships with the helpers and their services to the community in which both live.

ATTENTION SHOULD BE GIVEN, IN PARTICULAR, TO TOPICS THAT WILL BRING OUT THE ISSUES RELATED TO HUMAN INTERACTION, INDIVIDUAL RESPONSIBILITY, ORGANIZATION AND GOVERNMENT, HEALTH AND SAFETY, CONSERVATION OF OUR HUMAN AND NATURAL RESOURCES, AND THE LIKE.

The following outline on the community presents topics which have a good potential for decision-making situations.

COMMUNITY STUDY

I. The people in our community

   A. Where did they come from?
   B. Where do they live?
   C. How well do the people get along with each other?
   D. How safe and secure do they feel?

II. The needs of our community

   A. What do people living together need?
   B. How do they provide for common needs?

C. How successful is our community in providing for common needs?

III. The future of our community

A. Will our community grow?
B. What changes might take place?
C. Do you think you will be proud of our community in the future?

IV. Our community and other communities

A. In what ways is our community similar to or different from other communities you know about?
B. In what ways is our community better or worse than other communities?
C. Do communities depend on each other and work together in any way?

Following the same approach, a unit on Africa could be designed for the upper developmental levels.

AFRICAN STUDY

I. The land and the people

A. What are the physical characteristics of the continent of Africa?
B. What kinds of people live in Africa?
C. How do people in Africa use the land?
D. How could the Africans better utilize the land on which they live?

II. Political development in Africa

A. What types of government do the African nations have?
B. What are the relationships between various African governments?
C. What are the main problems facing today's African governments?
D. What appears to be the political future of Africa?

III. Africa and the world

A. What role do the Africans play in the United Nations?
B. How do the Africans respond to the worldwide ideological struggle?
C. In what ways are we in the United States influenced by African cultures?
D. How does the United States respond to the ambitions and needs of the various African groups?

(This outline is based on the African continent. To understand the cultures and problems of the several ethnic groups living there, a teacher needs to make other outlines to fit the desired goals.)

EACH OF THE QUESTIONS POSED IN THE TWO SUGGESTED UNITS SHOULD BE REDUCED TO TWO DISTINCT ELEMENTS: THE KNOWLEDGE THAT THE CHILD NEEDS TO ACQUIRE; AND THE UNRESOLVED ISSUES THAT SHOULD BE CONSIDERED BY THE CLASS.

The knowledge should be in the form of concepts and generalizations to be developed. *For example, in the case of the unit on the community:* In order for the child to be able to deal with the topical question, "Where do people live?" he needs to understand such concepts as *suburb* and *ghetto,* and such generalizations or relationships as "Most of the poor people in the metropolitan communities live in the inner-city area." *The same applies to the unit on Africa.* In connection with the topical question, "What types of government exist in Africa?" the child must understand such concepts as *colonial government* and *nationalism,* and such generalizations as "Independent and colonial governments in Africa are hostile to each other because of their conflicting aims."

At the same time, however, it is important that the child be exposed to and deal with the related issues: Is it right for people of different races to be segregated? Should everyone be allowed to live anywhere he wants if he can afford to do so? Should colonial governments, elected by white minorities, rule over African majorities? Questions of this kind were neglected by schools in the past because people didn't want their children to face controversy.

BUT LIFE IS FULL OF CONTROVERSY. CHILDREN WILL BE CALLED UPON AS MEMBERS OF SOCIETY, AS CITIZENS OF THE WORLD, OR AS INDIVIDUALS TO MAKE DECISIONS CONCERNING THESE CONTROVERSIES.

The sooner that children learn to make decisions, the better it will be for them, for their immediate society, and for the world.

SUMMARY

1. Maintain the old framework for social studies, if desired, but select topics that will lead children to situations requiring them to make decisions.
2. Reduce each topic to basic questions.
3. Determine the concepts and generalizations related to each topic by involving the children as much as possible.
4. Do the same for the controversial issues related to the same topic.

3. What About Inquiry?

Without inquiry there would be no decision making in the sense that is advocated here. To make a sound decision, the first thing a person needs is knowledge that is relevant to the problematic situation at hand. Suppose a child is faced with the problem of whom to vote for in the election for class president. He must first learn as much as possible about the candidates and their proposed programs. The same applies to adult situations.

WITHOUT ADEQUATE INQUIRY, DECISION MAKING IS IMPULSIVE.

If schools had a way of knowing the specific situations in which children would be called upon to make decisions throughout their lives, they could help students acquire most of the knowledge needed. Since this is impossible in terms of situations or knowledge, children must develop the skills required to obtain whatever knowledge they need, and when they need it. This can be accomplished by applying the inquiry method to teaching and learning.

Numerous books and many articles have been written in the last several years dealing with inquiry. Some authors have defined it in terms of what it is—an overall approach to teaching and learning that can be implemented in a variety of forms. Others have tried to put inquiry into very rigid forms, to the point that the teacher becomes a machine rather than the creative and imaginative director of learning that he should be. Also, much of the literature conveys the impression that inquiry has just been invented.

THE FACT IS THAT INQUIRY IS AS OLD AS SOCRATES. THROUGHOUT THE YEARS MANY TEACHERS HAVE USED IT, AND MANY MORE ARE CONTINUING TO USE IT.

One way to interpret inquiry is to consider the natural way of learning. The very young child does not wait for someone to tell him what to learn and how to learn it. The world around him is so interesting, apparently, that he feels compelled to take off on his own and to explore his surroundings. He uncovers things, touches them, and sometimes he breaks them. He smells things and moves them, or he makes them move. He observes the strange behavior of things and tries to make them behave the same way again. The child is often puzzled by what he observes. At times he is frustrated. In most cases he is rewarded through the satisfaction of his curiosity.

Anyone who has been around young children knows that they ask many questions. There are a lot of "What is this?" and "What is that?" types, but many questions are the penetrating kind that cannot be answered by looking at a dictionary, an encyclopedia, or the pages of a book. Typical of the questions asked by very young children are these three examples. *Why do the leaves fall? Why do bad people kill?* (Influenced by what the child has seen on television.) *How does the fire go out?* Through questions of this type, children are asking help to go beyond a mere awareness of things. They want an explanation for things they observe. They want to find out about relationships and what causes things to happen. Finding the answers to *why* and *how* makes learning exciting.

THUS INQUIRY, AS AN APPROACH TO TEACHING AND LEARNING, IS NOTHING MORE THAN THE IMPLEMENTATION OF THE NATURAL WAY OF LEARNING.

INQUIRY TEST FOR TEACHERS

If you want to find out whether or not you are teaching through inquiry, answer the following questions in reference to your present classroom situation and teaching practices.

1. Do you believe that children can learn by themselves and from each other? Do you guide them in this direction?

2. Is your classroom full of items that tend to excite children and arouse their curiosity to the point that they are anxious to explore and to study?

3. Does the learning environment that you have set for your children extend beyond the four walls of the classroom and into the outside world?

4. Does your teaching show that you are aware of differences in children? Do you provide a variety of avenues—reading, audiovisual aids, role playing, field experiences, and the like—for reaching the same objective?

5. Do you confront the children with, or assist them to ask, questions that go beyond repeating what they have read or seen? Are they stimulated to analyze, explain, and evaluate situations? Do you provide a variety of opportunities for them to apply what they are learning?

6. Do you allow your children to explore and even suggest solutions to social problems and important issues that have not yet been resolved? In other words, do you encourage open-endedness in your classroom?

IF YOUR ANSWERS TO THE ABOVE QUESTIONS ARE IN THE AFFIRMATIVE, YOUR STUDENTS LEARN IN A WAY THAT RESEMBLES THE NATURAL WAY OF LEARNING. YOU, TOO, HAVE DISCOVERED THE PROCESS OF INQUIRY.

As a matter of fact, you may already be an expert in the technique of inquiry teaching, even though you feel confused by the unfamiliar and seemingly complicated terms used by those who have been openly acclaimed as experts in the field of inquiry. Teachers who have avoided inquiry can be guided by the following.

INQUIRY REFERS TO THE KIND OF TEACHING AND LEARNING THAT IS BASED ON INVOLVEMENT AND INVESTIGATION ON THE PART OF THE CHILD. INQUIRY IS A PROCESS THAT USES A NUMBER OF SKILLS— OBSERVING, CLASSIFYING, ANALYZING, INFERRING, HYPOTHESIZING, REACHING CONCLUSIONS (GENERALIZING), AND SUPPORTING HYPOTHESES AND CONCLUSIONS.

To clarify the use of most of the inquiry skills just mentioned, two examples are presented, based on actual classroom work.

EXPLORING LOCATION

A primary teacher wanted his children to learn some of the elements of location theory. He wanted them to understand (*generalize*) that there are reasons for certain things to be located where they are. He felt very strongly, however, that this generalization would be more meaningful to the children if they developed it in connection with some decision that they were interested in making.

The problem was to decide whether or not their school was located in the right place in the neighborhood. The class became interested in the situation after the teacher had read a newspaper report about two children who had drowned in a lake located near a school they attended. To keep the children's attention on the problem, the teacher obtained a large photograph of their own school for the bulletin board. Underneath he wrote: *Is our school in the right location?*

As a follow-up, the teacher showed the class a large aerial photograph (it could be a pictorial map) of the neighborhood and asked them to describe it *(make observations)*. Lists were made of items mentioned, and these were placed in groups *(classified)* at the suggestion of the children with supervisory guidance from the teacher. Even though no children were visible around the school (in the picture), one child made this statement *(an inference):* "The children are in their classrooms." *At this point, the teacher took advantage of the opportunity to point out the difference and the importance of distinguishing between observation and inference.* Among the the things in the picture, the children located their homes.

The next task to which the children were directed by the teacher was to measure how many blocks away from the school each child lived *(analyzing)*. Some lived a couple of blocks farther than others but none of them lived very far from the school. The children agreed that the school was fairly well located in relation to its use *(reached a conclusion)*. Then the teacher took the children on an outdoor walk around the school to find out if there were any unusual hazards present *(analysis through field observation)*. The children were satisfied with their earlier conclusion that their school was well located. If they had discovered some hazard, the teacher would have directed the children to do something *(take action)* within their powers and capabilities.

But the first-grade teacher did not stop here. The children were shown pictures of other schools. The group was asked to decide whether the schools were properly located in relation to use or visible hazards. To make these judgments, first graders had to apply what they had previously learned. In subsequent lessons, they developed criteria for the location of food stores, fire stations, and shopping centers *(hypothesized)*. They tried to prove their hypotheses by examining pictures of these service areas, or by inspecting the locations during walking or riding field trips.

COMMUNITY VOTING

Students in the upper levels are capable of becoming involved in situations that have more social significance. Prior to an election year, sixth graders in a small town became concerned about the fact that everyone in their community traditionally voted for one party. They also knew that neighbors in nearby towns made fun of the community's voting pattern.

The sixth graders decided that they wanted to do something about this situation. With the help of the teacher, they outlined a strategy. Two teams were formed. By referring to newspaper articles and questioning individuals, the teams outlined the issues that the candidates from both parties were offering their constituents. After considerable work, the children presented the election issues to various civic and church groups.

Adult audiences were surprised by the children's work, sincerity, and enthusiasm. While the efforts of the sixth graders could not have completely reversed the voting habits of their elders that year, it is certain that the children developed valuable skills in the process. Hopefully, the experience will make a difference in their behavior as future citizens and voters.

IN CLOSING THIS SECTION, LET ME EMPHASIZE AGAIN THAT INQUIRY IS A NECESSARY PART OF DECISION MAKING. IT IS THE PROCESS THROUGH WHICH ONE GAINS THE KNOWLEDGE TO MAKE VALID AND SOUND DECISIONS.

However, if taken without some form of action in mind *(decision making)*, inquiry is simply an academic exercise which, like lecturing and textbook teaching, can turn children off as soon as the novelty of it wears out. This is especially true for the child who will never go on to college.

SUMMARY

1. Inquiry is a necessary part of decision making.

2. Inquiry resembles the natural way of learning. It requires involvement on the part of the learner, and the use of techniques which are investigation-oriented.

3. When unrelated to relevant decision-making situations, inquiry could become a boring routine, especially for the child whose future does not include college.

4. Decision Making and Values

Imagine two individuals faced with exactly the same decision-making situation. Both individuals may have inquired into the problem with equal vigor, and each one may know as much about it as the other. Yet, it is possible for each person to come up with a different decision. The factor that causes the two persons to react in different ways depends, to a large degree, on the values that they hold.

VALUES ARE THOSE UNSEEN FORCES WHICH INFLUENCE AN INDIVIDUAL TO BEHAVE THE WAY HE DOES AND MAKE HIM STRIVE FOR WHATEVER HE WANTS TO ACHIEVE IN LIFE.

CHILDREN'S VALUES

Children, like adults, also have values. Theirs grow and develop through interaction with the people and things in their environment. Since children live in different situations, they will naturally have differing values. During the last few years, this has become more evident in the United States as the result of acknowledging that our society is composed of important minority cultures.

The typical middle-class American child lives in a competitive society. When he goes to school, he feels at home because the typical American school is built upon the premise of competition.

THE NAVAJO CHILD, HOWEVER, LIVES IN A SOCIETY IN WHICH COMPETITION IS NOT CONSIDERED TO BE A VIRTUE.

As a result, Navajo youngsters feel out of place in a school that operates in the manner of the typical middle-class American school.

Even within the same block, children develop different values. For instance, a child whose parents follow fashions with compulsion may be very observant, and often critical, of the appearance of everybody around him. This will not be the case with another child in the same block if the family looks at clothes from a functional point of view and therefore dresses casually and informally.

Children's values are important in the educative process. This becomes more evident each day. There are social studies leaders who claim that values will dominate the social studies scene during the 1970s in the same way that concepts and generalizations did during the 1960s. Education literature includes numerous articles, and a few books have been published recently, dealing with values and value-related issues. Yet, we know very little about the kinds of values children have. As a matter of fact, educators are not in agreement on a clear definition of values.

SOME CLAIM THAT A VALUE IS ANYTHING A PERSON INTERNALIZES TO
THE POINT THAT HE ACTS UPON IT REPEATEDLY. IN THIS WAY, ONE
COULD END UP WITH NUMEROUS VALUES.

You could say that card playing, horseback riding, and taking drugs were
values just as much as cleaning the house, respecting all people as being
equal, honoring parents, and saluting the flag.

MILTON ROKEACH, A SOCIAL PSYCHOLOGIST, CLAIMS THAT VALUES ARE
LIMITED IN NUMBER AND ARE DYNAMIC IN NATURE.

As already pointed out, values are the forces that make people behave the
way they do. In his book, *Beliefs, Attitudes, and Values: A Theory of
Organization and Change* (Jossey-Bass, Inc., 615 Montgomery Street, San
Francisco, CA 94111), Rokeach has dealt mainly with adult values. Samples of these are: a comfortable life, a sense of accomplishment, a world
of peace, family security, happiness, and self-respect. He classifies them in
two categories which he labels instrumental values and terminal values.

ACCORDING TO ROKEACH, INSTRUMENTAL VALUES ARE RELATED TO
THE WAY OF LIFE A PERSON LEADS. TERMINAL VALUES REFER TO THE
ENDS FOR WHICH ONE REACHES IN HIS LIFE.

In an attempt to identify values of elementary school children attending
suburban schools, the author of this feature, with the assistance of a number
of teachers, used the Rokeach definition of values. Two questions were
designed and the children were asked to write their answers in compositions.
No other directions were given, and no discussion of the questions took place
in advance. The thought-provoking questions were:

1. What does a good life mean to me?
2. When I get old and gray, how would I like people to remember me?

An analysis of the free responses was indeed revealing, and eye-opening
for the teachers in terms of the values children hold. In answer to the first
question, children in one class valued these things most: a good job, family
life, happiness, a good house, having good friends, money, going to school,
travel, sports, health, not taking LSD and marijuana.

Answers to the second question revealed that the children in another class
would like to be remembered (when old and gray) as a good person, helpful
to others, honest, having loved animals, patriotic, dependable, as a famous
athlete, world-renowned author, nonviolent, a scientist who tried to make
life better for others, a person who actively worked for peace.

Children mirror their environment. What they eat, how they dress, how
they speak, and even how they think are merely expressions of that environment. Teachers should make every effort to get to know their students'

values, especially if the children come from minority cultures. In addition, a teacher should learn to respect differences in children's values. At the same time, he should ask himself whether their behavior is motivated by values that show concern for the general welfare, the rational process, and the dignity of man. If not, the teacher needs to find ways to help children build values which will make them happier individuals, and more responsive to the needs of others—now and when they are adults.

VALUING AND DECISION MAKING

Formerly, the school tended to force values on children. The current trend is for children to develop their own values so they will be more committed to them. *Consequently, the emphasis is on teaching the valuing process and not specific values.* Some sources even refer to the valuing process as the value-free process. A dangerous dichotomy is developing here, similar to the one about what to think versus how to think. One cannot learn how to think unless he is thinking about something. The same applies in the area of values.

ONE CANNOT ENGAGE IN THE VALUING PROCESS WITHOUT, AT THE SAME TIME, DEVELOPING SOME VALUES.

The school should play a role in developing new values and in changing some of the old if they work against the general welfare, the rational process, and the dignity of man. However, the school should do this through the application of the valuing process.

THE VALUING PROCESS IS THE PROCEDURE USED TO DEAL WITH THE CONTROVERSIAL ASPECTS OF LIFE AND THE CURRICULUM.

It consists of the following steps:
1. The students are presented with an unsolved controversial issue. *Example:* What could be done about poverty as we find it in the United States?
2. Students suggest as many alternative solutions as possible. *Examples:* Provide everyone with a basic annual income; let the government create jobs for the poor; encourage private industry to make an effort to develop jobs in poverty areas; move the poor out of poverty areas; find out which qualifications poor people lack for employment; provide educational opportunities to overcome these handicaps; and many others.
3. The students then consider the consequences of each alternative.
4. The children are given the opportunity to express their feelings about each alternative. This requires an open atmosphere so that everyone in the class can say what he is really thinking.
5. At this point each student should be encouraged to reach one or more decisions about solutions to the problem of overcoming poverty in this

country. In the future, it would be hoped that he would support or modify his decisions as he obtained more information and experience in solving this problem.

Obviously, there is a great amount of inquiry involved in the valuing process. As a matter of fact, the first three steps involve nothing but inquiry skills.

THE VALUING PROCESS BECOMES UNIQUE AT THE FOURTH STEP BE-CAUSE IT ALLOWS THE CHILDREN TO OPEN UP AND EXPRESS THEIR FEELINGS AND ATTITUDES.

No answer is right or wrong. Everyone is trying to articulate what he feels. The significance of this step lies in two important factors: *(1) The individual clarifies his own values.* Many times children are not clear what their values are even though these same values influence their behavior. It is difficult for a child to regulate his behavior unless he clearly understands what motivates it. *(2) The other important factor in the valuing process is the opportunity to express values after a thorough investigation of the alternatives and the consequences of each of the alternatives.* Weighing the pros and cons sharpens the child's ability to think and reason effectively.

In the exchange of ideas, a child has the opportunity, prior to expressing his own values, to evaluate them in the light of the evidence considered. He can also consider them in relation to the values expressed by classmates. In the process, it is quite possible that the child will modify his own values on some issues, or change them as he grows older.

APPLYING VALUING PROCESS

To illustrate the application of the valuing process, a classroom experience follows. A first grade was studying about the family. While the children were comparing family life in the United States and in other countries, they noticed that in some cultures grandparents lived with their children and grandchildren. As the first graders chatted about this, they found that most of their own grandparents were living alone in faraway places. Others were in old people's homes, or had their own apartments nearby or downtown.

Out of the discussion this question became paramount. *Should grandparents live alone?* Some children responded "Yes." Most said "No." The teacher helped the first graders to examine the consequences of each alternative. The chalkboard was divided into two sections, as outlined below, and the consequences were presented side by side.

If grandparents lived alone . . .
1. They can protect their homes.
2. They can fix their yard.
3. They will feel lonely.

4. They can have peace and quiet.
5. There will be nobody to take care of them if they get sick or fall.

If grandparents lived with their families . . .
1. They will be happy.
2. Children will make noise.
3. They can read stories to children.
4. They can babysit.
5. There will be too many people in the house if it is small.

When it came time to make a decision, most of the children were in favor of having grandparents live with them. Indirectly, the first graders conveyed the feeling that if grandparents, children, and grandchildren can be happy living together, they should have this opportunity to enjoy each other.

OBVIOUSLY, EMPHASIS ON VALUES AND THE VALUING PROCESS BRINGS THE HUMANISTIC ELEMENT INTO THE SOCIAL STUDIES PICTURE. ACTIVITIES OF THIS KIND PROVIDE CHILDREN WITH AN OPPORTUNITY TO DEVELOP A FEELING OF EMPATHY FOR CLASSMATES, AND FOR PEOPLE IN THE LARGER WORLD.

If we are to minimize conflict and improve our relationships with each other, the people in our society need to develop the skills of the valuing process. The elementary classroom is the place where we must begin, at all levels, to develop these skills.

SUMMARY

1. Values are inner forces which motivate behavior and life style.
2. Values play a vital role in a person's ability to make thoughtful decisions.
3. Children have values but until now no systematic effort has been made to determine what these values are.
4. The teacher should apply the valuing process in the classroom to help children develop values in accordance with the general welfare, the rational process, and the dignity of man.

5. Bridging the Old and New

There is no doubt that changes in social studies have been substantial, especially in the last ten years. The major changes, however, appear at two different levels—the theoretical and the practical. Changes at the theoretical level started with the various projects developed in the sixties, as mentioned on page 181. The changes in procedure and direction appear to be much ahead of what has been applied in the majority of classrooms observed. My contacts with teachers indicate that many feel the changes are beyond their means to adapt or utilize. One reason may be that the so-called new social studies has often been presented as something entirely new. Teachers look on the programs as something to replace what they are doing rather than as a set of underlying trends to improve traditional practices.

The purpose of this section is to show the teacher how to build a bridge between the old and new social studies by modifying the traditional unit plan to reflect the newer trend. In addition, it is expected that the teacher will apply the principles and suggestions about knowledge, inquiry, values, and decision making already explained in the foregoing sections of this article.

TRADITIONAL UNIT PLAN

I. *Title* Traditionally, the topics chosen followed a strict curriculum outline. They were not always related to each other. They may also have been topics in which the teacher had special interest or a greater sense of security when working with them.

BASED ON CURRENT TRENDS

All topics are unified on the basis of a common theme relevant to the contemporary scene in society. (*Example:* A number of units for third grade, related to the city, could be tied together with the theme, "Migration Toward the Cities" or "Comparing Old and New Urban Areas.")

II. *General Objectives* In the traditional plan, objectives are often stated in broad, unrealistic terms. (*Example:* Children will learn to develop pride in the democratic way of life.) In many instances it would be almost impossible to reduce the objectives to specific behaviors.

Under the modified plan, consider the structural elements of each topic such as the generalizations and basic controversial issues to which it can be reduced. (*Example of a generalization:* The population of the United States and other industrial societies is rapidly becoming urbanized. *A controversial issue:* Is the movement of people from the country to the city a healthy phenomenon for our nation?

III. *Specific Objectives* These are detailed statements of content to be mastered by the students. (*Examples:* Cities are centers of transportation and communication. Some of the largest cities in the world are in the United States.)

List specific behaviors through which your students will be able to demonstrate the development of generalizations basic to a particular topic. Also indicate in terms of behavior the types of knowledge you want them to acquire to deal with the issues listed in the general objectives. Include anticipated behaviors which show the development of skills which relate to inquiry and the valuing process and which culminate in the ability to make decisions. (*Examples:* Ask the children to give three reasons why more people live in the cities today than in the past. Children should also be able to list a number of consequences resulting from populations deserting the rural areas—consequences affecting both the city and the rural areas.)

IV. *Content* Traditionally an outline of subject matter, or an expansion of the statements listed as specific objectives. (*Examples:* Most of the railroads in the United States converge in the city of Chicago. O'Hare·and Kennedy are the two largest airports in the country.)

Formulate basic questions to which the content has been converted. These questions are intended to stimulate children to analyze situations, discover relationships, assess values, challenge positions on issues, and come face to face with decision-making situations. (*Examples:* What types of problems have developed when massive transportation facilities center in and around large cities? Should swamps or landfills be used instead of farm lands for new airports or longer runways? Examine all the possibilities and the alternatives in relation to how they will affect nearby residents and travelers using the airport.)

V. *Activities* Usually stated in broad categories—rarely specific enough to give direction to the teacher. (*Examples:* Children will engage in research activities. Children will view related films and filmstrips, and listen to records.)

In the modified plan, activities are specifically directed to the questions to which the content has been .converted. They are inspired by the inquiry method and the valuing process, and they provide opportunities for children to make decisions. They are in sufficient detail to be useful as procedure for specific phases of the project. Among the proposed activities are those which will allow for the children's individual differences. (*Example:* Read the book, *Let's Find Out about the City* by Valerie Pitts [Franklin Watts: 1968]. Based on the story, let the children list characteristics of a city. Follow with interviews to determine whether parents, grandparents, and other relatives have always [or ever] lived in a city. This information is then summarized in tabular form to illustrate movement to or from urban areas.)

VI. *Culminating Activity* Traditionally there are one or more activities to help summarize unit content and provide opportunities for the teacher to informally evaluate pupil behavior and achievement. (*Example:* Make a model of Chicago as a center of transportation.)

Under the modified plan, the culminating activity serves the same purpose. However, children should have the opportunity to make decisions about how well an urban transportation center solves or makes problems for the city residents and others who use it.

VII. *Evaluation* There are a variety of methods for evaluating pupil progress. Often there is an overemphasis on pencil-and-paper tests. Frequently the objectives of the evaluation are not clear.

Evaluation is more precise under the modified plan because it is directed toward the development of specific behaviors and values. A variety of evaluative techniques such as observation, discussion, checklists, and the like, are used. In this way, activities, programs, and teaching procedures are evaluated along with individual pupil progress.

Throughout the entire project, children work with various means of inquiry to provide the knowledge that will lead to opportunities for developing personal values and making decisions. The latter should be free expressions by the individual based on his reaction to evidence and reflecting his social background.

6. Criteria for Selecting Materials

The market is flooded with new materials that have direct or indirect application to social studies. Schools and teachers are constantly receiving advertising literature describing new textbooks, packages of materials, audiovisual aids, pamphlets, and so on. To make sure that the materials selected will benefit students in terms of current trends in social studies, the following criteria are presented to guide the decisions of selection committees.

The materials should clearly reflect an overall theme, a message that should be conveyed to the person using the materials.

The materials should reflect the multicultural character of our society and world.

The materials should be reality-oriented rather than presenting social situations from an idealistic point of view.

In the treatment of various topics, controversial issues should be emphasized as much as generalizations.

Inquiry should be presented as a means toward the development of decision-making skills, not as an end in itself.

The materials should have open-ended content leading to the study of the child's environment, and content should provide opportunities for students to make decisions.

The materials should afford occasions for the youngsters to assess society's values as well as their own.

The materials should take into consideration the individual differences within any group of children.

The materials should be based on and inspired by the social sciences as well as by the humanities.

The overall purpose of the materials should be directed toward the development of the entire individual so that he can become knowledgeable about and capable of coping with situations involving human relationships.

The swing toward decision making will be more realistic and productive when children have access to a wide range of material related to social problems confronting society.

Individualization Through Inquiry

THOMAS N. TURNER

John Holt launched his now famous *How Children Fail* with the following:

Most children in school fail. For a great many, this failure is absolute. Close to forty percent of those who begin high school drop out before they finish. For college the figure is one in three.

Many others fail in fact if not in name. They complete their schooling only because we have agreed to push them up through the grades and out of the schools, whether they know anything or not . . .

But there is a more important sense in which almost all children fail: Except for a handful, who may or may not be good students, they fail to develop more than a tiny part of the tremendous capacity for learning, understanding, and creating with which they were born . . .[1]

Such an indictment of the educational system is chilling; but teachers know that it contains more than a shred of truth. Many have seen the native

Thomas N. Turner is Assistant Professor of Education, University of Tennessee, Knoxville.

Reprinted from *Social Education* 34(1):72–73, 1970, with permission of the National Council for the Social Studies and Thomas N. Turner.

[1] John Holt, *How Children Fail.* New York: Pitman Publishing Corporation, 1964, p. xiii.

enthusiasm for learning of the young child dwindle, deteriorate, and finally almost disappear with the passing of years in school. Most persons who have taught have known the frustration growing out of struggling with students who fail to learn at a rate anywhere near their potential.

In the minds of many, an answer to this dilemma is individualizing instruction through inquiry approaches. Though certainly no panacea, learning by inquiry offers the promise of a giant step forward in the struggle against the failure of children as individual learners and effectively combats boredom with studies. Unlike subject-centered and textbook-centered instruction, the goals of investigation-oriented teaching are designed to reach the child as an individual learner rather than as a member of a large instructional group. The approach to learning is through proliferation of possible investigative situations to the extent that each individual has some topic, problem, or question to investigate that has high interest appeal for him, and about which he is curious.

For both those who would study man as a scientist and for those who would study him as a fellow creature with like passions as ours, the potential advantages of inquiry are great. Such instruction has appeal to the most content-oriented educator because, unlike the child-centered curriculum of the past, very well defined and specific areas of human studies can be taught through inquiry approaches. A continuing and well-articulated social studies curriculum, having an optimum degree of subject-matter stability, is possible.

Using inquiry approaches to individualize instruction implies, at least to some, the use of rather extensive information, resource banks as well as a wide variety of multi-media. A teacher who has experienced repeated difficulties in procuring such fundamental items as classroom dictionaries and globes may question whether such resources will ever be widely available to him. Greater resources probably do facilitate inquiry; indeed, they would probably make for better teaching, if used properly, in almost any approach. A key point, however, is that the inquiry idea represents the development of a set of attitudes in the instructor's mind rather than just a collection of materials. The difference is in basic assumptions concerning the role of the learner and the role of the teacher. The essence of beliefs requisite to successful inquiry experiences was caught by Nelson, who believes enthusiasm and success are stimulated when:

1. Students can be trusted to develop correct answers for themselves
2. Learning is an internal process
3. A teacher's role is that of a guider of learning who, at appropriate times, presents possible sources of information and alternative paths toward solution of problems
4. A teacher should be a sufficiently secure human being who is not threatened by, but rather enjoys, seeing students arrive at solutions without the "expert" giving him the correct answer or the exact way to arrive at his end
5. A teacher has the responsibility to capitalize on students' past experiences and to expose them to new experiences
6. A teacher must recognize and not be threatened by the fact that the inductive

approach may well produce learners who will go beyond him in the development of . . . concepts [2]

Teachers using inquiry to differentiate instruction need to believe in the capacity of children to think for themselves. They must be convinced that the freedom to think and autonomy in thinking are the prerequisites to effective thinking.[3] The classroom settings for inquiry most likely reflect this attribute when:

1. There is a focus on problems which are defined, probed, and labelled as relevant by the learners.
2. A definite aim is the development of judgment-making ability.
3. Questions rather than answers are stressed. Loughlin,[4] and Parsons and Shaftel,[5] and others have emphasized the importance of questioning in the teaching act. Inquiry approaches have sought to improve teachers' questioning capability, to shift question asking to students.
4. A range of alternatives is always possible for the learner.
5. The search is related to perplexities—problems where more than one "correct" answer is possible and there is more than one way of arriving at answers.
6. Much inquiry explores values and attitudes. Every individual's belief system is considered important and expanding and developing that system a major goal.
7. At no point does the teacher assume to know all that is important about what is being learned. He, too, is inquiring.
8. Emphasis on measurable comparison with peers is removed. The child is working with goals that are his own.

Differentiated instruction according to individual needs means children will vary widely in facts studied and learned, knowledge and concepts acquired, and generalizations made. Similarly differentiated will be skills, attitudes and values developed. Such wide diversity in learning outcomes need not mean utter confusion and probably is not confusing to the teacher who recognizes that the central purpose of inquiry is: children need to learn how to learn.

For educators willing to rethink basic patterns, investigation-oriented instruction can be a powerful aid in reaching the heretofore unreachable.

[2] John A. Nelson, "Inquiry as a Process in the Learning of Economics," in Dale L. Brubaker, editor, *Innovation in the Social Studies: The Teachers Speak for Themselves.* New York: Thomas Y. Crowell Co., 1968, p. 135.

[3] Theodore M. Parsons and Fannie R. Shaftel, "Thinking and Inquiry: Some Critical Issues," in Jean Fair and Fannie R. Shaftel, editors, *Effective Thinking in the Social Studies. 37th Yearbook of the National Council for the Social Studies.* Washington. D.C.: The Council, 1967, p. 136

[4] Richard L. Loughlin, "On Questioning," *The Educational Forum,* 25:461–2, 1969.

[5] Theodore M. Parsons and Fannie R. Shaftel, *op. cit.,* pp. 125–132.

It is hoped that the following postulates for individualizing instruction through inquiry may prove useful toward that end.

1. Have children formulate their own questions and hypotheses for investigation within the scope of the inquiry focus. If more than the nucleus of "Talkers" can be involved, the problems will be far more meaningful.
2. Give *each* child wide freedom of choice in the directions of his inquiry. In the practical interests of uniformity and to teach democracy, many very good teachers have done a great deal with group decision making and its majority rule. In doing so they have often reduced the potency of the very crux of democracy—an individual's decision.
3. Give each child opportunity and time to explore more than one topic for inquiry possibilities that are open to him. At some point the option to abandon or pursue a topic should be the child's.
4. Allow children the right to fail occasionally—in that they can test ideas to see if investigation is possible for them. Part of the enjoyment of learning is in the suspense involved in seeking to find what knowledge can be obtained and how far search can go.
5. Provide situations where decisions and choices must be made that are personal (and as such, personally important) to children.
6. Make any time limits a secondary concern, flexible according to the problem under study and the child studying it.
7. Attempt to insure that each child confronts problems in which his own "set" answer reactions simply will not suffice or even apply. Then guide investigations to areas in which worthwhile and alternate conclusions may be reached.
8. Promote independence in reaching conclusions by accepting and encouraging variation. (Remember that the decision to follow someone else's idea is made independently.)
9. Provide opportunity for each child to learn something that is uniquely his own. Help him recognize these distinctives and to take pride in them.
10. Provide a kaleidoscope of experiences to broaden and intensify children's interests. (Constantly extend and refurbish your own experience-bank as well.)

Questions That Teach: How to Frame Them; How to Ask Them

RONALD D. GIFFIN

For many teachers, the art of asking questions usually turns out to be not so artful after all. Most questioning is based upon the "who," "what" and "when" of a subject. The answers are necessarily descriptive.

The trouble is, though, that the answers don't really go any further. If they're right, that settles the matter then and there; and the teacher goes back to her lecturing or perhaps to another factual question.

What's being missed here is a chance to lead children into higher levels of thinking by being more persistent with the use of a definite method of questioning. "Probe" questioning is a technique that I use with a great deal of success in my own classes.

"Probe" questions ask for more than simple recall of factual information. They ask the student to manipulate information. They call for facts, of course. But, much more important, they make the child *use* facts to produce new facts and new ideas. Here's what I mean.

My class had been presenting oral book reports as well as written summaries of the science reading they had been doing. The work was good, but hardly profound. I thought they could do more with the material and I introduced a sequence of 13 probe questions to help them:

1. *Recount and recall.* I said to the children, "Each of you has read a book about science. Now please think of a sentence which will tell me something interesting about your book."

What I was after here was a simple listing of facts. But many of the answers I got were far from simple. They were vague and involved and far too long to list on the chalkboard. I narrowed down the children's answers by asking the following three questions whenever necessary: "Can you say that in fewer words?" "Does this say what the book is about?" "Are you satisfied with the wording in your sentence?"

When each sentence was sufficiently short and concise, I wrote it on the chalkboard. The end products looked like this: "Discovering light," "How power and energy are caused," "Sound around us" and "Life in a zoo." The total listing and questioning time took about 20 minutes.

Ronald D. Giffin is an elementary school teacher in Billings, Montana.

Reprinted from *Grade Teacher* 87(5):58–61, January 1970, with permission of CCM Professional Magazines, Inc. and Ronald D. Giffin. Copyright © 1969 by CCM Professional Magazines, Inc. All rights reserved.

That's all there was to my recount-recall questions. I was looking for a wide variety of answers which could serve as sort of a base for the rest of the probe questions, all of which required a higher level of thinking. To get this wide base, I deliberately made the recount-recall question broad enough so that every child would be able to contribute *something*. But I also made sure that the answers were short and concise so that we wouldn't have to spend a lot of time later on haggling over just what was meant.

When most of my youngsters had responded, I lifted the discussion to the next level with a collocation question.

2. *Collocation and grouping.* I was seeking more than just facts when I asked this question. I wanted each child to give an answer that would make him construct several sets of facts into a collocation. I didn't even care if the children argued about whether one fact could be listed with another. What better way of teaching children to accept one another's opinion?

Accordingly, I asked the collocation question: "Of the statements on the board, which ones might go together?"

The children pondered briefly, but soon many hands were waving. I kept track of the various groupings made by the youngsters by placing capital letters in front of all statements that the class decided should be in one group.

For example, the letter "A" was placed before these three statements: "Experiments in electricity," "Sounds around us" and "Galaxies and planets in space" (you'll see why when you get to the fourth probe question). The letter "B" was placed before four other statements, "C" before three statements and so on until all of the statements on the chalkboard had been taken care of.

Of course, there were arguments about the groupings. For instance, there was a debate as to whether snails should be grouped with spiders and insects. I resolved this argument by asking the child who had read the book about snails to seek further information and then to report back to the class as to whether a snail is indeed a spider or an insect.

There were other arguments, however, that could not be settled so easily. That's where the next probe question came in.

3. *Seeking explanations.* The purpose of this question was really to get the youngsters to know *why* they were grouping certain statements together. I didn't have to ask the explanation question very often—most students explained their groupings without being asked.

However, whenever a child failed to offer an explanation, and there was general disagreement as to whether a grouping was valid, I tried to make him defend his selection. I phrased it this way: "Why do you feel that 'galaxies and planets in space' should go with 'sounds around us'?"

4. *Classification.* Once all the facts had been placed into some colloca-tion, the next question was, "What would you call Group A if you were going to name it?" After several titles were given and debated, the young-sters decided to call Group A "Sources of energy." (If you still have doubts about the efficacy of asking probe questions, just consider for a moment what a gigantic leap in reasoning power *that* answer represents.) Each group was classified in the same way.

I didn't get as many student responses to the classification question as I did when I asked the first probe question. But that was only to be expected —it takes a higher level of thinking to classify than it does to recount and recall.

My more able students were bursting with energy at this point, which is pretty much what I thought would happen. But, to my surprise, a few of the youngsters who had been hesitant to react up to this time suddenly came to life. It was an encouraging development, since it meant that the probe questions were getting through—to more students than just the top few.

5. *Exact statement of classification.* In a few instances, we found that we needed the exact classification, and we were forced to examine the statements even more closely. The key word in this probe question was *all*—"If you were to put *all* of the items in this one group into one sentence, what would you say?" Here again, the purpose was to lift the youngsters' thinking into crystal-clear responses.

Once we had reached a decision—and had established that the titles were good ones that fit all of the statements they pertained to—the classi-fications were written on another area of the chalkboard. We were ready to go on to the next probe question.

6. *Total classification.* The final question for this class session on book reporting was, "Try to think of a sentence which states everything that we have discussed during this period." The response was light, but I listened to all answers. Three general labels were selected and written on the chalk-board: "Some facts about science," "Man's knowledge of life and power" and "Science and its discoveries."

You'll notice that I did not try to lump all of the many classifications under just one title. I could have, of course, but there were just too many subject areas that had been touched upon. A single, all-inclusive title would have missed that crystal-clear thinking we were aiming for in our question-ing sequence.

I found that I had to steer the youngsters away from giving me vague and all-too-general total classifications. They were all for titles like "Science books we've read" or "Modern science." Usually, these titles were the first things that came to mind. However, I kept after them until they had re-sponded with more precise titles.

It was time to call it quits for the day. The youngsters had been at it for some time now and a summing up of what we had discussed during our class session was an ideal place to stop. Besides, I wanted to attack the subject from a different angle with my next four probe questions.

7. *The focus question.* A good deal of preparation was necessary before the youngsters were ready for this probe question. I had given them an assignment: Construct a chart or perform an experiment that would prove the stand taken by their particular group when they had been asked the collocation question. (All of the children were in one group or another by virtue of the fact that the books they had read fell into Group A, Group B, etc.)

One student presented an excellent report and chart on kinetic energy. And the child who had been so uncertain about snails informed the class that snails were neither spiders nor insects, but mollusks.

It was time to narrow the focus again . . . and time for the next probe question.

8. *Pointing to the purpose.* During each presentation, I asked each reporting youngster a "why" question that related to the purpose of the investigation. In the case of the child who had read up on snails, at least one of the purposes had been to clear up the confusion about snails and insects. Accordingly, I asked him *why* a snail could be mistaken for an insect. He gave me two good reasons: the antenna and the size of the snail.

In the process of narrowing the discussion to a fine point, I found that many of the responses were becoming personal. I didn't worry about it, because it led me inevitably into the next probe question.

9. *A question that involves the pupil.* What I was trying to do here was involve the child's own feelings in the discussion. For example, I asked the children who had used experiments from a book how they would improve on the experiment if they had written the book.

Several youngsters indicated that certain materials need not be purchased from a store—as indicated in the book—since the materials were readily available elsewhere. (How's that for not accepting everything a textbook says as the gospel truth?) One girl who had used a lemon and salt solution to clean a dirty penny earnestly advised me that she would certainly use gloves the next time around.

When all of the youngsters had finished their presentations, we were ready for the final question of the day.

10. *Seeking a conclusion or summary.* This question was intended to lead to a resolution of everything we'd been discussing. It was phrased something like this: "All right then, what *did* we learn from the presentations?" The children came up with three conclusions:

- The charts and experiments make us wonder and desire to learn more.
- They lead to different ideas.
- They show that the person is trying new ideas.

The purpose of the first 10 probing questions was essentially one of interpretation. The children not only recalled facts but also interpreted them. I could have stopped then and there and still chalked up the questioning technique as a success.

But why stop when I could go on with a final set of three probe questions that deal with cause and effect? (This, by the way, was a time for fun, but I had to be careful to keep the discussion on a fairly serious level so as to make the cause and effect relationship appear rational.)

11. *The hypothetical question.* Because such a heated discussion took place about the sources of energy, I asked my class the following question during a science lesson: "What might happen if man could get energy from just one plant such as lettuce?" (See what I mean about keeping the discussion on a serious level, even though it's fun?)

The responses were quick to come. They were listed on the chalkboard as follows: "Everyone would buy lettuce seeds." (After each listing, I asked, "Then what?") "Stores would run out of seeds and lettuce." "Stores would close." "People would lose their jobs." "More poverty." "Those in cold climates move to warm climates." "Overpopulation of warm climates." "War over warm climates."

I had learned from past experience that a very curious thing happens when you ask a hypothetical "What might happen if" question. Usually, the responses become progressively more pessimistic. You'll notice that it happened here, too. After all, what could be more pessimistic than a progression from lettuce to a war over warm climates?

However, I was prepared for it and I had another probe question which was specifically designed to reverse the tide.

12. *The lifting question.* I simply inserted the word "good" into the discussion. I asked, "What *good* things will happen?"

The youngsters' responses began to creep back to a more optimistic level: "Land is finally divided equally among people." "Countries begin to cooperate." "Greenhouses are built in cold climates." "People move back to cold climates." "Stores reopen." "More jobs are available." "Age of prosperity begins."

On this high note, I ended the lifting questions. The stage was set for the final probe question.

13. *Substantiation.* I asked if the final statement—"the age of prosperity"—was a logical ending to our discussion. I immediately got a chorus of yeses. But I refused to accept the response. Substantiation was what I was after and that was what I was going to get. After thinking about it for a

while, the children gave me the proof I was looking for. They had been studying the Renaissance in history and they cited that period as a good example.

Fair enough, I thought, and that ended the complete sequence. I was certain that a great deal had been accomplished with these last three questions—much more, really, than we had accomplished in the earlier book reporting sessions.

But there's really only one way to find out if probe questions are for you, and that's to try them out on your own class. There's really nothing difficult about it. Just take the 13 probe questions, adapt them to your needs and use them for any topic you wish.

You'll probably be surprised at where the questions finally take you. But one thing is certain: Both you and your children will learn a lot and have fun while you're doing it.

Social Studies—From Facts to Concepts

VINCENT R. ROGERS

The key words in social studies during the past decade have been *concept, generalization,* and *structure.* Facts as such are belittled and scorned. In a way, this is as it should be. Surely few would defend the accumulation of facts for their own sake, and most would agree that the social sciences have developed at least some ideas that are much bigger, broader, more transferable; that really help people to understand themselves and society; that help to order and classify events; that even help us to predict. On the other hand, many teachers still find themselves confused about the relationship between facts and these bigger ideas, often labeled as concepts and generalizations; and it cannot be denied that the facts are still there.

A program such as EDC's "Man, a Course of Study" supplies teachers with facts (*data* would be a better word) carefully chosen to lead to the development of certain basic ideas about human behavior. Other programs (Minnesota, Greater Cleveland, Georgia Anthropology Project, for example) are also organized this way. The relationship between fact and concept is quite clear. The vast majority of American elementary school teachers are *not* yet using such programs, however, and they seem to find it

Vincent R. Rogers is Chairman of the Department of Elementary Education, University of Connecticut, Storrs.

From *Instructor* 79:60–61, 1970. Reprinted from *Instructor,* © May 1971, The Instructor Publications, Inc., used by permission of the publisher and Vincent R. Rogers.

difficult to help children make connections between facts and principles. What then does one do? How do we treat facts, if indeed we treat them at all? How do we deal with conventional social studies information in a way that may lead children to bigger, broader understandings? Let's examine a few classroom episodes that may provide us with some fairly specific answers to these questions.

Episode 1 (primary grades)

CONVENTIONAL TOPIC

How families live, including facts related to earning a living, saving money, borrowing money, and so on.

TO GO BEYOND FACTS

The teacher places on a flannel board a picture of a *man,* identifying him as Mr. Green. On Friday afternoon after work, Mr. Green receives his weekly salary *check* for $150 (add a check to board). On Saturday morning, Mr. Green goes to his neighborhood *bank* (add picture of a bank building) to cash his check. He receives *30 five-dollar bills* (add mimeographed play money).

The Greens have borrowed money from the bank to buy a *house* (add picture). Mr. Green takes $30 of the money to make his mortgage payment at the end of the month. (At this point, the teacher asks a member of the class to remove the picture of the house and six of the five-dollar bills. This is money that cannot be spent for other purposes.)

The Greens have also borrowed money from the bank to buy a *car* (add picture). Mr. Green takes $20 from his weekly salary to put aside for this payment at the end of the month. (A child detaches the car and four bills.)

Mr. Green decides to deposit $15 in the family *savings account* (an illustration of a savings passbook); and $5 in the *Christmas Club* (a picture of Santa Claus) to be used for gifts next December. (Again, a third and a fourth child take the savings passbook and three bills and the Santa Claus picture and one bill from the flannel board.)

When Mr. Green gets home from the bank, he gives *Mrs. Green* (a cutout of a mother) $25 for groceries (a photograph of a supermarket) and $10 to pay the *electricity bill.* (Add drawing of an electric light bulb. Two children pull off the grocery and electricity mountings and five and two bills respectively.)

After Mrs. Green returns from shopping at the supermarket early in the afternoon, she and Mr. Green ask their *children* (a picture of a boy and girl) whether they prefer to go to a restaurant for hamburgers, French fries, and milkshakes for dinner, or to eat leftovers at home and attend a drive-in movie. (The teacher pauses at this stage and holds up cutouts of *an eating place* and *an outdoor theater* and asks the class which choice they would make if they were the Green children. The class is told that either treat— the restaurant meal or the price of admission to the theater plus bags of popcorn—costs $5. The picture representing the children's choice could be displayed just long enough for another pupil to whisk it away with an accompanying five-dollar bill.)

On Sunday, the Greens attend church (add a picture of a church). They make their usual $5 contribution for church and Sunday school. (The church cutout and a bill are detached simultaneously.)

Next, the teacher asks how much money the Green family has left out of its weekly paycheck. The children count the remaining bills and report a figure of $35. The teacher then brings out a string long enough to reach the width of the classroom. The string is tacked on each side of the room just above the heads of the children. On this string pupils fasten illustrations depicting other items for which the Greens might spend the remaining $35. They might make a down payment on a portable television set; *or* on a piano, so the children could begin taking lessons; *or* on a vacation camping trailer. They could buy a small record player for the children, *or* a complete table tennis set, *or* new outfits for the boy and girl.

BIG IDEA EXPLORED

All families face the problem of relative scarcity, or unlimited wants and limited resources.

Episode 2 (intermediate grades)

CONVENTIONAL TOPIC

How the Maya, Aztec, and Inca Indians lived, including facts about religion, social organization, and so on.

TO GO BEYOND FACTS

On 3″ x 5″ cards, the teacher writes brief statements describing various human activities. Members of the class (or groups of three or four) each receive one of these "problem cards," which they are to investigate, clarify, and later explain to their classmates. At first, each activity appears to be somewhat strange, illogical, or mysterious. The task of the child (or group) is to *make it make sense,* i.e., to explain what people would have to believe in order to carry out such a practice. Sample cards might deal with such topics as:

A Northwest Indian potlatch ceremony in which an Indian chief burns his own canoes and destroys many other prized possessions in order to "defeat" a rival.

An Aztec, Mayan, or Inca ceremony involving human sacrifice.

A group that buries food, clothing, weapons, and so on, with a dead warrior.

A tomb erected in memory of an unknown soldier.

A man who purchases a new car every year, even though his previous car still runs perfectly.

A woman who sleeps on painful hair curlers all night long.

BIG IDEA EXPLORED

Every human cultural system is logical and coherent, given the basic assumptions and knowledge available to the specific community.

Episode 3 (intermediate grades)

CONVENTIONAL TOPIC

U.S. geography, including facts about America's natural resources.

TO GO BEYOND FACTS

The teacher begins by asking his class what a "natural resource" is. The pupils may have some difficulty defining "natural resource." Perhaps they recall from past study classes of natural resources (sunshine, air, water, soil, minerals, forests, wildlife) or specific examples such as rivers, coal, pine trees, and salmon. Without comment the teacher writes on the chalkboard all the examples given. Students often have no functional, transferable idea of why natural resources are given this label. They have learned to respond by rote. Next, therefore, the teacher asks his class to think about the items that have been recorded as natural resources and to see what they have in common. A pupil or two may arrive at a rather loose statement like, "Natural resources are things that have always been on the earth."

Now the teacher is ready to help the children refine and sharpen their thinking and see the relationship of their culture to natural resources. He underlines one of the words on the board, for instance *COAL,* and then makes an independent assignment. The class has access to a number of materials dealing with natural resources in general and coal in particular. Every pupil is given a series of questions such as these and asked to answer them in *numerical order:*

1. Is coal a natural resource?
2. Have we always had coal on the earth?
3. Have people always used coal whenever and wherever they found it?

4. Have people in different times and places always assigned the same value to coal?
5. If people had never used coal for any purpose, would they still list it as a natural resource?
6. What do people mean when they say "carrying coals to Newcastle"? Why and when did people start using this expression? Does this saying tell you anything about natural resources in general and coal in particular?
7. What are some of the things for which coal has been used? Have the uses made of coal always been the same over the years? Why?
8. Is coal more important, as important, or less important in the United States today than it was in the past? Why? Does your answer tell you anything about natural resources?
9. If all the coal in the world should be used up some day, what natural resources might be used to do some of the things which coal now does?
10. What is a natural resource? Can you write your own definition now?
11. What have you learned about natural resources through this activity that you did not know before?
12. What questions do you now have about natural resources for which you would like to find answers?

BIG IDEA EXPLORED

A society's value system, goals, organization, and level of technology determine which natural resources are prized and utilized.

Episode 4 (primary grades)

CONVENTIONAL TOPIC

Our community, including facts about where people live, how they get from one place to another, where they work, and so forth.

TO GO BEYOND FACTS

Virginia Lee Burton's Caldecott-Award-winning book, *The Little House* (Houghton Mifflin; 1942), is read to a group of first graders. The story concerns a house built on a hill, far out in the country. One day a road is built; soon new houses are constructed, and little by little the city creeps closer. At last the little house is surrounded by skyscrapers, apartment houses, buses, trucks, and an elevated railway. Following the reading of the story, the teacher discusses what happened to the little house and why.

Eventually the children are asked to look for evidence of changes in their own area, such as the construction of a new house, or the building of a bridge or tunnel, perhaps drawing pictures of such changes. The teacher puts the class drawings together on a bulletin board entitled "How Our Community Is Changing." He encourages his class to continue looking for examples of change in their neighborhood, adding to their bulletin board as the school year progresses and discussing at their level of maturity the ways in which such changes may affect their lives. Children may be asked to observe (on their way to or from school) all the changes *man* has made in their community or neighborhood.

BIG IDEA EXPLORED

Change is apparently one of the few constants in modern western society. Virtually no place is immune to change, and the lives of all are intimately affected by it.

It is difficult to describe accurately what really goes on in a classroom. It is even more difficult to assess what goes on in the mind of a child. There is no guarantee that children exposed to the teaching procedures just described are really grasping the "big ideas." Perhaps some merely play a word game, verbalizing "correctly" but actually understanding very little about the meaning of what they say. We often give children too much too soon, forgetting that they must have concrete experience before abstraction is possible. The parroting of concepts or generalizations is no better than parroting facts, and it is exceedingly difficult to know when a child is actually beginning to fit things together—to understand an idea or a principle. The problem is further compounded by the fact that children are different. They do not conceptualize at the same rate, in the same way, or at the same depth. Individualized approaches to learning and, more importantly, to the *assessment* of learning are crucial.

But most important of all—teachers themselves must be aware of the existence of ideas that go beyond facts. They need to understand the significance of "ordinary" events. They need to read, to listen, to be fully and richly alive. As I see it, there's no way out of this. No prepared program, however well conceived, can provide a solution to our problems that is any more effective than the classroom teacher who utilizes it.

Skills Teaching in the Primary Grades

The term *skill* is applied to the ability to do something with some degree of expertness in repeated performances. To have a skill or to be skillful, however, is usually something of a relative matter. The kindergarten child is highly skillful in his use of language when compared with a two-year old. We would say that he is less skillful in most things he does when compared with an upper-grade pupil. Adequacy of skill development must not only take into account the expertness of performance *per se,* but the age and prior background of the learner.

When children enter the primary grades, they have already developed a number of skills. They can carry on conversations with others, follow directions, take care of many of their personal needs, play simple games; some can read. Such skills are essential for ordinary living. Left unattended and untutored, the child will improve these skills simply through continued use. The refinement of the skills the child has when he comes to school and the learning of others that are introduced as a part of the curriculum will be greatly enhanced through careful and systematic instruction. From the moment the child enters school, his continued success in the school environment will depend to a significant degree on the extent to which he is able to learn and use essential skills.

There can be no doubt that well developed skills enhance the ability to do other school-related tasks. Conversely, poorly developed skills result in arrested school progress. Pupils who are off to a poor start in their skill development in the primary grades fall farther and farther behind in their overall achievement. Eventually the deficit accumulates to a point that becomes overwhelming to the pupil and nearly impossible for him to overcome. School dropouts at the high school level invariably present histories of skill deficiences that can be traced to the earliest grades in school. Skill competence strengthens the child's positive perception of himself, an important component of school success. The child uses skills to deal with the social world confronting him, and consequently, skills contribute directly to his social competence. It would be hard to underestimate the vital role primary grade teachers play in ensuring a successful introduction of the child to the skills program.

In the primary grades it is almost impossible to separate social studies

John Jarolimek is Professor of Education at the University of Washington, Seattle.

Reprinted from *Social Education 31*(3):222–223 ff., 1967, with permission of the National Council for the Social Studies and John Jarolimek.

skills from the skills objectives of the total primary grade program. There is no particular reason to label certain skills as being the unique province of the social studies, providing essential skills get the instructional attention they deserve. The advantage of singling out social studies skills in the curriculum is to ensure that they *are* included and taught systematically. Moreover, skills presented in a social studies context can often be taught in a more realistic and functional setting than when presented either in isolation or in the framework of another curriculum area, as for example, in the reading program.

In the first article of this supplement, Professor Carpenter has noted that in spite of the concern for social studies revision in recent years, no new skills have been identified. Essential skills persist in their importance in modern programs even though there have been some shifts in emphasis. Uniqueness in skills teaching does not come through the discovery of some new skill but in imaginative approaches to the teaching of those that have always been regarded as important. The social studies skills with which the primary grade teacher is concerned are less complex variations of skills that continue to receive attention throughout the total program.

One large group of such skills deals basically with a variety of intellectual operations. Thinking, asking questions, using language, solving problems, interpreting stories and pictures, and making simple analyses are a few examples of skills of this type. In most cases they are related to the informational content of the program. They do not deal basically with *getting* information but with interpreting, processing, and using information. In the following example, notice how the teacher is building thinking skills with her first graders:

The teacher selected a picture from a magazine advertising a dishwasher. The picture shows a young mother removing sparkling clean dishes from the washer while her daughter (about a six-year-old) looks on. One can see a bright, modern kitchen and the landscape greenery through the kitchen window. The teacher prepared the following questions in connection with this picture:

1. Is the mother taking the dishes out or putting them in the washer?
2. Is this a large or small family?
3. Does this family have a comfortable home?
4. What season of the year is it?
5. What might other members of the family be doing at this time?
6. Do you think the lady is the little girl's mother?
7. Is this a city home or a farm home?

The purpose of this exercise is not to establish right or wrong answers to the questions. Indeed, it would be impossible to determine precisely the rightness or wrongness of some of them. For example, one could not be sure about the size of the family by the number of dishes used; the family may have had guests, or the dishes may be an accumulation from more than one meal. Similarly, the season of the year could not be verified by the presence of greenery because some parts of the country are green the year around. Pupils could be expected to point out these possibilities, and while they may select what they think is the most likely answer, the door should be kept open to the consideration of other alternatives. In activities of this type, it is more important to consider a variety of possibilities and have pupils give reasons why a response is plausible than to agree on a right answer. (This degree of flexibility would not be acceptable, however, in considering factual questions where correctness can be established. Factual questions serve a different purpose from those designed to encourage reflective thought.)

Other examples of intellectual skills can be developed around such situations as these:

1. Identifying sequences—What happened first; what happened next; what happened last?
2. Considering alternative solutions—Can you think of another way to do it? What are some other ways the man could have solved his problems?
3. Differentiating between fact and fiction—What parts of the story are true and what parts are make-believe. How can we find out if something is true?
4. Developing sensitivity to words—Can you think of words that make you feel happy? Sad? Angry?
5. Predicting or speculating on outcomes of situations—How do you suppose the problem was solved? What do you suppose will happen next?

Telling pupils to think or admonishing them for not thinking are not effective methods for developing intellectual skills even though such practices in one form or another are fairly common. More productive approaches call for the pupil to respond to simple questions of the reflective type that may not have a single answer but force him to consider many alternatives, predict likely consequences of each, and decide the best course of action. There can be little if any thinking if the pupil does not have to consider alternatives in situations that involve choice or decision-making.

The importance of intellectual skills, and especially thinking skills, is often overlooked in the primary grades because of the widespread belief that one gains knowledge first and then uses that knowledge for thinking purposes at some later time. As a result the development of thinking abilities of young children has not always been the concern of primary grade teachers. Children at this level were expected to build literacy and work-study skills and expand their backgrounds of information. Thinking would come later. There is no evidence to support the notion that knowledge acquisition and knowledge use in the thinking process are separate and discrete functions. In fact, the practice of disassociating a skill from its functional context is rejected as unsound practice in most other realms of skill development. It is unfortunate that it should persist in teaching pupils the most important skill of all, namely, thinking.

A second large group of skills important to the primary grade social studies involves social relationships. They include ordinary social skills needed for harmonious living and working with others, as well as those more structured skills related to instructional processes, i.e., working on a small committee, contributing to a group project, participating in class discussions, and so forth. These skills are the concern of the total curriculum of the elementary school, of course, but the social studies provide excellent settings in which to teach them because of the nature of instructional processes associated with this area of the curriculum.

The most important point that could be made in connection with social relationship skills is that they *need to be taught*. It is often assumed that all that is required are activities in which pupils can apply and practice them. Consequently, pupils are forced to learn the skills of social interaction on a trial and error basis. In the process the teacher may become annoyed, isolate those pupils who were not "cooperative," and return the others to their seats to a more formal instructional posture. While there might be times when a child should be separated from the others, no child ever learned the skills of social interaction while he was in isolation. Neither do classes learn such skills in formal instructional settings where social interaction is not allowed or is discouraged.

A third category of social studies skills has to do mainly with the use of learning resources and tools including simple map and globe reading, knowing where to go for information needed, how to speak before the class, reading signs and symbols, and other similar operations. They are commonly called work-study skills. The need for instructional attention to these skills has been generally accepted through the years. Conventional reading programs ordinarily devote some instruction to work-study skills that are relevant to social studies.

It often happens that a specific activity can be used to attack several related work-study skills. For example, a third grade class may be collecting pictures that show the way of life in another country. Such an activity might be used to promote any or all of the following skills:

1. Locating appropriate pictures.
2. Explaining or telling the class something about the picture.
3. Classifying information—placing pictures in appropriate categories such as those that show home life, those that show work people do, holiday observances, or sports events.
4. Comparing information from one picture with another.
5. Learning and using new words and concepts represented in the picture.
6. Asking appropriate questions concerning picture content.

7. Planning and arranging an exhibit, such as a bulletin board.
8. Creating and writing appropriate captions and/or explanations to accompany the pictures.

Similarly, in the selection of activities for the development of work-study skills, the primary grade teacher can attend to intellectual skills and social relationship skills as well. For example, in teaching pupils how to use the school library, the teacher will undoubtedly stress such intellectual skills as listening to directions, observing carefully, asking questions, and knowing what information is wanted. If the activity involves going to the library as as class or in smaller groups, she will also use the experience as a way of teaching or reinforcing social behavior of pupils. Finally, in the process pupils will learn something about use of the library—how it is arranged, where to look for certain kinds of books, and how to check out a book. Although we separate these skills for discussion purposes and focus instruction on specific skills from time to time to ensure learning, the whole cluster of social studies skills is highly interrelated.

To a degree skill growth is related to the developmental pattern of children. Consequently, no matter how intensively skills are taught in the primary grades, there are definite upper limits on the level of proficiency that can realistically be expected of most primary grade pupils. It is advisable, therefore, to establish reasonable criterion levels of expectation and settle for those rather than to expend an excessive amount of instructional time in order to get small increments of improvement in performance. The growth curve on skills rises sharply to a point and then levels off; perhaps the optimum performance expectancy is just beyond the point where the curve begins to plateau. If adequate instruction on skills can be assured and reasonable expectancy levels set, there will be time to spend on other important dimensions of an effective primary grade program. Skills and skills teaching, while extremely important, should not entirely dominate the primary grade curriculum to the exclusion of art, music, poetry, literature, and other learnings vital to the total development of the young child.

The Psychology of Skill Development

A visitor enters an American senior high school social studies classroom where the students are completing their course in "Problems of American Democracy." He observes that the class is divided into several working groups, and his attention is drawn to one particular group of six high school seniors. They are seated about a table discussing a problem in American government. They are using maps, graphs, charts, books, periodicals, and data which have been collected from a variety of sources. One student is acting as the leader while another is taking notes. The group is discussing the problem intelligently, critically, and maturely. It is apparent to the observer that these students are utilizing a great number of social studies skills easily, naturally, and with proficiency.

When these same students entered school as first-graders some 12 years earlier, they could utilize none of these skills with any degree of facility. They could not read. Maps were unintelligible to them. Critical evaluation of abstract ideas was impossible. Group work consisted of self-centered activities performed in proximity to other persons. They were highly dependent upon the teacher for direction and social control. Linguistic development was immature; their language lacked most of the technical vocabulary which they use so easily now.

Of one thing the observer can be sure. The students did not develop these skills spontaneously as a part of the growing-up, maturing process. Neither did they learn them casually as an incidental by-product of school attendance. Behind this group of high school students is a thoughtfully and carefully planned program of skill development. The observer is simply seeing the cumulative effects of such a program, which was begun 12 years earlier and to which many teachers have contributed.

All schools want their students to complete their education with well-developed skills. In order to achieve this goal, it is important to know what kind of an educational program can be planned to bring pupils to a high level of competence in skills. It is important, too, to know how skills are developed and what kinds of experiences students need in order to grow in the utilization of skills. Finally, it is important to know how individual

John Jarolimek is Professor of Education at the University of Washington, Seattle.

This selection is Chapter 2 of *Skill Development in Social Studies,* 33rd Yearbook of the National Council for the Social Studies, Helen McCracken Carpenter, Editor, 1963.

Reprinted with permission of the National Council for the Social Studies and John Jarolimek.

pupils perceive the need for skills, what motivates them to want to learn skills, and the conditions which enhance or impede skill development for individual pupils.

The Nature of Social Studies Skills

The total social studies program is concerned with the development of important understandings, attitudes, and skills. Understandings have to do with conceptual learnings—with the development of concepts, generalizations, principles, and facts which comprise the basic content of the social studies and which are drawn from the social sciences. Attitudes relate to those values, appreciations, and ideals that the social studies program seeks to instill in the learner. Skills include ways of dealing with the social studies as a field of study and with other people in human association. Social studies skills make it possible for the learner to employ those intellectual processes necessary in obtaining or handling knowledge and to utilize those human-relations processes which lead to wholesome interaction with others. Social studies skills have been classified in a variety of ways, but in general they include *work-study skills* such as reading, outlining, map reading, and interpreting graphs; *thinking skills* such as critical thinking and problem solving; *group-process skills* such as those involved in leading or participating in other ways in group undertakings; and *social-living skills* such as acting responsibly, cooperating with others, and living and working in a group setting. It should be recognized in passing that other areas of the curriculum have a responsibility to contribute to the development of most of these skills.

In teaching the social studies, the three types of learnings—understandings, attitudes, and skills—are, of course, highly interrelated. To attempt to separate them from one another would result in grossly unrealistic teaching practices. But although they are interrelated they are not necessarily presented, taught, and learned in the same way. Teaching procedures which are appropriate in presenting conceptual learnings or attitudinal learnings are often inappropriate if employed in teaching a skill.

It is because of the kinship of social studies learnings that skills emerge as being fundamental and necessary. Skills are the basic tools of learning. They help the pupil learn. Inadequately developed skills foreshorten the opportunity to continue learning and lead inevitably to poor achievement in the social studies. It is simply impossible for a student to be deficient in skills and to excel in social studies.[1]

[1] Fay, Leo C. "The Relationship Between Specific Reading Skills and Selected Areas of Sixth Grade Achievement," *Journal of Educational Research* 43:541–47, March 1950.

There has been a tendency to associate the word skill with behavior which is somewhat habitual and mechanical in nature. Perhaps this is because skills are often identified with physical-motor behavior. When this narrow interpretation of skills is applied, responses are expected to be more or less automatic to certain stimuli, without the need for conscious mental activity. The performance of a skill by one who is expert in executing it does give the appearance of action without active thought or intention. It looks deceptively simple to the neophyte. The common belief is that practice makes perfect. Consequently, skills teaching has relied heavily upon drill techniques; and the abuses of drill procedures are so well known that the word itself has come to connote something in the way of malpractice in teaching. Educators today prefer to talk of practice and application—terms suggesting a functional use of drill.

For the most part, social studies skills are much more complex than such motor skills as handwriting, typing, throwing a ball, or jumping rope. In almost all cases, social studies skills are intellectual in nature and call for the use of cognitive processes. When the pupil is reading a map, for example, he should be thinking about what the map represents. When he is discussing a problem with his classmates, he is listening to and thinking about what others have to say and is reacting to it. If he is doing problem solving, he is thinking critically about various alternative procedures which might be employed in finding a solution. If he is writing a report or preparing to give one orally, he is thinking about what it is that he is going to say. To think of these skills as an accumulation of habitual responses is to misunderstand their nature and their complexity. Rather, effectively developed social studies skills are demonstrated in highly organized and integrated patterns of behavior.

To be skillful means that one is able to do something with proficiency in repeated performances. The standard of proficiency is determined by how well others can perform the same task. In other words, the measure of competency in a skill is the norm of the population of which the person is a part. We may, for example, properly say that a fourth-grader has demonstrated skill in preparing a report for social studies. The same level of performance by an eighth-grader or by a high school senior, on the other hand, would probably not be regarded as a skillful one.

Complex skills, such as those associated with the social studies, consist of several component elements or subskills. For example, the reading skill used by a high school sophomore in social studies calls into play many subskills related to the reading process. Early in the elementary school he learned how to recognize words and how to read selections with short sentences and simple words. Later he sharpened his reading-comprehension skills. He learned how to skim for a main idea and how to read intensively for details. Still later, perhaps in junior high school, he learned how to interpret a written passage to detect an author's bias. Somewhere along the line he should have learned to read creatively, that is, to react intellectually to the content by testing his own ideas against those presented by the author. Through the years his teachers have worked carefully with him so that he is now equipped with a vast array of reading subskills which have been integrated into a single act which is called a reading skill. The student is now able to approach a variety of reading tasks comfortably. Moreover, he will continue to extend his repertory of reading subskills each time he encounters a reading task which demands some variation in those already at his command. He will also learn to apply the ones he has with greater facility as he practices using them. This process continues not only throughout his years in high school but, indeed, throughout his lifetime.

Somewhat the same process applies to other skills as well. Map reading begins with simple, three-dimensional layouts and pictorial symbols in the primary grades and leads to the use of complex map reading and interpretive skills in high school. Group-process skills begin with simple parallel play and lead later to cooperative behavior and high-level intellectual interaction with others. In the case of these complex skills, it is apparent that the learner does not master them once and for all time but rather moves to more mature, more proficient, and more advanced variations of them.

To help pupils develop a skill to an advanced level, the component elements must be identified and arranged in a sequence representing levels of difficulty. The learner is then introduced to these components, one step at a time in a developmental pattern. These component elements should in themselves be functional in that the learner can apply them to social studies experiences at his present stage of development. That is to say, skills should not be broken down into fragmented elements which serve no immediately useful purpose.

It is important for the learner to know what is involved in a skill and what constitutes an adequate performance of it. This is precisely why demonstrations are so widely used in teaching physical-motor skills. The baseball coach wants his players to see a good swing at the plate when he is teaching them how to bat. The music teacher arranges for his pupils to see and hear a good rendition of a musical selection. These demonstrations are valuable because they establish clear goals for the pupil. They set the direction toward which his own efforts are to lead him. Demonstrations and explanations are important in directing and motivating the learner.

In explaining the meaning of a skill or in demonstrating it, the teacher should present a more advanced variation of the skill than the one with which the learner is presently familiar, yet the advanced variation should not be too far beyond the present stage of the learner. If it is, the explanation or demonstration is likely to overwhelm the learner and will not serve to motivate and help him in refining goals. In fact, it is likely to have the reverse effect. Models used at all stages of skill instruction should represent performances which are attainable by the learner.

In order to make skills meaningful to pupils, many authors have stressed the need to teach skills in their functional contexts.[2] In general, the more closely the skill can be taught and related to the situation involving its actual use, the better. However, it is easy to misapply or misunderstand this principle. Teaching skills in their functional settings is one thing; expecting to have them emerge incidentally without systematic instruction is quite another. Students who prepare reports; do reference work; use maps, charts, and graphs; or are engaged in small-group enterprises should be given instruction and guidance in the skills which inhere in those activities. If they are not given such guidance and instruction, the likelihood is great that learners will be getting firsthand experiences in performing skills incorrectly or, at best, in a slipshod manner. Whenever possible, teachers should avoid giving pupils an opportunity to reinforce incorrect responses.

However important it is for the learner to know the meaning of a skill, no amount of meaningful teaching will make him proficient in it unless the teaching is accompanied by practice with intent to improve. Practice makes it possible for the learner to become more discriminating in his responses; to perform them with greater ease and confidence. Practice in and of itself does not insure improvement—it merely provides the opportunity for the improvement of performance.

Krech and Crutchfield emphasize the need for kinesthetic knowledge in learning certain skills.[3] That is, the learner must get the "feel" of the situation. Suppose, for example, a teacher has taught reference skills to his students in the regular classroom. They have learned about the library and how to use the card catalogue. They become familiar with the Dewey Decimal System, special reference shelves, library procedures, use of indexes and guides, and so on. The pupils are thoroughly familiar with procedures in the use of the library, yet they have not visited it. Does this mean that the teacher can now take his class to the library and expect the pupils to use it skillfully? Probably not, because they will need to spend time browsing around, using the card catalogue, finding the special references, and getting the "feel" of the library setting. If they are to develop skill in the use of library references, they will need to have on-the-spot practice in using them.

Practice is one of the most essential aspects of skill development, and learners will not develop facility in skills without it. But if practice is to be effective, it must be performed under certain conditions. For example,

[2] See Burton, William H. "Implications for Organization of Instruction and Instructional Adjuncts." *Learning and Instruction.* Forty-Ninth Yearbook, Part I, National Society for the Study of Education. Chicago: University of Chicago Press, 1950. p. 246; Munn, Norman L. *Psychology.* Fourth edition. Boston: Houghton Mifflin Co., 1961. p. 424; Cronbach, Lee J. *Educational Psychology.* New York: Harcourt Brace and Co., 1954. pp. 377–78; and Kingsley, Howard L. (Revised by Ralph Garry.) *The Nature and Conditions of Learning.* Second edition. Englewood Cliffs, N.J.: Prentice-Hall, 1957. p. 518.

[3] Krech, David, and Crutchfield, Richard S. *Elements of Psychology.* New York: Alfred A. Knopf, 1958. pp. 448–50.

halfhearted practice, without a desire to improve, is self-defeating. Since the learner is not achieving success by improving his performance, there follows a deterioration in motivation to do the practice which is needed to learn the skill. If such a set of circumstances is allowed to persist over a period of time, the learner is likely to reject practice entirely and avoid situations where the skill is needed.

The purpose of practice is to improve performance. This is, of course, obvious, but it is nonetheless frequently overlooked in teaching and learning skills. Improvement occurs when the learner becomes conscious of the results of performing the skill. The teacher provides guidance to help the student discriminate between faulty performance and effective performance. If the learner repeats a response over and over in more or less the same way, does this constitute good practice? Under certain circumstances, it might. For example, his goal may be to increase the speed of his responses; that is, to do them in the same way but to do them faster. In this case, a more rapid response is a mark of improvement. One needs to be careful, therefore, of being too critical of repetitious practice because there are situations in which it is quite proper. The crucial question with respect to practice is whether it produces the intended results, providing, of course, that it is done under conditions which are not educationally or psychologically harmful to the learner.

Initial practice of a skill should be done under close teacher guidance and direction. This allows the teacher to clarify any points not understood by the learner. It also insures that the pupil is responding correctly. Careful supervision is important at this stage because if the learner practices the response incorrectly, he must unlearn the incorrect response before he can proceed with the correct one. This would constitute an unnecessary obstacle to learning. Immediately following the presentation and initial practice under close teacher supervision, frequent practice periods should be planned. Short, spaced practice periods seem to be more effective than those of longer duration but occurring less frequently. The practice sessions should be highly motivated in order to avoid having them seem like drudgery to the learner. The heavy loading of practice following closely the presentation will bring the skill up to a functional level for the pupil. Henceforth, less frequent practice periods will be needed but are nevertheless necessary in order to maintain and improve the skill.

Knowledge of success or failure is important in making progress in learning skills. Information concerning his success which the learner receives from any source is referred to as *feedback*. Feedback can be provided by the teacher, by classmates, by some mechanical device, or by the learner himself as he analyzes his responses. Feedback serves as a reinforcing agent, and as such has positive or negative values. Negative feedback tells the learner what he is doing wrong, and what he should avoid; positive feedback tells him what is right about his responses and reminds him of his successes.

Some caution is necessary in the use of negative feedback. It tends to be stress-producing and does not give the learner information concerning what he *should* do. It tells him only what he *should not* do. For example, a teacher's appraisal of a student's written report may point out errors but not indicate how the report could be improved or what was good about it. Likewise, negative feedback in the form of knowledge of failure on a map-reading test is not likely to be helpful in building map-reading skills unless the learner also knows the particular ways in which his performance was inadequate. If the only knowledge he has is that he failed the examination, he may devote additional study and practice to those aspects of the skill which he already does well and on which practice is not needed, while ignoring those aspects in which he is really deficient. This is not to say that negative feedback should never be used, but rather that it should be used in combination with positive reinforcement.

Positive feedback, on the other hand, tends to be stress-relieving, rewarding, and motivating to the learner. To be most effective, positive feedback should be fairly specific to the task being performed. For example, positive feedback could take the form of teacher praise or some other means of recognition for a good report or for successful participation in a roundtable discussion. This would be helpful to the learner. But such feedback would be of even greater value if the learner knew precisely what there was about his performance that had made it successful: for example, that he had had evidence to support his statements; or that his presentation had been well organized; or that he had spoken with conviction. Or, assume that a teacher has prepared a set of six questions intended to build skill in interpreting graphic data, each question being slightly more difficult than the last. The class might work these questions out, one at a time, with the teacher providing feedback for individual students *while* the skill is being performed. This means that the teacher must be able to diagnose the learner's status quickly, halt unsuccessful probing through negative feedback, and guide the learner to correct responses by providing him with positive feedback.

Feedback gives direction to the learner, steers him away from unproductive responses, and lets him know when he is on the right track. Without feedback the learner probably could not improve. If improvement is sought in such skills as reporting to the class, organizing information, participating in a discussion, or working together in a small group, learners must have their performances evaluated. In general, feedback is most effective in contributing to improved skill learning when specific and given during or immediately following the performance.

Individual Differences in Skill Development

Successful teaching of social studies skills cannot be achieved until the teacher comes to grips realistically with the problem of the wide range of abilities, interests, and backgrounds which exist among learners. These differences are often obscured by the practice of placing and keeping learners of similar chronological ages together in the same class. As the teacher faces his class, therefore, there is little to remind him that while he may be teaching a skill to a *class,* the skill is not learned by the class but by *individuals* within that class. Clearly, he will have to devise ways of helping individual students to learn through the use of group-teaching procedures much of the time.

Perhaps the most difficult concept of all to accept in teaching is that learners differ widely one from the other and that these differences are unavoidable. Teachers cling to the hope that all learners can do average work if they work hard enough at it and if they develop good habits of study. The tendency to look at effects of, rather than to seek causes for, poor achievement sometimes makes the learner the object of criticism by his teacher. Too often the teacher appears to think that his students have the same motivations, interests, ideals, and ambitions that he does.

A little-understood aspect of skills teaching is the extent to which a learner himself must be involved if a skill is to be learned. A learner will gain *some* knowledge and understanding simply by attending class and by listening to and seeing what is going on around him. He will learn certain attitudes through informal association with others. But because of the nature of skills, he cannot learn them in this way. In the case of skills, he himself must perform them. This means that he must want to learn them. Munn calls attention to this need for motivation in learning skills in the statement: ". . . skills, and especially complex ones, are not acquired casually. They are not learned unless something rather obvious is to be gained by learning them." [4]

A basic assumption in any teaching-learning situation is that the learner is capable of learning whatever it is that will be taught to him. This places the teacher in the position of having to plan his teaching in accordance with the preparedness of the learner, or of having to plan appropriate experiences for the learner which will prepare him for the new learning. Preparedness for learning a skill is related to the general maturity of the learner. Adults are prone to gauge the maturity of children by their physical size and chronological age. Thus, it is assumed that when youngsters reach certain ages and grades they are prepared for the introduction of certain learnings. A primary grade pupil is not expected to discuss a complex national or international problem, for example, but an eleventh-grader *should* be able to do so. Generalizations about what students should or should not be able to do at certain ages and grades are extremely hard to make with accuracy because maturity is a highly variable factor among learners. The teacher cannot assume, therefore, that all learners within a given class will be equally prepared for or receptive to some skill that he

[4] Munn, *Psychology.* p. 399.

plans to teach. Maturity relates not only to chronological age and physical development but has psychological and educational dimensions as well. Hence, some eleventh-grade students may be no better prepared for a complex skill such as organizing and evaluating information than some seventh-graders.

In addition to general maturity, life experience bears heavily upon a learner's ability to deal with certain social studies skills. The learner who has had broad experiences, travel, and close association with intelligent and educated adults is likely to have many advantages in learning social studies skills over a classmate who has not had this background. The learner who has developed a value system consistent with that of the school environment will find such a system helpful to him in learning social studies skills. Pupils who come from various subcultural groups often lack a background of life experience which will enhance their learning of important skills. For example, the student who cannot speak a single sentence correctly is not likely to be able to give much of an oral report to his social studies class, nor even want to give one. Pupils who come from hostile out-of-school environments are going to have difficulty developing competence in accepted human-relation skills. Young people who do not value reading in any form will not become excited about using references, locating and gathering information through reading, or organizing and evaluating information. This does not mean that teachers should not attempt to teach such youngsters—it only means that learning will be more difficult for them. In working with them, teachers will need to be more generous in their use of concrete rewards and approval, stressing the usability and practicality of the skill to be learned, and maintaining high motivation in the teaching process. Helping such pupils develop social studies skills is one of the greatest challenges to teachers today.

In dealing with the preparedness of learners for skill learning, there are three ways by which the teacher may proceed: First, he may defer teaching the skill until such time as the learners have developed sufficient maturity to handle it or have gained adequate life experience. Second, he may build into his teaching those experiences for learners which will hasten their maturity or provide them with background they will need to master the skill. Finally, he may present a simpler variation of the skill.

Deferring skills teaching until learners develop a preparedness for it on their own has both advantages and limitations. It is not economical from the standpoint of instructional time to labor the teaching of a skill which could be taught easily and in a much shorter time a few years later. On the other hand, if the teacher simply waits for the learner to mature or to gain background experience, the skill may never be taught. Where there is a gross lack of readiness for learning a skill, the teaching of it should be deferred. Along with such postponement, the teacher should take steps which will hasten the time when the learners will be ready for the skill. That is, the role of the teacher in such cases is not simply a matter of waiting passively for the learner to ready himself. For example, pupils may not be equipped to locate and gather information from a variety of references and incorporate such data into a polished oral or written report. They can, nonetheless, begin by using one or two books to supplement information obtained from their textbook and by contributing those ideas to class discussions. Or if pupils have been accustomed to formal question-and-answer procedures based on the textbook, the teacher can acquaint them with other ways of learning by planning a field trip, which will stimulate problem solving and critical thinking in a simple and concrete way. When primary grade teachers find pupils not ready for successful small-group enterprises, they can give pupil-committees minor responsibilities for housekeeping tasks about the room, leading gradually into small-group work in the instructional program, and thus preparing the pupils to do productive and responsible work in small groups in the middle and higher grades.

Part of the responsibility of the teacher clearly involves preparing the learner for the skill to be taught. Teacher attitudes reflected in such statements as "It should have been learned in an earlier grade" contribute nothing to good skills teaching. Perhaps the students should have learned it in an earlier grade, but the fact is that they did not. If the learning represents a critical prior element in the sequence of the skill, the teacher has no choice but to teach it before he can proceed. Similarly, the teacher must build experience backgrounds as a part of the teaching process when that need is indicated. Pupils will need many experiences in decision making, problem solving, group processes, and critical thinking if they are to build skills related to these processes. Moreover, they need to apply such skills to situations in which they are personally involved. In this way the skills will be of real significance in the lives of the learners.

Command of social studies skills is rarely an all-or-none affair. They can be performed at varying levels of sophistication. The skills one observes being utilized by high school students have their counterparts in simple forms in the primary grades. Consequently, the teacher can select that variation of the skill which is appropriate for individual learners. For example, a pupil in an elementary school may not be able to prepare an outline, but possibly can identify the three or four major ideas relating to a topic. Or a junior high school student may not be able to use a variety of library references to get information but can gather data through the use of nonreading resources. Perhaps the students are not able to think critically about current national issues but can apply critical-thinking skills to problems which confront them in their daily lives. Good skills teaching will place the learner in the instructional sequence at that point which is appropriate for him.

There are two sequences which must be observed in teaching skills: One is the logical sequence which inheres in the skill itself. In map reading, for example, a pupil learns that symbols on a map stand for real things on the earth before he learns that color is a special map symbol which can be used to represent elevation. The logical sequence is one which the learner must follow as he moves from one level of complexity of the skill to the next. The other sequence is psychological and is peculiar to individual learners. It has to do with what should be the next step in the learning *for the individual* in terms of his total background, experience, prior learning, and general maturity. It is obvious that a teacher following a strictly logical sequence of skills teaching may be offering experiences which are out of sequence for individual learners. The particular point from which further learning is to proceed is a highly individual matter. The teacher's task, therefore, is to synchronize the logical and psychological sequences for individual pupils in order that learning may progress in an expeditious manner.

Promoting Growth in Skills

Wherever one sees a good program of skill development in operation, he will find that the teachers regard skills teaching as an essential and important part of the total social studies instructional effort. The teaching of skills cannot be handled in an incidental or peripheral manner if good results are anticipated. Rather, it must be considered as one of the central purposes of social studies instruction. Often skills do not get the attention that they should because they are not identified carefully enough for the teacher. It is frequently assumed that every teacher knows what skills need attention and that every teacher will include instruction on them. Such an arrangement rarely works well in practice, because teachers often feel that their chief responsibility is to present the factual content which is designated for the grade or for the course rather than to emphasize skill development. Therefore, while everyone teaches skills to some extent, there is no real sequential program in operation for the development of skills. It would be hard to think of a situation which is less likely to produce learners who are competent in skills. The chance that important skills will be neglected or omitted entirely under this random scheme is very great indeed.

In order to attach some degree of importance to skills teaching, schools must identify specific skills which are to receive attention. The program of instruction at each grade, throughout the total 12 years of school, should clearly indicate what the teacher's responsibilities are toward maintaining and extending social studies skills. Pupil expectancies need to be spelled out and should, of course, be consistent with variation in learner abilities.[5]

Finally, frequent and regular appraisals of skill growth need to be made,

[5] Chapter 15 [of *Skill Development in Social Studies*] offers suggestions for planning a sequential program of skill development throughout the social studies curriculum. Further help is available in the chart entitled "Social Studies Skills: A Guide to Analysis and Grade Placement," that appears in the Appendix.

and a record should be kept of the progress of individual pupils. This should include test score data on progress in reading; in the use of maps, graphs, and references; and in communications skills for which standardized tests are available. It should also include teacher comments on and appraisals of the growth in group processes, human relations, problem solving, and study skills, for which informal evaluative procedures are more appropriate. Pupil progress in learning skills should be noted annually and kept as a permanent part of the learner's school record.

The necessity for direct teaching of skills needs to be emphasized. Because skills are associated with learning activities, it is often assumed that pupils will learn them simply by doing them. The handling of group-process skills affords a good example. Often learners are placed in group situations without any real instruction on how groups function, what the responsibilities of members are, what it means to be a leader, and so on. Or learners may be required to make use of a map or globe as a part of their social studies work but have not been adequately instructed in its use. In the case of such communications skills as writing, listening, reading, and spelling, the teacher may proceed under the tenuous assumption that pupils remember these skills from their language arts or, in the case of secondary students, from their English program. Better learning would result if teachers would reinforce, and reteach if necessary, such communications skills within the context of the social studies.

The heavy emphasis in educational literature on the need for "doing" on the part of learners should not be construed to mean that direct instruction is unnecessary. While it is true that pupils must perform skills if they hope to learn them, the learning can be more fruitful and efficient if the pupils are taught how to do them well. Perhaps the strongest programs are those which provide for instruction in skills within the functional framework of the topic studied. Thus the learner's attention is called to the need for the skill. He must learn the skill if he is to solve the problem which confronts him. The need for the skill is a real rather than an imaginary one. If the teacher utilizes such strategic moments of pupil need to give systematic instruction in skills, many opportunities for skill development exist in connection with on-going activities.

Instructional programs are weakened when teachers assume that pupils learn skills in the elementary school for later application in the secondary school. If instruction proceeds on this assumption, skills are apt to lack meaning for the elementary pupil, since he has little opportunity to apply them. It will also reduce the opportunities for the secondary student to build his skills to a high level of competence because his instructional program has been cut short. Actually, learning skills and applying them should be an important part of the program in all grades.

Practice situations and applications of a skill should provide the learner with a wide range of circumstances in which the skill is to be used. The learner must be able to adjust his application of the skill when he encounters situations in which its use varies somewhat from the one in which it was learned. Social studies skills are generalized patterns of behavior and should be taught by using specimen cases which represent a wide variety of examples of how skills are used. For instance, the individual will not learn reference skills if he always uses the same single source. Nor will he learn map-reading skills if he works only with one type of map. Neither can he learn to think critically if he limits critical thinking to certain problems in the social studies while accepting uncritically what is told him by his teacher. In the case of reading, teachers need to provide various types of experiences for the pupils and to teach them how to adjust the use of this skill to the reading task which confronts them.

Since social studies skills consist of many related subskills, the teacher should in most cases attack them on a modified part-teaching, rather than on a whole-teaching, basis. For example, one cannot teach map-reading skills on a whole-teaching basis because this skill consists of a vast array of elements and subskills. Map reading does not exist apart from such elements as noting directions, reading symbols, understanding scales, and so on. One learns to read maps by developing facility with these elements and by combining them into an integrated whole. In teaching elements of such a complex skill, therefore, it is important that the parts not become discrete and autonomous elements, but that they become functioning parts of the larger, more complex skill. This will make it possible for the learner to utilize the skill on a continuing basis in social studies activities.

Since learners vary to the extent that they do, a sound approach to skills teaching will allow for a wide range in the performance of skills. When expectancies are established, they should serve as guides to the teacher rather than as standards to be attained by all learners. In the lower grades there is a tendency to restrict the pupils' opportunities to move to more advanced levels of skills, while in the secondary school the inclination is to set unrealistic goals for low-achieving students. Pupils in the third, fourth, and fifth grades who are able to move rapidly on such skills as map reading, locating and gathering information, preparing reports, reading complex materials, and doing critical thinking should be encouraged and helped to do so. Sometimes teachers avoid the introduction of such skills because the course of study calls for their presentation in a later grade. There is little to justify this practice if teachers are well informed on the nature and extent of individual differences among pupils. Courses of study should not be so inflexible as to make adjustments in terms of individual learners impossible. The goal for the skills program should be continual growth for all learners. This means that skills performance can be expected to be variable rather than to show a rigid and fixed pattern. For some pupils, any progress, however small, is a mark of outstanding achievement.

A well-established principle in teaching is to ascertain what the learner already knows about whatever is to be taught, and to continue his instruction from that point. This being the case, teachers need to make careful appraisals of the status of skills learning of individual pupils before instruction is planned. A careful diagnosis of the skills-learning status of pupils will make it possible for the teacher to be more effective in properly gearing the instruction to the appropriate level of individuals within a class. A diagnostic approach to the teaching of social studies skills is essential if psychologically sound sequences are to be maintained.

A diagnostic approach to skills teaching underscores the continuous nature of skills growth. The complete learning of skills is not achieved in any one grade or set of grades. All teachers throughout the full 12-year program share the responsibility to introduce new skills or variations of skills; to maintain those which have been taught earlier and to reteach them if necessary; and to provide adequate practice and use of skills in order that they may be refined by the pupils. The teacher cannot fulfill his responsibilities along these lines unless he has a fairly complete and detailed knowledge of the learner's present level of proficiency. Schools need to explore ways of helping teachers get such information easily and quickly. More work needs to be done in the whole area of determining the existing status of learners with respect to social studies skills.

Conceptual learning is usually associated with the *content* of the social studies, while skills are often identified with the *processes* of learning. Skills learning does not necessarily result from the study of social studies subjects. For example, the teaching of history does not insure that students are developing a sense of time and chronology; nor does the teaching of geography necessarily indicate that pupils are developing a sense of place and space. A social studies unit may or may not help pupils develop group-process, problem-solving, or critical-thinking skills. The specific content has little to do with how well the skills are taught and used. A learner may read, evaluate, think critically, work in groups, use maps, and organize ideas equally well if he studies geography, history, economics, or government. In skills teaching, the vital elements are how the teacher organizes his class; what kinds of learning experiences he provides for his learners; how specifically he plans an instructional program to enhance skills growth; and the quality of human relations within the classroom; rather than the precise nature of the social studies content used.

This is not to say that content is unimportant in learning skills. The skills are the tools which the learner uses in his pursuit of conceptual learning in the social studies. The skills, therefore, cannot and should not be taught apart from a content framework. One does not read reading; he does not solve a problem unless one is identified; nor does he organize and interpret ideas that do not exist. Pupils do not learn to think critically by thinking critical thoughts about nothing in particular. Skills have no meaning if they are divorced from content. While skills are developed through the use of carefully selected teaching processes which will foster their growth, they are intimately related to the content of the program.

The ultimate object of the school's program is to prepare young people for life in a democratic society. The primary grade child who today is working with other children on a social studies project may one day be working with other adults on a community, state, or national problem. The high school student who is now reading his classroom periodical critically will one day be reading the editorial page of his local newspaper or reading a national weekly news magazine. The real test of the effectiveness of the school's program will come in the future, when the pupil of today must apply his skills as he encounters situations which necessitate their use. The school obviously cannot follow the student throughout his lifetime to appraise the quality of its skills program. What it can do, however, is to test the strength of its skills program by observing how well its pupils make use of those learnings within the school setting.

The school not only provides instruction in important learnings but also serves as a proving ground for the application of these learnings. Within the school environment, problem-solving and decision-making situations can be carefully controlled. Errors in judgment or wrong decisions rarely have disastrous consequences. In life outside the school, however, decision making and problem solving are much more critical. The skills needed to resolve many of the problems encountered in life are the ones with which the social studies deal. Consequently, the school seeks to bring the student's skill development to a level that will make it possible for him to do creative problem solving on his own throughout his lifetime. Perhaps much of what the pupil learns in the social studies will wear thin or become obsolete. But skills learned in school continue to be functional indefinitely, or for so long as they are used. Skills are among the most permanent of the learnings.

Section FOUR

Values and the Valuing Process

*T*he role of values and of the valuing process in social studies education is emerging as one of the major concerns of curriculum planners and teachers in this field. To a degree this emergence reflects the concerns of the larger society that has been struggling with a reexamination of its basic values in recent years. The whole matter of values education is extremely complex, partly because so little is known about how values are learned, partly because of the individual and personal nature of value preferences, and partly because of the lack of clarity of the role of the school in promoting preferred values.

Schools have often avoided dealing with the values question on the basis of maintaining a position of objectivity. Not infrequently when teachers have come to grips with values conflicts in a realistic way, they have done so at some considerable professional risk. There has been little to encourage a teacher to deal with social studies topics in ways other than those that would be considered "safe." It has been generally understood that there are certain issues and topics that are simply off limits for study in public school classrooms.

As thinking and decision making grow in importance as major outcomes of social studies education, it is clearly impossible to continue to avoid value issues. Indeed, value considerations are central to the whole thinking and decision-making process. This cannot help but have a desirable effect on social studies instruction. A major criticism of social studies programs of the past has been their blandness, doubtless arising from attempts to keep them "objective" and "safe."

The opening of the values area as a legitimate and necessary concern of social studies education does not, of course, provide the teacher with license to project his or her own value preferences on those he teaches. Neither

234

does it mean that classrooms will constantly be embroiled in bitter controversy arising from value differences. It does mean that the teacher and pupils must recognize that there is a value dimension to most of what is studied in the social studies and that to ignore it is unrealistic. It means, too, that pupils need to be provided opportunities to explore and clarify their own values relating to issues appropriate to their age and maturity. These and other issues relating to values and valuing are discussed by the authors in the articles that follow.

Values Education

JOHN JAROLIMEK

In the spring of 1970 on a small college campus in the West a group of students ran the American flag up a pole upside down. Another group objected and one of its members climbed the pole and brought the flag down. This precipitated a major altercation, and in the melee that followed, the flag was torn apart and local police had to be called to quell the disturbance. Although these young people were living in the year 1970 and had the advantage of thirteen to sixteen years of formal education, their ability to resolve value conflicts was evidently little better than that of their fore-bears who inhabited the earth many thousands of years ago—long before there were schools and formal education, to say nothing of social studies education.

It seems incredible that man has made so little headway in values educa-tion and conflict resolution considering the amount of attention that has been given to these matters through the years. All of the world's major religions concern themselves with values development. The writings of philosophers, poets, and playwrights are almost entirely values-based. Every society has established ideas about rightness and wrongness and devises ways to instill those values in its young and ways to enforce behavior codes based on those values. Almost without exception societies today, as they have for thousands of years, embrace a system of values that rejects killing, stealing, lying, and cheating. But men everywhere keep on killing, stealing, lying, and cheating. One can hardly believe that our own nation, which embraces and even demonstrates humanitarian values in so many ways, actually mass produces bullets, rifles, mortars, artillery, aircraft, and bombs designed specifically to kill human beings. Moreover, it maintains expensive and sophisticated training programs to prepare its men to do the killing. Thus, while we invest a million dollars on cancer research presumably to preserve human life, we spend billions on systems designed to destroy life. The same policeman who will risk a bone-breaking fall to rescue a stranded kitten on a rooftop will shoot and kill a fleeing burglar. The same society that becomes incensed over the killing of baby seals for their pelts seems unconcerned about living hells called prisons or, even more ironically, "correctional institutions." The same community that is aroused over the

John Jarolimek is Professor of Education at the University of Washington, Seattle.

This selection is the Preface to *Values Education,* the 41st Yearbook of the Na-tional Council for the Social Studies, Lawrence E. Metcalf, Editor, 1971.

Reprinted with permission of the National Council for the Social Studies and John Jarolimek.

spread of venereal disease among its young will not allow sex education in its school curriculum. The same citizen who proudly carries the flag as a patriotic gesture in the Fourth of July parade later in the week in the barber shop voices his views regarding what should be done with those who engage in protests: "Shoot the bastards!"

Thus we are brought to the profound enigma of the creature called "man." Why is it that our behavior individually and collectively is often inconsistent, or even contrary, to the values we profess? Is man by nature simply a scoundrel who cannot or will not conduct his life in accordance with humanitarian values? Or is man an inept learner when it comes to values education? Did man develop differentially, with his cognitive powers developing much more rapidly than his capacity to cope with corresponding value conflicts? Or have the exhortative strategies used to teach values through the thousands of years of man's history been inadequate or ineffective?

Among the recent finds in the archaeological diggings in Africa was a human skull crushed in a way to suggest that this man of antiquity had fallen victim to the evil ways of his fellow man. The same thing could happen and does happen almost any night in any of the large cities of this nation today. Surely a nation that can send men to the moon and return them safely should have the capacity to teach its people how to resolve value conflicts in more acceptable ways than crushing each other's skulls—either psychologically or literally.

The time is overdue when an all-out effort must be made to find productive approaches to values education and conflict resolution. In the yearbook, *Values Education: Rationale, Strategies, and Procedures,* a step is taken in that direction. Professor Metcalf in his Introduction cautions the reader that he may find it hard going. This is as it should be, for we are dealing with an incredibly complex subject. If the problem were an easy one, man would have solved it long ago. Too frequently simplistic proposals have been advanced as strategies for values education.

Valuing: A Curriculum Imperative

ANNA OCHOA

A free society is a multi-faceted entity. Its collage of individuals demonstrate an unfathomed range of interests, attitudes, opinions, and values. To most Americans this condition represents the fruition of democratic goals.

That individual commitments should be freely derived not only follows logically but is consonant with this nation's basic documents. It is especially startling then, that, after nearly two hundred years of the American experiment, vocal and vehement citizens will decry the fact that schools have failed to instill in the young a particular set of values prized by these critics. The fallacy of their position escapes them.

"The schools are not teaching loyalty."
"That teacher is a John Bircher and should be fired!"
"The schools are encouraging lawlessness."

Such comments are not rare or isolated. Any high school principal, social studies teacher, or school superintendent could document the fact that such criticisms are legion.

To argue that schools should teach loyalty, fire faculty who hold discrepant views, or avoid discussing vital issues directly violates free speech and denies the opportunity for free choice. Additionally, such arguments are predicated on a fear that the democratic system is not strong enough to stand the test of dissenting views. Failing to recognize this assumption, the advocates of such arguments would typically pride themselves as the most patriotic of citizens.

It is easy to scapegoat protesting parents as the cause of the school's inertia. However, educators who have not countered such views with a well-reasoned defense of school practices are equally to blame. Too often educators, themselves, have not clarified their own position on the role of values and of the valuing process in the curriculum. Consequently, they bend far too willingly to community critics.

Anna Ochoa is an Associate Professor of Social Studies Education at The Florida State University, Tallahassee.

Reprinted from *The College of Education Record* 35:69–74, 1969, with permission of the University of Washington and Anna Ochoa.

How Should the Schools Handle the Values Question?

Are there any values that are so fundamental to the development of individuals, as well as to the construct of a free society, that the schools must teach toward them?

With one significant contingency, the position supported here is that there are two tenets that are sufficiently basic that the school's curriculum must embrace them as instructional imperatives. Commitment to the *rational process* and to the *dignity of man* form the base of the school's focus on values.

Actions that have their basis in emotion, or those that unthinkingly accept the position of authorities, are not independently or intelligently derived. If one's personal behavior is predicated on the Puritan ethic, because opportunity to examine other ethical bases has been absent, such action cannot be described as the result of free choice. More pertinent for the school's purpose, if an individual adheres to democratic practices only because his significant-others (teachers, parents, and peers) have always told him to, he is not directing his own behavior. Instead, he is merely nodding passively to the pressure of authority. To rest one's behavior solely on beliefs acquired by faith, emotional conditioning, or authority seems to deny the potential of the human capacity for reason, for thoughtful analysis, and for objectivity.

This is not to suggest that man will not make some decisions on the basis of faith. It could well be argued that all human acts embrace an element of faith. Submitting to medical treatment serves as an appropriate illustration. In many cases a patient cannot know precisely why a given medical procedure will effect cure. Yet, he has no realistic alternative but to agree to treatment. Doing so, demonstrates an act of faith in the power of science and the expertise of his physician. Total knowing seems beyond man's power. However, support is given here to the maximum development of man's rational capacity. To whatever extent he is able, he must act on the basis of knowledge.

Further, the rational process facilitates choice. If man is required to make choices, a condition inherent in a democratic society, he should know why he chooses as he does. The rules of logic, the data and conclusions of scholarly observations, and the principles of objectivity give man the power to predict and examine the consequences of action in powerful ways. Equipped with such intellectual tools, the individual can be described as being in an independent and forceful position. He is no longer dependent on the views of others; he has the ability to frame and defend his own set of values.

Schools could profitably engage in an assessment of those procedures that ask youngsters to accept unquestioningly the decisions of authority. Young children are frequently told that some of their behavior is "good" or "bad."

They are seldom told why. Even more rarely are they asked to establish behavioral criteria of their own or to predict the consequences of their actions. Insisting on compliant behavior is not building independent, self-reliant, or rational behavior.

Individually, children will respond in a variety of ways to inculcative strategies. Those who have strong needs for adult approval will probably submit willingly to the authoritative demands. The approval received for such passive compliance will reinforce dependence and conforming behavior. From this writer's view, even if such strategies work, they cannot be used in schools that function in an open society without violating the basic assumptions on which both the schools and society are predicated.

Other children who demonstrate a sharper self-identity may at first grudgingly comply. Later they may quietly disobey or openly violate the wishes of authority. Eventually, they may drop out physically or psychically. Those who have "opted-out" appear to be an ever-increasing number of today's youth. If the school asks the young to act in unthinking ways, it is probably encouraging conformity, rebellion, and apathy–qualities that run counter to democratic beliefs.

Schools need to realize that emphasis on the rational process will expose certain public and personal practices. For example, denial of open housing or employment opportunities are two public practices that cannot be rationally defended. Neither can war nor police brutality receive reasonable support. Curricula that embody the rational process may find themselves at loggerheads with some traditions and norms in contemporary society.

The schools' attention to the rational process is itself subject to the rational test. This point is critical in defining a preferred value. If the rational process cannot defend itself, it is no longer viable. Before the completion of a school's curriculum, students should focus on an examination of rationalism. Such analysis demands comparison with other ways of knowing. The use of faith, intuition, and authority must be analyzed. Not meeting this provision results in the indoctrination of the rational process.

The other fundamental value submitted here as a basis for curriculum planning is the *dignity of man*. If values held by individuals would deny the individuality of others, they cannot be defended. The survival of an open society seems to rest on this notion. To make decisions without respect for other human beings serves to deny one's own humanity. Further, man's dignity is central to the democratic system. The dignity of man, as a value, must also be subjected to the rational test.

Valuing As a Curriculum Imperative

Valuing is a crucial component of the school's curriculum. Its essential quality rests on two functions. First, and most important, the valuing process is central to the establishment of individual identity. Second, the valuing process is fundamental to the development of social responsibility. Individuals need to feel capable of resolving value-laden issues before they can participate effectively in a complex and pluralistic society.

Schools have traditionally oriented their programs toward the development of good citizens. Much emphasis has been placed on instilling certain political and social norms in the young. The position reflected here emphasizes valuing not for the making of good citizens and not to serve societal ends directly; rather, it stresses that attention to valuing seeks to fulfill the needs of individuals.

Before an individual can function in an autonomous manner in an open society, he must be able to answer the central identity question: "Who am I?" If precision and uniqueness do not characterize an individual's self-concept, then his identity has probably not been clarified. An individual who does not perceive himself as having important qualities that distinguish him from others and who cannot describe these accurately, in all likelihood, does not have a clear understanding of who he is.

Raths, Harmin, and Simon [1] provide a continuum that describes the clarity of an individual's relationship to society on a clear to unclear dimension. They characterize individuals who fall near the clear extreme of the continuum as purposeful, positive, enthusiastic, and proud. Conversely, those who cluster in the unclear zone are flighty, uncertain, and inconsistent. These latter attributes can be too frequently evidenced in the composition of contemporary society. Individuals who lack a clear delineation of their value system are likely to exhibit ambivalent and contradictory behavior.

What, then, is essential for establishing identity? Predicating identity on uniqueness demands an answer to a more refined question: "How am I different?" The locus of one's difference lies in behavior. What does an individual do that makes him different? More importantly, what does he value that makes him behave differently? The ability to respond to this last question appears to be a fundamental condition for identity clarification. A valuing system and skill in the valuing process are the basis on which such personal identity rests.

What kind of behavior can be expected from an adult who can distinguish himself from others and who can explain why he believes as he does? Behavior that demonstrates this independence is seen when an individual has the courage to disagree when placed in a group of his significant-others. His disagreement will not be arbitrary or thoughtless. He will continue to hold his views only as long as he can defend them rationally.

Individuals who seldom or never deviate from the patterns of their group associations appear to be the product of one of two defective systems. On the one hand, some individuals demonstrate a conditioning to acquiescence. Fundamentally, they lack the emotional capacity and intellectual strength

---

[1] Louis E. Raths, Merrill Harmin, and Sidney B. Simon, *Values and Teaching* (Columbus, Ohio: Charles E. Merrill Books, Inc., 1966), pp. 1–12.

to challenge the group. Other individuals may "know better," but their lack of confidence inhibits their open disagreement. Both demonstrate cases of undefined identity. Eric Fromm forcefully describes the condition of modern man as he states:

> [Modern man] would be free to act according to his own will if he knew what he wanted, thought and felt. But he does not know. He conforms to anonymous authorities and adopts a self which is not his. The more he does this, the more powerless he feels, the more he is forced to conform.[2]

It is important to observe that the behavior that characterizes individuals with a clear identity is totally consonant with the assumptions that underlie a democratic society. A democracy asks that man act and choose freely. However, political ideology, legal documents, or judicial rulings cannot, by themselves, create a free society. If man is not emotionally independent, it is likely that he will default on the opportunities offered by his political system.

If this means-ends relationship between man's emotional component and his political behavior is a viable one, the purpose of schools, committed to serving the ends of a democratic society, should be clear. The realization of one's identity through the valuing process should become a central educational objective.

The accompanying diagram shows the school's dilemma.

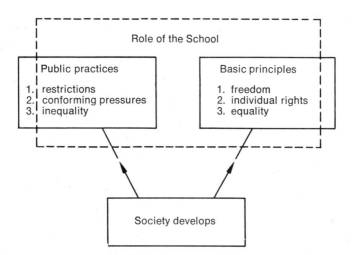

Society has developed, over the course of time, a set of guiding principles and a set of public practices. In some ways these are contradictory. How does the school establish its role? If it attempts to conform the values of students to basic principles, it contributes to allegations of hypocrisy. Stu-

[2] Eric Fromm, *Escape From Freedom* (New York: Holt, Rinehart and Winston, 1945), p. 281.

dents are later confronted with reconciling discrepancies on their own. Their resulting disillusionment may destroy the efforts of the school.

If the schools choose to accept the status quo—public practices—as their model, and do not relate these to the intended goals of society, they would be less than honest as well.

It seems clear that the school program must embrace both conditions. It should make clear the intent of societal goals and shortcomings of some of its practices. Colloquially, it must "tell it like it is" and compare this condition with basic principles. Contradictions and inconsistencies must be honestly faced and examined. Anything less will place the school in a false and hypocritical position.

Underlying the relationship between the school and society is society's strength to stand up to exposure. It appears that critics who charge the school with failing to instill certain values lack the capacity to face contradiction. A recent article in *Phi Delta Kappan* [3] focused on whether or not the position of conscientious objectors should be discussed in high schools. Those who oppose such open discussion are operating on an ostrich-like assumption. They conclude that if students are sheltered from unpopular ideas, these contradictory value positions will somehow fade away. If the public as a whole were to reflect such an attitude, this in itself would be conclusive evidence that the nation is not yet mature enough, nor strong enough to face the challenge of the rational process and human dignity.

The school's service to a society that seeks to become free and open is based on what it does for individuals. Seeking certain preferred societal commitments without allowing pupils to rationally examine controversy will contribute to forgetting the individual in the process.

The individual in contemporary America is faced by the impersonalization wrought by today's sophisticated technology. It is easy for identity to be lost in the operation of massive bureaucratic institutions. Government, as it enlarges, removes itself further and further from individual influence. The mass media, all too readily available, bombard citizens with canned opinions. If man chooses to live as an automaton, he can probably exist in today's society without ever having an independent thought. If man so chooses, both democracy and the individual have been denied. Schools must act in ways that enlarge the capacities of young people to confront these massive forces and deal with them intelligently.

---

[3] Dean Allen, "Responsibilities of the High School for Providing Information on Conscientious Objection to War," *Phi Delta Kappan, 50,* 145–48 (November 1968).

Values in the Curriculum

MICHAEL SCRIVEN

Two points are vital to the whole question of dealing with values in the curriculum, and both of them are almost completely at odds with common views about this problem. The first point is that the vast majority of value disputes are capable of settlement by rational arguments. The common slogan that "one person's values are as good as another's" is usually false and is usually an indication of insufficient training in empirical investigation or logical analysis.

The second point is that the analysis and resolution of value disputes is one of the most difficult intellectual problems that we ever put in front of the child in the course of the entire curriculum. A tremendous job lies ahead of us in developing methods and materials to teach teachers and children how to deal with this complex matter.

The Place of Ultimate Values

In disputes about what is "right," and what is "better," and what "ought" to be done, the discussion frequently ends with the disputants in disagreement about the issue, but in agreement that the argument cannot be carried further. A common conclusion is that "You can't dispute basic values." Let us use the common term "ultimate values" to refer to these values that are unarguable, in the sense that no further facts or logic can be mustered to show whether they are sound or unsound.

It is possible that there is no such thing as an ultimate value. One of the best philosophers in the country once said that he had never, in the course of any debate on any moral issue, found a disputant who could not be shown, at every point, to be appealing to yet further considerations of fact or logic. The stopping-point of value-disputes, then, is very often a point of disagreement about a complex matter of fact, such as the actual effects of pornography on grade schoolers, and not a dispute about ultimate values at all.

The question of whether ultimate values *exist* is not very important, however, if it is true, as the author believes, that *the great majority* of value

Michael Scriven is Professor of Education at the University of California, Berkeley.

Reprinted from the *Social Science Education Consortium Newsletter* 2:1–3, 1966, with permission of the Social Science Education Consortium, Inc., and Michael Scriven.

disputes can be settled by empirical investigation and logical analysis. The educational task is to push back the frontiers of analysis as far as possible, not to worry about whether there is a last frontier. There is an interesting analogy in the physical sciences. The status of determinism need not be settled before we agree that the right approach is to seek for causes of all phenomena with all our effort.

Education About Values vs. Indoctrination in Values

It follows from what has been said that most training of children in the realm of value disputes should have the purpose of helping them to become more skillful in clarifying issues, in verifying facts on which they believe their value judgments rest, in analyzing the soundness of the logic by which one value is based on another, and in examining the logical consistency among their values. This enormous task will keep us all busy for a long time to come, without bringing us to insoluble problems involving ultimate values. And one can only deny that this is the approach we should be taking by showing that ultimate values are encountered early rather than late in the process of tracing back the logical underpinning of everyday value disputes.

Let us take the hypothetical example of a sixth grade class discussing a particular issue about freedom of speech. Assume that, in the midst of an explosive social situation, the making of a scheduled political speech by a member of the opposition would involve a large risk of rioting and loss of life. Should the authorities prevent the speech?

A common approach, in the rare cases where this kind of material is discussed at all, is to earnestly ask the class what they think should be done. Should the sixth-graders' views on this subject be regarded as important, interesting, valid? No, no more than their views on the merits of Freudian psychology or the quantum theory. Can the teacher tell the children what the right answer is? Probably not, since her views may have no better factual and analytical basis than those of the children.

One way to begin to analyze the practical problem mentioned, where the value of life has to be weighed against the value of free speech, is to imagine what it would be like to abandon one of these values. If, for example, we abandoned freedom of speech as a value, what new institutions or system of rules would be required or possible to ensure a well-informed populace? What would be the logical consequences, for other values in our system, of abandoning the right to speak when speaking threatens life, limb, or property? What facts would be needed to assess the consequences of the change? How would it be decided whether to ban the speech? What redress for wrong decisions would exist?

The educational process suggested here has nothing to do with indoctrination in its usual sense of an effort to instill particular values or viewpoints other than by rational proof. In some contexts, indeed, indoctrination is taken to mean the instilling of particular values *plus* a resistance to rational examination of those values; sound educational policy must explicitly condemn indoctrination in that sense.

A third and perverse definition of indoctrination is sometimes encountered, according to which *any* process that affects the values held by individuals is indoctrination. By the first definition, indoctrination is nonscientific, which does not necessarily make it a bad thing. By the second definition, indoctrination is anti-rational, and therefore a bad thing for those who value rationality, as educators must. By the third definition, indoctrination is neutral with regard to rationality and morality, which may or may not be flouted by such indoctrination. Unfortunately, the term is all too often used without analysis, as a pejorative term to discourage the application of scientific methods to the study of values, and it then becomes a tool for irrational and immoral ends. Such use is irrational because it denies the use of rational methods to problems for which they are appropriate. It is immoral because it stands in the way of moral progress.

Our goal should be the straightforward development of cognitive skills for handling value disputes—not persuasion or indoctrination in the usual sense. Moral reasoning and the moral behavior it indicates should be taught and taught about, if for no other reason than that it is immoral to keep students ignorant of the empirical and logical bases behind the morality which is behind the law and the institutions which incorporate this country's virtues and permit its vices. But in addition to this intellectual payoff is the practical benefit to a society of possessing members who are skilled in making value judgments. Such a society becomes a moral community, offering important benefits to all of its members.

Values in the Curriculum

Values in the curriculum should not be a wholly separate subject, but should have the status of a pervasive substructure, like critical thinking and clear expression. Value analysis work should begin in kindergarten and continue, with problems of increasing complexity, through high school. We can begin at what may be called the level of practicality in value analysis—the evaluation of products. Then, we might go on to the area of personal problems where questions arise about behavior that is wise or foolish, sensible or not. We can talk about good and bad behavior, meaning, at this "prudence level," good or bad for you. We can then progress to the area of social problems—morality in law and politics—and finally to the level of international problems, where we come to the root question of whether or not international conflict is a domain for morality, a domain where moral judgments other than prudential ones can be given sense or made to stick.

Such a sequence suggests itself naturally, and presents many advantages. Even at the early level of the evaluation of consumer goods, there are rather sophisticated procedures and distinctions which will carry throughout the rest of the curriculum. But at that early stage, the basic moral problems do not yet need to be faced. As the student grows older and the subjects more complex, more practical ethical problems are introduced, in the course of teaching other things.

A Basis for a Moral System

As teachers and students push the logical analysis of values farther and farther, the question of ultimate values will arise more and more insistently and, eventually, perhaps even legitimately. If an ultimate value must be found, the best candidate for the position is "equality of rights." This is a value to which our schools and our nation are already politically committed, and thus has the great potential advantage of being reinforced by the prevailing mores. It is not open to criticism on the ground that appeal to it in the public schools violates the separation of church and state. Equally important, "equality of rights" is a value upon which a whole system of morality can be built, a complete rational system based on this single premise.

There is not time here to spell out the moral system that can be based on equality of rights, but one can say that it is a system very like the humanist tradition of this country, as well as much of the Christian and Buddhist traditions. Neither is there time to describe the full meaning of equality of rights, although it is essentially embodied in the provisions of our constitution and our laws on voting and due process. While there is no objection to giving "equality of rights" the temporary status of an ultimate value, a strong argument can be made for supporting this value on rational grounds, by appeal to probability, game theory and welfare considerations. As indicated earlier, it is still an open question whether any values are needed that go beyond that which is supportable by rational appeal to logical analysis.

Techniques

There are two dimensions to teaching how to handle values: the cognitive and the affective. We have been discussing mainly the cognitive side of values. In cognitive training, the methodology is that of the logician and the lawyer. In the analysis of legal systems, such questions arise as, What would be the conflicts if everyone followed this rule? What exceptions can be justified for this rule? and, What cases are subsumed under this general principle? Still other questions, the answers to which require factual materials from the social sciences, are, What would be the consequences of breaking this rule? What alternative rules might serve the same function? What is the significance of a particular custom to those who support it?

But there needs to be moral motivation as well as moral insight, which brings us to the affective side. The basic motivational training for a moral system based on equality of rights is closely connected with the training needed for understanding the positions and motives of other people. It requires seeing yourself in the other person's shoes and fostering of empathy and sympathy. Role-playing is appropriate in a great variety of historical, political and social situations. It encourages full use of materials available to support the role, and requires an active effort to understand the position of the person whose role is assumed; it is an excellent way to promote sympathy, and hence to promote moral behavior under the axiom of equal rights. Other techniques that will help to put the student into another's position are the use of graphic audio-visual materials, field experience, interviews and discussions.

Materials

With few exceptions, there should be no separate materials for value-training, just as there should be no separate subject matter. For the most part, materials should be multi-purpose. Some examples follow.

In elementary science, students could begin early to evaluate the relative merits of instruments. They could, for example, construct their own balances, and discuss with each other the relative merits of criteria of sensitivity, capacity, cost and ease of use.

Another example is the use of materials from American constitutional law. Constitutional law embodies much of the nation's moral code. It represents an attempt to create a just or moral society, and its legal aspects give good training in the study of moral analysis. Since constitutional law also reflects much of a nation's history, it provides for moral analysis an ideal entree to the schools' history offerings.

Conclusion

We need an approach to values in the curriculum which is pedagogically more explicit than at present, but not necessarily handled explicitly in a separate part of the curriculum. We should train students to assess alternative arguments about values in a consistent and intelligent way, and to push the rational analysis of values as far back as they can. Seldom if ever should a discussion of values end with the conclusion that the view of the student— or of the teacher—is as good as anyone else's. A value judgment is as good as the reasons for it, and as weak as the reasons that support alternative views.

A Strategy for Developing Values

JAMES RATHS

This paper deals with a strategy for helping children to develop their own values. Recognition of the importance of children's values has been with us for years. "A great and continuing purpose of education has been the development of moral and spiritual values" (5). With this pronouncement, the Educational Policies Commission opened its 1957 report. As important as developing values seems to be to the DAR and the VFW, to the FBI and the HUAC, the area is even more important to us as educators, it seems to me, because of its implications for the learning process. Let me briefly spell out some of these implications.

First, Kubie (12) suggests that learning is swift, spontaneous and automatic. At times, learning is blocked—many times by what Kubie calls preconscious motives and drives. He recommends that teachers concern themselves with developing self-knowledge on their students' part to remove blocks to learning—to free children so that they may learn in a spontaneous fashion. Second, Ginsburg (7) suggests that good mental health, assumed to be a necessary condition for learning, is merely a process of living up to a set of values. Finally, several researchers, following the ideas of Louis Raths, have identified pupil behaviors associated with a lack of values (9; 11; 13; 14). These classroom behaviors, including over-conforming, indifference, flightiness and several others, it is argued, interfere with concentration, involvement, and openness in the learning process. Therefore, value development, it seems, should be one of the many central concerns of teachers.

While the area of value development has been a major concern of edu-

James Raths is Chairman of the Department of Elementary Education at the University of Illinois, Urbana.

Reprinted from *Educational Leadership* 21:509–514, 544, 1964, with permission of the Association for Supervision and Curriculum Development and James Raths.

cators for many years, the public and many professional people, too, have had a feeling that our efforts in this area have not been too effective. The studies summarized by Jacob in his *Changing Values in College* tend to support this hunch (8). Teachers have been unable, it seems, to translate their genuine concerns about the value problem into effective patterns of action in their classrooms.

Essentially, there are four basic approaches to the development of values current in our schools. These methods include the teaching of values by the lecture method, by the use of peer-group pressure, by finding or setting examples for children to respect and emulate, and by a reward and punishment rationale. These methods are neither mutually exclusive nor exhaustive of all the approaches we use in schools, but they seem to me to be among the most prevalent in our classrooms.

Methods in Use

Perhaps the most common approach is the use of lecture methods. Teachers seem ever ready to tell students what they should believe or how they ought to act. It is easy to burlesque this method in harsh tones. Actually, it may be employed by the kindest, most sincere teachers as well as by the overly self-righteous, would-be reformers found on some school faculties. While it is possible to cite cases in which a lecture or even a "bawling out" did bring about changes in students' values, basically this method is not too successful. Attesting to this is the common cry of many teachers—"You can't *tell* those kids anything." In general, this remark has been found to be accurate.

Teachers' judgments and convictions seem, from a student's point of view, to be out of the framework of things. (Analogously, it may be akin to the feelings teachers in the field have of the "should's and should not's" of professors from schools and colleges of education.) Jones (10) has suggested a basis for explaining the ineffectiveness of the lecture method. He states that a teacher must be emotionally accepted by his students before he can contribute much to their development of self. By their moralizing and preaching, teachers may set themselves apart emotionally from their students. To the extent that teachers are not accepted by their students, it can be presumed that they will have little effect upon students' values. Students may leave the lecture all full of enthusiasm about what the teacher said, but they may not internalize what they admire and all too often they do not.

A second approach to the value development problem has been in the main popularized by exponents of the core curriculum. During a special period of the school day, students address themselves to self-evaluation and group evaluations. They are encouraged to speak freely, frankly and openly to the entire class judging their own behavior, criticizing group performances and perhaps pledging themselves to future improvements. In general, such statements are accepted by the teacher with little or no comment while other pupils are free to make suggestions, recommendations and comments.

The pressure of group approval or disapproval is a powerful force in bringing about changes in values. This method seems successful in some cases but it has some disturbing by-products. The most distressing of these is the tacit approval of the teacher of the notion that group consensus is correct or at least worthy of very serious consideration. This method, in effect, helps develop "other-directed" persons. Another disadvantage inherent in this group technique is the passive role of the teacher. In a sense, the insight, experience and skills of the teacher are muted. In their place, naive students play the dominant role in value development, and they do it quite unconsciously.

A third approach for developing students' values is one of acquainting students with examples of exemplary behavior. Instances of model behavior may be drawn from history, literature, and legend or, more directly, from examples set by teachers.

Literature for all levels of schooling has been selected for the past several hundred years on the basis of the ethical and moral lessons with which it dealt. As in other methods discussed previously, some students are truly inspired by these vicarious experiences but we have little evidence that attributes found in a student's reading are readily transferred to daily life.

Teaching values by a living example is a related tactic. Here it is assumed that "values are caught, not taught." It is argued that as teachers demonstrate values students will learn to prize these values. Surely people have been inspired by the goodness of a teacher with whom they have had the good fortune to be associated. However, teachers, especially in secondary schools, have little opportunity to demonstrate many key values. Problems that represent the real issues of life rarely present themselves in a 50-minute subject-matter period in such a way that students can observe their teacher's handling of them. It would truly be unfortunate if we had to rely on this approach as the only positive way teachers can help youngsters develop a set of values.

A fourth method deals with indoctrination and habit formation. Here it is assumed that when students are required to follow rules and regulations, when they are punished for infractions and praised for obedience, they will take on the values associated with the requirements. We are all familiar, however, with what students do when they are free *not* to obey the rules.

It is my contention that these four methods are rather ineffective. Perhaps their relative ineffectiveness arises partially because they are based on the assumption that the knowledge of ethical and moral choices necessarily leads to ethical and moral conduct. As pointed out many years ago by John Dewey (4), this assumption has little basis in fact.

Yet more important, these methods seem intent on utilizing external factors, such as lectures or peer-group pressures, to develop values. Frieden-berg (6) analyzes the current problems in developing values as follows:

> . . . it is the inner discipline that is lacking; the school fails to provide a basis for it. The undisciplined behavior which sometimes results is often a sign of the anguish which results from having no core *of one's own.* [Emphasis added.]

The most promising approach would seem to be one that attempts to help each student build his own value system. This idea is supported by Allport (2) who asserts that no teaching is more important than that which contributes to a student's self. Clearly, this statement echoes the ideas of Kubie mentioned in the opening paragraphs. Are teachers able to help children in this way? B. O. Smith has said that teachers use little psycho-logical knowledge beyond that found in common sense. What knowledge can we, as teachers, use in this area? Louis Raths has developed a teaching method designed to provide some direction for teachers who are interested in helping students develop their own value systems (15; 16; 17).

Use of Clarification Procedures

The teacher's role in this method is neither that of preacher nor that of passive listener. Instead the teacher strives to (a) establish a climate of psychological safety, (b) apply a clarification procedure. An elaboration of these procedures follows.

ESTABLISHMENT OF PSYCHOLOGICAL SAFETY

Nonjudgmental Attitudes. It has been said that teachers have difficulty responding to an idea without saying, "That's good," "That's bad," or "What good is it?" To provide an atmosphere in which children will feel free to express themselves without threat of ridicule and derision, teachers must refrain from making harsh unnecessary judgments. Of course at times some judgments become necessary in situations in which the health and/or safety of students are threatened in any real sense.

Manifestations of Concern. While the teacher may be nonjudgmental, it is important for him to be concerned with the ideas expressed by his stu-dents. If the concern is apparently lacking, then often the number of student ideas shared with a teacher tends to diminish. Perhaps students are reluctant to share their ideas with someone who is not interested in them. One of the most effective ways to show concern for a student's ideas is to *listen* to them. Busy teachers sometimes overlook this basic and effective technique for communicating interest to their students. Another method for a teacher's communicating his concern for a student's ideas is to *remember* them. As a teacher is able to cite a student's idea in a later conversation, the student cannot help but feel genuinely flattered and impressed.

Opportunities for the Sharing of Ideas. Teachers must organize their courses in such ways that children have the opportunity to express their opinions, purposes, feelings, beliefs, hunches, goals and interests, about moral issues. These attitudinal-type statements may then be examined by the child who expressed them with the teacher acting somewhat as a catalytic agent in the process. Some methods used by teachers in various researches by classroom teachers include: (a) question-answer discussion periods involving moot questions for the class to consider; (b) special written assignments; (c) role-playing techniques; (d) behavior manifestations of individuals or groups that may indicate attitudes, e.g., cheating or being tardy.

The task of finding issues that children may react to is no small problem. While our lives are filled with many, many moral and ethical questions to consider, even within our formal disciplines, it is difficult to find these issues in our textbooks, or Weekly Readers. Alexander (1), a textbook consultant for the New York City schools, has found that "few or no serious problems" are present in our current textbooks.

CLARIFYING STRATEGIES

Asking Questions. The teacher may attempt to clarify the ideas elicited from his students by asking probing questions. The key criterion for selecting these questions is that they must be questions for which only the student knows the answer. Of course, to be effective they must be asked in a non-judgmental manner. If a student seems seriously challenged by one of the questions, the teacher should make efforts to "save face" by accepting his bewilderment. For example, the teacher may pass on by saying, "That's a hard question for anyone to answer, isn't it?" "Let's think about it for a while and maybe an answer will come to us later." A list of questions that a teacher may ask is included below. Of course, this list is not exhaustive, and teachers may add to it as they become more fluent in the use of this procedure.

1. Reflect back what the student has said and add, "Is that what you mean?"
2. Reflect back what the student has said with distortions and add, "Is that what you mean?"
3. "How long have you felt (acted) that way?"
4. "Are you glad you think (act) that way?"
5. "In what way is that a good idea?"
6. "What is the source of your idea?"
7. "Should everyone believe that?"
8. "Have you thought of some alternatives?"
9. "What are some things you have done that reflect this idea of yours?"
10. "Why do you think so?"

11. "Is this what you really think?"
12. "Did you do this on purpose?"
13. Ask for definitions of key words.
14. Ask for examples.
15. Ask if this position is consistent with a previous one he has taken.

It is important that teachers ask these questions of students who express ideas with which they agree as well as with those students who express ideas with which they disagree.

Coding Written Work. Researchers have found the coding of written work very effective in value clarifying. Whenever students seem to express an attitude, belief, goal, purpose, interest, or aspiration, teachers may mark a V+ or V— in the margin to reflect this idea back to the student. This code works much like other more familiar codes we already use in our schools, e.g., WW for wrong word, or SP for misspelled word. There is one crucial difference. When a teacher marks WW in the margin, there usually is a wrong word. When a teacher marks V+ in the margin, it is understood that she is really asking, "Do you believe this?" or "Do you want to change it?"

Acceptance Without Judgment. It has been found that teachers feel awkward trying to draw the clarification exchange to a close. The verbal interaction between teacher and student is not to win an argument or to gain a debating point. The purpose of the exchange is to clarify students' ideas. It is important that teachers find a way to accept the students' ideas without communicating agreement or praise of them. In a sense, the exchange does not have an ending. Neither the teacher nor the student arrives at a conclusion. Neither is there a need for summarizing. Questions left unanswered are thought about and dwelt on by the student (and perhaps the teacher) at night before going to sleep, or during moments of quiet during the day. Some ways that have been found successful in closing an exchange are as follows:

1. Silence with a nod.
2. "Uh-huh."
3. "I see."
4. "I understand you better now."
5. "I can see how you would feel that way."
6. "I understand."
7. "I can see that it was difficult for you to decide that way."

In summary, the clarification procedure developed by Louis Raths attempts to elicit from students statements of an attitudinal nature and to clarify these statements for the student. By developing an emotional acceptance of himself on the part of his students, and asking students questions which will serve to clarify their own purposes, goals, attitudes, beliefs, etc., teachers can play an effective role in developing values in their classrooms.

This procedure can be time consuming or it may also take just a few seconds. For example, consider the following hypothetical exchange:

Student: I hate math.
Teacher: You have never liked math?
Student: Well, I did like it at one time.
Teacher: What changed your mind?
Student: I don't know.
Teacher: Oh.

Without trying to lecture the student about what he "ought" to like, without preaching about the dangers inherent in not liking math, the teacher is attempting to help the student understand his own preferences and values.

In passing, it may be appropriate to add that several researches (9; 11; 13; 14) have successfully attempted to test these ideas in classrooms in New York State and Wisconsin. Other studies are needed, of course, to test further the efficacy of this procedure. The experiences of a number of researches in this field suggest also that learning to use the process of clarifying is not easy. It is clearly a difficult matter to enter into a significant interaction with a student. The problem is much less that of identifying with a student, but one of identifying with the student's concerns, of listening, and of taking seriously what he has said and reacting thoughtfully to it.

It must be clear that teachers who apply the clarification procedure must have a tremendous respect for their students. As teachers agree or disagree with students' expressed ideas they must be able to consider them as tenable ones to hold. If teachers believe it is their role to "convert" students to a "right way" of thinking, then it seems they must basically disrespect the views their students hold now. The distinction I am trying to make is one between accepting and respecting. It would seem possible for me to respect the views of a colleague, let us say, without accepting those views. This is the spirit that I believe must dominate a teacher's conversations with his students. Of course, this statement must be modified to the extent that a student's views may threaten the health or safety of himself or society. It is my contention that such cases are rare in our classrooms. Yet there is still plenty of room for many safe differences of opinion and behavior between students and teachers.

Most of us have become accustomed to the association of teaching with changes in student behavior. Too frequently, quite without being aware of it, we look for "instant" changes. We hope for miracles on the "values front." We do not pay enough attention to the fact that it took many years for our students to learn their present almost valueless behavior, and that it may take a long sustained effort to help students to develop serious purposes and aspirations through the clarifying processes. For a free society, opportunities to clarify and to choose must be created again and again.

Norman Cousins (3) has written about his concern for the predatory quality of life in human form. He suggests that what makes our society so much like a jungle is the misfits who exert power over honest men.

There are those . . . who insist on projecting their warped ideas to the people around them. They are the agents of chaos. . . . Maybe this is what makes a jungle a jungle.

Cousins continues to say that the way out of the jungle is not just emptying it of these misfits. "There must be some notion about what is to take the place of the jungle. That is why ideals and goals are the most practical things in the world. They conquer the jungle, make men mobile, and convert humans from fawning and frightened animals into thinkers and builders." As teachers learn to develop the ideals, goals and values of students by applying the clarification procedures outlined in this paper, they may perhaps become truly "influential Americans."

References

1. Albert Alexander, "The Gray Flannel Cover of the American History Text." *Social Education 24*:11; 1960.
2. Gordon Allport, *Becoming: Basic Considerations for a Psychology of Personality*. New Haven, Conn.: Yale University Press, 1955.
3. Norman Cousins, "Hoffa, Hegel, and Hoffer." *Saturday Review*, April 20, 1963.
4. John Dewey, *Moral Principles in Education*. Boston: Houghton Mifflin, 1909.
5. Educational Policies Commission. *Moral and Spiritual Values in the Public Schools*. Washington, D.C.: National Education Association, 1957.
6. Edgar Z. Friedenberg, *The Vanishing Adolescent*. New York: Dell, 1962.
7. Sol W. Ginsburg, "Values and the Psychiatrist." *American Journal of Orthopsychiatry 20*:466; 1950.
8. Philip E. Jacob, *Changing Values in College*. New York: Harper & Row, 1957.
9. Arthur Jonas, "A Study of the Relationship of Certain Behaviors of Children to Emotional Needs, Values, and Thinking." Unpublished Ed.D. thesis, New York University, 1960.
10. Vernon Jones, "Character Education," in *Encyclopedia of Educational Research*, Chester Harris, ed. New York: Macmillan, Inc., 1960.
11. Albert Klevan, "An Investigation of a Methodology of Value Clarification: Its Relationship to Consistency of Thinking, Purposefulness, and Human Relations." Unpublished Ed.D. thesis, New York University, 1958.
12. Lawrence Kubie, "Are We Educating for Maturity." *NEA Journal*, January 1959.
13. James Raths, "Underachievement and a Search for Values." *Journal of Educational Sociology 34*:2; May 1961.
14. ———, "Clarifying Children's Values." *National Elementary Principal 62*:2; November 1962.
15. Louis E. Raths, "Values and Teachers." *Educational Synopsis*, Spring 1957.
16. ———, "Sociological Knowledge and Needed Curriculum Research." *Research Frontiers in the Study of Children's Learning*. J. B. Macdonald, editor. Milwaukee: School of Education, the University of Wisconsin-Milwaukee, 1960.

17. ———, "Clarifying Values." *Curriculum for Today's Boys and Girls.* R. S. Fleming, editor. Columbus, Ohio: Charles Merrill Books, Inc., 1963.

Values-Clarification vs. Indoctrination

SIDNEY B. SIMON

Whatever happened to those good old words we once used when we talked of values? Remember how comfortable it was to say *inculcate?* It was a nice, clean, dignified, closely shaved word if there ever was one. Then there was the old standby, *to instill*—usually followed by "the democratic values of our society." Doesn't anyone instill anymore? And what about the word *foster?* In schools, not so very long ago, we used to "foster" all over the place. But nobody does that much anymore. What has happened to the old familiar jargon of value teaching?

What happened was the realization that all the inculcating, instilling, and fostering added up to indoctrination; and despite our best efforts at doing the indoctrinating, we've come to see that it just didn't take. Most of the people who experienced the inculcation, instillation, and fostering seem not the much better for it. They appear to play just as much hanky-panky with income taxes as anyone else, and concerned letters-to-the-editor are not written by them in any greater profusion. They pollute and defoliate; move to the suburbs to escape integration; buy convertibles with vinyl tops that collapse in roll-over accidents; fail to wear seat belts; and commit all kinds of sins even while they are saying the very words that have been dutifully inculcated, instilled, and fostered in them. It *is* discouraging.

At this point, one might ask: "Is it all that bad?" "Aren't they also among the good people who go to the polls in November, read the current events weeklies, and pay their Bankamericard charges on time?" Yes, of course. But in these troubled, confused, and conflicted times, we need people who can do much more than that. We desperately need men and women who know who they are, who know what they want out of life, and who can name their names when controversy rages. We need people who know what is significant and what is trash, and who are not so vulnerable to demagoguery, blandness, or safety.

The indoctrination procedures of the past fail to help people grapple with all the confusion and conflict which abound in these baffling days. For

Sidney B. Simon is Professor in the Center for Humanistic Education at the University of Massachusetts, Amherst.

Reprinted from *Social Education* 35(8):902–905 ff., 1971, with permission of the National Council for the Social Studies and Sidney B. Simon.

example, in values-clarification, we apply a strategy which is deceptively simple. We ask students to spend some time listing the brand names in their home medicine cabinets. Just think of your own medicine cabinet as you are sitting reading this. What's in it? How many creams, ointments, and salves have you been sold? Do you use a brand-name, buffered product instead of plain old aspirin? How did you get started on that? What about the spray cans? How many are in your aerosol arsenal? What did you use before the product you now spray? How did all those brand names get there? Who bought them? What was the motivating force? How did you learn what to value as seen in your medicine cabinet? As long as you have the door to your cabinet open, why don't you pull out the cosmetic tray? How vulnerable are you to avoiding the hysteria surrounding all of us about getting a wrinkle? Getting old has become such a negative value. Who are the people who fear it?

In place of indoctrination, my associates and I are substituting a *process* approach to the entire area of dealing with values in the schools, which focuses on the process of valuing, not on the transmission of the "right" set of values. We call this approach *values-clarification,* and it is based on the premise that none of us has the "right" set of values to pass on to other people's children. Yes, there may be some things we can all agree upon, and I will grant you some absolutes, but when we begin to operationalize our values, make them show up in how we live our days and spend our nights, then we begin to see the enormous smugness of those people who profess they have the right values for others' children. The issues and hostility generated around hair length and dress and armbands are just the surface absurdity.

More dangerous is the incredible hypocrisy we generate when we live two-faced values and hustle the one right value to children. Think about the hundreds of elementary school teachers who daily stop children from running down the halls. I close my eyes and I see them with their arms outstretched, hands pressing against the chest of kids who put on their "brakes" in order to make the token slowdown until the teacher ducks into the teacher's room for a fast cigarette before all the kids get back to hear the cancer lecture. Think of those teachers preaching to children about the need to take turns and share. "We wait in lines, boys and girls, and we learn to share our crayons and paints in here. And, I don't want to see anybody in my class being a tattletale—except in cases of serious emergency, naturally." The words are all too familiar. I have used them in the old days. I have also seen myself cut into the cafeteria lunch line ahead of third graders. (Take turns? Well, not when we have so few minutes for lunch and always so much to do to get ready for afternoon classes.)

The alternative to indoctrination of values is *not* to do nothing. In this time of the anti-hero, our students need all the help we can give them if they are to make sense of the confusion and conflict inherited from the indoctrinated types. Moreover, we all need help in grappling with the chaos of the international scene, with the polarization of national life—not to mention the right-outside-the-door string of purely local dilemmas.

An approach to this problem is to help students learn a process for the clarification of their values, which is a far cry from indoctrination. The theory behind it can be found in *Values and Teaching* (Louis E. Raths, Merrill Harmin, and Sidney B. Simon, Columbus: Charles E. Merrill, 1966). In the remainder of this article, I will describe some of the strategies we are presently using to help students learn the process of values-clarification and begin lifelong searches for the sets of personal values by which to steer their lives.[1]

Five Value-Clarifying Strategies and Their Use

STRATEGY #1—THINGS I LOVE TO DO

Ask students (teacher does it with them) to number from 1–20 on a paper. Then suggest they list, as rapidly as they can, 20 things in life which they really, *really* love to do. Stress that the papers will not be collected and "corrected," and that there is no right answer about what people *should* like. It should be emphasized that in none of values strategies should students be forced to participate. Each has the right to pass. Students may get strangely quiet; and, at first, they may even be baffled by such an unschoolike task as this. Flow with it, and be certain to allow enough time to list what they really love to do. Remember, at no time must the individual's privacy be invaded, and that the right of an individual to pass is sacrosanct.

When everyone has listed his 20 items, the process of coding responses can be started. Here are some suggested codes which you might ask the students to use:

1. Place the $ sign by any item which costs more than $3, each time you do it.
2. Put an *R* in front of any item which involves some RISK. The risk might be physical, intellectual, or emotional. (Which things in your own life that are things you love to do require some risk?)
3. Using the code letters *F* and *M,* record which of the items on your list you think your father and mother might have had on their lists if they had been asked to make them at YOUR age.
4. Place either the letter *P* or the letter *A* before each item. The "P" to be used for items which you prefer doing with PEOPLE, the "A" for items which you prefer doing ALONE. (Stress again that there is

[1] Most of these strategies are from a soon-to-be-published book, *New Strategies for Clarifying Values* by Sidney B. Simon, Howard Kirschenbaum, and Leland Howe.

no right answer. It is important to just become aware of which are your preferences.)

5. Place a number 5 in front of any item which you think would not be on your list 5 years from now.
6. Finally go down through your list and place near each item the date when you did it last.

The discussion which follows this exercise argues more eloquently than almost anything else we can say for values-clarification.

STRATEGY #2—I LEARNED THAT I. . . .

This strategy fits in with the one above. After students have listed and coded their 20 items, the teacher might say, "Look at your list as something which tells a lot about you at this time in your life. What did you learn about yourself as you were going through the strategy? Will you please complete one of these sentences and share with us some of the learning you did?"

I learned that I. . . .
I relearned that I. . . .
I noticed that I. . . .
I was surprised to see that I. . . .
I was disappointed that I. . . .
I was pleased that I. . . .
I realized that I. . . .

The teacher must be willing to make some "I learned that I. . . ." statements, too. And they must not be platitudinous, either. Every effort is made for the values-clarifying teacher to be as honest and as authentic as possible.

"I learned that I. . . ." statements can be used after almost any important value-clarifying strategy. It is a way of getting the student to own the process of the search for values. It should be clear how diametrically opposed "I learned that I. . . ." statements are from indoctrination, although it is possible to misuse this or any clarification strategy to get kids to give back the party line. On the other hand, using this strategy can begin to build that lifetime search for personal meaning into all of our experiences.

STRATEGY #3—BAKER'S DOZEN

This is a very simple strategy which teaches us something about our personal priorities. The teacher asks each student to list 13, a baker's dozen, of his favorite items around the house which use PLUGS, that is, which require electricity.

When the students have made their lists, the teacher says, "Now, please draw a line through the three which you really could do without if there were suddenly to be a serious power shortage. It's not that you don't like them, but that you could, if you had to, live without them. O.K., now circle the three which really mean the most to you and which you would hold onto until the very end."

It should be clear that again there is no right answer as to what "good" people *should* draw lines through and circle. The main thing is for each of us to know what we want and to see it in the perspective of what we like less.

STRATEGY #4—"I URGE" TELEGRAMS

The teacher obtains blank Western Union telegram blanks. Or simply has students head a piece of paper with the word *Telegram*. He then says, "Each of you should think of someone in your real life to whom you would send a telegram which begins with these words: I URGE YOU TO. . . . Then finish the telegram and we'll hear some of them."

A great many values issues come out of this simple strategy. Consider some of these telegrams:

To my sister: "I urge you to get your head together and quit using drugs." Nancy. (All telegrams must be signed. It is our affirmation of the need to name your name and to stand up for what you believe in.)

To my Sunday School teacher: "I urge you to quit thinking that you are the only person to know what God wants." Signed, your student Rodney Phillips.

To my neighbor on the North Side: "I urge you to see that we have no other place to play ball and that you not call the cops so often." Signed, Billy Clark.

One of the things that students working with values-clarification learn to do is to find out what they really want. "I urge telegrams" help do that. Just think of the people in your own lives to whom an "I urge telegram" needs to be sent. The second thing students working with values-clarification learn to do is to find *alternative* ways of getting what they need and want. Take the case of Billy Clark's neighbor. The class spent some time brainstorming ways of approaching that neighbor. They talked about how to negotiate with a grouch, and how to try to offer alternatives in your drive to get what you want.

"I urge telegrams" are used several times during the semester. The students keep them on file and after they have done five or six, they are spread out on the desk and "I learned statements" made from the pattern of the messages carried by the telegrams.

Students also learn to use the "I urge you to. . . ." model to get messages across between student and student and between student and teacher.

An assignment I like to use, related to the "I urge telegram," is to have each student get a letter-to-the-editor published in a magazine or newspaper.

STRATEGY #5—PERSONAL COAT OF ARMS

Each student is asked to draw a shield shape in preparation for making a personal coat of arms. The teacher could go into the historical significance of shields and coats of arms, but the exercise is designed to help us learn more about some of our most strongly held values and to learn the importance of publicly affirming what we believe, that is, literally wearing our values out front on our shields.

The coat of arms shield is divided into six sections (see figure). The teacher makes it clear that words are to be used only in the sixth block. All the others are to contain pictures. He stresses that it is not an art lesson. Only crude stick figures, etc., need be used. Then he tells what is to go in each of the six sections:

1. Draw two pictures. One to represent something you are very good at and one to show something you *want* to become good at.
2. Make a picture to show one of your values from which you would never budge. This is one about which you feel extremely strong, and which you might never give up.
3. Draw a picture to show a value by which your family lives. Make it one that everyone in your family would probably agree is one of their most important.
4. In this block, imagine that you could achieve anything you wanted, and that whatever you tried to do would be a success. What would you strive to do?
5. Use this block to show one of the values you wished all men would believe, and certainly one in which you believe very deeply.
6. In the last block, you can use words. Use four words which you would like people to say about you behind your back.

The teacher can do several different things at this point. He can have the students share among themselves in little trios or quartets. He can also get the pictures hung up on the walls and get people to take each other on gallery tours to share the coats of arms. A game could be played which would involve trying to guess what the pictures represented. The class might try to make a group coat of arms to represent their living together in that classroom. In any case, the value expressions elicited in this nonverbal way are very exciting and lead to discussions which range far and wide. Incidentally, this strategy is a good one to use with parents to illustrate to them the power of the values-clarification methodology. It makes a meaningful exercise for an evening PTA meeting.

The Coat of Arms strategy illustrates quite well some things common to all of the values-clarification strategies. The teacher sets up an interesting way of eliciting some value responses. He establishes that there is no right answer. The strategy is open-ended and allows students to take the explora-

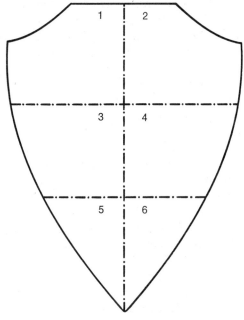

A Personal Coat of Arms

tion to whatever level they want to take it. Finally, there is a chance to share with each other some of the alternatives that emerge from our searching. This whole process allows each student to focus on areas where he has some work yet to do in order to keep growing. The Coats of Arms can be done several times during the school year and the various shields compared and seen as measures of a student's search.

CONCLUSION

The five strategies used as illustrations of what values-clarification is must raise some serious questions in the minds of readers who have more conventional views of what the social studies should be. For one thing, I have used no standard subject-matter content: there is no history, no geography, etc. Yet, if one thinks through what the outcomes of a course will be making use of the five strategies, he will see the student emerging with a deeper sense of who he is, what he wants, what is precious, and what is of most worth in his and others' lives. Have the social studies ever done more than that?

Values-clarification demands that we take a new look at what we have been calling the social studies. I feel more and more strongly that the most severe problem facing all of us is *HOW TO GET PEOPLE TO LOOK AT THE LIVES THEY ARE LEADING.* How can we get fathers and mothers to see that high college-entrance scores are not the end of a high school education? How can we get people to see that getting a high-paying job is not the final reward of a college degree? How can we get men and women to take on some larger share of their personal responsibility for the rampant racism in our nation? Or for allowing a senseless war to continue indefinitely? When will educators make a contribution towards helping people examine the head-long pursuit towards accumulating more and more material possessions and enjoying them less? Or what can we do about keeping our students from making drab and dreary marriages or being trapped into pointless jobs which they hate to go to each morning? It boils down to a concern for values, and yet we must not fall into the trap of believing that if only we could give boys and girls the right set of values to believe, they would avoid the mistakes of the rest of us. Nonsense!

Indoctrination is not the answer. The only thing that indoctrination did for people in the past was to help them postpone the time when they began the hard process of hammering out their own set of values. Values simply can't be given to anyone else. One can't value for other people. Each individual has to find his own values. One can memorize all the platitudes he wants, but when it comes to living and acting on the values, he needs to carve them out of carefully reflected experience. The skills necessary for doing this can be learned in values-clarification.

Perhaps when the reader and author acknowledge how little help they received from their own education about making sense out of life, maybe then they will be willing to help other people's children learn the *process,* a lifetime process, of searching for a viable set of values to live by and perhaps even to die for.

The author is convinced that he can leave his own children no greater inheritance than the gift of knowing how to negotiate the lovely banquet of life ahead of them. That is indeed something of value.

A Strategy for Exploring Values and Valuing in the Social Studies

AMBROSE A. CLEGG, JR., AND JAMES L. HILLS

The recent increase in crime rate in the nation and the large number of Americans enrolled in church groups and youth activities suggest an apparent contradiction in the values held by American society.

Crime in the United States increased 17 per cent during the first six months of 1967 in a country where the rate of population increase is but 1.15 per cent annually. On the other hand, more than 125 million Americans are affiliated with various church groups, 41 million are enrolled in Sunday and Sabbath Schools; and nearly 32 million young people are members of such groups as the Boy Scouts, Girl Scouts, and 4-H clubs (11: 902, 175, 641, 644).

Each year, similar compilations have contradicted the popular notion that the home, buttressed by the church and related character building agencies, is the most influential in developing sound values in the lives of young people. Nevertheless, newspaper editorials and public forums exhort the home and church to work harder and more effectively to prove their primacy in teaching values. They overlook the questions that should be asked.

Who shapes the attitudes and values of our youth? The school is one of the primary agents for inculcating values, especially those related to the political process, according to recent studies by Hess and Torney (2). They point out that pupil attitudes change markedly over the school years. Important shifts appear to take place beginning in the middle grades. Their evidence reveals clearly that by the eighth grade there is a remarkable similarity between the political values held by pupils and those held by their teachers on a number of variables. They conclude that the schools are one of the major forces responsible for shaping the political values of American youth through the eighth grade.

What value-laden problems must be handled by schools? If the public schools are to provide the type of education that makes intelligent civic participation possible, social studies curricula must be expanded to include a full examination of current value-laden problems. The list should include such topics as civil rights and responsibilities; the myriad problems of

Ambrose A. Clegg, Jr., is Chairman of the Department of Elementary Education at Kent State University, Ohio; James L. Hills is Chairman of the Department of Elementary Education at New York University.

Reprinted from *The College of Education Record* 34(4):67–78, 1968, with permission of the University of Washington and Ambrose A. Clegg, Jr., and James L. Hills.

minority groups including unemployment, segregation, and quality education; problems of poverty, housing, and health; pollution of air, water, and soil; and problems related to land use, taxation, and augmented social services. All of these pervade every level of the community: local, state, and national.

Which values must be taught? For years educators have been charged with the responsibility of teaching basic democratic values, such as those identified by Hanna *et al.* (1:63–68):

(1) Respect for the dignity and worth of the individual.
(2) Concern for the common welfare.
(3) Faith in the intelligence of common men to rule themselves.
(4) Use of reason and persuasion rather than force for solving problems and settling controversies.

Although the authors reported a number of school practices that evidenced acceptance of these values, the climate found in many classrooms might lead the serious observer to suggest that schools honor these values more often in the breach than in the observance thereof.

What is the problem? While lip service is publicly paid to such basic values as those cited above, private exceptions to these have often been observed in various aspects of American life. Over thirty years ago, Lynd pointed out this problem in his study of Middletown (5:60–62). He reported a number of apparent contradictions such as:

(1) Individualism, "the survival of the fittest," is the law of nature and the secret of America's greatness; restrictions on individual freedom are un-American and kill initiative.
   But: No man should live for himself alone; for people ought to be loyal and stand together and work for common purposes.
(2) The thing that distinguishes man from the beasts is the fact that he is rational; and therefore man can be trusted, if let alone, to guide his conduct wisely.
   But: Some people are brighter than others; and, as every practical politician and businessman knows, you can't afford simply to sit back and wait for people to make up their minds.
(3) Democracy, as discovered and perfected by the American people is the ultimate form of living together. All men are created free and equal, and the United States has made this fact a living reality.
   But: You would never get anywhere, of course, if you constantly left things to popular vote. No business could be run that way, and of course no businessman would tolerate it.

Because of the difficulties involved in these contradictory value positions, schools have tended to avoid value-laden problems in the curriculum that would be likely to produce controversy among students or within the community. It is "safer" to present the majority view as though it were the only one. This, in turn, has led to the disillusionment of many students when they became aware of evidence contrary to the majority view such as found in the inconsistencies pointed out by Lynd.

Further evidence of the contradiction in basic values was presented by Keniston in a recent study of alienated youth in American society. As he charted factors in the "alienated outlook," he found the "opposite outlooks" gave a recognizable portrait of the traditional American world view. Some examples, taken from his chart, make this clear:

Alienated Outlook	*Opposite* ("American Culture")
Low view of human nature	Human nature basically good
Futility of civic and political activities	Usefulness, need for civic and political activities
Rejection of American culture	Praise of American culture
Short-range, personally centered values	Long-range, universally grounded values
Intolerance, scorn	Tolerance, respect (3:79–80)

Which value position is "right"? Faced with community and student support for opposing positions on the points cited by Lynd and by Keniston, the teacher needs a validation procedure. He needs a strategy to help students arrive at their own position and be able to justify it. The subtle indoctrination implied in "Teacher says so" is the seed-bed of alienation when pupils are confronted by contrary evidence.

Scriven (7:7–10) has developed an excellent validation procedure based on a reasoned appeal to judgment that could be used along the following lines:

Suppose a class were studying economic conflict and the means to resolve a labor-management dispute. Suppose, further, that the controversy concerned public employees, such as policemen or teachers. Various approaches such as mediation, strike, or compulsory arbitration could be tested against the following questions as suggested by Scriven:

(1) If doing something (e.g., engaging in a strike or compulsory arbitration) will bring about a state of affairs that people value, that is a good reason for doing it.

(2) If there are good reasons for doing something (e.g., engaging in a strike or compulsory arbitration) and none against it, then we should do it.

(3) If there is a conflict of good reasons supporting one or the other proposed actions (e.g., strike or compulsory arbitration), then appeal must be made to a general moral principle such as the equality of rights of both parties, labor and management, to the dispute, as well as an appeal to the common good.

Obviously, many value factors are involved in this example. Children can be encouraged to examine and appraise the many alternatives, their consequences, and the conflicting value positions implicit in each. Ultimately, their choice of position must be based on their judgment of the greatest good for the greatest number of people, recognizing, at the same time, that their judgment may differ from that of other persons. Such a process is often called "valuing."

What instructional procedures are suited to the process of valuing? Taba's investigations in the cognitive domain have identified specific thinking tasks and appropriate strategies for developing higher thought processes. These have been widely reported (8, 9, 10). Krathwohl *et al.* have pointed up rather clearly the close relationship between the cognitive and affective domains (4:45–62). Looking more toward classroom application, Raths and his colleagues have recently published a collection of promising techniques for helping children deal with values. In their book *Values and Teaching,* Raths *et al.* identify three basic processes with seven subcategories (See Figure 1).

Choosing:	. (1) freely
	*(2) from alternatives
	*(3) after thoughtful consideration of the consequences of each alternative
Prizing:	(4) cherishing, being happy with the choice
	*(5) willing to affirm the choice publicly
Acting:	(6) doing something with the choice
	(7) repeatedly, in some pattern of life
	(6:28–30)

Figure 1.   Basic Value Processes

If nearly all cognitive objectives have an affective component (4:48), would it be possible to adapt the Taba tasks to accommodate the value dimensions? If Raths' processes are basic, could they be incorporated within the Taba cognitive tasks?

These questions led the writers to undertake an investigation to determine whether the three processes indicated (see asterisks, Fig. 1) could be employed in the classroom setting at the fifth-grade level, and what adaptations might be made to Taba's model of cognitive tasks to get at the values explored. The results of that investigation are presented below.

A MODEL FOR VALUING IN SOCIAL STUDIES

The Historical Episodes. Classroom materials were designed to present a variety of conflicting views based on historical episodes in the traditional fifth-grade social studies curriculum. For example:

Roger Williams—A tape-recorded narrative portrayed him as being insistent upon preaching his own narrowly conceived and fundamentalist view of God's covenant with man in the New Zion, even if some of its tenets threatened the social and political order of the New England theocracy. In opposition were John Cotton and the Puritan ministers and Governor John Winthrop, who were determined to maintain religious orthodoxy and the established order.

The Boston Tea Party—This multidimensional episode, with four groups of contending participants, was presented by means of a tape-recorded narrative, accompanied by a series of 35mm colored slides of the leading people and places. King George III and his prime minister, Lord North, were seen as determined to preserve the right of the Crown to rule its colonies and to levy taxes. The merchants of the East India Tea Co. and their consignees here in the colonies were pictured as anxious to protect their financial investments; they viewed the Crown as the best protector of these interests. Sam Adams and the "patriots" were portrayed as zealously determined to preserve the long-established right of local rule and self-determination in taxing. And, finally, Governor Hutchinson, caught in the middle, opposed the King's plan to tax tea, yet was determined to maintain order against the threats of the mob.

A Simple Model. The issue that developed between the Puritans and Roger Williams was investigated by means of a value continuum suggested by Raths. As a preliminary step, an adaptation of Taba's schema (9:73) depicting the formation of generalizations (Cognitive Task II) was made for the formation of value positions. (See Figure 2.)

Following this, separate continua were made for each position. These became cognitive maps of the discussion. An integral part of the discussion, they provided a visible summary of the alternatives and consequences expressed by the students. (See Figures 3 and 4.) The continuum depicting the Puritan's alternatives reveals that students offered alternatives, immediate consequences, and subsequent consequences. These "If-then" chains —"if we give him to the Indians, then the Indians might be on his side; if that could happen, we ought to sabotage him to prevent its happening"— provide a pattern which seems to incorporate certain aspects of the cognitive processes identified in both Task II and Task III of Taba's models (8, 9, 10).

A Complex Model. A more complex discussion was undertaken around the issues of the Boston Tea Party. This incident presented problems of scholarship because the text's simplistic stereotype of "good guys" (Patriots) versus "bad guys" (Loyalists) obscured the complexity of the real issues and the character of the individuals involved. Research revealed at least six positions that could be clearly identified around groups that were involved in the event.

Value continua for four of these were explored in the manner illustrated with Roger Williams and the Puritans. Analysis of the discussion indicated that the handling of these data was much more difficult for the pupils. The post-discussion analysis suggested a strong need for a data retrieval chart to facilitate the higher level cognitive operations necessary as a base for the affective component. A data retrieval chart was devised to facilitate such a discussion. (See Figure 5.)

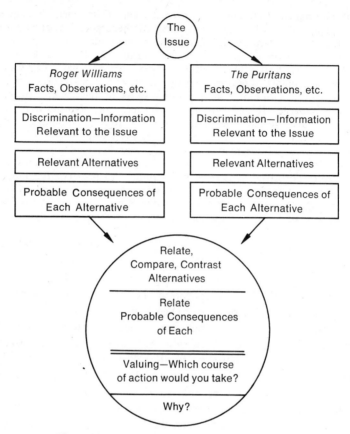

Figure 2.   Formation of Attitudes and Values

Since the data retrieval chart indicates six situations, instead of the two represented by the schema depicting the formation of values and attitudes (Figure 2) discussed earlier, a modification in strategy becomes necessary: The comparison/contrast of "Patriots" and "Loyalists" might be considered a reasonable first step. The comparison/contrast of the positions of Hutchinson versus the "Crown" might be the second step. Depending on the maturity of the class, the time available, and the extent to which the teacher wished to develop understandings of the economic forces underlying the issue, the positions of the colonial merchants versus the tea company could become a third step.

A Sequence of Learning. The order of pursuit for the paired comparisons mentioned may be optional. The crucial points are the following:

(1) Break the task down into component parts on which the students can easily focus.

(2) Take up the component parts one at a time.

(3) Tailor the tasks to the ability of the pupils.
(4) Help the pupils organize their data in a form which will facilitate the discussion tasks.
(5) Allow pupils to develop a number of alternatives.
(6) Encourage them to explore the probable consequence of each alternative and its effect on the parties involved.
(7) Urge them to identify the alternative that they would choose under the circumstances.
(8) Express the reason for their choice (get out the underlying value).

The affective sequence differs from that posed by Taba for the cognitive domain. (See 9:75.)

Such a complex subject should not be attempted during a single period. It could be taken up in segments over successive days. The paired comparisons mentioned above could be a useful basis for dividing the discussion into segments.

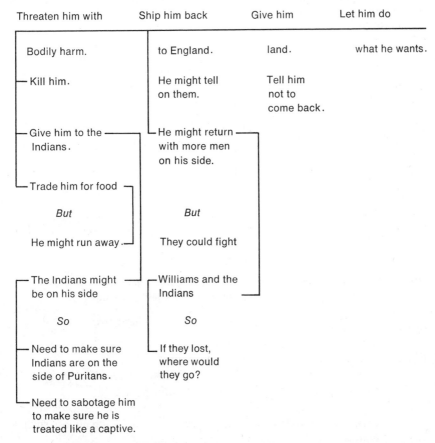

Figure 3. Puritans' Attitudes Regarding Roger Williams

Extension of the "If-Then" Questions to Value Positions. One of the important aspects of this exploratory study has been the extension of the "if-then" questions in terms of the value positions evident in the instructional materials. The nature of the eliciting questions dealt specifically with the alternative actions and probable consequences that had to be evaluated in terms of consistency with the expressed attitude and the likelihood of occurrence, given the anticipated action of one or more other participants whose views conflicted. In a sense the kind of intellectual activity involved here is somewhat akin to that of the chess player who learns to anticipate and weigh the multiple consequences of any of several moves open to him.

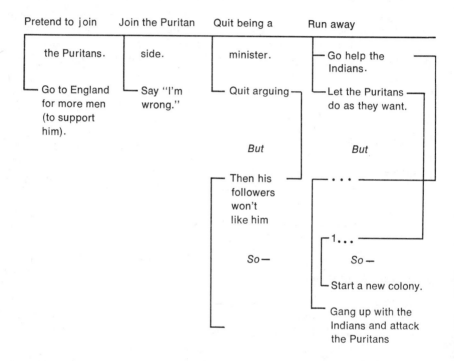

NOTE: [1]Omissions indicate that students jumped directly to long-range consequences omitting any plausible intermediate consequences.

Figure 4.   Roger Williams and His Alternatives

Eliciting questions such as the following were used:
  (1) What courses of action did Roger Williams have, if it were likely that the Ministers (or Governor Winthrop) would . . .?
  (2) If you were Roger Williams, what would you choose to do if you expected the Ministers would . . .? Why would you choose such a course?

(3) What are some possible alternatives that Sam Adams might have had, in light of the known views and probable alternatives open to the King, to Governor Hutchinson, and to the tea merchants? What do you expect would have been the probable consequences?

(4) How would you have acted if you were so-and-so? Why?

	Sam Adams and "Patriots"	"Loyalists"	"Crown" and Lord North	Hutchinson	Tea Company	Colonial Merchants
Who were they?						
What did they say (their opinions)?						
What did they do?						
What effect did it have (on each)?						
What was the final result (to each)?						

Figure 5.   Data Retrieval Chart for Value Discussion Focused on Boston Tea Party

Some Tentative Findings. Bearing in mind that this study was an exploratory one (hypothesis-seeking), some tentative findings, nevertheless, can be advanced. Preliminary analysis of the data seems to indicate:

(1) Many of the Taba's strategies for forming generalizations and applying principles in the cognitive domain lend themselves to adaptation for use in the affective context.

(2) Children need much more information and time to arrive at value judgments than was available during the experimental program. This suggests study in depth of a limited number of value issues, rather than a rapid survey of a large number of names, dates, and places.

(3) Eliciting questions need to be sharply defined and must focus clearly on the value element involved.

(4) Children appear to have considerable difficulty in choosing alternative courses of action when several variables are interacting simul-

taneously. This is especially true when the choice of alternatives is counterbalanced by the anticipated consequences of the alternative actions open to other participants (e.g., as in the Boston Tea Party).

(5) In complex situations, children's choices of alternative courses of action appear to be overly simplistic and tend to resort to stereo-typed or even improbable solutions, not unlike those found on Batman or Superman. This is probably due to lack of sufficient background information on which to base more probable choices.

(6) Many textbooks were found to be antiseptically neutral when it came to presenting conflicting value positions. For an approach of this sort a considerable amount of additional materials must be prepared such as slides, tapes, pictures, etc., that will adequately present the topic as a live issue.

Does This Procedure Have Relevance for Current Issues? When the valuing process is linked to historical people and events, the final data are available and the events are removed somewhat from the turmoil of strong emotional involvement in a contemporary issue. The use of historical episodes in the initial experiences, then, has the effect of muting the affective component to an extent sufficient to allow focus on the process. This approach was deliberately chosen by the investigators as a pilot study to permit exploration and mapping out of the process (see Figures 3 and 4), the dimensions of which have not been identified elsewhere.

The writers see this valuing model as having three rather distinct, but closely related dimensions: (1) learning to use the process described earlier in the paper; (2) learning the necessary content; and (3) developing value identification and commitment.

Since the process cannot be experienced without content, historical content appropriate to the setting was chosen. This would allow the primary focus to be on the *process* during the initial experiences. This is *not* a recommendation that valuing should necessarily start with a historical base. A non-controversial issue, such as flouridation in a community not strongly divided on the matter, might be fully as useful as a historical event for introducing the process.

It was hypothesized that this reduction of feelings of personal involvement in initial experiences permits the desired processes to be introduced and then reinforced sufficiently to allow subsequent transfer of the process to more emotionally laden topics.[1] The writers have conjectured that the processes delineated above, tentative though they be, will prove helpful to teachers who wish to deal with "hot" issues in the classroom such as "Black Power," racial violence, Viet Nam, or the draft.

[1] Krathwohl (4:57–62) has suggested that not only do cognitive factors shape affective learnings, but conversely, affective factors appear to influence cognitive learnings. Thus, the alternate hypothesis, that children can deal directly with current value-laden issues without prior training on historical materials, will be explored in a more rigorously controlled experimental study.

References

1. Lavone Hanna, Gladys L. Potter, and Neva Hagaman, *Unit Teaching in the Elementary School.* New York: Holt, Rinehart and Winston, 1963.
2. Robert D. Hess, and Judith V. Torney, *The Development of Political Attitudes in Children.* Chicago: Aldine, 1967.
3. Kenneth Keniston, *The Uncommitted: Alienated Youth in American Society.* New York: Dell, 1965.
4. David R. Krathwohl, Benjamin S. Bloom and Bertram B. Masia, *Taxonomy of Educational Objectives,* Handbook II. Affective Domain. New York: McKay, 1964.
5. Robert S. Lynd, *Knowledge for What?* Princeton: Princeton University Press, 1939. For a more extended list, see *Middletown in Transition,* Chapter XII, by Robert S. and Helen Lynd. New York: Harcourt, 1937.
6. Louis E. Raths, Merrill Harmin, and Sidney B. Simon, *Values and Teaching.* Columbus: Merrill, 1966.
7. Michael Scriven, *Student Values as Educational Objectives.* Publication No. 124 of the Social Sciences Consortium, Purdue University, Lafayette, Indiana, 1966.
8. Hilda Taba, "Implementing Thinking as an Objective in Social Studies," Chapter II in *Effective Thinking in the Social Studies,* Jean Fair and Fannie Shaftel, editors. 37th Yearbook for the National Council for the Social Studies. Washington, D.C.: The Council, 1967.
9. Hilda Taba, *Teachers' Handbook for Elementary Social Studies.* Palo Alto, California: Addison-Wesley, 1967.
10. Hilda Taba, "Teaching Strategies for Cognitive Growth," Chapter 3 in *Conceptual Models in Teacher Education,* John Verduin. Washington, D.C.: American Association of Colleges for Teacher Education, 1967.
11. *1968 World Almanac,* Luman H. Long, ed. New York: Newspaper Enterprise Association, Inc., 1968.

Can Children's Books Change Children's Values?

ERIC A. KIMMEL

Are a child's attitudes and values affected by his reading? In the same manner, one might ask, can a child's character be shaped by careful selection of the books he reads?

Educators have been concerned with these questions since the end of the First World War, when the need for interracial, international, and interreligious understanding became apparent if future wars were to be prevented. Needless to say, the questions are just as challenging in our own time, and probably more so.

Recently it has begun to seem as if the belief that a child's attitudes can be affected by his reading is considered almost as an act of faith among teachers, librarians, parents, and publishers, who have certainly acted on their hopes. Never before have there been so many books of high quality for children dealing with varied races, nationalities, and religions, having as their theme the importance of sympathy, kindness, and understanding between people all over the world. Black, Spanish, and Oriental faces peep from the pages of the once staidly all-white basal readers.

A quick glance through the professional journals reveals article after article proclaiming the need for overcoming prejudices through an appropriate program of reading and discussion. The *Reading Ladders for Human Relations* program, under the editorship of Muriel Crosby, is a noteworthy example, providing many useful bibliographies for teachers and librarians.

Like Euclid's parallel lines which never meet, the assumption that books can be a positive force for sound character development seems to be axiomatic. Unfortunately it is too axiomatic, for by definition an "axiom" is a statement believed to be true, but which cannot be positively proven beyond a doubt to be so.

Most ideas about the affective potential of children's books are based on assumptions which have not yet been proven. Ironically, it appears to be a common pattern that the amount of objective evidence cited in an article seems to be in inverse proportion to the degree of certitude expressed by the author that children's books can or do mold a child's character. In light of the amount of concern with the problem, it comes as quite a surprise to

Eric A. Kimmel is Teaching Assistant in the Elementary Education Department at the University of Illinois, Urbana.

Reprinted from *Educational Leadership* 28(2):209–214, 1970, with permission of the Association for Supervision and Curriculum Development and Eric A. Kimmel. Copyright © 1970 by the Association for Supervision and Curriculum Development.

the reviewer to find that objective studies of the affective qualities of children's literature are few, open to question, and sometimes contradictory.

Three Forms of Research

This research falls into three basic forms: content analysis, general effects, and overcoming prejudices.

The content analysis is the most common type of study dealing with children's literature, possibly because it is the easiest to conduct. Two of the most significant studies in this area were performed by David Gast (1967) and Alma Homze (1966).

Gast, investigating minority stereotypes in recent children's books, came to the conclusion that although the more objectionable minority stereotypes have disappeared, stereotypes (meaning an oversimplified, often inaccurate view) still predominate. For example, a book may deal with Negro children, but there may be nothing especially Negro about them or the problems they face to distinguish them from the average suburban white child. Gast also noted that while Negro and Japanese children are usually depicted as living within the mainstream of American life, Chinese, Mexican, and Indian children are depicted as set apart, either in Chinatown, in the sleepy adobe pueblo, or on the reservation.[1]

Homze, in a much more extensive survey, examines children's literature from 1920–60 and notes many of the same factors as does Gast, particularly that the "middle class white" child dominates the field. She also finds evidence for considering children's books a mirror for changes in American family trends over the 40-year period. The more recent books, she points out, stress reliance on self-sufficiency and good relations with the peer group in contrast to older books, which emphasize the importance of family and the need to depend on adults for guidance.[2]

The problem with content analyses of children's books is that they represent an attempt to build the house by working from the roof down. It is impossible to gauge, for example, the significance of a large or small percentage of Negro characters in recent books until we know what effect the presence or absence of Negro characters will have on children. Until we know that, mere content analysis can provide little more than knowledge of the books themselves and trends within them. A researcher might just as well study the number of fat characters, or children who wear red shirts. Yet the content analyses remain the best studies in the field, and certainly

[1] David K. Gast. "Minority Americans in Children's Literature." *Elementary English* 44: 12–23; January 1967.

[2] Alma Homze. "Interpersonal Relations in Children's Literature." *Elementary English* 43: 26–28, 52; January 1966.

the ones least open to question. Norine Odland, in *Teaching Literature in the Elementary School,* states the problem perfectly:

It is also possible that, with the sophisticated and refined statistical treatments currently available, work with affective responses and content analyses has not been encouraged or approved. It is difficult to assign a mathematical score to a six-year-old's response to the story of Mike Milligan.[3]

The content of books, at least, can be measured and recorded statistically. The response of children to books cannot.

Fehl L. Shirley (1969) attempted to get around this dilemma in a study of the general effects of reading on concepts, attitudes, and behavior. Although the books to which the subjects responded were not children's books (e.g., *Black Like Me, Peyton Place, None Dare Call It Treason*), the methods of the study and its findings are worth noting.

Shirley asked 420 Arizona high school students to "report any changes in concepts, attitudes, and behavior that they had experienced as a result of reading." [4]

Reactions to reading ranged from "The Indifferent," who admitted to never having been influenced by any sort of reading, to the "Decision Maker," who was influenced to make a specific change in his behavior through something he had read. The example given is that of a student who decided to give up smoking as a result of reading a magazine article linking smoking to cancer.

Of the 420 students, only 16 reported no personal influence traceable to reading. Of 1,184 different influences reported, 45 percent were new concepts, 40 percent new attitudes, and 15 percent behavioral responses. Also significant were the following findings:

1. No difference in influence between fiction and nonfiction.
2. A positive relation (significant at .01 level) existing between the number of total influences and the intelligence, vocabulary, and comprehension levels of the subject. The better readers were more apt to be influenced by books.
3. Students were more influenced by voluntary reading than by assigned readings.[5]

Shirley's findings are significant for teachers and researchers. Only 15 percent of the reading influences resulted in a behavioral change, the type most easily measured by our present methods. The overwhelming number of changes occurred in the cognitive areas of concepts and attitudes. Certainly these will result in changes eventually, but changes much more subtle,

---

[3] Norine Odland. *Teaching Literature in the Elementary School.* Champaign, Illinois: Educational Resources Information Center, 1969. p. 23.

[4] Fehl L. Shirley. "Influence of Reading on Concepts, Attitudes, and Behavior." *Journal of Reading* 12: 369–72, 407–13; February 1969.

[5] *Ibid.,* p. 411.

and probably much more important, than one individual's decision to give up smoking.

The slower readers seem to be least influenced by books; most likely because they enjoy reading less and read fewer books. It would be interesting to find out whether they would read more if their reading skills were improved, or if their reading skills would improve if interesting, mature, yet easy-to-read books were more available than they are at present.

The finding that voluntary readings seemed to be more influential than assigned readings ought to be a warning to teachers and librarians. No matter how good a book is, a child is unlikely to benefit from it if he feels himself pressured into reading it.

In spite of the value of these findings, there are some reservations about the study. Faced with the problem of recording and measuring cognitive effects, Shirley took the "bull by the horns" and took the most direct course of action: asking subjects to record their personal responses. This raises the old problem of whether or not the best way to learn something about somebody is to ask him about himself. The main problem with Shirley's method is that it bears too much resemblance to overworked composition themes inflicted upon students by harried English teachers: "How a Book Changed My Life," "My Favorite Story," "The Best Book I Ever Read." By the time he reaches high school, even a minimally able student can grind out an acceptable theme whether or not the book really influenced him. In some cases he might not have read the book he writes about. Many of the responses suggest students writing what the teacher wants to hear. A great number are rather trite. Some are peculiar, such as the girl who notes that *Peyton Place* influenced her negatively because ". . . it made me want sex." [6] One of the most original responses came from a boy who was classified as an "Indifferent Reader," who, after admitting that he did not read much and preferred to spend his time hunting in the desert, noted that ". . . if people read all the time, they'd dry up and blow away." [7] I am sure most of our finest authors would agree!

The problem is that there is no way to determine the accuracy of the subjects' self-assessments; yet without these assessments, 85 percent of the influence of their reading would have gone unrecorded.

The third major research area deals with the effect of children's readings on influencing and overcoming their prejudices. The greater number of general writings on the effect of children's literature on children's thinking concern themselves with this subject, but only a small portion of the research studies do.

The most recent and certainly one of the most thoughtful reviews of research in this field is J. W. Schneyer's "Effects of Reading on Children's

[6] Fehl L. Shirley. "Influence of Reading on Adolescents." *Wilson Library Bulletin* 43: 256–60; November 1968.

[7] Fehl L. Shirley. "Influence of Reading on Concepts, Attitudes, and Behavior," *op. cit.*, p. 409.

Attitudes." In this report, he calls attention to three studies dealing specifically with the problem of children's prejudices and reading. They are: R. H. Tauran's "The Influences of Reading on the Attitudes of Third Graders Toward Eskimos" (1967), F. L. Fisher's "Influence of Reading and Discussion on Attitudes of Fifth Graders Toward American Indians" (1965), and Evalene P. Jackson's "Effect of Reading Upon Attitudes Toward the Negro Race" (1944). Of the three, so far as the reviewer can determine, only Jackson's study has appeared in a journal. The other two are unpublished doctoral dissertations.

With variations, the method used by each of the three investigators was basically the same. The subjects were divided into experimental and control groups and their attitudes toward the particular ethnic group in question were recorded by means of a questionnaire. A story or stories dealing with the ethnic group were then read to one or more of the groups and their subsequent attitudes were measured with another questionnaire.

Significant variations in methodology are as follows:

1. Working with two matched groups of Southern white children of junior high age, Jackson read a story favorable to Negroes to the experimental groups. She did not read to the control group.
2. Tauran did not make use of a control group. Favorable and unfavorable stories dealing with Eskimos were read to two groups of third grade classes.
3. Fisher worked with three groups of fifth graders. To the first group, six stories favorable to Indians were read. In the second group these stories were read and discussed. The third group acted as a control and stories were not read to them.

Children's stories appear to have a positive effect, at least for a while. Tauran, Schneyer reports, found that children's attitudes toward Eskimos were definitely shaped by the stories they heard. Positive initial attitudes were reinforced by the positive stories.

This is in line with Fisher's finding. Favorable stories about Indians resulted in favorable attitudes toward Indians. Discussion of the stories seemed to make the children's attitudes even more favorable.

Jackson noted the same positive reaction to the favorable stories. However, unlike Tauran and Fisher, Jackson administered the same attitude test again two weeks later. Whatever favorable attitudes toward Negroes the children had gained through the story were lost over that period. After two weeks there were no significant attitudinal differences between the experimental and control groups.

Schneyer's evaluation makes note of leading questions in all three questionnaires which may have biased the responses, and raises certain doubts of how effective an instrument the attitude test is, particularly when used as both a pre- and post-test. He makes a third general point which is especially significant for this and for future research:

One important element which needs further explanation is the influence of the home, community, and peer group in reinforcing or opposing the original attitude.[8]

The three studies might well be examined in this light, and also in light of certain investigations of the effect of mass media (TV and movies) on children's attitudes, as noted by Martin and Lois Hoffman:

Himmelweit and associates offer the generalization that children are more likely to be influenced by the media the less complete their knowledge is from other sources. This view would be consistent with the Peterson and Thurstone experience. . . . While the point has not been fully demonstrated, it is reasonable to suppose that in value areas where the parents have strong, explicitly stated views, and where the parents serve as models for their children's actions, the media would have little effect. The values and attitudes which should be most vulnerable to media influence should be those concerning which the significant people in the child's life have not taken a stand. Furthermore, children in homes where the parents do not interact frequently with their children should be more susceptible to media influence than children whose relationship with their parents is more intense.[9]

With these ideas in mind, it is regrettable that the Tauran and Fisher studies did not make use of an evaluation after a period of time. One might, however, make certain hypotheses in the hope that they will be tested in the future.

Considering Tauran's study, one might expect the effect of the stories to be quite long-lasting, since Eskimos are a group with which few children have any firsthand contact, and one about which, outside of Alaska, there would not be strong parental, peer, or community knowledge or feeling.

In the same light, Jackson's study is extremely encouraging in that she was able to elicit a positive response toward Negroes at all. In this case one would expect peer, parental, and community attitudes toward Negroes to be well-defined and fairly rigid, effectively discouraging deviation. Under these circumstances, one would hardly expect a single story to have a lasting effect.

Fisher's study raises an interesting question. Some homes and communities, especially in the Far West, foster negative attitudes toward Indians, but considering the nation as a whole, most are probably indifferent, as not many people have direct contact with Indians or know very much about them. A great many unfavorable attitudes toward Indians are generated by television and movies. Fisher's study seems to show that initial attitudes can be overcome through the use of selected readings and a well-planned discussion program. As in the case of Tauran's study, the question remains how long children retain these new attitudes. One might well explore the

[8] J. W. Schneyer, "Effects of Reading on Children's Attitudes." *The Reading Teacher* 23: 49; October 1969.

[9] Martin L. Hoffman and Lois Wladis Hoffman. *Review of Child Development Research,* volume 1. New York: Russell Sage Foundation, 1964. p. 342.

problem of whether or not a reading-discussion program can overcome and correct attitudes derived from TV and movies.

Looking over the total field of research into how children's readings affect children's values, one can conclude that books *may* play a significant part in shaping and reshaping an individual's thinking; yet the means by which they do this and the total significance of their role are matters still determined largely by the observer's intuition. In many cases children's readings might momentarily affect their responses, but how lasting these effects are remains to be determined.

Reflections on Moral Education

PETER F. CARBONE, JR.

One of the curious things about moral education is that while nearly everyone approves of it, we seem to have great difficulty in working it into our educational system. As Ralph Barton Perry observed some years ago:

> Schools and colleges, designed for educational purposes, leave it to the home, the church, the Boy or Girl Scouts, or other private and more or less impromptu organizations. But even these agencies hesitate to assume responsibility. The home passes it on to the school, and the school passes it back to the home.[1]

The literature on the subject, moreover, clearly tends toward the view that what little time and effort the school *does* invest in moral education is relatively unavailing. On that account, there is certainly no scarcity of articles pointing out the contemporary "breakdown" of moral standards and urging upon the schools the obligation to revitalize the nation's moral strength, the implication being, of course, that educators are not performing the task satisfactorily at present.

It seems to me that whether or not one subscribes to this view depends in large part on one's conception of moral education. It is doubtless true that we rarely allot a place in the curriculum for a formal course in the subject. Nor, as a rule, do we get very deeply into moral issues, even when we do attempt to provide at least a smattering of moral education on an informal basis. On the other hand, any experienced teacher can testify that the school takes some pains to reinforce those norms and values that are

Peter F. Carbone, Jr., is Professor of Education at Duke University, Durham, North Carolina.

Reprinted from the *Teacher's College Record 71*(4): 598–606, 1970, with permission of Columbia University and Peter F. Carbone, Jr.

[1] Ralph Barton Perry. *Realms of Value.* Cambridge: Harvard University Press, 1954.

generally accepted in society at large. This is usually accomplished not by direct instruction in moral precepts, but rather by various indirect methods which stress example and illustration in a variety of contexts. The means employed are diverse and somewhat haphazard, perhaps, but the task can hardly be said to be ignored. It can, however, and frequently is said to be ineffective, but here again the assertion is somewhat ambiguous. If our criterion of effectiveness is the child's ability to recite the values and norms he is expected to abide by as the result of moral instruction, then I should say that the school, in conjunction with home and church, is fairly successful. For how many school children would deny that they should be God-fearing and patriotic; that they should tell the truth, be honest, and keep their promises; that they should love and respect their fellow men (communists, anarchists, and miscellaneous "leftists" excepted, of course); that they should value liberty, equality, and, above all, free enterprise?

Appropriation and Indoctrination

The charge of ineffectiveness may refer, however, to actions, to what children do as opposed to what they say, in which case the criticism could be well-taken. For as Scheffler has so ably pointed out, it is one thing to appropriate a norm in the verbal sense and quite another to possess a tendency to act in accordance with it.[2] This being the case, it might seem at first glance that the solution lies in forging patterns of behavior consistent with the normative principles we wish to impart, using whatever behavior-influencing devices we may have at our disposal. Now the obvious objection to this strategy is that it smacks of indoctrination, and as Frankena notes after considering techniques along these lines, "We conceive ourselves as having put them behind us."[3] And so we have—but not completely, of course. Here again, those most familiar with what takes place in our classrooms would concede, I believe, that this sort of thing is hardly unknown in the American school.

Of course the indoctrination charge may refer to the content as well as to the process of moral education. This issue obviously emerges when we raise questions about which moral principles we should be expected to teach. As I indicated earlier, we do present long-standing norms and values to children as being worthy of adoption. This is part of what is meant by passing on the cultural heritage. But it will not do to construe the transmission of culture as the whole of moral education, since it is always appropriate—in fact it is incumbent when one is engaged in moral inquiry—to question the legitimacy

[2] Israel Scheffler, *The Language of Education.* Springfield, Ill.: Charles C Thomas, 1960.

[3] William K. Frankena, "Toward a Philosophy of Moral Education," *Harvard Educational Review,* Vol. 28, No. 4, Fall 1958, p. 302.

of custom (and, indeed, of law or any other guide to conduct), and it is this feature more than any other, perhaps, that sets ethics or critical morality off from custom or conventional morality. In other words, an individual might understand perfectly well which norms are valued in his culture and yet reject some of them on the grounds that they are unacceptable from the moral point of view. As Benn and Peters have observed in this connection, "Morality arises when custom or law is subjected to critical examination." [4]

Value Conflicts

Thus, it is inappropriate, at least with older children, to teach morality the way we teach the multiplication tables, or the characteristics of chemical elements, or, for that matter, the behavior of crowds. Morality is not primarily an "information-dispensing" subject, in which content can be distributed in neat factual packages. "What distinguishes morality from the formal and natural sciences," says R. F. Atkinson, "is that in it different and opposed first principles are readily conceivable, and are in fact accepted by morally serious people." [5] It is important, I think, for students to grasp this fact. Similarly, it is important for them to realize that in a given situation dispute is entirely possible, even among those who subscribe to the *same* first principles. As Isaiah Berlin reminds us:

> In life as normally lived, the ideals of one society and culture clash with those of another, and at times come into conflict within the same society and, often enough, within the moral experience of a single individual; . . .[6]

This point seems to have been missed by those writers on moral education who exhort us to present prevailing norms and values to children as though we *were* teaching the multiplication tables, as though moral principles, like the rules of mathematics, never conflict with one another. Apart from the indoctrination issue, it is worth noting in this connection that even if we decided to heed this advice and ignore the problem of validation, we would still fall short of the mark from a practical standpoint. We would fall short because our students would be unprepared to cope with situations involving conflict between values. That such conflict is not only possible but rather commonplace needs to be clearly understood.

More than that, it is important, I believe, to emphasize that considerable disagreement exists with regard to the very nature of ethical propositions.

[4] S. I. Benn and R. S. Peters. *Social Principles and the Democratic State*. London: George Allen Unwin Ltd., 1959.

[5] R. F. Atkinson, "Instruction and Indoctrination," in Reginald D. Archambault, Ed. *Philosophical Analysis and Education*. New York: The Humanities Press, 1965.

[6] Isaiah Berlin, "Equality," *Proceedings of the Aristotelian Society*, Vol. 61, 1955–56, p. 319.

Consider, for instance, the claim that a given act is right, wrong, or obligatory; or that a certain character trait or motive is morally good or bad; or that an experience or a material object is valuable (in a nonmoral sense). Can such claims be said to be true or false? Are they even meaningful? Are they empirically verifiable or logically demonstrable? Are they self-evident, that is, can their validity be seen intuitively? Or are such judgments merely matters of personal taste or opinion? Can they be described as purely subjective, emotional utterances? Or, finally, do they function neither as descriptive propositions nor as arbitrary assertions of personal preference, but rather as prescriptions which can be defended on rational grounds, though not verified to the degree possible with empirical or logical propositions? Turning to moral philosophers for guidance, we find, alas, that most if not all of these questions have been answered both affirmatively and negatively by competent thinkers.

From Acceptance to Criticism

To grasp this characteristic open-endedness, to understand that there are no absolute, invulnerable guidelines to the "virtuous life," that no moral theory has preempted the field, is to begin to discern something about the structure of morality; and assuming that such discernment is helpful when one engages in moral discourse, I should think that it ought to rank high on our list of priorities. I am not suggesting, however, that we can dispense entirely with the inculcation of norms. The fact of the matter is that we cannot wait until the child has reached the point at which he is capable of abstract reasoning before we begin to introduce him to the norms and values that are part of his cultural legacy. The school could "officially" disclaim all responsibility for providing moral instruction in the lower grades, of course, but teachers would continue to impart norms in one way or another simply by virtue of their roles as authority figures in the lives of younger children. Thus it is unrealistic to argue that we can avoid confronting the inculcation bugbear merely by postponing moral education until the child is old enough to benefit from a more sophisticated treatment of the subject. The real issue is not whether, but how moral instruction should be provided in the elementary grades; and since the research of Piaget and his colleagues [7] indicates that youngsters at that age are incapable of grasping the rationale for moral principles, or even perceiving the appropriateness of demands for justifying reasons, it would appear that we are left with little choice at this stage but to present the rules as though they were part of the natural order of things. I am not overlooking, in this context, the heuristic

[7] Jean Piaget, *et al. The Moral Judgment of the Child.* New York: The Free Press, 1965.

educational value, particularly in the "factual" areas of the curriculum, of Bruner's interesting claim that "any subject can be taught effectively in some intellectually honest form to any child at any stage of development." [8] Given Piaget's findings, however, it is not at all obvious that this principle can be applied to the moral education of the very young without placing undue strain on the term "intellectually honest." The problem, then, is to avoid destroying the child's capacity for later critical evaluation of the norms he has been led to accept uncritically during his most formative years. Referring to this situation as "the paradox of moral education," Peters has described it as follows:

> Given that it is desirable to develop people who conduct themselves rationally, intelligently, and with a fair degree of spontaneity, the brute facts of child development reveal that at the most formative years of a child's development he is incapable of this form of life and impervious of the proper manner of passing it on. [9]

It is necessary, in short, to instill norms and habits of behavior before children are capable of thoughtful appraisal of what they are absorbing. Now it is very difficult for us to admit this necessity because the admission is so much at variance with our popular ideology. Indeed, a good deal of our educational rhetoric is utilized to deny this very assertion. The danger here, it seems to me, is that we can get so caught up in our own rhetoric that we fail to perceive the extent of, and the reasons for, our involvement in the practice of inculcation. Consequently, we tend to obscure the difficult problem of how norms may be implanted in children and yet not so firmly rooted that they will be permanently immovable under any contingency whatsover. If, as Piaget and Peters seem to suggest, some inculcation is inevitable in the lower grades, then the question is, how much of it can we tolerate, and how can we avert its potential adverse effects? Hopefully, we may turn to the educational psychologist for assistance here, but such help is not likely to be forthcoming unless we ask the right questions. And in order to do that we must first face up to the problem.

The Socialization Phase

What I am suggesting, then, is that it might prove fruitful to conceive of moral education as including two fairly well-defined levels or phases. At the first level our chief concern should be to contribute to the socialization of

[8] Jerome S. Bruner. *The Process of Education.* Cambridge: Harvard University Press, 1963.

[9] R. S. Peters, "Reason and Habit: The Paradox of Moral Education," in W. R. Niblett, Ed. *Moral Education in a Changing Society.* London: Faber and Faber, Ltd., 1963.

the child by inducing him to accept (in the active sense) the values, attitudes, and standards of behavior that prevail in his social environment. (There will be some conflict here, of course, but even in a society as pluralistic as ours, there are basic values that transcend group differences.) As I have already indicated, a certain amount of imposition is unavoidable at this level, there being no other way to initiate the young into their culture at the time such initiation must begin. By "imposition" or "inculcation" I do not mean what Sidney Hook calls "irrational" means of persuasion such as the systematic use of spurious arguments, for example, or the suppression of pertinent facts in order to support a debatable point of view.[10] This sort of approach is to be avoided at all levels. On the other hand, what Hook refers to as "conditioning" or "nonrational methods of inducing belief," presenting norms straight-out, that is, without benefit of elaborate supporting statements or possible counter arguments, seems to me to be an acceptable method of instructing younger children who are not yet proficient in dealing with abstractions. Even at this early stage, however, we need, as Hook cautions, to be alert to opportunities for cultivating the child's critical abilities, and we should present to him on a nonrational basis only those norms that we are convinced will stand the test of reflective evaluation later on.

Towards Reflectiveness

In the second phase of moral education, our objective is, of course, to advance the child beyond the level of relatively passive acceptance of norms, merely because they are prevalent in his surroundings, to a point at which he is capable of critical, independent judgment in these matters. In a word, we are interested at this level in developing reflective moral agents, people capable of furnishing a reasoned justification for the principles that guide their behavior. For as Frankena comments,

> Morality fosters or even calls for the use of reason and for a kind of autonomy on the part of the individual, asking him, when mature and normal, to make his own decisions, though possibly with someone's advice, and even stimulating him to think out the principles or goals in the light of which he is to make his decisions.[11]

A good deal of the literature on moral education centers on the problem of how best to carry out what I prefer to think of as the preliminary part of the task. There is much debate about what means are most effective, whether, for instance, time should be set aside for direct instruction in

[10] Sidney Hook. *Education for Modern Man: A New Perspective.* New York: Alfred A. Knopf, 1963.

[11] William K. Frankena. *Ethics.* Englewood Cliffs, N.J.: Prentice-Hall, Inc., 1963.

moral precepts, or whether the so-called indirect methods—teacher example, illustrations drawn from the study of literature and the social sciences, inspirational school assemblies, object lessons arising out of classroom or extracurricular activities, etc.—will yield better results.

These are questions worthy of serious consideration, certainly, but a more important issue in my view, as I have already intimated, and one that does not usually receive the attention it deserves, is the problem of how to facilitate the child's transition from the first to the second phase of moral education. For surely we cannot rest content with simply furnishing instruction in whatever moral principles happen to prevail at present. Surely a second phase is needed if we take seriously the goal of producing autonomous moral agents. To continue on indefinitely with the techniques appropriate at the first level, I should say, is to fail to advance from moral "training" to "teaching," both of which have their place in an overall program of moral education. An adequate analysis of this distinction would take us far afield, but roughly, "teaching" is more restrictive than "training" in terms of acceptable methodology, and it demands more of a cognitive emphasis on the part of both teacher and learner. "To teach, in the standard sense," Scheffler remarks,

> is at some points at least to submit oneself to the understanding and independent judgment of the pupil, to his demand for reasons, to his sense of what constitutes an adequate explanation . . . Teaching, in this way, requires us to reveal our reasons to the student and, by so doing, to submit them to his evaluation and criticism.[12]

"Training" on the other hand, connotes processes of drill, rote-learning, habit-formation, and the like. It is more permissive, less scrupulous about the means used to bring about a change in behavior or in attitude. It fails, in sum, to engage the child's rational capacities to the extent that "teaching" does, and is therefore unequal to the assignment once moral education has advanced beyond the introductory stage.

Teaching Principles

Much more could, and no doubt should, be said by way of clarification here, but perhaps the point regarding the difference in emphasis between the first and second levels is evident at least in outline form. I have already commented on the need for further research to inform our efforts with respect to the preliminary phase. Assuming that this additional information will be provided, and that we *can* guide the child through his early moral training without placing too great a strain on his incipient critical capacities,

[12] Scheffler, *op. cit.*

we can sketch in some of the characteristics of moral education at the second level. Most of these characteristics, e.g., the emphasis on reasons and justification, the awareness that moral principles frequently conflict with one another, the realization that there is considerable disagreement even among moral philosophers concerning the meaning and cognitive status of moral propositions, have already been mentioned. In addition, we need to convey something about the nature of moral discourse, I should think, and perhaps some understanding of how it differs from the "language" of other disciplines. This, I suggest, is partly what we are groping for when we talk about providing children with the intellectual tools that are a prerequisite for clear thinking. Further, we need to confront our students with moral issues that force them to re-examine and re-evaluate their own moral principles. "What we do, if we are sensible," Hare writes,

is to give him [the learner] a solid base of principles, but at the same time ample opportunity of making the decisions upon which these principles are based, and by which they are modified, improved, adapted to changed circumstances, or even abandoned if they become entirely unsuited to a new environment.[13]

Admittedly, it is somewhat unsettling to subject one's basic moral beliefs to the kind of challenge implied here; but, as Peirce and Dewey taught, the irritation of doubt frequently serves as a prod to genuine inquiry. It may be argued, however, that youngsters of high school age are not sufficiently experienced or psychologically stable enough to engage in this sort of thing, that such considerations should be taken up only on the college level.[14] Personally, I feel that this view grossly underestimates the maturity of contemporary 16-, 17-, and 18-year olds, who have practically been weaned on moral controversy as a result of their constant exposure to the mass media. And though it may be true that adolescence is not the most psychologically tranquil period in one's life, it is also true that it is the time when one is most likely to seriously question and demand justification for the moral rules and standards one is expected to honor. Under these circumstances, we do the adolescent no favor in attempting to shield him from difficult moral issues at a time when he is searching for a personal philosophy of life. What he needs at this point is guidance on a journey that he is very likely determined to undertake, whether we approve or not.

Most of the procedures suggested above are rather familiar, to be sure, yet with possible rare exceptions, one does not find them being implemented in our schools. Their absence is partly attributable, in my opinion, to the misconception that once the notion of moral absolutes is discarded, *any* attempt to provide moral education becomes an exercise in indoctrination. And while we might be willing to concede that a limited amount of indoc-

---

[13] R. M. Hare. *The Language of Morals.* London: Clarendon Press, 1952.

[14] View expressed in George Herbert Palmer and Alice Freeman Palmer. *The Teacher.* Boston: Houghton Mifflin Co., 1908.

trination in Hook's "nonrational" sense may be unavoidable in the lower grades, most of us rightfully have serious misgivings about extending its application to older students. Thus we simply neglect to provide a coherent program for this age group. In my view this is a classic example of throwing out the baby with the bath water. The perceived danger can easily be averted by recognizing that at the second level our primary emphasis must shift from the transmittal of moral propositions to their application, justification, meaning, and genre. I am inclined to believe that such a shift in emphasis is mandatory if moral education is to reflect the essential character of moral philosophy, and that some such reflection is necessary to ensure the integrity of moral education.

In concluding, I should acknowledge the many practical problems that I have neglected to consider in this brief essay, problems relating, for example, to implications for teacher education, to the possible introduction of new courses, and to the relationship of moral education to the "factual areas" of the curriculum (for obviously factual information is a necessary condition for the intelligent application of moral principles). I realize, too, that some of the concepts and terms employed in this discussion would benefit from further explication and analysis. But each of these tasks would require extended treatment, and my purpose here was merely to suggest a concept of moral education which might contain enough initial plausibility to be taken up for further discussion. In attempting to do so, I have drawn freely from the writings of a number of philosophers who have made significant contributions to our understanding of the ways in which moral philosophy is relevant to the problems of moral education. If drawing together some of the more promising and provocative features of their work contributes anything worthwhile toward the developrient of an adequate conception of moral education, I am confident that the practical problems can be worked out by specialists in the areas of learning theory and curriculum development.

Philosophic Dimensions of Character Education

HAROLD A. WREN

Character education has arrested the attention of philosophers for centuries. The Socratic query "Can virtue be taught?" remains as much in
controversy as it did when Aristotle attempted to outline a means for an
answer through providing instruction and habit formation. Throughout the
ages, religious teaching has relied upon the weight of rigid authoritarianism,
and virtue was a gift of God or of the pagan gods. The absence of virtue,
according to our Puritan ancestors, provided a reason for conformity and
curbing our evil ways. More recently, a rigid permissiveness has depended
upon the natural goodness with which a child was believed to be born. This
is frequently indicated in the present day in the secularization of education.
The old nature-nurture conflict, as usual, adds heat without light. Finally,
about a generation ago, the Character Education Inquiry showed that there
was no valid character education school program in operation.

Character is a tonal word. When you look at a painting you recognize its
tone. The blending and harmony of the colors, the effects of the light upon
the composition bring out the quality, meaning, significance, depth, feeling,
a host of characteristics that give the painting its individuality. This is what
character is. In the person, it is that which is the moral and mental self as
expressed by behavior and habits. Character is not an aggregate of habits
or traits, but a merging of each feature of the personality into an identifiable
whole.

Character is a molar word. It connotes wholeness. When a kind person
does an unkind thing, we say his action is "out of character." We expect
kind actions from a kind person. As contrasted with the molecular, or
particularized, or partial view, the over-all presentation of a person provides
us with an identification of his character.

When character development is viewed in the light of educational philosophy, the axes, upon which its dimensions are scanned, lie in the following
areas: the nature of the individual to be taught, the relation of the educative process to the social order, the acquisition of knowledge, how learning
takes place, and the formulation of a value system.

The four DIMENSIONS of the educative process that provides the
guideposts for character education are:

Harold A. Wren is Director of the School of Education at Our Lady of the Lake
College, San Antonio, Texas.

Reprinted from the *Character Education Journal* 1(2):14–15 ff., 1972, with permission of the Character Education Project, San Antonio, Texas, and Harold A. Wren.

1. the *integration* or one-ness of the person
2. personal *decision making* with its dual source of input
3. examination, *evaluation,* reinforcement or inhibition *of behavioral outcomes* through operation
4. *contextual behavior* of the individual interwoven into a pattern of living.

The drive for integration of the various elements of our society too frequently causes neglect of the concept of individual integration that is intrinsic. It would be patently foolish to strive for an integrated society of dis-integrated individuals. When a person's behaviors are in harmony with his purposes, we say that person is integrated; when they are in disharmony, that person is headed for the psychiatrist's couch. Frequently, the change need be one of purpose, not behavior. The determination of and insight into the "whys" frequently provides happiness. The character education program must ultimately provide insights into personal integration.

No single element of character education is more important than decision making. The making of wise volitional choices is dependent upon the validity of intellectual judgments that are part of the input determining choice. These judgments that influence decisions have their source in cognitive learnings, and cognitions are dependent upon the information or data received. When cognitive knowledge has been put to the test by the use of reasoning, it may terminate in judgment. When there are errors in information, or its transmutation into knowledge, can we have sound judgments or wise decisions?

Again, not all decisions are rational. We talk about "gut" choices. Fully as powerful as reasoning is the influence of emotions and feelings. The bodily appetites, the ideals and attitudes, are frequently stronger than reason or judgment in decision making. The sorting out of one's feeling, when a decision is impending, is difficult.

Then, when intellect and emotions have supplied their inputs, a decision can be made. Decisions cannot be made in a vacuum.

Essential in character education is the necessity of exposing the process of decision making. Delaying a decision until all the data have been judged, or until the influence of the emotions has been weighed, prompts the formation of a character that will be consistent in its behavior.

When character is translated into behavior its meaning is difficult to assay. The significance attributed to a behavior must be made in relation to the generalized structure of consistent behaviors of the individual. It is often meaningless to ascribe connotation to a specific behavior. What does a smile mean? Is it a friendly, cynical, embarrassed or hostile reaction?

One of the few facts that have been established in the psychology of learning is that rewarded behavior is likely to persist. It would seem reasonable, therefore, to reinforce desired learnings as expressed by behavior. If character education depends upon platitudes or even derived principles without translating them into activities, its lessons might be shallow.

Herein lies the difficulty. The inference that is made regarding the behavior, that it is a choice made on the basis of volition involving judgment and feeling, may range from sheer speculation to conviction. How can the teacher gauge the behavior that is to be reinforced? There seem to be three criteria: (a) it is a desired and desirable response, (b) it is consistent with previous behaviors, (c) the existence of a cognitive background seems likely.

Finally, character education is expressed in terms of contextual behaviors interwoven into a pattern of living. In the present-day, "life styles" is commonly used to indicate different ways of living in our society. In a former day, differences in the lives of individuals were believed to inhere in their socio-economic circumstances or levels. People on lower economic levels, in general, held many of the same or similar values and ideals as those on higher socio-economic levels and planned their lives to approach or reach the kind of goals for living held by those on higher levels.

In the present day, the individual values that are held are more a function of character than of socio-economic level. A value such as "human dignity" covers the spectrum of the socio-economic scale. People expect to have their persons respected, regardless of circumstance. Each child must learn not to transgress the person of another individual. The respect to be accorded a person because he is a human bears no relation to any other facet of the person: race, religion, educational level, social status, nationality, etc. It has taken human kind a long time to achieve this value, and it has become part of every "life style."

Any list of values commonly held by most people in the present day will produce some that had different interpretations a generation ago. *Pluralism* may illustrate the idea. A present-day concept of the value would indicate that all citizens must accept pluralism. One single religion for all people in the United States is as unthinkable as one single political party. Each person respects the choice of each other. A generation ago, the "peculiarities" associated even with nationalities were held to scorn. A character education program of the present day recognizes the validity of differences.

When "democracy," "self-realization," "personal freedom," "equity," and a host of other values become part of one's personality and function in living, these values can be said to have become part of one's character. In a world where the number of recurrent and stable values are diminishing, and where many values are recognized as changing, the difficulty of directing the functioning of values, in behavior geared to the context of a life style, is great, indeed. The goal of character education, however, is as great as its charge.

In this short paper, I have tried to delineate the dimensions of character education while avoiding the pitfalls of topics such as moral education, religious education and stereotyped character formulae. The conscientious teacher will find in these dimensions the challenge that enlarges the scope of the problem but promises the hoped-for rewards.

But Who Bends the Twig?

JOHN JAROLIMEK

One of the truly fascinating things about human beings is their diversity. Linguists estimate that the world's people speak some three thousand different languages. If one includes dialects, the figure soars to many times that number. People range throughout the world to make their homes. They can be found in the most hostile environments on earth, from the bitter cold of the far north to the scorching dry deserts—and everywhere in between. Similarly, human beings meet their basic needs in diverse ways. Here again there is a full range of activity from those who convert work to money and then to needed goods and services, to those who grub their food, clothing, and shelter directly from their immediate environment. But wherever or however people live, it is significant to note that their children grow up behaving and acting as they are expected to behave and act in their society. Left in their home environments, it would be impossible for a French child to grow up to be an Uzbec, a Chinese child to grow up to be an Englishman or an American child to grow up to be a Congolese.

How can we account for this incredibly complex and diverse set of folkways, mores, values and life styles we find among the people of the world? Morphological or physical differences cannot explain these variations in human behavior. Any human being of any racial, national or ethnic group could function equally well in any of the many societies of the world if he were placed there at birth. The evidence is overwhelming that these interesting variations in human beings are learned behaviors. Wherever human groups live, they develop a culture, and from that culture they learn their particular way of life. In short, human beings build a culture, and correspondingly, that culture shapes and forms those human beings that are a part of it. This is an idea of profound importance in understanding human behavior.

If a society is to transmit important elements of the culture from one

John Jarolimek is Professor of Education at the University of Washington, Seattle.

Reprinted from the *Character Education Journal* 2(2):14–15, 23, 25, Winter 1973, with permission of the Character Education Project, San Antonio, Texas, and John Jarolimek.

generation to the next, ways must be devised to teach the young. Thus families traditionally have been and continue to be one of the most important teachers of young children. As a culture becomes more complex and learnings more extensive, special institutions are established to take over a portion of the responsibility of educating the young. These special institutions are, of course, schools. In a society such as ours with highly developed school systems there is a natural inclination to mistake *schooling* for *educating* of children.

In our own country we find that schools were established by the early colonists in the 1600s. Quite naturally the nature of these schools has changed greatly in the past 300 years. Nonetheless, from the earliest times to the present, it has been generally understood that elementary schools should do at least three things: (1) provide training in the basic skills of literacy, namely, reading, writing and arithmetic, as needed for everyday living; (2) provide education for intelligent and loyal citizenship in order that self-government might be enhanced and enlightened; and (3) provide moral education in order that education would be applied to good rather than evil purposes. Character education obviously is a part of the third purpose listed and to some extent is a part of the second as well. In both cases a considerable amount of controversy has been generated with respect to how these purposes are to be achieved.

In early times schooling was clearly an extension of the training the child received at home. Moreover, persons living in the attendance area of an elementary school were relatively homogeneous in terms of values, religious beliefs and life styles. In such settings there is not likely to be a problem in teaching moral values preferred by the community in public schools. Even today there are pocket communities here and there that are homogeneous to the extent that Bible reading in school, for example, though illegal, is not only allowed but encouraged.

As communities became more heterogeneous, a gradual shift in emphasis took place in the responsibilities of schools. Rather than schools being an extension of home training, the home and school have become two institutions serving related but nevertheless different and separate functions. Increasingly, schools have attended to cognitive learning, i.e., basic subject matter and related skills, an area relatively "safe," meaning free of controversy. Schools have steered farther and farther away from affective, moral and values education. Perhaps this is inevitable in a society that is highly diverse and where so little apparent consensus exists on moral and value issues. Be that as it may, the present emphasis on cognitive learnings with a corresponding lack of attention to affective, moral and values education must be considered a serious shortcoming of American education today. It is impossible to deal with character education in any meaningful way if these dimensions are not considered.

It can be argued that affective, moral and values education are responsibilities of the family, not the school. But the life styles of the modern family do not lend themselves well to this dimension of the child's upbringing either. For the most part the extended family is extinct as a functioning unit. Modern employment patterns frequently remove both parents from the home for eight to ten hours or more each day. Single parent families are common.

We find, therefore, another set of organizations designed to assist with the character education of the young. These are groups such as Boy and Girls Scouts, Bluebirds, Brownies, Cub Scouts, Indian Guides, Little League and so on. They provide legitimate social activities for children, but fundamentally they are concerned with character building (i.e., "A Scout is kind, A Scout is trustworthy, etc."). Additionally, parents will send their children to religious classes with the expectation that they will thereby not only be better prepared for life in the hereafter but also that such training will have some impact on their moral and ethical behavior in the present.

The way of life in modern America has resulted in a high degree of segregation of children from adults. Adults will go to great expense and effort to do "anything for the children." They will also do almost anything to exclude children from the activities of the adult world. Children are left with baby sitters as parents go out to dinner. There are children's matinees at theatres. Children are sent away to summer camp. Some churches have special services for children or may reserve the last few rows of pews for parents with young children at regular services. The practice of providing "baby sitting service" at large department stores and church and club functions is becoming common. Adults can check their children at the door as they do their coats and go about their business unencumbered. Parents breathe a sigh of relief when their children return to school after a holiday. Those who bring their children to social affairs invite criticism. There can be no question that our society has systematically separated its adult population from its child population, a practice that is completely at variance with both conventional wisdom and research on the upbringing of children.

Not only are children separated from adults, but older children are segregated from younger ones. In schools, for instance, typically pupils are grouped in grades on the basis of age. In out-of-school club groups, age is ordinarily a prime prerequisite for membership. Those who are too old or too young cannot be Cub Scouts, Brownies or Campfire Girls. In some cases the mixing of older and younger children is not only discouraged, it is not allowed. Likewise, children are encouraged to associate only with their own age groups and those who do not are suspected of being deviant. The old-fashioned one-room rural school had obvious limitations as an educational institution, but it did provide a cross-age mix of children that had many advantages for the total development of young people.

If we examine these practices within the context of character education, we must conclude that they are leading us in the wrong direction. Character education is closely related to the socialization process; indeed, it is an important component of it. Socialization is the capacity to function in many statuses or roles. These statuses and roles must be modeled for the learner. They have to be made concrete if he is to observe them. As the child matures and intellectualizes value concepts, he can benefit from the reading of biographies and case studies of idealized types. But he cannot deal with these ideas at such an abstract level during his early years.

All the evidence we have points to the fact that these socialization skills take form early in life and are learned from association with significant adult figures. The kind of adult we expect a child to become is almost entirely governed by the adult models with whom he associates as a young child. Thus a society that systematically removes adults from the lives of young children is depriving them of the most important means of becoming socialized into the society. The child can obviously learn many social skills by associating with his peers. But he cannot and will not learn to internalize those values embraced by the adult society in this way. In order to achieve these learnings, he must have extended and close contact with adults who model those values in their life styles.

Character education, including moral education, values education and ethical education is in deep trouble today. It will remain so until this society begins to think broadly and profoundly about what it means to provide a proper upbringing for children. It cannot be achieved by providing special programs in truth and goodness for children who are shunted away from the adult world. It cannot be achieved by inserting a few units on values education or character education in the social studies curriculum. It cannot be achieved by Bible reading alone nor by sending children off to religious classes.

More than anything else, the practice of segregating children from adults must be discouraged. Responsible prestigious groups, educators, psychologists and public officials should speak out against this practice and work toward the development of more accepting attitudes toward adult-child interactions and associations. Adults need to become more aware of the fact that they are always teaching the young in any contact they have with them. Children must be valued as human beings who will one day occupy responsible adult roles in the society.

School and pre-school experiences will need to include many more adults than is the case today. In view of present day family patterns (as opposed to traditional extended family arrangements), the practice of having one teacher with 30 children for several years in the elementary school is very questionable. The school experience should provide for close contact with many adults of varying ages, both sexes, in many occupational roles. One could imagine an elementary school, for example, that had as many adults as children associated with it, with adults ranging in age from sixteen to eighty. This does not mean that all of these adults and children would be physically present in the school building all of the time. It means simply that over a two to three-month period the child would have close contacts with many adults on and off the school grounds, in work roles, in play situations, in sharing experiences, listening, seeing, learning.

Because adult models are as critical as they are in the character shaping of children, and because society has highly segregated children from adults in ordinary living, new methods need to be invented to bring adults and children together to ensure the wholesome upbringing of the young. Clearly the traditional institutions and procedures are not able to deal adequately and competently with the task.

Section FIVE

The Learning Environment: Learning Resources for Social Studies

The increased quality and quantity of instructional materials coupled with modern teaching strategies are producing a shift from the traditional "audio-visual aids" approach to the more comprehensive and efficient *learning resources* concept. This broadened concept of media is predicated on the assumption that if effective learning is to be promoted, the child must have easy access to a wide range of learning resources. In applying this principle, therefore, an array of media is brought to the classroom. Naturally, use is made of the conventional materials such as books, motion pictures, film-strips, and study prints. But beyond these, other educationally valuable media are used, including some newer and more exotic innovations such as simulation and gaming, programmed instruction, multimedia kits, and com-puter-based instruction. Multisensory-assisted learning is especially worth-while in social studies because of the abstract and complex learnings in this field.

As the learning resources idea flourishes in the schools, it can be expected to cause changes in the methods of housing, distributing, and utilizing educational media. It will become imperative to streamline the distribution-utilization system in order to close the gap between pupil need and avail-ability. With this in mind a number of elementary schools across the nation have already converted libraries into learning resource centers. Collections of books and other printed materials have been augmented by the addition of other learning resources. Thus, with ready access to all needed learning materials, the pupil can be expected to shoulder greater responsibility for selecting resources than he does now. With utilization on an immediate and highly individualized basis, he will no longer need to wait for nor depend on the teacher to present a particular resource to the entire class before he can make use of it.

Learner-centered use of resources will present teachers with some new responsibilities, too. One of the most important of these is to assist in selecting good items for the school collection. Unlike the experience of a generation ago when his counterpart faced a barren desert of materials, today's elementary teacher confronts a bumper crop. Great claims are often made for the value of new instructional materials. However, solid evidence to support such claims is frequently lacking. The problem is the plethora of materials and the resultant necessity to separate wisely the wheat from the chaff. Quite obviously the classroom teacher needs to be involved in making such choices.

Materials must be selected with care so that they not only instruct but instruct appealingly. With disturbing regularity, investigators have directed attention to the indifference with which many youngsters regard elementary social studies. The source of objection is not the content *per se,* but the manner in which the content is taught. One effective approach toward vitalizing social studies instruction is through the use of carefully selected and wisely used instructional media. Media that provide information in a clinically sterile and uninteresting way cannot be expected to contribute positively to increasing the appeal of social studies.

The essays that follow provide an overview of current thinking regarding the use of learning resources in elementary social studies. The technology of education is producing new and exciting innovations in media at a rapid pace. These new resources along with improvements in the old ones should materially assist the teacher in his work and enhance the learning of the pupils who use them.

Learning Resources for Individualizing Instruction

HUBER M. WALSH

There are several reasons why teachers who have proper learning resources at hand can meet individual learning needs in a superior manner. First, instructional materials make it possible for the classroom teacher to "stretch" his time. When resources such as auto-instruction media are utilized to perform the rudimentary instructional tasks like drill, the teacher is freed for other functions demanding more creative, human teaching. Second, children *do* have different learning patterns which necessitate using various instructional modes to "reach" them successfully. Books and other printed materials are the most effective keys to understanding for most pupils, but individual learning patterns may make viewing a motion picture, hearing a tape recording, or working with self-directed programmed materials more profitable for others. Many pupils will require all of these and perhaps others in combination. The point is, we have yet to discover a universal skeleton key to use in unlocking children's minds. No single best way to reach every student exists; hence, the need is created to find and to use the right material(s) tailored to the particular needs of particular individuals. Third, good instructional materials seem to have built-in child appeal—a kind of intrinsic glamor and fascination that tend to intrigue youngsters. At least in the beginning, they find most new media attractive and, consequently, are motivated to use them. This phenomenon tends to vitalize social studies instruction and make it more enjoyable. Fourth, certain of the learning resources now available are well suited to individualizing instruction in the fullest sense of the term. That is, these devices can provide instruction on a fully self-directed basis allowing the child to investigate and discover on his own when there is no teacher present to assist him. Innovations in technology have simplified equipment operation to such an extent that pupils can use machines easily. Such refinements have made it possible for children to use motion pictures, filmstrips, and tape cassettes as their own personal tutors.

Reviewed below are several important resources that hold the promise of effectively "reaching" children of varying abilities in social studies—the slow learner, the culturally different child, the nonverbal youngster, the retarded reader, the gifted learner, and others. An attempt has been made

Huber M. Walsh is Professor of Education at the University of Missouri, St. Louis.

The original version of this article appeared in *Social Education 31*:413–415 ff., 1967.

Reprinted with permission of the National Council for the Social Studies and Huber M. Walsh.

to focus on salient new developments that provide refreshing, innovative approaches to individualized instruction. Most of these are already available to the classroom teacher; others, however, are in the developmental stage and will become available later on.

8mm Cartridge Systems

Because of its compactness, lightness, and simplicity of operation, the 8mm cartridge projector is particularly valuable as a tool for individualizing instruction. It can be used easily by youngsters in the classroom or at home for independent study because the problem of threading film is eliminated. Film is housed entirely within a plastic case and formed into a continuous loop making rewinding unnecessary. Using the projector is as simple as inserting the cartridge, turning a switch, and making minor focus adjustments.

A variety of film loops pertinent to social studies is available, with most designed to teach a single concept. Moreover, teachers as well as the students themselves can film their own motion pictures tailor-made to the particular learning requirements of their classes. This is done using a conventional 8mm camera. The processed film is then sent to the Technicolor Company where it is formed into a loop and mounted in a cartridge.

The ordinary film runs for about four minutes, then repeats itself as many times as desired. This continuous presentation feature makes it a particularly valuable resource in meeting the needs of individuals requiring much repetition for concept mastery. Such children, on their own, can view and review the film as many times as is necessary to fully grasp the idea. The films are also advantageous for slow readers and children with restricted language backgrounds such as those coming from culturally different environments.[1]

A new version of 8mm cartridge is used for commercially produced films with sound. These films, which require a special projector, are used extensively in Man: A Course of Study. The sound system has the same simplicity of operation and continuous projection features as the silent system, though of course, its cost is much higher.

The Multi-Media Kit

Multi-media kits are rather complete learning-resource packages containing a wide variety of audio and visual media, printed materials, artifacts,

---

[1] For additional information, contact The Technicolor Corporation, 1985 Placentia Avenue, Costa Mesa, California 92627.

and other learning tools related to various social studies units. They will be particularly welcome in those classrooms where a wide diversity of individual learning needs exists. Each kit contains something beneficial to and usable by almost every child, whether he learns best visually, aurally, or tactually.

Usage of kits simplifies the often vexing problem of instructional materials procurement, for it is simpler for the teacher to procure one package containing an array of media than to have to order each item separately. Its most important contribution is what it provides in individualization of instruction. In a multi-media kit on Mexico, for instance, one could have at hand the following resources: (a) information brochures on Mexico City (these are appropriate for use by gifted children); (b) filmstrips with accompanying records (these could be used for research by average children); (c) photographs (slow readers could use these to advantage); (d) a collection of Mexican toys and other artifacts of the culture (nonreaders and nonverbal children could make discoveries from studying these articles).

Multi-media collections have proved popular to the extent that a number of school systems have produced them for their teachers. In addition, some teachers create their own kits. They find art galleries and museums an excellent source of supply for inexpensive reproductions of the world's great sculpture and paintings; ancient jewelry and other artifacts; color slides; books, and other useful items.

Programmed Materials

The array of programmed materials for social studies instruction is an additional resource useful in meeting individual learning needs. Though many of these are intended for total-group use, perhaps their most significant contribution to learning is made when they are used to individualize instruction on a single-pupil basis. Programmed materials become particularly valuable for reviewing, reteaching, and reinforcing knowledge already presented by the classroom teacher. Used in this way programmed materials do not supplant human teaching, but instead provide a way to meet special needs of a given learner without necessitating the expenditure of a disproportionate amount of the teacher's time.

One set of programmed materials provides instruction in map and globe skills. This kit, like the two described immediately below, uses very much the same color-coded, sequential approach as is used in the SRA Reading Laboratory Materials. The map program consists of materials to teach basic concepts, study-exercise materials, and self-checking devices.

An organizing and reporting skills kit is a program designed to provide instruction in reporting, note-taking, and outlining. Its companion set of materials is a graph and picture skills program intended for the upper-elementary grades. Skills in interpretation and application of graphic materials such as photographs, editorial cartoons, diagrams, charts, and the like are included.[2]

A study skills library will answer the need of many pupils for individualized instruction in social studies reading skills—especially those needing remedial instruction. Comprised of seven different sets of materials, the library encompasses reading levels III through IX. Within each is a series of sequential lessons predicated on a self-directed reading exercise followed by a self-checking activity. Individual lessons are designed to teach such specific skills as interpretation, judging relevancy and significance, verifying accuracy, and finding and organizing ideas.[3]

Automatic Projection Center

A fascinating idea that is destined to capture the imaginations of creative social studies teachers is the Automatic Projection Center. Capable of a myriad variety of multi-media presentations, the device consists of two sound motion-picture projectors (16mm and 8mm); three slide projectors, and a stereophonic tape recorder.

The heart of the center is a punched paper tape that programs the presentations. Equipment is started, paused, stopped, and reversed on command of the tape. Slide projectors may be programmed to operate individually, to project in 1-2-3 order across the screen to illustrate a step-by-step process; or all three may be used in concert to produce a cinema-scope-like, wide-screen panoramic view. Inclusion of the 8mm projector makes it possible for teachers to augment commercial film presentations with their own inexpensively made films. The flexibility of tape programming produces almost unlimited possibilities for individualizing instruction. Using the same projection materials, for example, one program can be prepared appropriate to the learning requirements of the gifted learner; another can be made for slow learners; and yet another can be developed for use by average pupils. Though the same instructional media are used in each case, such factors as order of presentation, and provisions for repetition and review are varied according to need differential. Although the APC is not yet commercially marketed, its components and plans for its construction are available.[4]

---

[2] For additional information on these three programs, contact Science Research Associates, 259 East Erie Street, Chicago, Illinois 60611.

[3] For additional information, contact Educational Development Laboratories, Huntington, New York.

[4] For information contact Eastman Kodak Company, Rochester, New York 14650.

Videocassette Systems

Videocassettes (videotape recordings housed in plastic cartridges) will make it possible to tap for educational use a vast reservoir of network documentary and other television programs. In a videocassette system, the sights and sounds of a recorded program are reproduced on a classroom television set in the same way an audiocassette system reproduces sounds. This is accomplished by attaching a videocassette player to the T.V. receiver.

Given an appropriate library of cassettes, the television set could function as a tool for individualizing social studies learning. Videocassette systems are distinctly advantageous for their potentially enormous range of subject matter. One supplier claims to have the rights to over $20 million worth of programs, with new titles being added constantly. Cassette programs, which are said to cost about one half as much as film, can be either purchased outright or rented.[5]

Computerized Programming for Individualization

A future possibility more than a present-day actuality is the prospect of using automated data processing to aid teachers in individualizing social studies instruction. For example, given data on what a pupil learned yesterday, on his learning needs for tomorrow, and on his optimum learning pattern, data analysis could be used to identify the most promising learning activities and resources to be used with that particular child. For one, this might indicate an individualized session with some kind of electronic teaching device; for another it might mean a small-group work session with the classroom teacher, or perhaps the beginning of some kind of construction project. For others additional work in textbooks might be prescribed. One type of learning resource would be suggested for the gifted, another for the average, and a different one for the slow reader, and so on, accommodating each according to his special needs.

Study-Print Packages

A review of new learning resources for individualizing instruction would be incomplete without at least brief mention of the packets of study prints

---

[5] For details on the videocassette player, contact Sony; for information on video-cassette programs packages, write to Videorecord, Videorecord Building, Westport, Connecticut 06880.

now available. The typical set contains a coordinated collection of large, full-color photographs centered about a topic or theme such as "Life in the Heart of the City." Although they are good media to use with all pupils, they are especially appropriate to the needs of the slow learner, the retarded reader, and the nonverbal child. Slow learners, for instance, can use them for independent research, recording on tape the information discovered from carefully studying the content of the pictures.[6]

Audiocassette-Visual Systems

Audiocassette recordings have enjoyed widespread acceptance by teachers who have found them to be inexpensive and effective media for entire-class teaching as well as individualized instruction. While a wide variety of commercially prepared tapes is available to the social studies teacher, many have created their own especially designed presentations to meet the particular needs of their students.

Until recently, adding a coordinated visual element to such teacher-made audiocassette presentations has been difficult. Now, however, teachers can very easily produce their own synchronized "sight and sound" presentations using a specially designed projector. The projector uses standard audio-tape cassettes in conjunction with regular carousel slide trays. Up to 140 standard or super 2 by 2 inch slides can be used. The sound can be reproduced by earphone for individual use, and the picture is projected on a self-contained 9 by 9 inch screen. An additional possibility for individualized instruction offered by this equipment is that of allowing students to create some presentations on their own.[7]

The resources described are illustrative of products available to individualize instruction in social studies. In the final analysis, however, it is not the addition of more hardware to the classroom that will, in and of itself, effect greater individualization of instruction any more than adding hardware in the kitchen produces gourmet meals. Indeed, the critical factor is not a mechanical but a human one. The key point is *how* these media are put to work in individualizing instruction by the classroom teacher. And so, in a very real sense, the most important single resource in individualizing instruction still is the creative teacher.

---

[6] Further information on Study-Print Sets can be obtained from producers such as Silver Burdett Company, Park Ridge, Illinois; and Society for Visual Education, Inc., 1345 Diversey Parkway, Chicago, Illinois 60614.

[7] Contact the Singer Company for information on the Caramate Projector.

Ideas and Objects: The Artifact Kit

DAVID G. MENSER

Teachers and students alike know that history teachers are very wordy. Dealing so much in words, both written and spoken, we are like the man who painted himself into the single remaining corner in the room. Our paint is the sticky goo of too many words. Like the man in the corner, our dilemma is painful. We have tried desperately to contrive props and walkways to escape.

The whole range of audio-visual materials available today is an attempt to find a way out of the word prison. In the hands of a skillful teacher a filmstrip can hold attention much better than words alone, bringing details of technology, costume, and architecture to the class. Through films a class can visit Williamsburg, Monticello with its many wonders, or stand by Concord Bridge. A record can capture some of the flavor of putting to sea. Surely "The World Turned Upside Down" speaks the feelings of the British at Yorktown. Yet all of these are flat. They have no dimension. They cannot be touched or held.

More serious than the lack of size and shape, films and records lack a time dimension. They are not old. The things that they show are not the same as they were. The colors are too bright. The grass is too well trimmed. The new techniques help in many ways, but they, like words, have no dimension.

Many museums have attacked the bars of the word prison. Most have education departments. They are eager to cooperate with the schools and share their collections. For example, the Marine Historical Association of Mystic, Connecticut, sends out wooden chests containing many artifacts of nineteenth-century whaling. Colonial Williamsburg plays host to thousands of children each year in a well organized and enjoyable educational experience. But, of necessity, the museums have had to rely on people coming to visit them. This leaves the majority of teachers where we found them—in the corner. The teacher who could not go to the museum now or ever is left with the current audio-visual aids and words.

Last winter the American Studies Research Project, a part of the Wemyss Foundation, decided to design and build teaching kits:

We are anxious to develop teaching kits which would bring a third dimension reality to the history class. They would include artifacts (especially those used

David G. Menser is a history and government teacher at the Mount Pleasant Junior High School, Wilmington, Delaware.

Reprinted from *Social Education* 30:343–345, 1966, with permission of the National Council for the Social Studies and David G. Menser.

in America between 1800 and 1830) telling how men lived and worked in the young Republic.

. . . hand tools and nails from which America was built; pieces of textile and homespun by which men were clothed; samples of the food on which they were nourished.

Starting with this general idea, a kit research team composed of a director, an anthropologist, and three high school history teachers was established. Working under the supervision of Marshall Fishwick, the team assembled five kits: a peddler's kit, a Civil War soldier's kit, a covered wagon kit, a technology kit, and a seaman's kit. Each has its own container so that it is easily portable. Each can be reproduced in limited quantity.

Before the work could begin, several questions had to be answered. The answers were worked out by the team. Four tests were established. The answer in each case had to be "yes" before an object could be included in a kit. Is the artifact authentic? Would a sailor have had one of these? Nothing was to be included that could not be documented.

Does the object illustrate a teaching point? Here the difference in the museum and kit approach begins to·show. In the kits the point to be illustrated was decided and then the object tracked down. We had no collection to draw on.

Is the artifact unique? A student's attention is most easily attracted by things that are different. Some early sailor's tools are unique enough that many students have never seen them. A palm and a fid (a tool used in splicing rope) drew nothing but blanks from a ninth-grade class. Yet both tools were bought in a well-known marine store in their own city. These objects made in 1965 are the same as the fid and palm made in 1765. Not only are the tools unique, the teaching point is there. Today these are the tools of the yachtsman. Today's leisure was yesterday's toil.

Is the object available? It defeats the whole purpose of the kit if the objects in it are so rare that teachers and students are constantly worried about breaking them. No amount of talk will convince a boy that the Civil War musket he is holding is for real if he is constantly being admonished to treat it as though it were an egg from a whooping crane's nest. He must feel its weight, shoulder it, sight down its barrel, and aim over its sights at someone. It helps if it goes bang.* Only then can the student really identify what he has in his hands with the musket of the lad of Gettysburg or Fredericksburg.

Touchability is the heart of the matter. Where it was possible, the teams used objects that could be used and handled the way they were intended to

---

* *Ed. Note:* All firearms are potentially dangerous. They must be handled with extreme care. *No* firearm should ever be pointed at another person. The high explosive power of present-day ammunition, coupled with the relatively weak metals used in manufacturing antique firearms, makes it dangerous to fire old weapons.

be used. In two kits there is a piece of hardtack. Our students can touch and taste it. An old fashioned ax, were it included, should have a log for chopping.

Touchability presented a problem that had to be answered before assembling the kits could begin in earnest. Does the kit include antiques, facsimiles, reproductions, or all three? In the end, the teams decided to use only antiques and facsimiles. To bring in reproductions would have let in an *ersatz* quality that nobody wanted.

It was not difficult to define antique—something made during the period. The kits needed some antiques or they would not have the time dimension that was part of the original plan. It was equally obvious they could not be made completely of antiques. Availability, ease of replacement, and cost were all factors to be considered.

Facsimiles eased the problem. A facsimile is an artifact made in the same way as it would have been made in the past. The seaman's kit includes a set of checkers cut from the top of a discarded leather boot. They were made this summer using the same materials that a sailor used to make a set of checkers now in the Smithsonian Institution.

There are two advantages to be gained from the use of facsimiles. They help to keep down cost and they can be easily replaced if they are accidentally broken. A clay pipe bought for fifty cents and then covered in a sailor's stitch, says just as much about a sailor's humanity and ingenuity as an antique pipe. If broken, it can be replaced. Students can make facsimiles themselves. In this way, they can participate in history. Facsimiles lack only the patina of age. Too many facsimiles can make a kit as phony as the too bright colors of the well trimmed grass at the Bridge.

My project was the sea chest. It is a composite; no single sailor would have had all the things in it. I had hoped to be able to assemble the things that a boy would have had when going to sea for the first time. I gave this up, for in limiting the kit, many useful and interesting artifacts would be left out. The kit illustrates traits that were found in many of our early seamen.

I wanted to emphasize that these seamen were human beings. They were alive; they chewed tobacco, played an occasional game, and had aches and pains. They had certain skills and used particular tools that were peculiar to their work. I wanted to show how the American was different from his European counterpart with his class mobility. I felt it was important to capture some of the discomfort that one feels in the fo'c's'les of ships like the *Constitution*.

The task of finding what belonged in a sea chest took me to many museums. Everywhere I found people eager to help. Mystic furnished details on chests and clothing. New Bedford's library has an excellent collection of old ships' account books. There are many curiosities of the whaling trade on Nantucket. The Peabody Museum at Salem provided valuable advice and several antiques. The libraries in Washington as well as the Smithsonian, cooperated in opening non-public rooms and collections.

Once the research was done, I began collecting artifacts for the kit. I had never really gone antiquing. The kit was not to be a treasure chest. The criteria for inclusion at the beginning of the summer remained. Did the artifact say something? Was it accurate? Was it available? Since cost was a fact of life, some interesting and illustrative objects could not be included. There is no clothing in the chest. A sailor's clothes belong in the chest, but to have had accurate reproductions would have cost as much as all the other items in the chest together. Clothing just does not say that much. On the other hand, an antique quadrant accounted for almost half of the cost of all the artifacts. For what it says of hopes and dreams, it was worth the cost.

The last task was to prepare a teacher's manual to go with the kits. In the manual is a description of the objects in the box. No teacher could be expected to know why some things were included and others were not. Each manual contains background information for the teacher who uses the artifact kit. At the end of each manual is a bibliography including fiction and non-fiction, records, films, and filmstrips. There is also a list of suggested student projects.

What happens now is anybody's guess. It was somewhat humbling for me to be told after presenting my kit to a group of local teachers that "this is nothing new. I've been doing this with my classes for 18 years." We don't claim that the artifact kits will make anyone an inspired teacher. They are not an aluminum catwalk to climb out of our corner over the wordy paint on the floor. They are more like an open window letting in a breath of fresh air to clear out some of the fumes.

Instructional Media for Teaching About Values

DONALD R. GREER

Faced with the task of teaching about values, educators are often prompted to ask rather direct questions concerning instructional media: What's new? What's good? What's useful? Response to the first of these queries is provided simply by introducing the latest available methods and material in the values area. Were answers to the latter two questions as easy to come by, it would be a great source of satisfaction; however, there are major controversies surrounding these last questions which prohibit

Donald R. Greer is Assistant Professor of Educatonal Psychology and Instructional Resources at the University of Missouri, St. Louis.

Reprinted from *Social Education* 35(8):911–915, 1971, with permission of the National Council for the Social Studies and Donald R. Greer.

absolute, all-inclusive replies. Deliberation on "what's good" and "what's useful" in instructional media for teaching about values hinges on two fundamental issues. These should be examined by those teaching about values before judging the good and useful media resources. The first of these involves the process by which values are acquired, and the second involves a consideration of what makes up the legitimate content of value instruction.

Value Acquisition—A Controversy

The first major issue deals with the question of how values are acquired and the kinds of mental processes called for as the learner acquires these values. Psychologists tend to divide into two groups of opinion on this issue. The first describes the process associated with value acquisition as a simple one. The child simply engages in certain behaviors, then receives some reward which increases the probability he will engage in that behavior again. The child acquires values by conceptualizing what is desirable and then being rewarded for engaging in appropriate behavior. All that is necessary to teach values is to define or illustrate what is desirable and then reward behavior which is consistent with that description.

A second group of psychologists views the acquisition of values as a much more complex process. The key element is establishment of a warm, supportive relationship wherein *empathic identification* takes place between the child and an individual or a group. The child receives his reward, real or imagined, by engaging in behavior consonant with the values of the "significant others" in his environment. This position, as well as the first, relies on a system of rewards, but here the reward comes from the empathic relationship wherein the child has internalized feelings associated with the values of others. The child acquires values because he is able to feel as others do.

The above description of the two major positions on how the learning of values takes place is directly related to the conception of which mental processes are involved in each. The first involves exclusively those mental processes which fall into the cognitive domain. The child may first have to analyze before he responds, but, most likely, he needs only to recall the appropriate action before responding. Values could be changed by simply describing what new behavior is to be acquired and then receiving a power-ful enough reward to change behavior. Under this position, things are judged as good or bad to the degree they conform to the prescribed behavior.

The second major position involves the affective as well as the cognitive processes. The child is asked how he "feels" and how he thinks another would feel under the same circumstances. Cognition is involved to the degree that it makes the person aware of the feelings of others; and affect is involved to help establish empathy with others.

The design of instructional media is classified as being related to one or the other of the two positions and learning goals, for use of such material also favors one or the other position. Techniques of role playing offer an illustration of this point. Since the materials designed to elicit various cognitive responses are obviously such that can be used to describe a desired behavior associated with a given value, so role playing can be designed to fit the cognitive end. In such a case, role-playing activities are formulated not to arouse feelings but simply to present information for analysis. On the other hand, however, role playing can be designed to elicit empathic feelings and to aid in the process of identifying with others. Materials associated with either of these positions might well be labeled as role playing but would be drastically different in purpose and design. Consequently, evaluation of "good, useful" role play and other forms of instructional media must reach beyond the activity itself and should instead be determined by careful examination of the *intended* purpose.

Value-Teaching—Value-Processing Issue

The value-teaching—value-processing issue is a refinement of an older argument questioning the teacher's right to teach values. Today, the issue is whether specific values should be taught or whether the value-processing techniques are the proper end results of instruction. One school of thought proposes that there are certain transcultural values, present in all cultures, which the school system is obligated to teach. This viewpoint is exemplified in the 1965 Progress Report of the Social Studies Curriculum Center of Syracuse University.[1] The authors point out that, while these universal values change within the various cultures, it is the presence of values that provides cultural stability in the midst of change.

The counterposition is stated in the argument that it is precisely because of this characteristic of change that no specific set of values can be prescribed. Further, since there is no truly universal set of values, and since the present values are undergoing change, the only truly productive activity for teachers is the teaching of value-processing skills. The child must be afforded the opportunity to inquire, to examine, and to discover what values he and others hold and what are the factors associated with their formation. The processes of clarifying values and of resolving conflicts are important skills to be acquired. To fail to teach these skills is to fail one's responsibilities.

[1] Price, R. A., W. L. Hickman, and G. G. Smith, *Major Concepts for Social Studies*. The Social Studies Curriculum Center, p. 21.

The issue is confronted by one group urging the teacher to teach a common set of values, and by the other group, with equally strong exhortations, stressing the teaching of those process skills which develop in the child the ability to analyze, to classify, and to resolve value conflicts. To the debate over what to teach is added the dilemma concerning determining materials that are most effective. The decision the teacher makes concerning what to teach helps resolve the instructional media problem, since design of materials, consciously or not, tends to identify them with one or the other of these major positions. Those tending toward the value-teaching positions will stress identification of a common set of values; and materials tending toward the value processing will stress the analysis and clarification of values as well as the resolution of value conflicts.

The issue associated with the processes involved in the acquisition of values or the modification of existing ones and the controversy associated with the value-value process issues are not mutually exclusive approaches in instructional media. Indeed, materials designed to establish empathic relationships with an individual or a group, while stressing specific values, could, nevertheless, easily border on indoctrination. Materials designed to deal with the identification of values could be coupled with a reinforcement as to the "correct response." Thus, a child may be able to analyze his values but be unable to identify with the position of others. A coupling of the empathic skills would lead to a cognitive-affective experience where one might "feel" how it is to be involved in a value conflict between two strong values.

With these two issues in mind, we are reviewing below some media designed for teaching about values. Although there can be no claim for comprehensiveness of coverage, it is believed that the materials selected for review constitute a fairly good cross section of items currently available. It may also be mentioned that the word "media" is used in the broadest sense to include value drama or role playing as well as other simulated situations.

Instructional Media

A variety of formats for materials is available, but one in the traditional textbook form is *The Human Value Series* authored by Arnspiger, Brill, and Rucker. Designed for kindergarten through upper elementary, the series consists of stories centered around eight major values which the authors feel should be a part of the social studies curriculum. Accompanying the stories are illustrations which add some color and interest. Quite plainly the series is designed to teach particular values and would tend strongly to the value-teaching side of the continuum. The method of instruction tends to be based on the description of values and rewarding appropriate responses. Although the stories are of some interest to children, there is no attempt to establish an empathic relationship. The approach to the teaching of values leans heavily toward learning the "right" thing to do.

Another series of materials is titled *SRA Social Science Laboratory Units,* by Lippitt, Fox, and Schaible. These are to teach social studies through the inquiry approach. Values are explored through the application of certain inquiry techniques. The authors state that the teacher's role is not to teach values *per se,* but rather to guide each child toward clarifying his personal values, to deal with value conflicts, and to become aware of those factors which are related to the values of others. The program consists of situational stories illustrated by photographs. Role playing is used as a teaching technique, but its primary function is as a vehicle for presenting data for examination and not for the purpose of establishing an empathic identification. These materials appear based on the description-reward concept, with the child doing his own describing. The teacher's role is to help him clarify his description. There is no attempt to indoctrinate the child, but it is expected that he will discover those values that are appropriate for him.

An inquiry approach is also utilized in a program soon to be published. Authored by Byron Massialas, the program deals with the entire social studies curriculum drawing concepts from the seven major social science disciplines. The approach is based on a student interaction model utilizing large photographic prints and student workbooks. The role of the teacher is to help the students deal with values, his own and those of others. These materials, as would be expected, tend to the value-processing orientation and the teaching techniques are based on the reinforcement position rather than that of empathic identification. The program is more fully described in *Today's Education* (May 1969).

Schools, Families, and Neighborhoods, by John Michaelis and Richard Gross, is a multimedia kit based on an inquiry approach in which "the values, attitudes, and interests important for rational inquiry and for living in the United States in the last decades of the twentieth century" [2] are explored. The materials, short strips, filmstrips, records, large study prints, as well as wall charts, are provided to accompany the texts. The kit is designed primarily for postkindergarten and is probably best suited for beginning first grade. Role playing is utilized as a teaching device. The purpose of this technique is to lead the child to the discovery that all peoples have values which determine their behavior. In addition to the *Schools, Families, and Neighborhoods,* other kits are planned for later publication to accompany the text series and will follow the same format. The materials tend to strike a midpoint between the opposite ends of the value-teaching–value-processing issue, but perhaps are closest to the value-processing end. Role playing is designed to clarify values and to present information. The suggestion for teaching would place the materials towards the midpoint of

---

[2] Promotional material—New Field Social Studies Program. Field Educational Publications, Inc.

the reinforcement-empathic identification issue but still towards the descriptive side with the act of discovery providing the reinforcement for the child.

A series of text materials which are referred to as "a complete social studies program for meeting the value crisis" [3] is the *Man and Communities* series published by the Fideler Company. It is basically a series of texts which begins with a series of photoprints for the K–2 level entitled *Families.* The basic approach stresses that there are certain values held by families which make life together possible. The series deals with values in each of the texts along with the factors which have influenced the establishment of certain values. These are clearly value-process oriented, but utilize a "discovery" approach wherein a child is rewarded by discovering these values for himself. No attempt is made to use the materials to establish an empathic relationship.

There are a few materials designed to establish an empathic relationship. The values films adapted from the Shaftel and Shaftel book, *Role Playing for Social Values,* are designed for this purpose. The three films in the series, *Paper Drive, The Clubhouse Boat,* and *Trick or Treat,* deal with open-ended situations which are designed to involve the viewer in the dilemma of a value conflict. The teacher's role is to involve the children in exploring their own feelings as well as those of the characters and to look at ways people may react to a given situation. As a follow-up activity the children are to engage in role playing to dramatize what the consequences of a given decision will be. A discussion follows the role playing which leads to replaying a revised or new-role situation. There are also suggestions for the use of discussion only without the value drama. The purpose, however, is the same, to involve the children in a situation in which there is a conflict between the two values. The films are designed for the upper elementary grades and the principal characters are all within this age bracket. The teaching technique is to establish an empathic identification with the characters. The children then explore the value conflict involved and propose solutions. These materials are clearly classified as utilizing an empathic identification approach to learning and are also clearly on the value-process end of the value-value process issue.

Another set of materials specifically designed to involve the child squarely in a value dilemma is that developed by Harold Berlack and T. R. Tomlinson. These materials, which will be published by the E. W. Singer Company in the fall of 1971, are a multimedia approach to an array of social studies concepts associated with value conflicts. The intent is plainly to establish an empathic identification with the characters around which the units are organized. There are slide-tape programs, transparencies, student activity books which contain self-teaching exercises, programmed reading exercises, as well as role-playing activities and simulation games. Although certain

---

[3] Promotional material—*Man and Communities,* The Fideler Company.

values are presented in the context of the materials, the primary purpose is to show how these are brought into conflict with other values. The emphasis of the materials is to teach the value-process skills in analyzing and clarifying values and resolving value conflicts.

The materials reviewed vary from teaching specific values to teaching specific value-process skills. They range from relying heavily on the cognitive aspects of learning to reliance on the affective. They are either simple or complex in design utilizing either a single or multimedia format.

When evaluating materials, judgments must be based on the teacher's own frame of reference. Instructional media which are technically flawless and beautifully packaged are of little value for this reason alone. Materials like specific methods become useful only to accomplish those objectives for which they were designed. In the case of media the design is related to how values are acquired and what is the legitimate content of value instruction. Once the teacher has clarified his own position on these issues then the questions as to "what's good" and "what's useful" can be answered to some degree of satisfaction. The ultimate decision like the ultimate responsibility rests, in the final analysis, with the teacher. In any event, the prospect of value instruction utilizing new materials promises to be nothing less than exciting and rewarding.

Individualizing with Responsive Spatial Environment

DONALD LANG

No one will deny the importance of every person realizing his place and potential within the networks of man-made and natural elements which collectively we call the environment. Both societal survival and personal success rely on this fundamental task. Yet the problems of the technical urban systems within which most people must live grow more complex daily. The residues of these technical systems increasingly threaten the greater natural order within which they attempt to function. It is no longer possible for us to lull ourselves with notions that specialized technocrats hold the keys to understanding the environment and will be able to effect the action necessary to sustain the smooth day-to-day performance of our urban systems within a balanced natural context. All of us must become our own

Donald Lang is Co-Founder and Director of the Penny Museum, Inc. (Children's Workshop and Research Project), Washington, D.C.
Reprinted from *Social Education* 36(1):62–66, 1972, with permission of the National Council for the Social Studies and Donald Lang.

environmental mechanics to make the adjustments required to keep our own domains in working order. To take on such a role requires a clear understanding of the environment in simple *operational* terms. The educational system must undeniably confront the responsibility of transmitting this understanding. Education must provide each of us with the operational skill necessary to sensitively control and adjust our environment, before it grows totally incomprehensible.

Operational knowledge, as opposed to figurative or verbal knowledge, simply is *how* things work. This type of knowledge is in a form useful for solving real problems. Accommodating environmental situations of any scale demands this type of "nuts and bolts" expertise. Understanding the environment in terms of its inner workings, which has allowed us to harness the power of the planet, is not a detached academic study; on the contrary, operational knowledge is the direct product of grappling with our environment in everyday situations, of trying new solutions and finding new patterns. *Operational* knowledge is a realistic index for effective intelligence, but it is quite distinct from the rote learning and verbal skills which too often characterize our programmed learning centers. We must acknowledge and respond to the importance of operational concepts in designing and programming learning facilities. Learning centers will then become the true microcosm of the overall learning environment. It will become the environment's true focus, a place for children to operate on, manipulate, construct and reconstruct their environment.

Looking Back—A Corollary

An analogy might solidify this somewhat philosophical plea into useful operational reality for the classroom. For 3000 years, architecture has been the continual *reshaping* of our living space across the planet's surface to suit changing needs. This metamorphosis ultimately progressed and became sophisticated because man became more facile at operating on his environment with each attempt. Through his activity, he gained usable (operative) knowledge about both the interior complexity of his environment and himself, as he strived to articulate his needs clearly enough to accommodate them within the limits of his environment. This progressive development of architecture points out a direct corollary to a learning process.

We should all become competent architects or *reshapers* of the sections of the environment over which we have dominion. This obviously does not mean we should all be qualified as city planners, but it does mean that we should at least know how to work with what we have to adjust and maintain our familiar environment finely tuned to our needs.

Looking In—The Where to Learn the How

The educator's familiar environment focuses on the classroom. Like the overall environment, the classroom space must be periodically *reshaped* and adjusted to keep it finely tuned to the needs of its participants. If neglected, it can become an atrophied inventory of books and child holders. The classroom space must be structured so that both teacher and child can operate on it. Only by operating on it can the child learn the *hows* of his environment. The potential of the classroom's full three dimensions must be utilized to create a place where a child can come to act on, manipulate and shape his environment with the advantage of expert guidance. A learning environment with these qualities is truly responsive to the needs of young learners. It is much more than a closed container for two-dimensional activities involving words and numbers.

Looking Ahead—Optimizing the Where

Creating a responsive environment within the classroom space is by no means a formidable or expensive proposition. However, there is one major opponent to responsiveness which constantly interferes. He stands on eight legs and is called the chair and desk set. This villain has long dominated students, teachers, school boards, architects and building departments. He qualifies the interior structure of all classrooms and even established the formula for the quantitative areas required for classroom space. (Each chair and desk set, with or without child, requires 20 sq. ft. including aisle space in a rank and file arrangement.) Once he is established in a classroom space, three-dimensional activities are all but impossible and a responsive environment is lost.

Certainly any creative teacher can find another use (or place) for these immutable relics. Perhaps they can be recycled into articles more appropriate for environments responsive to the needs of young children. Once cleared of these obstructions, a classroom space can be transformed into a three dimensional context for problem solving, a place for the child to act on and manipulate the environment to accommodate the needs of his activities. *The child learns about his environment from constructing and reconstructing it.*

The problem for the architect teacher is to restructure the classroom space to allow the child to operate on it. To accomplish this merely requires that the environment contain useful elements which can be safely manipulated by the child to create or structure an environment suited to his own needs. These needs are demonstrated by the personality of the individual child and by the spatial requirements of the various task settings which compose a daily class schedule. The concept of a responsive spatial environment can be integrated synergetically with any preconceived curriculum.

Each activity of the curriculum can be analyzed to determine its spatial requirements. The simplest breakdowns are for tasks requiring: (1) *individual* work: folder tasks, writing, computation, etc.; (2) *small group* projects: reading, discussion, art work; (3) *communal* or large group participation: story telling, forums, demonstrations, movies, or activities where children move around. Different task settings such as these would have differing spatial requirements. With guidance, a child can learn to optimally construct an environment best suited to executing these tasks. With more experience, children can learn to cooperate in these activities to see how their needs relate to the needs of their fellows. Attempts may be crude at first, but as in the analogy to the development of architecture, progress is only a matter of time.

Besides the quantitative spatial breakdown for various task settings, other qualitative aspects of space can be dealt with. Openness and closeness, separation and proximity, personal and public, and quiet and activeness are qualities which can be incorporated in a manipulable environment. For instance, a certain child may perform one task best in an enclosed space in one corner of the room, while another child may perform the same task best in an open space in the center of the room. A manipulable environment affords both students an equal opportunity. We must remember though that increased performance is not the ultimate justification of such an environment. The child must be allowed to find out about his environment and about himself as he relates to it by constructing and then reconstructing it.

Seeing Space—Knowwhere

The application of a responsive environment is not limited to allowing a child to solve the functional spatial requirements of curriculum activities. The responsive environment lends itself to a diagnostic application. If a child is allowed to experience and manipulate his space in a free discovery process (e.g., in games or animated play), the degree of sophistication by which he perceives his space can be noted. The child's developing perception of space has its beginnings with an awareness of simplistic topological (me-to-it) relations and progresses toward an understanding of the complex Euclidean concept of space in three dimenions (X, Y, Z coordinates).[1] By

---

[1] Jean Piaget describes a developing awareness of the complexity of space by the child's maturing intellect as he interacts with his environment. The development begins with topological perception, then to projective relationships, and refines to an awareness of the complex Euclidean space of simultaneous three dimensions.

observing the child as he interprets his space, the type of individual guidance he needs to systematically operate on it can be extracted. This type of free interpretation of the classroom space can be initiated by simply asking the children to make the room the way they would like it.

Once organized, a responsive classroom environment can be utilized as the specific context for three-dimensional problems involving the mathematical aspects of space. These problems can be designed to stimulate conceptualization, cooperation, gross motor coordination and reversibility of operations. The best problems are those which do not have immediately visible solutions. The child must use his own ingenuity to experiment with possible solutions. The complexity of such problems can be controlled by organizing them around a developing schema whose basis is a singular point. The simplest problems would then be organized around a singular location. Concepts involved here would include *over, under, next to, between, high* or *low.* These are concepts which define a location.

The second phase of the development would include two points or linear concepts, i.e., from here to there. Simple or complex problems can be designed which involve movement through space on a line. "Bridging" exercises are very successful. One way of doing these, from which many variations can be drawn, is to somehow designate two singular point areas in the room. Place five or six elements of the responsive environment at one point and instruct a small group of children to move themselves and the elements to the other point (using the elements as bridging devices). This exercise can be done by recycling the elements over and over as stepping stones, carrying along the surplus. The group should not be allowed to walk on the floor in executing their assignment.

Children have enjoyed this exercise, and it involves the conceptualization, coordination and cooperation mentioned previously. Many variations to this exercise are possible by differentiating the allowed uses of the different elements, or by increasing the number of points. For instance, start with four points on the floor plane identified, and all the equipment at one point. Either by shape or by color, instruct the children to move certain elements to certain points. Identify the points as base, red point, blue point and yellow point. All equipment is placed at base point (Fig. 1.) There are several lines along which the children can move themselves and the color-coded equipment to the appropriate point. To finish, all equipment must be left at its appropriate destination with no pieces left over.

These exercises do not have to be limited to the floor plane. Vertical bridging can be tried, etc. In communicating the concepts involved with these exercises, simple definitions and instructions are required. An essential vocabulary could include definitions such as: (1) a *point* is a place, (2) two places show a *line,* (3) a *plane* is between, and (4) what's under the floor is *volume.* In this form, the definitions have an accurate meaning in terms which children can easily understand. They are the conceptual basis for an understanding of space as a *referencing system.*

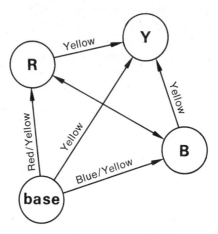

Figure 1   Complex Bridging

Using the four elements of *point, line, place* and *volume* as organizing points, a teacher can create many simple exercises for the classroom besides the bridging problems described. Once an understanding of the potential of a responsive environment is acquired by a teacher, the number of specific applications possible is limited only by scheduling. Any exercise is relevant if it involves the child manipulating or constructing the environment to solve a problem.

Besides developing the child's awareness of the workings of space and the environment, there are certainly subtler psychological implications for a child, who is given the ordinarily denied opportunity to control his environment.

In experiments done with a manipulable system of modular cardboard components, even the most withdrawn children became animated when they participated in the responsive environment.

The equipment needed to create a responsive environment in the classroom need not be as sophisticated as a modular system. The critical element in applying such an environment to the classroom is the understanding by a teacher of how it can be used. Any available objects can be used which are safely manipulated by a child. In the designated modular system, abstract sculptural forms were used because they did not have immediate functional uses associated with them. This allows broader interpretations for their uses by both child and teacher. A variety of objects can be used which share this characteristic, the more diverse textures, shapes, and weights the better. Paint buckets, cartons, wooden boxes, spools, barrels, cushions, plywood, foam rubber scraps, or heavy cardboard are appropriate. These objects can be painted by the children to code them, allowing discrimination by both their color and shape. The children themselves can gather the needed items: large, small, flat, round, heavy, light, hard, soft objects to be on top of, next to, or inside of. Again, it is important to use items not having singular functional implications (e.g., chair and desk set) for the child.

A teacher who attempts some of these ideas in his own classroom will be able to refine and enhance this description of an environment more suited to developing children with a real need to understand and manipulate their environment. The structure of our learning environments must engage active participation on the part of the learner, not merely demand dull compliance. They must be real "knowwheres."

Bibliography

Piaget, Jean and B. Inhelder. *Child's Conception of Space*. London: Routledge and Kegan Paul, 1956.

Simulations, Games, and Related Activities for Elementary Classrooms

R. GARRY SHIRTS

"I'll start with a hint—strawberry is a Queen Anne."
"Is cherry a Queen Anne?"
"Yes."
"Is beet a Queen Anne?"
"Right again."
"Is a Queen Anne any red fruit or vegetable?"
"Tch, tch, tch. It's against the rules to guess the rule. You can only ask if such and such is a Queen Anne. I'll give you another hint, though: Tree is a Queen Anne."
"Tree is a Queen Anne? Oh no, it can't be!" [1]

So goes Barry Barnes' introduction to the games and activities developed for primary school children at the Far West Laboratory.[2] Following the Queen Anne game, he shows the teachers a rectangular box (looks like

R. Garry Shirts is Staff Associate at the Western Behavioral Sciences Institute in La Jolla, California.

Reprinted from *Social Education* 35(3):300–304, 1971, with permission of the National Council for the Social Studies and R. Garry Shirts.

[1] In this game a Queen Anne is any word with a double letter. In other games a Queen Anne might be any item that can be defined by a general rule.

[2] For more information, write to Far West Laboratory for Educational Research and Development, 1 Garden Circle, Berkeley, California 94705.

an old cheddar cheese carton) with a lid that slides back. Inside are cards with numbers on them. He slides the lid back and exposes the numeral three.

"What do you think the next number will be?"
"I say four."
"No, it will be two."

After almost every number from one to twenty has been guessed, he slides back the lid and exposes the number 6. More guesses, but everyone finally agrees that the next number will be 9. He pulls back the lid. It's twelve. And now everybody knows the pattern. Everyone, that is, except one or two art teachers who still look a little puzzled in the back of the room. Then he asks the group to tell him what the next letters in this series will be: OT, TF, FS, SE. Can you do it? [3]

Following this he challenges them to a contest. He has nine numbers written in a tic-tac-toe figure hidden from view (see Figure 1). For every number he has to tell the group, he gets a point; for every number they guess, the group gets a point. He wins the first contest, and from then on it always ends five to four in favor of the teachers.

2	4	6
3	5	7
4	6	8

Figure 1

These are only a few of the numerous games, puzzles, and related activities that have been developed for elementary children [4] at the Laboratory, which can be applied in a wide variety of classroom situations.

The NASA game is another simple game to execute, yet it can produce surprisingly sophisticated discussion in children. They are asked to assign a numbered priority to fifteen items for inclusion on a moon expedition, first as individuals, then by consensus in groups.

Frederick Goodman [5] gives sixth-grade students some marbles, a stack of blocks, and a few directions, and in a short time they are building coalitions, establishing governments, police systems, and political machines. A game with profound implications for our time, yet very simple to execute.

[3] NT for *N*ine, *T*en.

[4] An additional source of information for children's games is the free catalogue distributed by Creative Publications, P.O. Box 328, Palo Alto, California 94302.

[5] Instructions for "They Shoot Marbles, Don't They?" can be obtained from Frederick L. Goodman, Department of Education, 4023 University School, University of Michigan, Ann Arbor, Michigan 48104.

Rex Walford, in his book *Games in Geography,*[6] presents examples of different types of geographical games, most of which require only a piece of paper and a pencil. They are oriented towards the geography of England, but can easily be adapted to reflect local or regional concerns.

Jay Reese [7] of Eugene, Oregon, has created a game called *Explorers*. He drew a grid of three-quarter inch squares on a sheet of 3 × 4 foot tagboard. Each vertical line of the grid was numbered and each horizontal line was lettered. On a smaller grid an imaginary continent was drawn which was kept out of the sight of the students. The class was divided into groups which represented explorers from different nations. They were to start on the right-hand side of the area and explore the unknown region to the left. Each team could move three grids per day. At the end of each day the teacher drew on the large map, using his smaller master map as a guide, whatever they would have seen in their travels that day, e.g., water, coastline, or nothing because of poor visibility. When they discovered the coastline they had to decide whether to stop and settle the area or to continue exploring the continent. Those groups that decided to settle the area were required to obey a set of laws imposed on them by the mother country. Inevitably, there were disputes with the other exploring countries and the mother country.

Not all of the games and simulations require so little equipment and advance preparation. For instance, the Community Land Use Game (CLUG)[8] has been used successfully by sixth graders. It is a classic game that has spawned several generations of land use games. To use it one would have to do more than the usual amount of studying and preparation. Yet the learnings that can come from the game are so useful it would be a shame not to expose the children to the game merely because it required extra work for the teacher.

These are but a very few examples of games and simulations that have been created the last few years. Until now, it has been very difficult to get information about what is available, but in the fall of 1970 *The Guide to Simulation Games for Education and Training* [9] was published. It gives full particulars on games currently available. I would highly recommend that your school library buy a copy. It is the "Sears and Roebuck catalog" for the simulation and game field.

Games are not new to elementary teachers. They have been using them in their classes for years, but simulation is a relatively new activity that has

[6] Rex Walford, *Games in Geography*. London: Longmans Green Ltd.

[7] For more information write to Jay Reese at 3235 West 17th Avenue, Eugene, Oregon 97402.

[8] Players' instructions available Free Press (Macmillan Publishing Co., Inc.), 866 3rd Ave., New York, New York 10022.

[9] David W. Zuckerman, Robert E. Horn, Paul A. Twelker, *The Guide to Simulation Games for Education and Training,* Information Resources, Inc., 1675 Massachusetts Avenue, Cambridge, Massachusetts, 02138.

somehow gathered great clouds of mystery around it. No two "experts" can agree on what simulation and related terms mean. But for the sake of discussion it is necessary to venture a ball park definition. The essence of simulation is the creation of an experience which models a process or condition in the real world. If the simulation is a model of a process that is gamelike, such as the stock market, a political contest, or a war, then the simulation takes on gamelike characteristics. Role playing is one form of simulation in which a person simulates being in the position of another person. However, role playing and simulations are generally considered to be different processes. The difference is that in role playing the forces to which the participant reacts largely come from the initial description of the situation, the person's imagination, or from the other people in the role playing exercise, whereas in a simulation, the participant is also bound by reality as it is represented in the rules and structure of the simulation. In other words, the participant in role playing has great freedom; he can imagine any condition, make any decision, or create and shape the situation as he wills without suffering "tangible" consequences to his actions. By contrast the environmental forces created by the rules and structures of the simulation put one in a position of "living" the consequences of his actions: he may be thrown out of office, win or lose an election, make a profit for his corporation, not be allowed to pass Go, be defeated in battle, fail to get a job, or suffer any one of a variety of results depending on the nature of the simulation.

Building Your Own Simulation

When considering what simulations to use in the classroom, it is helpful to think of them as belonging to three categories. In Category I we have those simulations which require special training or a computer before they can be used by a "stranger" (person other than the developer). The second category contains simulations which are easily exported; they do not require special training or computers in order to be used by a stranger. In the third category are those simulations that require the presence of the developer.

Developing a simulation for one's own use is quite a different matter from developing one that can be exported. In the home-grown simulation or game, the teacher or some other person serves as an umpire determining the consequences of the action of the participants on the basis of his knowledge and experience. When a problem arises, the teacher thinks through the experience with the students and arrives at an answer that allows the simulation to continue. He models reality out of his personal experience and knowledge. Because he is free from the hard work and inhibiting effects of formalizing the model in writing, it is possible to develop simulations in the classroom which are surprisingly rich in detail, content, and process.

Furthermore, I would predict (if it were possible to measure) that there is no correlation between the level of a simulation's complexity and its effectiveness as a teaching device. Indeed, when considering elementary students it may well be that there is a negative correlation: that the students learn more from the less complex than the complex experience. On the other hand, I am confident that the *designers* of the more complex simulations learn a great deal more than the designers of the Category III experiences, but that is another matter.

The main point here is that the teacher-designed simulations, even when they are relatively less complex than commercial versions, may be just as instructive and valuable as those experiences which have cost thousands of dollars to build and years to design. If you add to this the enjoyment and learning that results when one creates his own experience, then the answer to the frequently asked question "Should we try to design our own simulation experiences?" becomes yes, yes, most emphatically, yes.

There are several approaches to building a simulation. One is to turn the entire classroom into a simulated environment. For instance, each year Wesley Stafford, now teaching in Africa and formerly of the La Mesa-Spring Valley School District in California, had his students land on a deserted island or an unknown planet and build a complete government and culture from the ground up. The year I visited him, the students were living on a heretofore unknown planet. They had labored for weeks over a constitution for their new civilization, trying to find one which was fair to all concerned yet made it possible to accomplish something. They invented their own language which was used during a certain part of each day. The face of the clock and all other numbers in the room were changed to a base five numbering system which was adopted as their official measure and which several of the students became especially adept at manipulating. To protect themselves from alien visitors a password was developed (the principal was turned away several times until he got next to some of the students and learned the magic words). The room itself was decorated by the students to reflect the new environment. One entered through a cave and was confronted with a "live" volcano and a mural on the wall depicting the flora and fauna of this new world. The total simulated environment approach created a strange feeling in adults who visited the class for the first time, as they heard children speaking a different language, reading time from a weird clock, and having to say a strange password before entering. Possibly the feeling is similar to those of the child as he tries to navigate in the adult world.

The mechanics of building a simulated environment were dealt with by the class and the teacher as they developed. Some of the ideas came from the students, some from the teacher. The teacher had the final say as to whether or not an idea would be implemented, but he rarely had to invoke that power. The students agreed to, and did in fact, work extra hard to accomplish their regular work so they could devote themselves to their simulated environment. It is likely that the required work faded from their memories within weeks of the ending of school but I doubt that many have forgotten the year they spent on another planet.

The ungraded class of Doreen Nelson at the Westminster Avenue Elementary School in Venice, California provides us with another approach. Using a cardboard base, styrofoam, and other materials gathered from the classroom, home, and industries in the area, the class rebuilt their neighborhood as they would like it. First, they recorded representative structures of the area on film. Then with a couple of architectural students as consultant and a lot of thinking, planning, and creative fun, they constructed a new environment to reflect their wishes. All cars were eliminated and replaced by a monorail and a system of conveyor belts. More area was available for parks and playgrounds and in general an esthetically pleasing environment was created. All construction plans had to be passed by a democratically chosen planning commission, city council, and a nine-year-old mayor.

Donald Love and associates of the Meadowbrook Intermediate School in Poway, California, were interested in having their students develop an understanding of some basic principles of economics. One class was given the scissors, brushes, and the duplicating machine, another class the paint, paste, and art paper, and the third class, construction paper, duplicating paper, and spirit masters. When any of the three classes undertook a project that involved materials which they did not own, it was necessary for an economic transaction to take place. At first, every transaction resulted in an elaborate haggling session worthy of the best skills of the proverbial horse traders. Then the students became annoyed with the amount of time required to carry on such transactions and developed a standardized rate of exchange, i.e., 32 sheets of construction paper equals 18 spirit masters, but that also quickly proved cumbersome. Then one class hit upon the idea of printing money, which they did. It looked like a breakthrough, but the other two classes would not accept it for payment. But the idea caught on and it was decided that there should be one currency for all three classes. It then became obvious that a government was needed to control the amount printed, whom it was distributed to, etc.

Unfortunately, these experiences cannot be packaged and exported to classes all over the nation. They depend on the creativity, interest, and experience of the specific teachers and their classes. However, it is possible for teachers to take the basic idea and create their own world, and of course that is what we are encouraging here.

To help you build games, you will probably want to pursue the appropriate chapter and references to game building in the books cited in the following section. A word of caution, however. Frequently, when I point out to a teacher that he has created a simulation-type experience, the response is, "Oh, I'm sorry, I didn't know that was what I was doing. I was just trying to create a good experience for the kids." Had he known that there were people who were "experts" in creating and analyzing such experiences, he probably would not have felt that he had the right to undertake the task. We are conditioned to honor and sanction the "territorial" privileges of special knowledge, and new disciplines generally develop a specialized jargon and rites of membership to protect their new territory. So accustomed are we to respecting these "territorial" privileges—medical doctors are the only people who can practice medicine, lawyers are the only ones who can practice law, plumbers are the only ones who can plumb—we are frequently shamed out of using our creative talents. This is not to say that special knowledge can't be helpful, but it is better to attempt a creative act in ignorance than to refrain from trying because of lack of knowledge.

Basic Reading List

In addition to the books already cited for special information, I would suggest as general background a small pamphlet edited by William Nesbitt called *Simulation Games for the Social Studies Classroom,*[10] or Alice Kaplan Gordon's *Games for Growth.*[11]

Related Reading List

If you are a primary teacher and have not been exposed to the fantasy-filled fun of theater games, I urge you to order Viola Spolin's *Improvisation for the Theater.*[12]

If you are interested in role playing, and perhaps even more importantly in values, I would strongly recommend Fannie and George Shaftel's *Role-Playing for Social Values: Decision-Making in the Social Studies.*[13]

---

[10] William Nesbitt, *Simulation Games for the Social Studies Classroom,* Foreign Policy Association, 345 East 46th Street, New York, New York 10017. (price one dollar).

[11] Alice Kaplan Gordon, *Games for Growth,* Science Research Associates, College Division, Palo Alto, California.

[12] Viola Spolin, *Improvisation for the Theater.* Evanston, Illinois: Northwestern University Press.

[13] Fannie R. Shaftel and George Shaftel, *Role-Playing for Social Values: Decision-Making in the Social Studies.* Englewood Cliffs, New Jersey: Prentice-Hall, Inc.

The Role of Reading in the Social Studies

PAUL A. WITTY

During the past decade, there has been widespread criticism of reading methods and materials of instruction used in our schools. It has been shown that some of the criticisms are unjust. Children are, on the whole, reading better and more widely than ever before. However, some of the criticisms are valid and merit the serious consideration of teachers and administrators. It has been clearly shown, for example, that permanent interests in reading are *infrequently* developed in children and youth. Far too many people who *can* read do not choose to read books. They have failed to develop a strong interest in reading.

Not long ago, The American Institute of Public Opinion reported a poll in which six out of ten adults questioned stated that the last time they had read a book other than the Bible was a year or more ago. Moreover, one out of four college graduates had not read a book during the last twelve months.[1]

Lack of interest in reading has been demonstrated again and again in studies of children, young people and adults. And numerous speculations concerning the causes have been advanced.

It has been indicated, too, that there are unjustifiably large numbers of poor readers in our schools. Some studies do show large amounts of reading retardation. For example, in the South Side High School, Newark, New Jersey, of the 247 entering freshmen who were tested in September, 1952, more than 50 per cent tested at or below the sixth grade level.[2] This study reveals a higher frequency of poor reading than is generally reported in such investigations. Yet, other studies show that 15 to 20 per cent of entering high school pupils in some schools read less well, according to test results, than the typical seventh grade pupil. It has been found that most of these pupils can be helped to read more effectively.

However, it should be noted that in most studies of entering high school pupils, *many* superior readers are reported. Such data should make us aware

Paul A. Witty is Professor Emeritus from Northwestern University, Evanston, Illinois.

Reprinted from *Elementary English 39:*562–569, 1962, copyright © 1962 by the National Council of Teachers of English. Reprinted by permission of the publisher and Paul A. Witty.

[1] *Reader's Digest,* March, 1956, p. 23.

[2] Vivian Zinkin, "A Staggering Reading Problem." *The Clearing House, 28,* November, 1953.

that in our zeal for helping students with reading problems we should not overlook the special needs of superior and gifted students. These pupils are frequently neglected or inadequately challenged. Such pupils are often potential leaders, much needed in the area of human relations. As Harry Passow states: "The daily press and professional journals alike are clamoring about shortages of scientists and engineers. . . . Perhaps our most frightening shortages are not in the general supply of scientists but in those rare persons with imagination, creativity, motivation, competence, and education who can contribute something fresh and basic to our understanding of man's relation with man." [3] To the development of such understanding, the role of reading in the social sciences is essential and unmistakably evident.

Dull Material Discourages Child

Some critics are convinced that certain teaching materials, especially primers and first grade readers, are unnatural and repetitious, and contribute vitally to the inefficient instruction, and lack of interest in reading.

Writers assert, too, that a concern for the interest factor should be shown not only in the primary grades but also at every level of instruction.[4] The desirability of this approach is emphasized by George Norvell who, after analyzing the selections taught in New York high schools, concluded that "To increase reading skill, promote the reading habit, and produce a generation of book lovers, there is no other factor so powerful as interest." [5]

The primary objective of a developmental reading program should be recognized clearly at all times: we should seek to help children to become skillful, self-reliant, and independent in using the library and other resources for satisfying interests and needs. This objective will be achieved only if students are enabled to enjoy the act of reading and the results.[6] The first part of this aim will be achieved through an efficient, systematic program of reading instruction. The second part will be realized by the association of reading with interests and needs. Accordingly, children and youth will become skillful readers and will probably continue to enrich their understandings and satisfactions all their lives.

[3] Harry Passow, quoted in *Education Digest,* March, 1957.

[4] Paul Witty, "The Role of Interest," Chapter 8 in *Development In and Through Reading,* Nelson B. Henry, ed. 60th Yearbook of the National Society for the Study of Education, Part I. Chicago: University of Chicago Press, 1961.

[5] George W. Norvell, "Some Results of a Twelve-Year Study of Children's Reading Interests." *English Journal 35:*531, 1946. See also George W. Norvell, *What Boys and Girls Like to Read.* Chicago: Silver Burdett, 1959.

[6] See Paul Witty, "Reading Instruction—A Forward Look." *Elementary English,* March, 1961.

Formal Instruction Necessary

Many school administrators and teachers will doubtless agree that a developmental reading program should be initiated throughout our schools. Instruction in reading today should not cease at the sixth grade level. Help and guidance should be given to all students in studying and reading efficiently the materials of each subject field.[7] Remedial instruction should be offered as a temporary expedient only.

There is a great need to extend opportunities in reading so that children's interests will be satisfied and their needs met judiciously through reading. Accordingly, a balanced reading program includes not only a variety of textbooks and practice books, but also an assortment of narratives, biographies, magazine articles, and factual presentations on many topics.[8] Such needs as the ability to understand oneself and to appreciate one's social environment can be met to varying degrees through the use of printed materials. This approach recognizes the significance of using interesting, varied and individually suitable materials of instruction at every level. And it recognizes too the need for a definite program of instruction designed to apply and extend reading skills in the content fields.

To offer the most helpful guidance and instruction, the teacher requires considerably more information about each pupil's reading than that obtained from tests. For example, the teacher of social studies needs to know the nature and extent of the pupil's specialized vocabulary in this area. This appraisal is not always included in a standard test of reading. Nor do standard tests usually contain measures of the pupil's familiarity with, and ability to use, source materials. Moreover, most tests do not examine the ability to read critically.

To be an effective guide, the teacher needs also to know the pupil's rate of reading different kinds of materials. In addition, he should ascertain the nature and extent of each pupil's reading experience. It is clear, then, that to understand a pupil's status in reading, the teacher will employ data from standardized tests and will assemble additional information revealing the pupil's vocabulary, his ability to read and use various types of materials, and the amount and nature of his reading experience.

In offering reading instruction, the teacher requires not only facts about

[7] Elizabeth Simpson, *Helping High School Students Read Better*. Chicago: Science Research Associates, 1954.

[8] Paul Witty, Chapter 2 in *Reading in the High School and College*, W. S. Gray, chrmn. 47th Yearbook of the National Society for the Study of Education. Chicago: University of Chicago Press, 1948. See also the discussions in Henry P. Smith and E. V. Dechant, *Psychology in Teaching Reading*. Englewood Cliffs, N. J.: Prentice-Hall, 1961.

each pupil's reading, but also information pertaining to his interests and to his personal life and social adjustment. Some procedures such as the use of interest inventories, anecdotal records and various forms of observation are helpful in obtaining data of this type. Interest inventories (which include inquiries concerning play activities, hobbies, vocational preferences, wishes, etc.) may yield clues of value in understanding pupils' attitudes, problems, and adjustment.[9] An interest inventory may be used advantageously in studying groups as well as individuals. These data may be employed in association with others to afford a sound basis for planning appropriate and profitable reading experiences for a class or for an individual. Such data will reveal each pupil's readiness for reading at different levels of growth.

Reading in the Content Fields

In considering the role of reading in the content areas, W. S. Gray pointed out that various attitudes range from complete acceptance to total rejection of the idea that "every teacher is a teacher of reading." He also noted that this slogan, which appeared in the 36th Yearbook of the National Society for the Study of Education, *The Teaching of Reading: A Second Report,* was unfortunate in that it designated responsibility without indicating reasons, goals, or methods to achieve objectives. What are the functions of the subject teacher insofar as reading is concerned? W. S. Gray states:

The basic view presented in this paper is that teachers of different curriculum fields become concerned about reading problems as reading assumes importance in attaining the aims of teaching in those fields. The three major duties of such teachers with respect to reading are to provide optimum conditions under which acquired reading ability may be used in attaining worthwhile goals, to promote growth in many aspects of reading which are unique to given fields, and to provide specific training in reading when for any reason they assign reading materials that are above the reading level of the pupils in their classes. The final level of reading competence attained by pupils in elementary and secondary schools is the product of the effort of all teachers. Whereas the reading teacher lays the foundation of good reading habits, the content teachers play a highly significant role in extending and refining the reading efficiency of pupils in specific areas.[10]

[9] See Witty-Kopel-Coomer Interest Inventories, Northwestern University. See also questionnaires used in Paul A. Witty, Ann Coomer, Robert Sizemore, and Paul Kinsella, *A Study of the Interests of Children and Youths,* a cooperative research based on a contract between Northwestern University and the Office of Education, U.S. Department of Health, Education and Welfare, 1959.

[10] W. S. Gray, "Theme of the Conference," Chapter I in *Improving Reading in Content Fields,* Supplementary Educational Monograph, No. 62, compiled and edited by W. S. Gray. Chicago: University of Chicago Press, 1947, pp. 4–5.

And we might add that special emphasis should be placed on flexibility and ready adaptation of reading skills in order to attain success in the subject fields. A. Sterl Artley states:

> It is not enough to develop proficiency in specific abilities—to teach the child how to locate materials, to select material and evaluate it in the light of the problem at hand, to read at various rates. We might say the job is half done when these abilities have been developed. The second half of the instructional job is that of teaching the child to recognize his particular reading needs and to adapt to those needs the necessary skills—developing the attitude that reading is not a static, inflexible activity, but a dynamic, modifiable activity that changes as conditions change.[11]

We have stressed the importance in a developmental program of the ability to read in the subject fields through effective application and extension of reading skills. Such applications result from emphasis on the ability to adapt reading skills readily to varied needs and purposes.

As a pupil proceeds in school, he encounters a wider and wider range of materials. In modern schools, reading of science and of social studies materials is often introduced in the primary grades. The pupil must learn how to read and to study such materials effectively. Soon he will have elementary books on these subjects to employ for varied purposes. He will increasingly utilize library resources in association with experience units and investigations of various kinds. In the intermediate grades, the program in the subject fields becomes intensified and greater demands are made on the pupil for the selection and application of varied reading skills. He must therefore develop flexibility in applying reading skills. It is clear that a good foundation in basic reading skills is one of the safeguards for successful reading in the content fields. However, beyond these basic skills, there are applications and extensions necessary in each field.[12]

It is worth nothing that Guy Bond and Miles Tinker conclude: "The correlations between general reading tests and reading tests in the content fields range from about .30 to .50." Furthermore they state that "there are many reading abilities (that operate) somewhat independent of each other." [13] A student may be competent in reading materials in one area and not in another. In the elementary school, there are four areas in which reading presents problems because of new vocabulary and concepts, readability obstacles traceable to style of writing, differences in typography, and so forth. The areas include social science, science, mathematics and literature.

---

[11] A. Sterl Artley, "Influence of the Field Studied on the Reading Attitudes and Skills Needed," Chapter V in *Improving Reading in Content Fields, op. cit.*, p. 42.

[12] See David H. Russell, *Children Learn To Read,* 2nd edition. Boston: Ginn, 1961.

[13] Guy Bond and Miles Tinker, *Reading Difficulties: Their Diagnosis and Correction.* New York: Appleton-Century-Crofts, 1957, p. 352. See also L. C. Fay, "What Research Has to Say About Reading in the Content Areas," *The Reading Teacher* 8:68–72, 1954.

One of the most valuable aids in the "teaching of essential study skills and the improvement of reading in the content areas" is the *EDL Study Skills Library* which is "planned as a sequential twelve-year program." The materials stress the skills of interpretation, evaluation, organization, and reference in the areas of science and social studies.[14] The use of these materials is especially valuable in providing the needed application and extension of reading skills in the content areas.

Bond and Tinker point out that within the social studies, difficulties are occasioned by factors such as the temporal sequence of events portrayed, unfamiliar content unassociated with present-day happenings and experience, and necessity for reading and interpreting maps, graphs, charts, etc. Similarly in geography, they indicate that understanding of reading material may depend on the possession of a special vocabulary based on conditions related to housing, food, or occupations; to physical features of the land; and to climate or agriculture in various, often unfamiliar places throughout the world. The interpretation of maps and "interrupted" reading involving reference to materials on various pages also require types of adjustment not previously emphasized. Mathematics presents other unique reading problems with its strong use of a technical vocabulary, symbols, diagrams, complex concepts, and verbally stated problems.[15]

Responsibility for Developmental Reading Program

A developmental program requires the co-operation of administrators, supervisors, and teachers. A primary responsibility of the administrator in a secondary school is to encourage all-school participation in the work. The formation of a committee to study the total reading situation and to make plans for the development and maintenance of the program is a good initial step. This committee should include representatives from every subject field.

In the planning of extension of reading instruction in every area, certain conditions must be met. The reading demands or objectives of each subject should be set forth. We have chosen the social studies field for illustration. In this paper we shall limit our discussion to the following acquisitions: (1) vocabulary and concepts, (2) ability to see relationships between facts, (3) capacity to organize information, (4) tendency to read critically, and (5) ability to use source materials effectively.

[14] H. Alan Robinson, Stanford E. Taylor, and Helen Frackenpohl, *Teacher's Guide, Levels 4-5-6, The EDL Study Skills Library*. Huntington, N.Y.: Educational Developmental Laboratories, 1961.

[15] Bond and Tinker, *op. cit.*

Some Reading Proficiencies Essential in All Social Studies

The above list includes some of the skills essential for reading successfully in the social-studies area. In every subject, similar, more detailed lists may be assembled. This is perhaps the first step in embarking on a developmental program that stresses successful reading in the content fields. And it is a step which a teacher or a group representing each subject might follow. Lillian Gray and Dora Reese have discussed effectively and in detail such acquisitions for geography and history, the two social studies subjects commonly studied in elementary and secondary schools. For example, they have attempted to identify the varied skills needed for effective reading of geography content. They suggest that pupils be taught directly to:

1. Sense space relations. A thousand miles is a distance difficult for children to understand even though they can easily read the words. . . . To teach directions, children must be taught the location and significance of *north,* and not conceive of it, for example, as the 'top of the map.'
2. Understand how geography influences people and events.
3. Prepare detailed, well-organized reports for class discussion from materials read in different books.
4. Get the facts straight.
5. Sense cause and effect relationships.
6. Recognize generalities, such as the fact that increased altitude indicates a cooler climate.
7. Find the main ideas in an involved paragraph containing cross references and extraneous details.
8. Recognize supporting details.
9. Understand terminology. . . .
10. Classify geographical concepts according to basic human needs: food, shelter, clothing, occupations, recreation, communication, transporation, aesthetic appreciation, government, education, and religion.
11. Compare statements and draw accurate conclusions.
12. Read graphs, maps. . . .[16]

Although we recognize the need for detailed analyses and emphases such as that just given for geography, we shall in this paper limit our discussion to the five items previously cited.

[16] Lillian Gray and Dora Reese, *Teaching Children to Read,* 2nd ed. New York: Ronald Press, 1957, pp. 379–380. Cited by Henry P. Smith and Emerald V. Dechant in *Psychology in Teaching Reading.* Englewood Cliffs, N. J.: Prentice-Hall, 1961, pp. 360–361.

1. VOCABULARY AND CONCEPTS

One of the most important needs of pupils in successful endeavor in social studies is an understanding of the specialized vocabulary employed. The teacher should provide the background of experience and the related activities which help children to understand these words thoroughly and to have clear concepts of them.

This development should be planned with care. The teacher should be alert from the first to detect and correct misconceptions. Significant terms in each unit of instruction should be assembled, studied and discussed. The use of direct experience, photographs, filmstrips, and motion pictures will aid in building backgrounds essential for understanding many new words and phrases.

Discussion techniques may be used to advantage. By encouraging extensive reading, the teacher can help pupils obtain facts or illustrations upon which clear understanding of many terms depends.

The use of films and film readers is another way of providing a common background of experience for children. The phenomenal success of children employing film readers suggests their value in improving the efficiency of reading instruction, especially in clarifying the vocabulary employed and in fostering clear interpretation. Some teachers have reported considerable gains in fluency in silent reading and unprecedented gains in reading skill attending the use of the combined approach.[17] These results and indorsements will require validation by careful research. However, there already is clear evidence that the teacher will find the use of the film and the film reader an effective way to foster gains in reading skills.

2. ABILITY TO SEE RELATIONSHIPS BETWEEN FACTS

Pupils also need help in seeing the relationships between facts encountered in different contexts as well as in varied sources. Simple exercises such as the following may help somewhat in the acquisition of this skill. Dates and significant events in an historical presentation may be arranged in two columns in mixed order. The pupils are asked to connect the associated items with lines. However, more important and subtle relationships should also be stressed. For example, the teacher may encourage the students to find the chief products of certain countries and to determine the amount and rate of production. Discussion and objective tests may be used to determine the accuracy of their conclusions. More complex relationships

---

[17] Paul Witty and James Fitzwater, "An Experiment with Film, Film Readers, and the Magnetic Sound Tract Projector." *Elementary English,* April, 1953.

between such factors as resources and productivity or form of government and attitudes of different peoples may also be stressed.[18]

3. CAPACITY TO ORGANIZE MATERIALS

Some pupils appear to have little expectation that they will be required to do more than reproduce a few facts from the accounts they read. They give scant attention to the sequence of ideas and do not differentiate significant items from unimportant details. It is necessary, therefore, to encourage pupils to react more intensely to the content in social-studies presentations. Some pupils may be helped by practice in making outlines in which they differentiate main topics from subordinate themes. Practice in summarizing will also assist pupils to react to ideas as they read and to organize the information they acquire from reading. Since sources of information are so numerous and varied in worth, it is necessary for pupils to learn to evaluate presentations and to submit their findings in well-organized compact form.

4. TENDENCY TO READ CRITICALLY

Charles B. Huelsman has summarized the critical reading skills that were mentioned in one or more of fifteen articles on the topic:

1. To define and delimit a problem
2. To formulate hypotheses
3. To locate information bearing on specific problems
4. To determine that a statement is important for a given purpose
5. To distinguish the difference between facts and opinions
6. To evaluate the dependability of data
7. To recognize the limitations of given data even when the items are assumed to be dependable
8. To see elements common to several items of data
9. To make comparisons
10. To organize evidence that suggests relationships
11. To recognize prevailing tendencies or trends in the data
12. To judge the competency of a given author to make a valid statement on a given topic
13. To criticize data on the basis of its completeness and accuracy
14. To criticize a presentation on the basis of the completeness and logic of its reasoning
15. To suspend judgment until all evidence is assembled and evaluated.[19]

[18] See also Guy Bond and E. B. Wagner, *Teaching the Child to Read.* New York: Macmillan Publishing Co., Inc., 1960.

[19] Charles B. Huelsman, Jr., "Promoting Growth in Ability to Interpret when

Several studies show that many elementary and secondary school pupils lack the ability to read critically. Pupils should be encouraged to study and to contrast the attitudes and points of view of various authors, as well as their sources of information. Attention should also be given to the extent to which authors are impartial and objective in drawing conclusions and in interpreting data.

In the development of "critical reading," specialized approaches have been devised by some teachers. For example, Spencer Brown employed "documentary techniques" to encourage pupils to seek accurate information on which to base their statements.[20] Pupils of varied nationalities and backgrounds visited the homes and neighborhoods of various "racial" groups found within a school district. After discussing their findings and observations, the facts which had been "documented" were utilized in writing a play entitled "America Is Only You and Me." Many elementary school teachers have found that this approach adds authenticity to information obtained from books and leads to a critical attitude toward the printed page. There are many other efforts to help pupils gain skill in critical reading as shown in booklets designed to aid junior and senior high school pupils improve their reading as well as in books designed to foster effective reading of the newspaper.[21]

5. ABILITY TO USE SOURCE MATERIALS EFFECTIVELY

Prevailing practice often neglects the wide range of reading abilities within classes. If a single textbook is prescribed for all pupils, little can be accomplished since a typical class contains pupils of widely differing abilities. In the upper grades of the elementary school the differences in ability between the poorest and the best pupil will probably equal a range of from four to five grades, according to test scores.

The following approach is being used by some teachers in recognition of the range of ability within classes. First, the teacher selects the topics or units to be treated in the social-studies program. For each topic, varied

---

Reading Critically: In Grades Seven to Ten," in *Promoting Growth Toward Maturity in Interpreting What Is Read,* Supplementary Educational Monographs, No. 74. Chicago: University of Chicago Press, 1951, pp. 149–153, cited by Smith and Dechant, *op. cit.,* p. 358.

[20] Spencer Brown, *They See for Themselves,* Bureau of Intercultural Education Publication Series, Problems of Race and Culture in American Education, Vol. III. New York: Harper, 1945.

[21] (a) Paul Witty, *Streamline Your Reading,* Life Adjustment Booklet, Chicago: Science Research Associates, 1949. (b) Paul Witty and Harry Bricker, *You Can Read Better,* Junior Life Adjustment Booklet, Chicago: Science Research Associates, 1951. (c) Paul Witty and Edith Grothberg, *Improving Your Vocabulary,* Chicago: Science Research Associates, 1959. (d) Edgar Dale, *How to Read a Newspaper,* Chicago: Scott, Foresman and Co., 1941.

source materials are assembled to meet the abilities within the class. The variety of materials includes factual accounts, biographies, story materials, magazine and newspaper articles, as well as reference sources such as encyclopedias, atlases, and almanacs. Fortunately, there is a substantial and growing amount of literature on every topic of significance in this field.[22]

Co-ordinating the Reading Program—A Concluding Statement

The foregoing concept of reading instruction differs, in some respects, from views previously held. We have seen that modern approaches to reading instruction include emphasis on the reading skills needed in the subject fields. The teacher of every subject has a responsibility for helping the child to read effectively the varied materials employed in instruction, for developing special vocabularies and for building concepts, for providing diversified materials so as to encourage growth for every pupil, for cultivating critical reading, and for fostering reading from varied sources.

When such practices are widely followed in our schools, co-ordination of the reading program will occur. Co-ordination will be facilitated further by the consideration on the part of all teachers of the interests and "developmental needs" of boys and girls and the selection of appropriate, related subject matter and experience.

These procedures are being followed with success in some schools. Not only are they leading to greater skill in reading, but they are helping students appreciate and enjoy the subject matter of the special fields. It is to be hoped that increased numbers of superintendents and supervisors will be led to initiate developmental reading programs in their schools. Certainly there appears to be a great need for stressing reading in the content fields in most schools. Moreover, efforts of this kind have proved abundantly rewarding.[23] This is an approach which when widely followed promises to increase greatly the efficiency of instruction in the modern school.

[22] The use of the *EDL Study Skills Library* previously described seems particularly appropriate to provide differentiated instruction within classes.

[23] K. B. Rudolph, *Effect of Reading Instruction on Achievement in Eighth Grade Social Studies,* Teachers College Contribution to Education, No. 945, New York, 1949. See also Bond and Wagner, *Teaching the Child to Read, op. cit.*

Museums and the Schools

SUSAN PURVIS

Rural students in Illinois are programed through a mobile art unit by automatically timed lighting and tape recordings.

As school children in Manhattan wander through an exhibit on the "Artist's Workshop," they swing color wheels; push buttons for recordings, filmstrips, and movies about artists' tools and techniques; peer through peepholes; and compete on a push-button machine to test their knowledge.

A small child gazes at the beehive in the Bedford Lincoln extension of the Brooklyn Children's Museum and asks, "Gee, lady, where can I get one of these?"

At Boston's Museum of Science, elementary teachers compete to be admitted to an annual seminar for nonscience majors.

In Washington, D.C., teachers work with curators from the Smithsonian and 20 children to develop a curriculum on man and animals.

Dayton, Ohio, creates an art museum for children in the basement of a school.

These are just a few examples of what is happening as school systems across the nation are turning to the museum to supplement what the classroom can provide. Traditional perfunctory school-museum contacts—special-occasion class museum tours, for instance—are giving way to activities that make museum experiences a regular part of the curriculum. All over the country, museum curators and teachers are working out ways to open channels of cooperation between people-filled schools and treasure-crammed museums.

Not all museum-school programs are new. In Boston, the Museum of Science claims to have started public school science programs in the nineteenth century, and the Children's Museum there has offered natural history and social studies programs since 1914. Every year for over a decade the Houston Museum of Fine Arts School has provided space and materials for a hundred high school children who study under artist-teachers paid by the Houston Independent School District.

Children in Boston and Houston have been unusually fortunate in this respect, however. To many city children, going to the museum has meant

Susan Purvis is a teacher and sculptress in Washington, D.C.

Reprinted from *Today's Education* 57:14–17, 1968, with permission of the National Education Association and Susan Purvis.

having to pay bus fare in order to put in a dreary hour or so in vast, poorly lit, cold halls, peering at displays labeled DON'T TOUCH! For their part, many children in rural areas or small towns have had no opportunity for museum experiences of any kind.

Now, this is changing. Museum education directors, a new breed of professionals, are gearing exhibits to appeal to children and, through branch or mobile museums, are making the exhibits accessible to all of them.

What is more, they are finding ways to help teachers make their students' museum experiences meaningful. Some museums provide manuals for teachers who have groups scheduled for museum tours; others arrange teachers' seminars and workshops.

Some cooperative relationships between schools and museums are informal; others, highly structured. In Cleveland, the board of education assigns three public school art teachers to the Cleveland Museum of Art to act as liaison teachers. They conduct classes for the city's public school students at the Museum and also use materials from the Museum to teach art appreciation in the schools.

In New York City, the school board provides two full-time teachers to coordinate the Metropolitan Museum of Art's Junior Museum's exhibits, tours, and classes with the school curriculum.

The art department of the St. Louis public schools expects teachers to take their classes to the City Art Museum at least once a year, and supplies the Museum with three art historians to lecture to students.

The city government of Newark, New Jersey, provides an operating budget for the Newark Museum. In 1967, 42,025 young people were given guided tours in the galleries.

In Birmingham, Alabama, a U.S. Office of Education Title III grant supports a school-museum program. Instructors from the Birmingham Museum deliver slide talks to high school art, English, and history classes. For elementary schools, the program calls for visits by an art mobile as well as a Thursday tour for eighth graders and classes and workshops for teachers and pupils.

A staff of liaison teachers in Baton Rouge have prepared audiovisual materials relating to some important exhibits at the Louisiana Arts and Science Center. Other functions these liaison teachers perform are visiting schools to work with classroom teachers to prepare students for museum tours; coordinating tours; and conducting follow-up activities. One liaison teacher works full-time on developing a sixth grade humanities program involving art, drama, music, history, literature, and architecture. Another concentrates on astronomy, encouraging use of the planetarium at the Center.

The North Carolina Museum of Art houses the Mary Duke Biddle Gallery for the Blind. Its permanent collection includes such touchable objects as a bronze Egyptian cat, a cast of Rodin's "Hand," and an Etruscan helmet. Since the gallery opened in 1966, blind students have enjoyed special exhibits on such diverse subjects as "Musical Instruments of the World," "Chinese Jade," and "Athletic Figures."

Nathaniel Dixon, director of the Office of Academic Affairs of the Smithsonian, a schoolman turned museum educator, believes "the whole concept of museum utilization is changing a great deal." Recently, he instigated a summer project wherein suburban and metropolitan education boards paid teachers to work out projects in museum teaching to enrich the curriculum of various grade levels. "We [in the museums] must be sensitive to emerging curriculum patterns; at the same time, curriculum makers should be sensitive to our resources," says Dixon.

The museum tour is no longer a passive experience. These days, "touch" sessions, free discussions, lively demonstrations, and workshops immediately follow lectures. For school groups viewing its paintings, the Metropolitan includes a creative art workshop in the schedule; the Smithsonian makes available special classrooms equipped with papier-mâché, microscopes, plants, live animals or small models, and standard audiovisual equipment for follow-up probing and unhurried discussion of new concepts after a museum visit.

According to Mr. Dixon of the Smithsonian, exhibits there are designed "to upset the attitude that behavior in a museum should be the same as in a public library." Purposeful noise and activity on the part of museum visitors are regarded as signs of successful stimulation. The exhibits themselves aren't static. Visitors hear the whistle of a locomotive, the sounds of machinery in the machine shop, and soon, they will be able to hear the trumpeting of an elephant. The machine shop smells of machine grease; the replica of an old-time confectionery shop gives off the aroma of chocolate.

Museums are using imaginative techniques to lure the children in. Boston's Museum of Science, for example, publishes a brochure entitled "Take Off to Wonder." "Adventure at every turn," it boasts. "See how you were born. . . . Hear a talking transparent woman whose organs light up as she explains her bodily functions. . . . Play tic-tac-toe with a computer. . . ."

This Boston institution provides a highly dramatic program on a selected topic each year, using special, staff-designed demonstration devices. Youthful visitors to the museum are encouraged to wander through the halls on individual tours of discovery and to watch brief demonstrations there.

At the Milwaukee Museum, students get to play games. A youngster entering an exhibit hall may rent, for a dime, a portable tape recorder and programed learning machine. A recorded voice guides him through the exhibit, telling him about the various displays and quizzing him about what he is learning. He must answer the question on one part of the exhibit correctly before he goes on to another. He responds by pushing buttons on the learning machine. The machine lights up like a pinball machine for correct answers; goes black for wrong ones.

"For children, this is terrific," says the director of the program, C. G. Screven of the University of Wisconsin-Milwaukee Psychology Department, adding that teen-agers will stand in line half an hour for a chance to play. Rewards for good performance may be refund of the dime or a small prize, although the ideal outcome is for the child to realize early that learning is its own reward. Testing has shown impressive increases in learning through game playing as opposed to unstructured encounters with the same exhibit.

Museum programs for inner-city children of all ages—Head Start through senior high—are proving to be especially valuable. In many cases, museum branches have been established right in inner-city neighborhoods. The Whitney Museum of American Art in New York, for example, runs an Art Resources Center in a warehouse in Manhattan's lower East Side. Students from nearby schools come here on a released-time basis to work on art projects. Observers report that participating in the program has improved the behavior of some boys who have been discipline problems. The youngsters themselves are enthusiastic. One boy said, "Here, I am treated like an artist—like somebody special. At school they treat us all the same."

In Washington, D.C., the Smithsonian operates a neighborhood museum in Anacostia, a low-income, high-density, largely black section across the river from the Capitol. This is no stamp-sized replica of the parent institution, but a facility especially designed for the community it serves. From the start, citizens from the area, including teachers and administrators, have advised and helped to run it. School groups tour exhibits, such as a recent one on African culture, and afterwards, during workshop sessions produce art objects or artifacts related to what they have seen.

Bedford-Stuyvesant district in Brooklyn, a section similar to Anacostia, has its neighborhood museum, too. When the Brooklyn Children's Museum closed its main building, fifth graders from the area carried part of the collection there to a new home in their own neighborhood—a building that was formerly a poolroom and automobile showroom. Muse, as the branch museum is called, houses widely varied displays, a small planetarium, classroom space, and a library. Teen-agers act as junior curators.

Swarms of youngsters come to Muse to look and touch and listen and learn. Some come on their own, to participate in art, science, jazz, or writing workshops; attend the evening programs, Saturday and after-school events; or take part in preschool programs. Others come in school groups to attend lectures by staff experts and remain for the discussion and workshop sessions that follow.

Mobile museums are making various kinds of museum experiences available to children right at their own schools. The Virginia Museum sends four traveling galleries loaded with art treasures to visit even the remotest areas of the state. The Mini-Natural Science Museum of the Philadelphia Academy of Natural Sciences features a live animal show and a conservation movie.

The Art Resources Traveler is the name the Illinois State Board of Education has given to its traveling museum. This is a specially designed and equipped trailer unit, financed by federal funds. Its first exhibit, to which several museums lent works of art, was a survey of art from Egyptian through contemporary. Before the Art Resources Traveler visits a school, teachers there receive materials to use in preparing their classes for the show. During the actual visit of the Traveler, the program includes in-service lectures for teachers and programs for adults in the community as well as carefully planned experiences for children.

The Mobile Gallery of the Wichita, Kansas, Art Museum brings an exhibit of original works to communities in 13 unified school districts for a stay of from one to three weeks. An art educator-curator accompanies the exhibit and serves as guest lecturer, art consultant, and visiting instructor to schools and community during the stay, conducting preparatory meetings, workshops for elementary teachers, and postvisit activities for the children. One child found the experience particularly worthwhile. He said he planned to be a writer and appreciated the chance to look for an artist to illustrate his books.

Some museums are cooperating with schools by making available kits that let teachers turn their classrooms into mini-museums. The Boston Children's Museum, for example, offers school-tested, boxed materials developed under a USOE contract. Called MATCH (materials and activities for teachers and children) Boxes, they contain artifacts, models, audiovisual materials, and teachers' guides around which a teacher can plan various lessons. One kit contains a portable press, type fonts, paper, ink, and instructions for printing and binding a book. Another enables a class to "excavate" an ancient Greek villa.

The Newark (New Jersey) Museum distributes catalogs listing over ten thousand 3-dimensional objects available for use by schools.

The State Historical Society of Colorado sends out kits within the state. One of them on mining includes gold pans, ore samples, oil lamps, and jacks and drills.

A few schools have permanent museums of their own and have developed programs to go with them. One of these schools is Calvert Elementary School in Lincoln, Nebraska. Here, two mothers, both former art teachers, sparked donations for a $50,000 collection of painting and sculpture and organized extracurricular programs for the pupils.

New Visions Museum in Dayton, Ohio, a Dayton Public School Project operated under ESEA Title I, was developed and designed to challenge the imagination and thinking of children through the use of their five senses. The uniqueness of this museum is that children are aware that the atmosphere was created for them. They begin to know themselves by using all of their senses in exploring and discovering artifacts of many cultures. The Museum's program is not intended as an end in itself, but as a means of opening doors during the early years.

In the Pac-A-Pic program in St. Louis, individual schools own reproductions of famous paintings with information about the artist and the work of art on the back. A child can select a favorite, tote it home in an Army-surplus canvas bag, and keep it for two weeks.

By one means or another, more and more American children are having the opportunity to have the firsthand cultural and scientific experiences that well-planned museum programs can give them. The museum is coming into its own as an important educational agency.

Section SIX

Pupil Backgrounds:
Social, Cultural,
and Ethnic Variables

As the educational community became sensitive to differences between and among learners, it first focused its attention on the slow learners and pupils with other forms of exceptionality, including the gifted. Then during the decade of the 1960s much was done to improve educational opportunities for children from disadvantaged backgrounds. All of these efforts have sharpened the perceptions of teachers and educators to the broad range of social, cultural, and ethnic variables that affect the success of children in school. The essays selected for this section do not deal exclusively with the education of disadvantaged children but reflect the wide range of factors that are responsible for the interesting variations found between and among pupils.

Of course, the children who are products of disadvantaged environments present the teacher with the greatest challenges. Of all school subjects the social studies can and should be the one most important to pupils who come from disadvantaged environments, because it is through the social studies that the pupils' range of encounters with society and culture can be extended. Vicariously and directly the pupil can experience contact with cultural models otherwise unknown to him. Because of limited experience with various segments of society, these pupils are often unfamiliar with the range of life choices that are possible and available to them. It is fair to say that social studies programs for pupils from disadvantaged environments have not been innovative or imaginative. In most cases they represent minor modifications of the programs for all pupils.

The problem of deprivation exists everywhere. It is found in the rural sections of the nation, in the slums of the large cities, in the towns and hamlets throughout the land. In recent years there has been an increased awareness of the magnitude and extent of this problem, and, as a result, tremendous amounts of money and energy have been allocated to the improvement of educational opportunity for disadvantaged pupils. Whatever the success of such programs has been to date, there can be little doubt that these investments in human resources will pay large dividends to society. It is only through education that pupils who are victims of deprivation can be converted into contributing and responsible citizens of this nation.

This nation has long been known as one that represents a confluence of world cultures. In the past, school programs have done little to highlight the cultural contributions of various peoples of the world to America. This is now changing, and there is a renaissance of interest in heritage studies. Social studies programs can be greatly enriched by capitalizing on the natural interest that pupils have in their own personal heritage. This will not only help them learn more about themselves but will help them develop a deeper understanding and sense of appreciation for their nation as well.

Imperatives in Ethnic Minority Education

JAMES A. BANKS

As we approach the threshold of the twenty-first century, our nation is witnessing technological progress which has been unparalleled in human history, yet is plagued with social problems of such magnitude that they pose a serious threat to the ideals of American democracy and to man's very survival. Environmental pollution, poverty, war, deteriorating cities, and ethnic conflict are the intractable social problems which Americans must resolve if we are to survive and create a just, humane society. Our society is becoming increasingly polarized and dehumanized, largely because of institutional racism and ethnic hostility. The elimination of conflicts between the races must be our top priority for the seventies.

One of the founding principles of this nation was that oppressed peoples from other lands would find in America tolerance and acceptance, if not a utopia for the full development of their potential. People who were denied religious, economic, and political freedom flocked to the New World in search of a better life. Perhaps more than any nation in human history, the United States has succeeded in culturally assimilating its immigrants and providing them with the opportunity to attain the "good life." The elimination of differences among peoples of diverse nationalities was the essence of the "melting pot" concept.

While the United States has successfully assimilated ethnic groups which shared a set of values and behavior patterns of European origin, it has blatantly denied its black, brown, red, and yellow citizens the opportunity to share fully in the American Dream because they possess physical and cultural characteristics which are non-European. Ethnic minority groups have been the victims of institutional racism in America primarily because of their unique physical traits and the myths which emerged extolling the intrinsic virtues of European civilization and describing non-European peoples as ruthless savages. European and white ancestry have been the primary requisites for full realization of the American Dream. For most colored peoples in the United States, the dream has been deferred. The shattered dream and the denial of equal opportunities to ethnic minority groups have been the sources of acute ethnic conflict within America; it has now reached crisis proportions. The flames that burned in Watts, the blood

James A. Banks is Professor of Education at the University of Washington, Seattle.

Reprinted from *Phi Delta Kappan* 43(5):266–269, 1972, with permission of Phi Delta Kappa and James A. Banks.

that ran in Detroit, and now the Attica massacre are alarming manifestations of our inability to resolve conflicts between the majority and ethnic minority groups in America.

No sensitive and perceptive student of American society can deny the seriousness of our current racial problems. In recent years they have intensified as blacks and other powerless ethnic groups have taken aggressive actions to liberate themselves from oppression. Reactions of the white community to the new ethnic militancy have been intense and persisting. A "law and order" cult has emerged to eradicate ethnic revolts. To many white Americans, the plea for law and order is a call for an end to protests by ethnic groups and alienated youths. The fact that many law and order advocates demanded that Lt. Calley go free after a military jury convicted him for killing numbers of civilian colored peoples in Asia indicates that many "middle" Americans do not consistently value law, order, or human life. The law and order movement is directed primarily toward the poor, the colored, and the powerless. One example is the "no-knock" law in Washington, D.C. Although promises to bring law and order to the street often ensure victory in public elections, the most costly and destructive crimes in America are committed by powerful syndicates, corrupted government officials, and industries that pollute our environment, not by the ghetto looter and the petty thief. Also, few constructive actions have been taken by local and national leaders to eliminate the hopelessness, alienation, and poverty which often cause the ghetto dweller to violate laws in order to survive. As our nation becomes increasingly polarized, we are rapidly becoming two separate and unequal societies.[1]

Because the public school is an integral part of our social system, it has been a partner in the denial of equal opportunities to America's ethnic minorities; it has served mainly to perpetuate the status quo and to reinforce social class and racial stratification. Sensitive and perceptive writers such as Kozol and Kohl, and researchers like Pettigrew and Coleman, have extensively documented the ways in which the public schools make the ethnic child feel "invisible," while at the same time teaching the American Dream. Such contradictory behavior on the part of educators makes the ethnic minority child, as Baldwin has insightfully stated, run "the risk of becoming schizophrenic." [2]

Despite the school's reluctance to initiate social change, despite its tendency to reinforce and perpetuate the status quo, whenever our nation faces a crisis we call upon the school to help resolve it. Obviously, this is not because schools have historically responded creatively and imaginatively

---

[1] *Report of the National Advisory Commission on Civil Disorders.* New York: Bantam Books, 1968, p. 1.

[2] James Baldwin, "A Talk to Teachers," *Saturday Review,* December 21, 1963, p. 42.

to social problems. It is because many Americans retain an unshaken faith in the school's *potential* for improving society. *I* share that faith. The school does have potential to promote and lead constructive social change. In fact, it may be the only institution within our society which can spearhead the changes essential to prevent racial wars and chaos in America. I would now like to propose a number of changes which must take place in the school if it is going to exercise a leadership role in eliminating ethnic hostility and conflict in America.

Because the teacher is the most important variable in the child's learning environment, classroom teachers must develop more positive attitudes toward ethnic minorities and their cultures and must develop higher academic expectations for ethnic youths. Teacher attitudes and expectations have a profound impact on students' perceptions, academic behavior, self-concepts, and beliefs. Many teachers do not accept and respect the diverse cultures of ethnic youths, hence ethnic students often find the school's culture alien. The "cultural clash" in the classroom is by now a cliché. Studies by scholars such as Becker, Gottlieb, and Clark indicate that teachers typically have negative attitudes and low academic expectations for their black, brown, red, and poor pupils. Other research suggests that teachers, next to parents, are the most "significant others" in children's lives, and that teachers play an important role in the formation of children's racial attitudes and beliefs. A study by Davidson and Lang indicates that the assessment a child makes of himself is significantly related to the evaluation that "significant" people, such as teachers, make of him.[3]

It is necessary for *all* teachers to view ethnic groups and their cultures more positively, whether they teach in suburbia or in the inner city. The problems in the ghetto are deeply implicated in the larger society. Our future presidents, senators, mayors, policemen, and absentee landlords are taught in suburban classrooms. Unless teachers can succeed in helping these future leaders to develop more humane attitudes toward ethnic minorities, the ghetto will continue to thrive and destroy human lives.

The research on changing teacher attitudes is both sparse and inconclusive. It suggests that changing the racial attitudes of adults is a herculean task. However, the *urgency* of our racial problems demands that we act on the basis of current research. To maximize the chances for successful attitude intervention programs, experiences must be designed specifically for that purpose. Programs with general or global objectives are not likely to be successful. Courses which consist primarily or exclusively of lecture presentations have little impact. Diverse experiences, such as seminars,

---

[3] Helen H. Davidson and Gerhard Lang, "Children's Perceptions of Their Teachers' Feelings Toward Them Related to Self-Perception, School Achievement, and Behavior," *Journal of Experimental Education*, 1960, pp. 107–18; reprinted in James A. Banks and William W. Joyce (eds.), *Teaching Social Studies to Culturally Different Children*. Reading, Mass.: Addison-Wesley, 1971, pp. 113–27.

visitations, community involvement, committee work, guest speakers, movies, multimedia materials, and workshops, combined with factual lectures, are more effective than any single approach. Community involvement and contact (with the appropriate norms in the social setting) are the most productive techniques. Psychotherapy and T-grouping, if led by competent persons, are also promising strategies.[4]

Teachers must help ethnic minority students to augment their self-concepts, to feel more positively toward their own cultures, to develop a sense of political efficacy, and to master strategies which will enable them to liberate themselves from physical and psychological oppression. There is a movement among ethnic minority groups to reject their old identities, shaped largely by white society, and to create new ones, shaped by themselves. The calls for black, red, brown, and yellow power are rallying cries of these movements. However, despite the positive changes which have resulted from these identity quests, most ethnic minority youths still live in dehumanizing ghettos which tell them that black, brown, and red are ugly and shameful. They have many hostile teachers and administrators who reinforce the negative lessons which they learn from their immediate environment. Ethnic youths cannot believe that they are beautiful people as long as they have social contacts within the school and the larger society which contradict that belief. While current research is inconclusive and contradictory, the *bulk* of it indicates that recent attempts at self-determination *have not* significantly changed the self-concepts and self-evaluations of most ethnic minority children and youths.[5]

Despite the need for ethnic studies by *all* youths, ethnic content alone will not help minority youths to feel more positively about themselves and their cultures, nor will it help them develop a sense of control over their destinies. A school atmosphere must be created which values and accepts cultural differences, and ethnic youths must be taught how they have been victimized by institutional racism. They must become involved in social action projects which will teach them how to influence and change social and political institutions. One of the major goals of ethnic studies should be to help ethnic minority students become effective and rational political activists. We must provide opportunities for them to participate in social action projects so that they can become adept in influencing public policy which affects their lives. We now educate students for political apathy. They are taught that every citizen gets equal protection under the law, that racism only exists in the South, and that if they vote regularly and obey laws our

[4] For a review of this research, see James A. Banks, "Racial Prejudice and the Black Self-Concept," in James A. Banks and Jean Dresden Grambs (eds.), *Black Self-Concept: Implications for Education and Social Science*. New York: McGraw-Hill, 1972, pp. 5–35.

[5] For a research summary and review, see Marcel L. Goldschmid (ed.), *Black Americans and White Racism: Theory and Research*. New York: Holt, Rinehart, and Winston, 1970.

benign political leaders will make sure that they will get their slice of the American Dream pie. The powerlessness and widespread political alienation among blacks, Chicanos, Indians, Puerto Ricans, and other poor peoples are deceptively evaded in such mythical lessons about our political system. We must teach ethnic youths how to obtain and exercise political power in order for them to liberate themselves from physical and psychological captivity. Their liberation might be the salvation of our confused and divided society.

There is also an urgent need for ethnic studies to help white students expand their conception of humanity. Many whites seem to believe that they are the only *humans* on earth. To the extent that a people excludes other humans from their conception of humanity, they themselves are dehumanized. Racism has dehumanized many whites and caused them to exclude ethnic minority groups from their definition of humanity. The differential reactions by the majority of whites to the killings of blacks and whites in recent years indicate how whites often consider blacks and other ethnic groups less than human. During the racial rebellions that broke out in our cities in the early 1900s, the 1940s, and the late 1960s, hundreds of blacks were killed by police because they were protesting against injustices and grinding poverty. Many of these victims were innocent bystanders. In 1969, two black students were shot by police on the campus of a black college in South Carolina. The majority of white Americans remained conspicuously silent during these tragedies; a few even applauded. The tragedy at Kent State evoked strong reactions and protest by many white Americans, but no similarly strong reactions followed the tragedy at Jackson State. Reactions of the majority of white Americans to the My Lai massacre and the Attica incident were not as intense as the reaction to the Kent State tragedy.

Each of these dehumanizing events—the killings of ghetto blacks, the incidents at Kent State and Jackson State, the My Lai massacre, and the Attica tragedy—should have caused *all* Americans to become saddened, anguished, and outraged. The American dilemma which these incidents illuminated is that Americans are capable of reacting to the killing of human beings differently because of differences in their skin color and social class. While people may start treating others in dehumanizing ways because of their skin color or social class, the dehumanizing process, once started, continues unabated. Unless aggressive efforts are made to humanize white students, future incidents such as Kent State may leave the majority of Americans emotionally untouched. The issue of helping students become more humanized ultimately transcends race and social class. However, helping students see ethnic minorities as fellow humans is imperative if we are to eliminate our racial problems.

Ethnic content can serve as an excellent vehicle to help white students expand their conceptions of humanity and to better understand their own cultures. Since cultures are man-made, there are many ways of being human. The white middle-class life-style is one way; the Spanish Harlem culture is another. By studying this important generalization, students will develop an appreciation for man's great capacity to create a diversity of life-styles and to adapt to a variety of social and physical environments. Most groups tend to think that their culture is superior to all others. Chauvinist ethnocentrism is especially acute among dominant groups in American society. By studying other ways of being and living, students will see how bound they are by their own values, perceptions, and prejudices. The cultures of our powerless ethnic groups, and the devastating experiences of America's oppressed black, brown, red, and yellow peoples, are shocking testimony to the criminal effects of racism on its victims. Ethnic content can serve as an excellent lens to help white America see itself clearly, and hopefully to become more humanized.

We must construct new conceptions of human intelligence and devise instructional programs based on these novel ideas to improve the education of ethnic minority groups. Brookover and Erickson have summarized the conceptions of human intelligence on which most current educational programs are based: "1) that ability to learn is relatively fixed and unchangeable and 2) that it is predetermined by heredity. . . . These beliefs assume that ability is unaffected by external social forces. Another common assumption is that fixed ability of individuals can be measured with reasonable accuracy by intelligence tests." [6] These pervasive and outmoded assumptions have led to unfortunate practices in our schools. Ethnic minority youths are often placed in low academic tracks, classified as mentally retarded, and exposed to an unstimulating educational environment because they perform poorly on I.Q. and other tests which were standardized on a white middle-class population. These practices result in the self-fulfilling prophecy: Teachers assume that these pupils cannot learn, and they do not learn because teachers do not create the kinds of experiences which will enable them to master essential understandings and skills.

The traditional conceptions of human intelligence have been recently defended and popularized by Arthur S. Jensen. Jensen's research is based on unhelpful and faulty assumptions (he maintains, for example, that intelligence is what I.Q. tests measure). His argument is only a hypothesis, and should never have been presented to the general public in a popular magazine such as *Life* (since it is only a hypothesis) in these racially troubled times. I believe that *the hypothesis is immoral, misleading, and irrelevant.* Since we have no reliable and valid ways to determine innate potential, a moral assumption is that *all* students have the ability to master the skills and understandings which educators deem necessary for them to function

---

[6] Wilbur B. Brookover and Edsel L. Erickson, *Society, Schools, and Learning.* Boston: Allyn and Bacon, 1969, p. 3.

adequately in our highly technological society; we should search for means to facilitate their acquisition of these skills and understandings and not spend valuable time trying to discover which ethnic group is born with "more" of "something" that we have not yet clearly defined. As Robert E. L. Faris, the perceptive sociologist, has stated, "We essentially create our own level of human intelligence." [7]

Teachers must obtain a more liberal education, greater familiarity with ethnic cultures, and a more acute awareness of the *racist* assumptions on which much social research is based if they are to become effective change agents in minority education. Social science reflects the norms, values, and goals of the ruling and powerful groups in society; it validates those belief systems which are functional for people in power and dysfunctional for oppressed and powerless groups. Research which is antithetical to the interests of ruling and powerful groups is generally ignored by the scientific community and the society which supports it. [8] Numerous myths about ethnic minorities have been created by white "scholarly" historians and social scientists. Many teachers perpetuate the historical and social science myths which they learned in school and that are pervasive in textbooks because they are unaware of the racist assumptions on which social science research is often based. Much information in textbooks is designed to support the status quo and to keep powerless ethnic groups at the lower rungs of the social ladder.

Teachers often tell students that Columbus discovered America, yet the Indians were here centuries before Columbus. The Columbus myth in one sense denies the Indian child his past and thus his identity. Many teachers believe that Lincoln was the great emancipator of black people; yet he supported a move to deport blacks to Africa and issued the Emancipation Proclamation, in his own words, "as a military necessity" to weaken the Confederacy. Primary grade teachers often try to convince the ghetto child that the policeman is his friend. Many ethnic minority students know from their experiences that some policemen are their enemies. Only when teachers get a truly liberal education about the nature of science and American society will they be able to correct such myths and distortions and make the school experience more realistic and meaningful for *all* students. Both pre- and in-service training is necessary to help teachers to gain a realistic perspective of American society.

The severity of our current racial problems has rarely been exceeded in human history. The decaying cities, anti-busing movements, escalating poverty, increasing racial polarization, and the recent Attica tragedy are alarming manifestations of the ethnic hostility which is widespread through-

[7] Robert E. L. Faris, "Reflections on the Ability Dimension in Human Society," *American Sociological Review*, December, 1961, pp. 835–42.

[8] For a perceptive discussion of this point, see Barbara A. Sizemore, "Social Science and Education for a Black Identity," in Banks and Grambs, *op. cit.*, pp. 141–70.

out America. Our very existence may ultimately depend upon our creative abilities to solve our urgent racial problems. During the decade which recently closed, much discussion and analysis related to ethnic minority problems occurred, yet few constructive steps were taken to eliminate the basic causes of our racial crisis. Educators must take decisive steps to help create a culturally pluralistic society in which peoples of different colors can live in harmony. Immediate action is imperative if we are to prevent racial wars and chaos and the complete dehumanization of the American man.

Cultural Differences and the Melting Pot Ideology

ROGER D. ABRAHAMS

Today, many are recognizing that the melting pot ideal is just another ethnocentric concept. The image of the melting pot implies that there is a "consensus culture," a way of life which all Americans can learn, subscribe to, and live by. In theory, this culture of "mainstream America" is a conglomerate of the lifeways of all of the groups who have entered into the building of America—and in many ways this is true.

Yet what this perspective does not take into account is that, though consensus culture has indeed borrowed elements from various European groups, and from Indians, from Blacks, and from Chicanos, there remain many groups in our midst who live by a different culture. That is, though Euro-American culture has borrowed heavily from Afro-American, Mexican American, and Native American lifeways, these other groups have remained culturally distinct as they have remained socially apart. The continuing existence of such distinct ethnic enclaves puts the lie to those who would argue that the melting pot has really worked.

Consensus culture cannot be taught to these other groups as long as what is being purveyed is only in the realm of ideals. For culture to be taught, there must be institutions which support cultural ideals, and members of these so-called minorities have never been allowed equal access to the mainstream institutions, especially on the economic and political levels.

However, the alternative being proposed, *pluralism,* asks us to do the

Roger D. Abrahams is Director of the African and Afro-American Research Institute at the University of Texas, Austin.

Reprinted from *Educational Leadership* 29(2):118–121, 1971, with permission of the Association for Supervision and Curriculum Development and Roger D. Abrahams. Copyright © 1972 by the Association for Supervision and Curriculum Development.

very same thing—to accept an ideology on the value level without indicating how this is to operate on the institutional or the interactional levels. By this I simply mean that we are given as an alternative to the "One Great American Culture" idea the "Many Great American Subcultures" program of pluralism, without any indication of how we are going to provide equal access to the sources of power for all, or how we are going even to learn each other's ways of interacting and communicating.

Education for pluralism is as great a bowl of mush as melting pot education if we do not take into consideration that pluralism means the full recognition of cultural differences (on *all* levels of culture) and the devising of educational strategies whereby a cultural equality can be made meaningful.

This means, among other things, that we must recognize that our present classroom procedures are an intensification of our own middle class ideals and institutions and therefore operate in many ways as exclusionary devices against those who come from other cultures. What do we know of the ways in which the poor, the Black, the Chicano, the many Indians learn and interact? Have we, as teachers, bothered even to learn the ways in which we embarrass our students by not understanding these cultural differences— much less the reasons that we cannot teach them effectively?

What I am arguing is that if we are (and I hope we are) really committed to a pluralistic ideal of education, then we have to recognize ahead of time what we are up against in engineering change. And the one fact that we must contend with is that there is no case on record in the past in which cultural pluralism of the sort we are discussing has ever existed. That is, there is no country that we know of which has a cultural mix which does not have one dominant culture, the others subordinate—at least as far as access to the major economic and governmental institutions. So if we are to devise such a system it would be a unique social experiment. The United States has, however, engaged in such enterprises before.

What Happened to the Melting Pot?

One way of beginning is to see what was wrong with the melting pot image. From our contemporary perspective, the melting pot implied a racist ideology because it never included as part of the formula for the proper mix the truly culturally different—Afro-Americans, Chicanos, Indians, etc. These groups were never accorded status as full human beings, so they were not considered as fit candidates for the melting process. The idea of the melting pot was a reaction to the massive introduction of non-Anglo-Saxon European immigrants to America in the last half of the 19th century. Though aimed ostensibly at extending American beneficence and the American ideals hinging on individualism and rationalism, in retrospect the melting pot argument looks suspiciously like a knee-jerk reaction to the forming of Irish and Southern and Eastern European ethnic communities within the East Coast cities. Such ethnic communities, through their maintenance of community and language and cultural differences, threatened the fragile unity of the nation. The melting pot ideology then has always been an essentially nationalistic one, and thus an argument subject to uses by any group, benevolent or malevolent, which preaches Americanism at the expense of ethnic, regional, or even social class identification.

Yet even with this nationalistic thrust, used as an argument against the continuation of linguistically and culturally different European-Americans in the cities and towns, the practice of melting for the pot never included the other (and darker) Americans until the Civil Rights movement began. And then it happened only because the members of these ethnic communities suddenly demanded to be recognized as human beings. Before that time they were relegated to animal status.

The reader will be saying at this, "Now wait a minute! That is going too far." Perhaps it is, but let me demonstrate what I mean. I do not mean that slavery and its attendant chattel status continued to operate. Rather, the dehumanization process functioned on a less legalistic plane, one we know best through the operation of stereotyping.

The Operation of Stereotyping

What is stereotyping? It is primarily the imposition of traits on a group which are purported to be characteristic of the group. Now occasionally these traits may be the result of real observations on the part of the stereotypers. Blacks *do* have more rhythm, for instance, because they have more complicated and overlapping rhythms in their dances and songs. Yet even when these cultural differences are observed, the question is what we do with them. With Black rhythm, for instance, we tie this in with a certain earthiness and by extension to a basically immoral (or amoral) and child-like perspective.

The other stereotype traits imposed on Blacks (and other "minorities" and groups of poor people) all revolve around these primary traits of childishness and immorality. Laziness, thievery, inability to contain sexual urges, strange eating habits, having too many children and raising them without any sense of proper family life—all of these and more emphasize the inability of members of the group to live by the proper rules.

The implication (sometimes it becomes an explication) is that people from these groups have no sense of order. Now *culture* is, if nothing else, the agreed upon ways in which a group orders things—the rules and manners of the group. If members of a group have no sense of order, then they have no culture, and the acquisition of culture is what divides adults from children and human beings from animals. So when the stereotype is involved, it means that the stereotypers are assuming that the stereotyped are a group of children or animals without actually always saying so. And defining a group as *culturally deprived* or *disadvantaged* does exactly the same thing— it defines the culturally different by our own norms and finds them lacking.

Any time members of a group are derogated in regard to where they depart from another group's norms and practices, they are being stereotyped. Until very recently, this was the only approach to Blacks and other culturally different groups by an overwhelming majority of Euro-Americans, an approach institutionalized in our educational system (except in rare cases). This is what I meant when I said that non-Euro-Americans have been treated as animals—not wild ones, but the kind we like to keep around the house and yard.

Today suddenly the bases of stereotyping are eliminated and we can no longer generalize on such groups (at least officially). And so now the old melting pot ideology is trotted out, for if these others *are* human beings they must be assimilable. The ethnic Euro-Americans that have been thus assimilated now preach, "We have done it; why can't you?" The answer, of course, is why should they have to? By any standard of equality, being forced to adhere to an alien cultural mold is both iniquitous and, without structural changes in national institutions and goals, clearly impossible.

Cultural Relativism in the Schools

This position of cultural relativism which I am espousing for the schools is a difficult one to accept at best, for it means questioning the absoluteness of our own values and practices. In the task of devising a pluralistic perspective, it is equally as important to maintain one's own cultural sense as it is to recognize that of others.

One of the major by-products of adopting the relativistic position is that one begins to question the values of one's own culture, when one sees that one's values and practices are not immutable and the only right solutions to our human problems. To reject out of hand one's own values is folly indeed. One cannot educate effectively without a firm knowledge of oneself. The task, then, is to question and investigate cultures without totally rejecting one's own and developing a defeating sense of self-doubt.

A procedure which my colleagues, Mary Galvan and Rudolph Troike, and I (of the Texas Education Agency's East Texas Dialect and Culture Project) have found meaningful is to teach other cultural ways by making teachers more conscious of their own culture. First of all, this means that we must demonstrate how deep stereotyping goes, and that this is just one way people with culture project and protect their own sense of groupness and sharing. Then, however, it is necessary to show that we live by a lot of other unexamined ordering processes, especially by rules of interaction— those ways in which we make haphazard behavior into ordered manners or decorum.

To show how deeply rule-involved we are and how much of our sense of personal worth depends on living by these rules, we attempt to embarrass each other. It is only in embarrassment situations that we can demonstrate how we have learned and internalized certain practices, developing expectations for a wide range of interactions, and how much we are threatened when these expectations and orders are broken.

Then, because we are dealing with teachers who minister to both Afro- and Euro-American students, we demonstrate how patterned and predictable the ways are in which the two cultures do not fit, producing the same embarrassment situations repeatedly. To get this message through, however, we must convince the teachers that their students, no matter what age or color, have culture and can therefore be embarrassed. To do this, we describe Black language use, both in terms of phonological and morphological differences and in the ways language is utilized in personal exchanges. We also cover what is known about Afro-American culture, not only in speech use but in child-rearing and family patterns, peer grouping, religion, allocation of time and money, and so on. To do this we give over a large part of our in-service programs to teaching teachers how to observe, notate, and use language and cultural differences.

Our aim throughout is to permit recognitions of differences at all levels of culture. Only by developing the powers of observation about oneself and others will it be possible to regard the culturally different as culturally different and nothing more. In this sense a truly pluralistic education will provide the most profound American Revolution in 200 years.

The Schools Can Overcome Racism

DELMO DELLA-DORA

In our country, *every school* is the best place to work on overcoming racism, whether the school is all-white, racially mixed, or all-black. *Every* educator is in a position to make a real difference. *Now* is the best of all times to work on it. One reason for this is that teachers and other staff members are in contact with youngsters for a longer portion of most days than anyone else—including parents. Equally important, maybe more so, schools are quite likely the single most important cause and source of racism which young people experience in our nation.

Some will object to that last statement. Isn't that "simplistic labeling" or ". . . an unfair and exaggerated blanket indictment of schools generally"? Others already accept the validity of the generalization and say, "It's true, but what can any one person or a few people do? It's a societal phenomenon and too big for me." The fact is that every one of us is an active participant in racist practices daily, usually unintentionally and unconsciously. It is also a fact that each of us is the only one we can count on to change racist behaviors in the ways desired.

Racism in the Society

If you're still saying "Who? Me a racist?," consider this. Schools could be *racist* in nature without having a single staff member who harbors racial *prejudice* or commits racially discriminatory acts. (That is unlikely, but possible.) Racism, prejudice, and discrimination are related but different. Racial *prejudice* means to prejudge people on the basis of their race and, usually, to *feel* that one race is inferior to others. Racial *discrimination* is an *act* of behaving differently toward people based on their race and reflects the feeling of prejudice.

On the other hand, racism in America is a word which describes prevailing practices in our society and its major institutions. Racial prejudice

Delmo Della-Dora is principal of the Edna Maguire Middle School, Mill Valley, California.

Reprinted from *Educational Leadership* 29(5):443–449, 1972, with permission of the Association for Supervision and Curriculum Development and Delmo Della-Dora. Copyright © 1972 by the Association for Supervision and Curriculum Development.

and discrimination have now become ingrained into the everyday practices and operations of all our major societal institutions. After 350 years of institutionalized racism, most white people and many black people are not consciously aware of the racism which pervades almost every waking moment. The most unaware seem to be whites in all-white communities or schools, particularly those who say, "Of course, we don't have that problem here" (meaning there are no other races present in the school or community) or who refer to "your" problems when referring to racially mixed communities. There are still some who even talk about racial problems as "the Negro problem."

The fact is that the curse of racism is *there* most of all, in the ever increasing number of all-white schools. Further, our racial problems in this country are primarily a "white problem," because white people are in power everywhere that counts, and it is *their* institutions which affect black, yellow, brown, Chicano, American Indian—and whites themselves—adversely.

For a more complete description of the nature and development of racism in our society, there are several excellent fairly recent publications including ones from the U.S. Commission on Civil Rights,[1] by white psychiatrist Joel Kovel,[2] by black psychiatrists Price Cobbs and William Grier,[3] the many excellent articles and books by Lerone Bennett, Jr., Senior Editor of *Ebony* magazine,[4] and the National Book Award-winning historical analysis *White Over Black,* written by Winthrop Jordan.[5]

Racism in the Schools

How are school people involved in racism and what can they do about it? Institutional racism in schools appears in all major functions and operations, for example, (a) textbooks and other instructional materials, (b) the content of the curriculum, (c) knowledge, attitudes, and behavior of the student body and staff, (d) personnel selection and promotion procedures, (e) major organizational and instructional practices (grouping, testing, etc.).

[1] Anthony Downs. "Racism in America and How To Combat It." U.S. Commission on Civil Rights. Clearinghouse Publication, Urban Series No. 1. Washington, D.C.: Superintendent of Documents, U.S. Government Printing Office, January 1970.

[2] Joel Kovel. *White Racism: A Psychohistory.* New York: Pantheon Books, Inc., 1970.

[3] William H. Grier and Price M. Cobbs. *Black Rage.* New York: Basic Books, Inc., Publishers, 1968.

[4] Too numerous to list, but noteworthy among them is: Lerone Bennett, Jr. *The Negro Mood.* Chicago, Illinois: Johnson Publishing Company, 1970.

[5] Winthrop Jordan. *White Over Black.* Chapel Hill: University of North Carolina Press, 1968.

TEXTBOOKS

Check out the reading series and the social studies textbooks in particular. They are not necessarily worse than the others, but their defects are usually more readily obvious. Simply count the total number of illustrations in one book and then the number in which black people and other minority groups appear. In how many of the latter do they appear as equal to whites or in a favorable status? How much of the world history book or world geography book is devoted to black and yellow people (who constitute a *majority* of the world population)? These are simple *quantitative* indices. For qualitative indices, see analysis sheets such as that used by the Detroit Public Schools.[6] Even a cursory analysis will show that *every* textbook now in use seriously distorts by omission and commission.

What can we do about it? Some examples of low-risk actions would include: (a) having students examine the textbooks they use to discover for themselves the bias and distortion exhibited there; (b) telling every book salesman why his company's textbooks are not adequate, then writing those sentiments to the superintendent, local board of education, state board of education and president of the book company; (c) developing a supplement to correct the deficiencies and/or purchasing supplementary books; and (d) establishing in-service education to upgrade staff knowledge in this field. Some high-risk actions would include: (a) refusing to use the textbooks because of their deficiencies, and/or (b) establishing protest groups to halt teaching in any subject for which the instructional materials available are inadequate because of significant omissions or distortion.

CONTENT OF THE CURRICULUM

Does your curriculum include coverage of the nature of institutional racism in the U.S.A. as part of the required program? Does this treatment include local practices (including its existence in the schools), as well as examination of state and national manifestations?

What part of the curriculum is devoted to race-relations problems internationally, nationally, statewide, locally, and in the school itself?

Are the nature of racism and examination of race-relations problems covered in early elementary, later elementary, middle grades, and high school?

If the answer is "no" to any of the foregoing, what can we do about it? It can be as simple as asking those questions of other staff members individually, in committees, or at staff meetings, or writing letters to the central administration, the board of education, and "letters to the editor" of local

---

[6] Intergroup Relations Department. *Textbook Report.* Publication 1-112. Detroit, Michigan: Detroit Public Schools, 1968.

newspapers, as well as raising the questions at PTA meetings and other public places.

Higher risk actions would be unilaterally to decide to add such study to your classroom or school curriculum, or to insist that no curriculum committee on which you serve has completed its task until these issues have been incorporated effectively into its work.

KNOWLEDGE, ATTITUDES, AND BEHAVIOR

Does your school or district have an accurate assessment of what the students and staff *know* about racism, race-relations problems, and contributions of minority-group people in our country's past and present life?

Is there any kind of systematic attempt to determine what the attitudes and behaviors of staff and students are in relation to racism and race relations?

Is anybody trying to do ·something about inadequate knowledge and inappropriate attitudes and behaviors?

These questions are even more significant for an all-white setting than for a racially mixed or all-black one. It is there that such questions can more easily be ignored and therefore can result in entrenched ignorance, more biased attitudes, and most inappropriate behaviors outside of school and after school days are over.

Concerned educators can, with little effort, determine the degree of student awareness in a classroom (or school) simply by discussing the issues involved with staff or students or by making up their own questionnaires. The same can be done as part of self-examination by any group of interested staff members and, preferably, by the total staff.

Higher risk actions would include making such assessments of staff knowledge, attitudes, and behavior a demand on the board by the local teachers or administrators group or by requesting a board policy along these lines. Even better, any bargaining unit could demand that in-service training for all staff be mandatory in such matters.

PERSONNEL SELECTION AND PROMOTION PROCEDURES

Does the composition of the staff at each school and in the central office reflect national racial distribution, as a bare minimum, or local area racial composition (where higher) as a desirable minimum?

Are racial and ethnic minority group members properly represented at each echelon of administration and on the board of education?

Do promotion practices and procedures systematically work in favor of, or against, any racial or ethnic group?

As in other areas, we can at the very least raise these questions whenever and wherever we have the opportunity.

Other helpful actions would include formal requests that no additional whites be hired or promoted until some specified minimum of racial and ethnic composition is reached. The request could be escalated to a bargaining demand. A higher risk move would be to organize interested parents and students to protest present practices and insist on immediate changes.

ORGANIZATIONAL AND INSTRUCTIONAL PRACTICES

Testing and grouping are probably the two most insidious racist practices in the field of school organization and instruction.

All test-makers and most educators know that tests are biased in favor of white middle class people. The published results help reinforce the sick notion that white middle class children are superior and all others are inferior. Grouping based on test results makes the most of a bad thing. With the formation of so-called "ability" groups, we now "see" (literally) that poor children of racial and ethnic minorities are "stupid" and should be kept separate so as not to interfere with the learning of those better-dressed and (generally) better-behaved children. This feeds the paranoia of racism in racially mixed communities. Ironically, ability grouping continues in the face of 30 years of research which shows it to be ineffective at best, and even harmful in some cases.[7]

Testing results are increasingly being published at the demand of state legislatures (including California and Michigan). Some black educators see this as a way of pointing out to "whitey" how poorly he has done by black students. The conclusion is undoubtedly correct, but the use of biased, distorted, and narrowly limited testing devices is a dangerous and misguided means for so doing.

Educators can help with low-key approaches, such as (a) reporting research from scholars concerning the inadequacies of testing and grouping, or (b) setting up local research designs to determine the efficacy of either. We can also refuse to test or to set up ability-grouped classes, whether we be teachers or administrators. The *Hobson* v. *Hansen* U.S. District Court decision is one indication of legal support for such a position.

In summary, every educator in our country is part of the racist society. We can recognize this and cry "mea culpa" while doing nothing—or just do nothing. No one will notice, particularly in an all-white community. In so doing, we would have ample company in history and in hell with the Germans of World War II who lived just outside the gates of Belsen or the Americans of World War II who saw innocent Japanese placed in "internment" camps or die under a mushroom cloud at Hiroshima and Nagasaki—and who did nothing and said nothing.

Or, we can decide that we are part of the problem and must do some-

[7] Miriam Goldberg, A. Harry Passow, and Joseph Justman. *The Effects of Ability Grouping.* New York: Teachers College, Columbia University, 1966.

thing—every day, wherever we are, whoever we are. It can be quiet and subdued or loud and angry. Each person has to decide what he can and should do. To "do nothing," however, is to maintain all the evils we see about us. There is no neutral ground. To act will be painful at times, in direct proportion to the effectiveness of the action.

There is the likely risk of losing some friends and the possible risk of losing a job. Racism is costly to black people and other minority racial groups in terms of health, income, education, and general quality of living. Giving up the "benefits" of racism can be costly in material benefits to whites. The question is, how much are we willing to pay for equality and justice in this land? No one else knows the answer for any of us. Each of us must provide his own.

A Rebirth of Interest in Heritage Identity

ANTONIO GABALDON

Never before have such great numbers of Mexican Americans flocked to the golf courses of the United States. What is the cause of this phenomenon? Likewise, their television sets are flicking on every Saturday and Sunday to watch the heroics of their college and professional football heroes.

Yes, Lee Trevino, Homero Blancas, and Chi Chi Rodriguez have certainly made an impact on the golfing world, as have the two great Chicano quarterbacks, Jim Plunkett and Joe Kapp. The last two individuals mentioned picked up German last names somewhere along the line (probably grandfathers), but there is no question in their minds or in the hearts of their admirers that they are Chicanos, through and through.

We admire the unselfish decision of quarterback Jim Plunkett, son of blind parents, who postponed for one year a lucrative professional football career, in order that he might remain with his teammates and enhance their chances of playing in the Rose Bowl. What a year it was for him as well as his teammates!

What is the reason for this clamor in the use of adjectives in describing these young men as Mexicans or Chicanos? It seems that just a few years ago the word "Mexican" was coupled with being dirty, lazy, or greasy,

Antonio Gabaldon is Principal of the Charles W. Sechrist Elementary School, Flagstaff, Arizona, and Arizona State Senator, District 2.

Reprinted from *Educational Leadership* 29:122–124, 1971, with permission of the Association for Supervision and Curriculum Development and Antonio Gabaldon. Copyright © 1971 by the Association for Supervision and Curriculum Development.

and it was more often than not that all were used together. While the term "Mexican" has gained a degree of respectability, there are those (including a few Mexican Americans) who shudder and tremble with *horror* at "Chicano." These are the people who equate "Chicano" with Brown Power and fear the militancy attached to that movement.

Yes, times are changing and feelings also. Sensitivity in allowing people to be what they are and what they wish to be certainly falls within these changes. It was not too many years ago that some of my best friends insisted that I must be "Spanish" instead of "Mexican." They did not realize that in encouraging me to deny my heredity, they were insulting me instead of complimenting me. (Still that thought about "Mexican" being a dirty word.)

Indeed, there was a time when we all insisted that black people were colored. (Did that mean the rest of us had a lack of color?)

It has taken many years for us to begin to tell the story of the American Indian in the way it really happened.

This desire for heritage identity is not something new for this melting pot called the United States of America. Many of the European ethnic groups, such as the Irish, German, Swedish, and Polish people, went through the same turmoil and difficulties that are now faced by blacks, Indians, and Mexicans. The only thing that made their "melting in" process a little smoother was the color of their skin. Having overcome their language problems, they were allowed to assume their roles as *real* Americans.

Pride in Group Identity

A few years back when these old Americans (remember Indians, Mexicans, and blacks have been around for some time) made their first moves toward establishing pride in their identity, it was members of these European ethnic groups who resisted their efforts by insisting that they forget their identity and become "just Americans" and "all Americans" immediately.

There is nothing wrong with this eventual goal of one nation and one people. However, to force people to lose their identity by giving up their cultures and especially their pride, even before it has been established, is despicable. Once a person has gained this pride in his group culture and his group identity, let it become an individual matter as to how he or she will navigate within the mainstream of the large current. However, to force people (as has been attempted) to lose their identity out of shame is deplorable and can only make the individual miserable within himself. Eventually he will really not be able to contribute his full and most worthwhile efforts to the fundamental goal of a strong nation.

Having hopefully established the validity of pride in heritage identity, let us discuss what the schools can do to help children gain it.

A Mexican, black, or Indian child's self-esteem must include pride in being what he is. He must know who he is and know that his cultural heritage is a noble one. Many minority children know little or nothing of their cultural heritage. In fact, some Mexican children are ashamed of being Mexican and try to hide this fact.

We must teach these children that being a Mexican is something of which to be proud. Teach them that Mexicans have contributed a great deal to the American Culture, especially in the Southwest. Mention the many cities with strong Mexican influence, such as Los Angeles, San Francisco, Nogales, Santa Barbara, San Antonio, El Paso, San Jose, San Diego, and many others. Mention the many Mexican American political leaders, such as Dennis Chavez; U.S. Senator Joseph M. Montoya, from New Mexico; Edward R. Roybal, Congressman from California; Raul Castro, successful U.S. Ambassador to South America, a strong contender for governor of Arizona.

Point out that in the future many well-trained Mexican Americans, Indians, and blacks must be available if America is to be a successful plural society. Mention the rich historical background of Mexicans stemming from the colorful Spanish conquistadores, and other romantic figures such as the great Indian Emperor Montezuma.

Be sure to acquaint your minority children with people from their culture who are "successful" people. I am sure there are people in your community who fall in this category and would eagerly accept an invitation to visit your classroom and give your children a lift.

Acceptance and Support

These children must learn and be made aware that they are bearers of cultural heritages esteemed by their teachers and their classmates. They must see that they, as individuals, are well regarded and that they are accepted by their teachers and peers, and are important to the school life. Given this acceptance, along with a teacher's support when his "minority" ways need understanding, a boy or girl will learn in school despite the fact that, initially, he may have approached school with apprehension, distrust, and frequently insufficient ability to communicate with others.

Most parents of these children want them to learn all they can in our schools, but they also want them to remain Mexican, black, and Indian. They want them to hold on, whenever feasible, to their culture and to their way of life. They want an education which will help them to find a way to combine the best from two cultures. A number of European ethnic groups in our country have retained many of their traditions, celebrations, foods, religions, and other ways of life, yet they think of themselves as basically Americans. These ideas are commendable and likewise should be accepted for our people who are now struggling to do the same thing.

The school which effectively mobilizes its resources to provide disadvantaged boys and girls with the education which will help them to realize their maximum potential will be distinguished by an administrator whose competence is manifested in vision and sensitivity combined with emotional security, intelligence, and drive.

Only in a school in which the teacher has this kind of administrative support can the teacher fulfill his or her role as the most influential part of a child's learning. Most of the child's school hours are spent in contact with his teacher. This contact is continuous in affecting the child's attitudes and responses to the learning situation. The teacher's personality, as much as the teacher's knowledge, will determine how the child learns.

The teacher not only represents the adult world, but is also the model for growth, a mirror in which the child sees himself reflected. A good teacher for disadvantaged boys and girls will view himself as an educator who defines education as the liberation of individuals into new levels of emotion as well as intellect—levels where they can achieve new capacities and insights. Teaching to him becomes a creative art, an example of humanity thinking and bringing ideas to life.

The wisest educators, as they work with these children, will conscientiously ponder the following questions: What strange ways must these children learn in order to live in today's society? How can they absorb the technical knowledge necessary for their survival without disrupting the whole fabric of their lives? How much of their old pattern of life can be preserved? How can the human values by which they live be conserved in the heritage of all humanity?

Certainly by doing this we will not only be fostering pluralism in our society, but also fostering a climate of humaneness in our schools which will endow our nation with the strength necessary to survive these troubled times.

The Thousand Indignities of a Spanish-Speaking Student

FRED DIAZ

Me gustaria hablarles en Espanol completamente pero como hay muchos aqui que no hablan Espanol, tengo que hablarles en ingles.

Some of you may now be reacting as many children are reacting in our schools today. There are many migrant students who do not speak English as their first language, and it's a traumatic experience when they walk into that first grade classroom. Picture yourself as a first-grader having to go through this.

I am concerned because I see what's happening to the kids. I am concerned as a parent. I am concerned as an educator. I am concerned as a human being as you should be, because my philosophy of teaching kids is that I do not see how teachers can reach children whom they do not understand—of whose cultures they have no knowledge. This is important because these cultures produce conflicts of values.

Only in the past few years has there really been a great concern for Spanish-speaking students. You may say, so what? Let me quote a few statistics to give you an answer to your "so what?"

Some of you may wonder, what does he mean by Mexicans? Who are they?

Mexicans, for the most part, are people born in Mexico.

Mexican Americans are people born in the United States of Mexican descent.

Spanish Americans are people born in the United States, descendent from Spain.

There is a great difference. Some of you say Spanish American, Mexican American. But these are not synonymous terms. Some will fight you over the term. Mexicans don't care too much for Spaniards and Spaniards don't care too much for Mexicans. This goes back to the conquest of Mexico by Cortez. This carries down in their poetry, in their language, and in their culture. They don't care for each other. So don't use the terms synonymously.

Chicano is the term that is probably most seen and used. Chicano is the

Fred Diaz is a teacher and migrant consultant in the Pajaro Valley Unified School District, Watsonville, California.

Reprinted from *Washington Education* 82(8):20–22, 1971, with permission of the Washington Education Association and Fred Diaz.

term that came from the Nahuatl language which was the original language of Mexico. In that language all the x's were pronounced "ch" so that the people from Mexico were Mechicanos. Mexico was Mechico. Drop the first syllable "me"—you have Chicanos. This is the group that wants self-identity and change. This is the group that you see in the paper. Many people see Chicano; they think it's synonymous with Mexican. It is *not!* There are Mexican Americans who do not like the term Chicano. There are people from Mexico who do not like the term Chicano. So don't assume that "Chicano" represents all Spanish-speaking people.

There are other terms such as hispanic. The hispanic term refers to people from the Latin American countries, from Portugal and Spain.

There are other terms that you will probably never see—manitos and pochos. Who are we talking about? You've got to play it kind of cool with these terms because they are like Okies and Arkies. What are pochos? Mexican Americans born in California. What are manitos? Mexican Americans born in New Mexico. For all practical purposes, these are the most important terms with which you will come in contact.

The big concern about migrant education has come within the last few years because federal funding is available. Fifty per cent of the Mexican Americans were dropping out by the eighth grade. Only two per cent of the Mexicans go to college—this is nationwide. Less than 15 per cent graduate from high school. These statistics of the last two years are from the United States Office of Education and Mexican Affairs Unit in Washington, D.C.

Let's take Texas for an example. Texas has 500,000 Spanish-surnamed youngsters and 80 per cent of these are dropping out by the 12th grade. That's a lot of humanity there. Look at the Indians. Five years ago, the dropout rate was shocking: but we made a lot of progress. Now we've got only around 70 per cent dropping out nationally—really great!

Why the problems? Where do they lie?

The number one major problem of Mexican migrant education is oral language development. What does that mean? Those are fancy words. Oral language simply means that we get a lot of kids here in our country who don't speak English. You may say again, so what? Of the Mexican Americans, 80 per cent nationally, *eight out of ten,* have to repeat the first grade.

The second problem of migrant education is basic content. The curriculum is not relevant. I think of my own education. Think back when you were in the first, second, third and fourth grades. Think of the things you used to study. We teach units on coal; but how many know what the heck coal is and what it's used for? We hardly use coal any more.

In first grade you see a picture showing father. He's dressed in a coat, a suit, a necktie; he carries a briefcase; looks great. This isn't father to the Mexican! This isn't father to the black! This isn't father to the Indian! He's no more father than the mailman.

You see other pictures to which kids cannot relate. The one that really gets me is health. Health—that one really shakes me up. When I was in school, the teacher used to say, "All right, tomorrow everybody is going to give all of the calories of everything he ate." The next day you make a report. Oh man, all the Chicanos would say. Oh no, not that again; but that is what happened. Everybody went home and spent a half-hour lying. You hate to be the first because you know everybody is going to laugh at you that knows. All the Mexican kids are going to laugh at you. So you get your little paper. "For breakfast I had grapefruit," and that starts it, man! (Que mentiroso—what a liar. I know what he had.) And he goes on: bacon, hash browns. I never saw hash browns until I joined the Navy. I didn't even know what they were. All these lies going on about these calories and everybody laughing in the background.

Recently I taught in a sixth grade where I had a lot of Mexican kids, and I made it a point when we came to health to figure out the calories of what they really eat at home—how many calories there are in tortillas, chile, sopa, frijoles, papas. These kids told me what they had; and they weren't ashamed.

In high school you brought your lunch and where did you eat? You didn't eat in the gym. You ate out under the bleachers if you could so they couldn't see you eat your tacos. Sometimes it was raining and you couldn't go under the bleachers; so you're up in the gym. I remember to this day a very good friend of mine was sitting there and some Anglos were around him. He was waiting to eat lunch and I knew he was hungry. I said to him, "Por que no comes, por que no comes?"—meaning "Why don't you eat?" "I am not hungry," he said, the clock getting closer to one o'clock. Finally just before the bell rang, he grabbed his lunch and threw it in the garbage can, and you know tortillas and tacos have a distinct sound. Chicanos know what it sounds like—sort of a thud! So he dropped his lunch in the garbage can and thud! "I'm not hungry," he said. And all us Mexicans thought to ourselves, there goes that poor guy's tacos!

The third major problem of migrant education is attitude—teacher attitude. As far as I'm concerned, this is the most important because you can have all this other jazz, you can have all these books with everything in it, you can have techniques in oral language, but if the attitude is poor and if it isn't in here—forget it! Kids can spot phonies just like that, and they will. They'll spot a phony and you've lost the battle.

Some of you know about the research with rats. People said that these rats are real intelligent; so the scientists went at whatever they had to with rats and treated them the way they would teach someone that is real intelligent. The rats performed well above average at the end of the designated time. So they tried it with kids. They walked in and told the teachers, all right, Juan, Maria, so and so, these kids have it. Teachers with that attitude-set taught, and the kids performed, above grade level.

Attitudes of teachers are very, very important. Know what you expect of kids. The expectation level of kids is very important. Don't expect miracles.

It's pretty hard to teach a kid how to read in first grade if he has a language problem; and yet this is expected in a lot of our grade schools.

Let me cite another example of what can happen because it's happening right now and will be happening every spring and summer when the migrants come in. I talk to teachers who say, "Well, I don't do this and I don't do that." Sometimes just a gesture can really do a lot of destruction. You've got 35 kids in a classroom, and I'm not knocking teachers completely because there are a heck of a lot of good teachers and they're doing the best they can. But when the principal comes in bringing the migrant kid and says, "Here's a student for you, Mrs. so and so," sometimes just the facial expression of, "Oh no, not *another* one," just that reaction or expression can do a lot to destroy this kid's feelings about himself. His self-image is very important.

Some of you may be saying: Where are you going to get the bilingual teachers to teach kids? Who's going to train them? Where are you going to get the money, the books? These are just a few of the problems that arise. I think one of the best ways is to bring bilingual education into the area where it is needed. When you say "bilingual education" to administrators, a lot of them figure "here comes another one." They figure, "All right, if we give it to the Mexicans, we've got to give it to the Filipinos; we got to give it to the Japanese; we've got to give it to all the groups that demand it." They don't understand what bilingual education is and what the philosophy is all about.

Bilingual education simply means that you are going to be teaching in two languages according to the needs of the community.

If you're in Louisiana, you probably would teach English and French because of the large French population. If you're in the Great Lakes area, you'd probably teach German and English. Teach Ubangi and English if you want. Teach according to the needs of the kids! And teach kids, not books!

Bilingual education means that there is going to be a mixture of everybody in the class and they're going to learn two languages, probably Spanish and probably English. This is contrary to our philosophy of education today: You can't teach concepts unless they speak English. I have personally seen this disproved. I have done it myself with first- and second-graders. We don't wait too long because if you don't reach Mexican migrant kids by the third grade, research shows that these kids will probably drop out. You've got to reach them before the third grade. So we have some districts that have no kindergarten. And they wonder why more than 50 per cent, as I said before, of the Mexican American children have to repeat the first grade. Bilingual education is a terrific motivation. It helps keep kids in school. It also brings up the self-image.

I recall one time a sixth grade student's talking to another Mexican child. He didn't know that I was Spanish-speaking and they were arguing, "si habla Espanol, no habla Espanol." Finally one of the students came up to me and said, "Mr. Diaz, you speak Spanish, don't you?" So I said, "si como no, soy Mexicano." The kid looked at me kind of shocked and said to me, "But I thought only Americans could be teachers." There are many kids who feel this way. There are many people who feel that they are second- and third-class citizens. This is what prejudice does. You start hammering this at people and pretty soon they start believing it. This is the sad thing about it. It affects students this way and this is where change has to be made.

How can we solve some of these problems? I would recommend the following:

First, in areas of high Mexican migrant influx, introduce bilingual education.

Second, assess the needs of the individual districts according to the migrant population. Some places have a modified bilingual education in reading and language and then the rest of the course is in English. But if you should do something now—get it started, maybe English as a second language if you have a lot of non-English speakers. Bilingual education has a lot of merit, and I'm sold on it.

The colleges begin offering courses to students, to teachers, to citizens on cultural awareness of oral language. It gripes me to see who come out of colleges with Spanish majors and I say to them, "All right, let's be honest with each other. Do you really feel qualified to go in there? Let's say you've got a bunch of Chicanos in your class and you've got some Anglos who can't speak a word, and all at once they're in there in the same class. What are you going to do?" And they say: "Well, you know, I have to be honest, I've had a lot of courses in Latin American, the poems and the poetry and that jazz; but when it really gets down to the nitty gritty of what I'm going to do, I really didn't learn what I wanted. I really wasn't prepared," they answer.

Or for example, if you're teaching Mexican migrant students and you don't know that in the Spanish language all the words end in ten letters. They end in ten letters only—vowels, l, r, s, n and d and that's it. In English they end in about 40. So we're talking about 30 sounds that these migrants can't hear. This is where you get "shicken" and "shurch." They can't pronounce yellow—instead they say jello. Now if you know this and there are ways of remedying these problems and you're *taught* in college, then you're going to solve a lot of their problems. But if we don't face up to the problems, these kids are going to continue to drop out of school.

Many of you who speak Spanish, for example, right now will argue with me about this next statement. Whenever a word starts with a "v" in Spanish, it takes a "b" sound whether you want to admit it or not—"beinte" not "veinte". It's "baca" not "vaca". This is why kids don't say "very," they say "bery"—bery good.

Let me talk a little about the differences in culture. You've got to know some of these things before you can really reach the child. In some cultures some things are just completely opposite to the dominant Anglo culture. If you learn nothing more in a culture course or whatever it's called, if you learn this one concept—that your culture is *good* for *you,* somebody else's is good for him, and yours isn't any better than his, if you learn that, you've come a long way.

One time, I was at the University of Kansas. A friend of mine from Latin America was walking across campus, and I wanted that character to come over to see me. I didn't like to yell across campus because everyone looks at you thinking, "This guy's kind of nuts." So I gestured him to come and I kept doing this and this guy kept going away from me. I kept thinking, "What's wrong? He's trying to tell me something." Afterwards we found that our gestures were completely opposite. Our gesture for hello and our gesture for good-by were complete opposites. I didn't find this out until we talked.

When you scold a child, some cultures demand that he not look you in the eye. When we correct kids, we think, "You better darn sure look at me when I correct you!" Or else we figure, "This kid is a wise guy."

Mexican custom is to learn in groups. But we can't have *that.* No sir, we've got to have it by rows; you stick to your seat, do your work and keep your mouth shut. But if you work with a group, you're cheating, the kid is cheating. Cultural conflict. They learn better in groups. If we're really concerned, let them learn the best way they can. That is what should be the important thing.

Mexicans share everything. There is no such thing as his toy and her toy. They want to think there is but there isn't. They mix everything together. So if I see a pencil on your desk and I take it and use it, I'm going to bring it back. In the Anglo culture that's stealing.

You need to know about the *machismo* in the Mexican American family. Machismo means the male domination. The woman's voice, they don't pay much attention to it. You get a child in school and you get a woman teacher (which you usually have in the elementary grades) and you've got problems. Especially in sixth, seventh and eighth grade—they're going to eat her up unless she's really strict and knows what she's doing and lets them know who's boss. Usually you get too many conflicts there. You get a male teacher in there and half your battle is won.

A change is needed. Look at the dropout rate and that tells you something. We've got to change. When we talk about bilingual education, don't get shook up if you're an administrator. Why get shook up? Russia has more than 700 bilingual schools. Europe is crying now for multi-lingual schools. We're still back here with this idea of English or else . . . . You don't like it? Shape up or ship out. We've got to quit thinking that way.

We've got to pool our resources, everybody—everybody from Black Panther to Brown Beret to the Establishment to—everybody! If we pool our resources, then we're going to solve the problem. But until we do that, we're going to have one hell of a big problem like we're having right now.

The Teacher and Latin American Culture

DAVID TAVEL

The Brazilian streetcar is a unique institution. Down the streets of Rio de Janeiro it miraculously is making its way, open sides supporting scores of people who, unable to board the vehicle because of the number of riders, find a hold for one foot and one hand and travel suspended over the street in defiance of gravity and passing autos. Indeed, with such daring occupants on both sides from front to rear, the trolley itself is remarkable for not splitting down the middle, dashing its riders to the pavement, and burying them under wood and iron. Such is the streetcar portrayed by artist, travel agent, and tour director. Spotting an approaching streetcar, one group of forewarned tourists grabs for cameras. But this particular vehicle is not bulging at the sides; it has less than a dozen passengers. Quick thinking is called for. The conductor slows the vehicle to a stop, smooths down his wind-blown hair, dons the uniform hat lying by the controls, and with a broad smile pushes his head half through an open window. The passengers rise as one, move to the near side of the trolley and, waving gaily, all lean out over the street. Miraculously the "real" Rio streetcar has appeared. Honks of dissent are heard from autos stopped behind the trolley, but the conductor and his vehicle remain unmoved until the cameras stop clicking.

A friend departs for a journey and I tell him: "Have a good trip and enjoy yourself." I myself have been told by a Mexican counterpart, "Vaya con Dios, y nada pasa." (Go with God, and may nothing happen.) In a Lima specialty store the manager smiles at me, "Please, sir, I must apologize, but it is noon and my family will be waiting for me. I must close. Would you be so kind as to return in three hours? I am sure we can provide what you are looking for at that time." The *maitre d'* in a Quito restaurant apologizes for overcharging me, saying he can do nothing about the bill now, but *when* I come for dinner that evening he will make it up to me. I come, and without a word he takes care of things. And in a hotel in a Mexican state capital the bar is closed. The governor, it seems, was unable to obtain the best suite in the hotel, and by way of retaliation or possibly to uphold his honor he orders the bar shut down.

David Tavel is a Professor of Education at the University of Toledo, Ohio.
Reprinted from *Social Education 34*(6):663–666, 1970, with permission of the National Council for the Social Studies and David Tavel.

These descriptions, while not offered as typical, do reveal, however, values clearly different from those to which we are accustomed. Yet none of these examples was drawn from one of those formulaic, quiet villages with its pajama-clad peons in wide-brimmed straw hats leaning against an adobe wall taking an all-day siesta—villages conjured up by such hackneyed terms as underdeveloped, developing, or emerging area. They were drawn from life in twentieth-century cities with high rise buildings, street after street of business establishments, neon signs, and traffic jams—cities where pajama-clad peons are hard to find, and where the only time you ride a horse-drawn carriage or get to shout "Arre, Burro" is when the family decides to do something out of the ordinary on a free weekend.

This is the Latin America which deserves to be the focus of study in the elementary grades. The exotic, the strange, and the unusual have their place, but giving them primacy will result in a picture of Latin Americans no more real than one of North Americans based on study of reservation-dwelling Indians, the Okies and Pineys, and the Alaskan Eskimo. Furthermore, in a very real sense Latin America is a land of cities—large, medium, small. In contrast to the North American experience, the first Europeans planned and built cities, some on the ruins of the civilizations they destroyed. (This is also literally true of many churches, government buildings, and homes whose Late Gothic or baroque forms can be seen resting on a pre-Columbian foundation.) In Spanish America cities began and remained as centers of political, social, and economic power. Even today homes of the wealthy are found "in town," while the poor live on the hills fringing the city. In general, North American patterns tend to be the reverse.

The geography of Latin America has isolated communities from one another, and contributed to a provincialism which often results in identifying more with one's city than one's nation. The city acts as a magnet on all classes, with the possible exception of the Indian who has voluntarily withdrawn from contact with the European-American. The wealthy landowner works his holdings just enough to permit him to live in the city with its luxuries and conveniences. The poor from the rural areas migrate to the city as the only place where they can better themselves and provide opportunities for their progeny. Finally, the national capitals, most notably Montevideo, contain such a disproportionately large segment of the population, industry, and commerce that they are comparable, not to a Washington, D.C., but to a Washington–Philadelphia–New York–Boston–Los Angeles all rolled into one. The Latin American culture referred to in this article is mainly the culture of the city.

One final qualification is necessary. Just as there are North Americans who do not fit into the "WASP" category, so is there diversity south of the border. Latin America, however, is marked both by greater diversity and a greater mixing of diverse elements. This is truly the "mestizo" continent (the term basically referring to the mixture of white and Indian elements), and throughout Latin America exists diversity of race, of social class, of wealth, and of custom far more pronounced than in the United States. The Carioca in Rio de Janeiro can leisurely sip his coffee in an open coffee shop and watch the pretty girls walk by. The Paulista, his counterpart two hundred miles away in São Paulo, gulps down his coffee standing at a counter and hurries on his way. Lost in Andean valleys of Peru and Colombia may be found completely unassimilated colonies of Europeans. (In the major cities one occasionally meets a European who first emigrated to the United States but who, unhappy in his new surroundings, went on to Latin America where he found a more hospitable environment.) The following discussion should, therefore, not be viewed as descriptive of what will be found in almost every case. It is an attempt to describe, not the unique, but that which is general in the uniqueness found among our southern neighbors.

The Family in Latin American Culture

The youngster born into a Latin American family is entangled in a web of relationships—obligations, responsibilities, and privileges—which has no counterpart in Anglo-Saxon America. It is in stark contrast to the two generation family in the United States with its "mother-in-law" jokes and the home-which-is-where-you-hang-your-hat concept. The impact of industrialization has yet to shatter the traditional family—a family of grandparents, parents, children, close relatives, distant parents, and godparents. This family is not just a network of people related by blood, or even blood and patronage. Each member knows he can call on any other member in time of need, and he knows others will call on him. Obligations are lifelong and they are reciprocal. Nepotism in government and business is a well-known side effect subjected to considerable criticism by outsiders. So numerous may be the demands made by so many family members on a well-established individual that charity both begins and ends at home. To a person outside this family group he feels no obligation. He has little sense of community responsibility. (This is basic to any understanding of the political problems in the young Latin American nations of the immediate post-revolutionary period.)

This extended family does make a significant positive contribution. It is the cement which keeps society from utter fragmentation. Combine the sense of uncertainty in life, a distrust of organization, an intense individualism, and pessimism and fatalism, and the expected result is social chaos and a withdrawal from society such as is occurring today among some younger age groups in the United States. In this country, those who withdraw are in part balanced out by our penchant as joiners. Anglo-Americans are great joiners of clubs, societies and associations of every description. Such organizations are few in South and Central America, and those which do exist tend to have resulted from contacts with North Americans.

What the unions, the lodges, the neighborhood organizations, and even the government provide in the way of social cement in the United States is provided in Latin America by the family. The family provides a feeling of belonging, of not being all alone. It gives a person a place to turn to in time of crisis, something to fall back on when one's own efforts become impotent. In short, the family keeps society together. This, incidentally, happens to be true not only in the twentieth-century city but in the Indian community far removed both in miles and spirit from the Latin culture. By the time today's Latin American elementary school youngster reaches adulthood, he may be inclined to dismiss as old-fashioned the sense of extensive family responsibility. The political parties, the service clubs, and even the labor unions, all mustering support less from the older families than from the new middle class, may in time become successors to the extended family, but at present they appear to lack both the organizational maturity and the magnetism to play that role today.

Latin American Politics

A most fruitful area for contrasts and comparisons is that of politics. Many North American children learn that nearly everyone is either Democrat or Republican, and the difference between the political parties is that one has the good guys, and the other the bad guys. The choices available to the Latin American are greater both in number and variety. The individualistic tradition of Spanish culture makes every man potentially his own political party. Where limited value is placed on cooperation, compromise is often treated as a surrender of one's beliefs and ideals, and organization is not necessarily a good thing, the result can be several political parties competing for Juan Pueblo's vote (assuming, of course, the freedom of parties to organize and campaign). An increased number of parties means an increased likelihood that no one of them will gain a clear majority triumph. Compromise thus becomes necessary if a governing coalition is to be established, but the very factors which accounted for the existence of several parties in the first place now tend to work against effective compromise. Little wonder that so many governments have come to power through sheer force.

In determining his own political orientation, the Latin American tends to rely on personalities or an over-arching principle such as nationalization, land reform, or anti-clericalism. By way of contrast, in the United States where the two major political parties attempt to make a nationwide appeal, platforms, policies, and even personalities tend to be of secondary importance to organizational effectiveness. If the North American becomes politically cynical because his words carry no weight in the vast impersonal political organizations of his country, *his* southern counterpart turns cynic for different reasons. He *knows* the *government* runs the country. Those in government are likely to take care of their own and none outside their own, "their own" referring to the extended family as previously discussed and to the capital city. In the absence of accepted regular procedures for replacing a government, the only way to get rid of one you don't want is to forcibly overthrow it. When seen in this light, the *coups d'état* and bloodless revolutions become an understandable part of Latin American life.

The Arts in Latin American Culture

If the North American is too busy moving up to or ahead of the Joneses to have time for artistic creativity, his Latin counterpart is less swept up by the egalitarian fetish, the need to constantly be proving to others that one is as good as they are, especially in terms of the material aspects of life. The Latin is not too busy to enrich, rather than merely add to his life. This helps explain why Latin American accomplishment in the arts has been disproportionately great. Considering the relatively limited number of Latin Americans whose social, economic, or educational level provides them with opportunity for concerted attention to the arts, the productivity of the nations to the south is all the more noteworthy. In architecture, literature, sculpture, and painting, Latin Americans have received universal recognition. Accomplishments in the other fine arts, most notably music, while not so widely acclaimed, are still considerable.

The Spaniard did not come to America merely to exploit the resources and convert the natives. Were that the case there would be no need for carefully planning and building so many cities—some on the sites of native cities, some on good harbors, and many in mountain valleys reminiscent of the Iberian homeland. Each city began with its central plaza, from which led the major streets. Fronting on the plaza were the government buildings and a cathedral or church.

For the design of his buildings the Spaniard brought ideas from home, but giving these ideas form in the new world meant being influenced by climate, topography, available materials, and the craftsmanship of the native laborers. To the extent that form is influenced by function, sixteenth-century buildings were designed with the view they might be called upon to serve as defensive bastions. Thus medieval Gothic forms, characterized by sheer size, pointed arches, and ribbed vaulting, were popular, most notably in cathedrals and churches, even though Renaissance classical architecture was taking hold in Spain at that time.

The classical influence held sway briefly in the Americas in the late sixteenth century, gave form to the Cathedral of Mexico City and those of Mérida and Oaxaca in the same country, and then was succeeded by the more ornate baroque styles so appropriate as a vehicle of expression in the hands of skilled craftsmen desirous of giving each work an individual touch. From the cathedral at Zacatecas, Mexico, moving southward, each colonial area contributed its own unique refinements. Thus we find thicker walls in areas subject to frequent earthquakes, regional flora and fauna serving as ornamental patterns in the tropics, and even a Moorish emphasis where the Spaniard was most secure and comfortable as in the city of Lima in Peru.

When the Spanish colonies gained their independence there was an even greater cultural break than occurred in North America. France succeeded Spain as the source of cultural inspiration, and neoclassical models from Europe were combined with the indigenous American craftsmanship. The result was an architecture evident today throughout almost all of Latin America, with its finest representatives in Mexico and Brazil. The capitals of Argentina and Chile (not to mention that of the United States) clearly reveal the neoclassical influence. The Argentine Congress and the United States Congress meet in buildings the uninitiated could easily mistake for one another.

It is in the twentieth century, as the idea of being a nation has taken hold, as governments have increasingly played a role in the cultural life, and as economic and social changes are tending to widen effective social participation, that Latin America has achieved its position of prominence in the arts. The Mexican revolution brought to the fore the architects, muralists, sculptors, and painters to whom belongs the credit for the magnificence of the National University and the Olympic Stadium, but active government support since the 1920s made such developments possible. The genius of Oscar Niemeyer and Lúcio Costa has made its greatest impact with the construction from scratch of an entirely new capital city in Brazil. It is to the credit of Niemeyer, chief architect of Brasília, that if any nation of the world has in our day developed a national architectural style, that nation is Brazil.

Although perhaps somewhat more difficult to incorporate into classroom study, Latin American literature is a most fruitful source of understanding of our southern neighbors. Themes which have indelibly influenced the history and culture of these nations are revealed in the prose and poetry. One such theme is the impact of the natural environment. Man does not exploit nature in Latin America, he battles it. This battle is vividly portrayed by Rómulo Gallegos in *Doña Barbara,* and by José Rivera in *The Vortex.*

A second theme well expressed in the literature is that of violence, and the sadness which accompanies it. Nature is not the only source of cataclysm. It was men from Europe who destroyed aspects of the pre-Columbian civilizations; it was the United States which severed half of Mexico.

"Go with God, and may nothing happen." This theme pervades *El Señor Presidente,* an attack on dictatorships by the Guatemalan Miguel Asturias; Euclides da Cunha's *Rebellion in the Backlands,* set in rural northeastern Brazil; and José Hernández's epic poem of the Argentine gaucho, *Martín Fierro,* available not only in several translations, but also in prose. (All the works mentioned are available in translation.)

Music, drama, and religion have thus far been ignored. In appropriate circumstances they do have instructional value, but it is questionable whether they would be as useful as the areas discussed. Music is readily available in recorded form, and Latin Americans in the field are widely recognized—composers Carlos Gómez, Heïtor Villa-Lobos, Carlos Chávez, and Ernesto Lecuona; artists Claudio Arrau, Guiomar Novaes, Jesús María Sanromá, and Bidu Sayão.

This article has merely hinted at a few of the cultural differences between Anglo and Latin America. Examination of Latin American culture can provide our children with an opportunity to see vivid contrasts in values and life styles. These contrasts can lead to comparisons with North American culture, which in turn can promote a greater awareness and a critical view of our own culture. Why study Latin America? To learn that ours is not the only set of answers provided to the problems European man found in this new world. With this increased awareness we may then be more willing and able to examine our own answers, and the beliefs and values lying behind them.

A Classroom Resource Library on Latin America for $25.00

Alexander, R. J., *Today's Latin America,* 2nd ed., Doubleday, Anchor Books, $1.45.

Castedo, L., *A History of Latin American Art and Architecture.* Praeger, $4.95.

Freyre, G., *New World in the Tropics: The Culture of Modern Brazil.* Vintage Books, $1.95.

Gibson, C., ed., *The Spanish Tradition in America.* Harper Torchbooks, $2.45.

Hanke, L., ed., *Do the Americas Have a Common History?* Knopf, Borzoi Books, $2.75.

Nava, Julian, *Mexican Americans: A Brief Look at Their History.* Anti-Defamation League of B'nai B'rith, $.75.

Pendle, G., *A History of Latin America.* Penguin Books, $1.25.

Ramos, S., *Profile of Man and Culture in Mexico.* McGraw-Hill paperback, $2.45.

Tannebaum, F., *Ten Keys to Latin America.* Vintage Books, $1.65.

and a subscription to *Américas.* Pan American Union, $5.00/year.

Teaching About Jewish History

GLADYS ROSEN

The melting pot is the image that has always been at the heart of any American credo. As a theory of history, however, it has often obscured more than it has revealed, for ignoring the uniqueness of ethnic and racial minorities in our country not only distorts history but also contributes to the kinds of prejudices which are abhorrent to American ideals.

Strong feelings of ethnic awareness and identity have emerged in America today in the wake of the black civil rights movement. To direct this ethnic awareness toward mutual understanding rather than divisiveness and hatred, citizens need deeper understanding of cultural pluralism. In this connection, the teaching of social studies is crucial, since its purpose is "to give a measure of knowledge for understanding contemporary society."

Unfortunately, research reveals that many instructional materials now in use fail to give every thread in the "seamless web of history" its just consideration. The lack of concern with Jewish history is distressing. But for the use of the unexplained and unilluminating phrase, *Judeo-Christian,* most textbooks regard the Jew as an archaeological relic whose day ended with the advent of Christianity.

Jews do not fit neatly into any conventional definitions of nation, culture, ethnic group, religion, or civilization, for their historical development includes aspects of all of these. The nature of the Jewish experience has always been that of a continuing dialectic between a people and its tradition on the one hand and tradition and a foreign-host culture on the other. This dual process enabled Jews to enrich their internal culture and institutional life by selective assimilation even under difficult conditions of persecution and economic hardship. At the same time, they made vital contributions to the cultures that surrounded them.

From the period of early exile in Babylonia, the Jews participated (when permitted) in all branches of cultural and economic life in most countries where they settled. During the early medieval period, they achieved a practical monopoly in the important areas of financial management and international trade. In Spain in this same period, their translations of the

Gladys Rosen is a program specialist in the Jewish Communal Affairs Department for the American Jewish Committee, New York City 10022.

Reprinted from *Today's Education* 61(4):47, 1972, with permission of the National Education Association and Gladys Rosen.

classics into Arabic and Hebrew helped to keep alive culture and the Greek and Roman tradition.

Yet, despite the unique nature of the Jewish contribution, most world histories show ignorance of or little interest in Jewish history. Also, most American history textbooks currently in use are notably *judenrein*—except for a brief mention of the contributions of individual Jews like Haym Salomon, the revolutionary patriot, and Louis D. Brandeis, the Supreme Court justice.

In order for the student in the United States to understand American Jewry as an integral element in American society, he must acquire some awareness of how and why Jews came to America; the various immigrant settlements; and Jewish beliefs, institutions, and cultural and economic contributions to American society. Material about the Jewish role in American history can be included in social studies units on colonial and local history, immigration, minority-group relations, economic history, and so on. Emphasis should be on the Jewish group role rather than on outstanding individuals who, of course, can be included whenever their particular contributions are germane to the subject.

This kind of treatment presupposes the improvement and revision of textbooks and the availability of supplementary materials that will effectively illuminate the unique development of the Jewish community within America. In-service training of teachers will help to ensure the successful use of such materials, which should be integrated into social studies courses for all students.

A proper understanding of the Judaic role is an essential part of a well-rounded liberal arts education and a sine qua non in helping the non-Jewish student to understand his Jewish neighbors.

The Jews can serve as a paradigm of survival for our age. Their sense of tradition and the meaning of their history are especially timely today. As John Dos Passos wrote: "In times of change and danger, when there is a quicksand of fear under men's reasoning, a sense of continuity with generations gone before can stretch like a lifeline across the scary present."

The Cultural Dilemma of American Indians

LORRAINE MISIASZEK

American Indian culture is unique in this nation today because it has endured almost five hundred years of exposure to the predominant Euro-American culture, with all the accompanying social and economic pressures to change and to conform to middle class white American culture. The worth of any culture lies in the values of that culture, so it might be enlightening to examine the values of Indian culture to learn why, after so many years, Indian people are still influenced in varying degrees by their cultures and why they have not assimilated into the "mainstream of American life" as quickly as ethnic groups have who immigrated to the United States.

Indian Standards and Values

The economy of any social group determines the kinds of rules that must be maintained if that group is to survive. American Indian tribes, particularly in the Northwest, depended for their existence on their ability to hunt, fish, gather roots and plants, and to trade for items unavailable to them in this region. They relied on nature to make food available and depended on themselves to acquire food and clothing.

Because nature cannot be regulated, Indian tribes formed a cooperative way of life to function in harmony with nature. Traditions were followed religiously, and tribal values were taught the children by the elders of the tribe—the grandparents—who passed their wisdom and knowledge to the new generation often through legends and songs. To be old was synonymous with being wise.

Although individual autonomy was accorded high priority, the greatest values were placed on generosity—sharing and giving to others of the tribe. Bravery, courage, physical stamina, and endurance were greatly admired characteristics essential in this region where one had to cope with the elements of extreme cold and rugged terrain to exist.

Lorraine Misiaszek was formerly a Consultant for Intergroup Education at the State Office of Public Instruction, Olympia, Washington.

Reprinted from *Social Education* 33(4):438–439 ff., 1969, with permission of the National Council for the Social Studies and Lorraine Misiaszek.

The tribe to which one belonged was considered in terms of an "extended family." Cousins, however distant, are still often referred to as one's brothers or sisters because many of the Indian languages have no words or expressions to make the distinction between cousins and brothers or sisters.

Strong family ties were maintained in the tribes and were reinforced through the values placed on sharing, individual autonomy, and the practice of utilizing the talents of all age groups for the continuance of the tribe. A strong sense of humor prevails amongst Indian people today, for they were once a very happy people living in harmony with themselves and the universe.

Just as the positive virtues were rewarded by admiration, the negative ones were punished through ridicule. More stern measures were applied— even death—if the offense was great. The traits that were discouraged included boasting of one's accomplishments, loud behavior, being stingy, and lying. A person's word was as good as that person.

The Indian in Today's Society

Today's society in which American Indians find themselves is based on an economy that calls for highly competitive ability with the ultimate goal understood to be financial success and upward social mobility. It follows that an entirely new set of standards and values is imposed on Indian people today, and there is some doubt in their minds if they want to accept these new standards, especially because it means that they must repudiate all the deeply ingrained values of their culture if they are to conform to the new. It is safe to state that many are going through the motions outwardly, but they have not really accepted these modern values. Quite a number of Indian people have developed a deep hostility toward society as a whole.

There is little doubt that a serious conflict exists for the Indian; a conflict manifested by a growing alcoholism problem and an increasing number of broken homes, both major elements that contribute to the poverty cycle. It appears that there is no easy or immediate solution in sight for this troubled people.

Because the values of a given culture are often unconsciously accepted and applied, today's Indian is not aware of what is taking place in his own situation or what is causing the conflict within himself. At no time in his educational experience has he been taught anything about his past rich culture. He is unaware of how deeply he is influenced by his cultural values that conflict with the work day world concept of an 8 A.M. to 5 P.M. schedule that he must function in daily. Traditionally, he followed the "present" oriented way of his tribe, and today the Indian does not concern himself too seriously with tomorrow, next week, or next year. Furthermore, he does not see anything wrong in sharing whatever he has with others of his "extended family" if he has more than they have. He can see little merit in boasting about his abilities or talents in order to impress a prospective employer. Because Indian people do not easily adopt a competitive spirit in the employment area, they have been labeled lazy.

On the other hand, the individual Indian who has established himself economically through his own efforts finds that he must repudiate the tribal value of sharing with others. Because he is seen by his friends and relatives as not being generous and even as stingy, he is alienated from them. As a consequence, this person tends to reject his race and his ethnic identity entirely. I cite this as an example of the common pressures confronting the American Indian in his daily life as he attempts to earn a livelihood and provide for his basic needs.

Helping the Indian Child to Adjust

The American Indian can be assisted in making an adjustment to today's society through education. A good adjustment can be made if the changes are implemented on the basis of what the child believes and follows of tribal values. Therefore, emphasis ought to be placed on the kind of pre-school educational experiences offered the Indian child. Because the early part of his development takes place in the home, he is apt to absorb his basic cultural values long before he enters the classroom. The difficult task facing the teacher will be to build on the foundation already established. If that foundation is destroyed in the process of introducing the new values, the Indian child will experience great difficulty in making a good adjustment and is likely to fail scholastically. Ultimately, he will drop out of school. This has already happened far too often as evidenced by the high drop-out rate in the public schools amongst Indian children throughout the nation. Reports show an average 50 percent drop-out rate. Some schools have an 80 percent rate, and a few reflect a 100 percent drop-out ratio for Indian children.

It is obvious that the Indian child will be confronted with a cultural conflict when he begins to associate with his peer group and the teacher in the classroom. It is at this point in the child's life experience that the teacher can make the most progress in introducing new concepts. It would be valuable if the teacher knew what kind of a home environment the child came from. In view of the cultural conflict experienced by most adult Indians, one or both of the child's parents may suffer from an alcoholic problem, and the family income may be unsteady and frequently is non-existent.

Often a grandparent, an aunt, or another relative is raising the child. The child is usually treated permissively and is loved by his parents and relatives.

The trait of respecting an individual's autonomy is applied to the child at an early age, so he does very much as he pleases with little regulation of his activities. In reference to my own childhood, punishment or displeasure was expressed by my parents in a frown and a scolding for unacceptable behavior, but never was I given a sound spanking, which I would have preferred to a scolding. Physical punishment for Indian children was not a part of their cultural pattern.

People in the role of authority such as law enforcement officers, doctors, or nurses usually appear to the child in an unpleasant or unfavorable light because of an experience with some member of the family. Instead of considering these people as friends, he sees them as an enemy who should be avoided whenever possible. The teacher may easily be placed in this category if the child's first contact with the teacher appears to him as a negative experience. Although the teacher may act in an impersonal manner, the child may define this as unfriendly and not respond readily to friendly gestures at a later time.

Most Indian children are taught to be seen but not heard when adults are present. This training is likely to affect the child's behavior in the classroom, and if this happens, he will not respond easily unless he is specifically asked to answer a question or give his opinion. Many teachers regard such behavior as sullen, but more often than not, the child is really quite shy and exhibiting the cultural trait he has learned at home.

Experienced teachers of Indian children relate that it is not uncommon to ask a pupil a question in class, and if he doesn't know the answer, the other Indian children will declare that they do not know it either, even though they might. This reaction relates to the non-competitive aspect of Indian culture and concern for the individual by not causing him to lose self-esteem. However, this is not the only behavior pattern that Indian children demonstrate today. There are some who exhibit and express hostility by being a show-off, using shocking language, or being a bully. In these ways they are attempting to compensate for feelings of inferiority and frustration in an unstable, changing environment. The child's shyness or hostility can be overcome easily by praise and admiration for something he has done.

Indian children do respond well to programs emphasizing art, music, nature studies, and athletic activities. Traditionally, there is not a great deal of verbalizing in the Indian home and, as a result, the child will develop his ability to perceive meanings that underlie facial expressions, gestures, or tone of voice. Programs that relate to perceptive ability often prompt successful achievement more rapidly than do the academically oriented subjects. The Indian pupil will profit from special language and reading helps to assist him in developing verbal expression.

If an understanding teacher-pupil relationship can be established successfully early in the school experience of the Indian child, the chances are immeasurably improved that this child will achieve scholastic success at a level comparable to non-Indian children.

As the teacher strives to gain a better understanding of the response behavior of the culturally different, his efforts will be facilitated by first examining his own responses and attitudes. He must question the basis of his expectations relative to pupil achievement and evaluate his classroom practices in an objective way. By recognizing the degree to which his own culture has conditioned him, the non-Indian teacher can begin to understand the problem in clearer perspective. He is better prepared to commence building on the cultural foundation that has shaped this child prior to enrollment in school.

I have endeavored to present, from the American Indian's point of view, the stronger values of a native minority culture as they are manifested in the behavior and feelings of Indian children, while these children attempt to find a place in the system developed by a dominant non-Indian middle-class society. These enduring cultural values have offered many strengths to the individual while at the same time have caused a conflict that frequently leads to self-destructive behavior. Such behavior lends credence to the negative stereotyped image of the contemporary American Indian as he is viewed by his fellow Americans, and so the cycle continues. I trust that one day soon American society will see that its strength lies in the differences of its multi-racial membership and that respect for individual differences will become the rule rather than the exception.

Creating Group Cohesion in Inner City Classrooms

FRANK P. BAZELI

New teachers in inner city schools badly need, but seldom receive, any practical guide to surviving in the classroom. The culture shock which most suffer upon their first encounter with what seems like uncontrollable gangs of pupils, totally disinterested in education, but gleefully intent on the harassment of teachers, effectively prevents the creation of viable learning environments and secure teacher-pupil relationships. Unfortunately, love and a well-planned lesson do not insure success. To become a skillful inner

Frank P. Bazeli is an Associate Professor in the Department of Secondary Professional Education at Northern Illinois University, DeKalb.

Reprinted from *The Clearing House* 45:547:550, 1971, with permission of *The Clearing House* and Frank P. Bazeli.

city teacher requires a bitter apprenticeship. It need not be so long nor so painful, however, with some forethought and preparation.

While little will be said here about curriculum, it must be understood that nothing will work for long if what is taught is not plainly useful and relevant. Teachers must look at their subject matter and materials with a ruthless eye. Anything inappropriate or without obvious value must be excised. Disadvantaged children need too many things for teachers to mourn the passing of beloved anachronisms.

Authority

Children are socialized by their sub-culture through complex patterns of coercion. While there is extensive overlap, three basic models might be identified. One pattern utilizes the love-withdrawal technique, in which the child is channelled into appropriate behavior through the threat of withheld love and acceptance by persons who are important to his comfort and happiness. A second model is based on the status of the socializer; the child must conform to the demands of someone who occupies a position of power, and who will exercise that power punitively when necessary. A third technique rests on the consequences of behavior; the child may make choices but must live with the consequences.

Most disadvantaged families tend to use the status technique (1). Physical strength, cunning, and daring are prized; ganging for protection and exploration is appropriate behavior, and challenge to authority if successful brings status. This creates a series of problems for teachers in inner city schools, since most are alien to its methodology and repelled by its values. However, like it or not, the teacher must become skilled in status control. But control through a dominance-submissive pattern is brittle and needs to be systematically reoriented toward group self-discipline and cooperative learning in order to avoid a possible breakdown requiring drastic remedy, such as removal of the teacher or disbandment of the group.

Preconditions

While many kinds of teachers are successful in inner city schools, one determinant seems to be the degree to which the teacher becomes involved with the children. Alert teachers concentrate on learning to recognize each of their pupils as quickly as possible. Ordinarily, this is done by close observation, asking questions, and generally talking to each child at every opportunity, especially outside of class. This entails learning their speech patterns.

These language patterns, while colorful, are restricted. Disadvantaged children seldom are precise in communication; they depend on body English, facial expressions, intonations, and context to convey meaning, and use colloquialisms new to the teacher (2). A study of the dialect of the sub-culture avoids many discipline problems arising from mistakes in perception and communication.

In addition to speech, special attention must be paid to the life style of the students. When disadvantaged children exhibit physical aggression, choose practical skills over abstract learnings, demand immediate rewards, and show direct and even primitive interest in such things as sex and material possessions, they are acting out the methods found best by their sub-culture for the satisfaction of needs and goals (3). The most successful teachers are aware of these conditions and move easily from one value structure into another without prejudice. They learn that their job is not to propagandize middle-class values but to provide children with the means to success in any society (4).

Before turning to relationships with pupils, however, consideration must be given to classroom organization. While avoiding regimentation, class management should be systemized to the point where it operates with minimum effort and maximum efficiency. Everything from books to erasers ought to have a special place and a well thought out plan of distribution and collection. These preparations have nothing to do with the personality or teaching style of the instructor. No class will even begin to function if the learning environment is disorganized.

New teachers are always amazed to find that everything worn, said, or done is under intense observation by the class. In a short time the children will be able to point out with accuracy the teacher's strengths, weaknesses, and eccentricities. The only recourse is to abandon pretence and be as natural and relaxed as possible.

Classroom Control

The first few moments of each period are by far the most dangerous to order. Children entering the room bring an accumulation of tensions and experiences built up over the course of the day. The best place to begin the control procedure is at the door. A set routine of entry, seating, and commencement of work establishes the structure disadvantaged children often need for security. Any evidence of tension, hostility, or over-excitement must be observed and quickly attended to. Since an unstable group is easily lost, it is much better early in the year to spend the bulk of class time on activities which limit free movement. After control procedures are functioning good pedagogy requires opportunities for free movement and team learning.

Directions are best given one at a time in an unhurried clear voice; each step should be completed before the next one is presented. Continuous but relaxed movement affords excellent opportunities for observing the children from different angles and brings many undercurrent activities to the teacher's attention. Practice in identification of room sounds tunes the teacher into the real world of his pupils; one often far more important than the official learning activity for the day.

When undercurrent activities are discovered, they need not to be made into an issue. A relaxed, secure room atmosphere is not created by prison-like regimentation, but the teacher should often let the pupils know he is aware of potential disruption preferably through the use of some mysterious, psychic power or third eye. That is when control becomes non-threatening, amusing, but still effective.

Confrontations sometimes will occur. They are emotionally explosive situations requiring the will to act in the face of challenge. When the need arises for enforcement of rules, however, the teacher must act with good nature and concern for the dignity of the pupil. The infraction should be made quite clear in terms of its hindrance to class objectives, and the process of retribution should be ritualized with all parties performing their required duties with no personal animosity involved.

Promoting Group Cohesion

Maintaining status control is necessary, but it is only a preliminary to group self-discipline. In order to achieve this the teacher must devise experiences which create group cohesiveness and mutual support.

Establishing a good learning environment generally progresses through three overlapping stages of development. In the first stage each class member becomes identified by the others as a unique and worthy individual; in the second stage the group identification is developed and a sense of belonging is encouraged; finally, the third stage sees the creation of a strong commitment to group goals, a secure learning environment, and group self-discipline.

The first part of any new year should be devoted not to course content but to the pupils and their group climate. Not only is the teacher responsible for an intensive study of each child, but every class member should become acquainted with his mates. Through game activities and associative learning techniques, names, addresses, interests, and other pertinent information which establishes a unique image for each child should be required learning for everyone. Having a map of the school community with flags locating the homes of each child, posting individual and group photographs, and developing an organizational chart on which each pupil is given responsibilities for the smooth operation of the class, are examples of techniques which can be used to identify the children with the group.

A sense of territory is highly important in the organization of groups. All organizations, from nations through street gangs, to clubs and homerooms are strengthened by having a headquarters and a differentiated territory (5). The classroom, then, must be personalized to create such an effect. The importance of pupil work, decorations, and exclusive use of storage and work spaces must be recognized and attended to.

Team spirit and cooperative learning are brought about by incorporating supportive learning and total group activities. After the teacher has established good status control, pupils should be given increasing time each day to learning in pairs, then in threes, and later in larger learning teams. Individual competition might be largely replaced by team competition, and every opportunity utilized to take the class into competition against other groups in sports, contests, and other activities. With careful, total group planning, the class should be able to find some degree of success in this competition, which will transfer into a sense of loyalty and cooperation in the classroom.

When a student group possesses cohesion, a protective association is established which provides security for everyone—including the teacher. Under these conditions learning can take place and discipline problems are minimal.

References

1. Hess, Robert D. and Virginia Shipman, "Early Blocks to Children's Learning," in Staten B. Webster, ed., *The Disadvantaged Learner: Knowing, Understanding, Learning* (San Francisco: Chandler, 1968), pp. 276–285.
2. Bernstein, Basil, "Social Class and Linguistic Development: A Theory of Social Learning," in A. N. Halsey, J. Floud, and C. A. Anderson, eds., *Education, Economy and Society* (New York: The Free Press, 1961).
3. Epstein, Charlotte, *Intergroup Relations for the Classroom Teacher* (Boston: Houghton Mifflin, 1968), pp. 83–90.
4. Goldberg, Miriam, "Adapting Teacher Style to Pupil Differences: Teachers for Disadvantaged Children," in Joe L. Frost, and Glenn R. Hawkes, eds., *The Disadvantaged Child: Issues and Innovations* (New York: Houghton Mifflin, 1966), pp. 345–362.
5. Berne, Eric, *The Structure and Dynamics of Organizations and Groups* (New York: J. B. Lippincott, 1963), pp. 56–60.

The Self-fulfilling Prophecy and the Teacher

Can a belief, no matter how false or unreal, become true, or fulfilled, as people begin to act as if they believed it? Can one's expectations of his fellow man, either positive or negative, fulfill themselves as one acts in accordance with his expectations? Yes, say the proponents of the self-fulfilling prophecy, and a great amount of recent research supports their position.

According to Robert K. Merton,[1] the self-fulfilling prophecy begins as a false definition of the situation and proceeds toward self-fulfillment as more and more individuals come to believe the false definition of the situation and act accordingly. The result is that the initial false definition becomes true as self-fulfillment occurs. As an illustration of the self-fulfilling prophecy, Merton presents the example of a good, sound bank becoming insolvent because of a "run" on it. (Of course, the temporal setting for the illustration is prior to the establishment of the Federal Deposit Insurance Corporation.)

At the outset the bank was sound, but as more and more people began to believe the rumor of the bank's shaky financial condition, and, *to act* upon their belief by withdrawing their deposits, the true condition of the bank began to deteriorate. The original false definition of the situation in the rumor became the true condition of the bank.

The phenomenon of the self-fulfilling prophecy is frequently seen in the school. Here it is usually related to the expectations teachers hold for students and colleagues. A language arts teacher may lament, "I don't know what I'm going to do with that class. Not one student in the entire class can write a complete, grammatically correct sentence. They cannot learn."

Another teacher may say of the same students, "What a challenge this class presents! Not one of them can write a correct sentence. I hope I can help them before the end of the term."

Both teachers are making self-fulfilling prophecies. The former is predicting failure and non-achievement; the latter is looking toward some degree of success in teaching the students to write correctly. At the outset,

Roy Sanders is an Assistant Professor of Education at the Northwest Missouri State College, Maryville.

Reprinted from *School and Community* 57(5):10–11, 1971, with permission of *School and Community* and Roy Sanders.

[1] Merton, Robert K., *Social Theory and Social Structure,* (New York: The Free Press) 1957, p. 423.

both teachers' predictions are false definitions of the situation, but either can become "true" as the teacher's expectations for the class unfold. The teacher who predicts non-achievement will fulfill his prophecy, because his teaching will be geared toward containment of the class rather than toward achievement. But the teacher who expects some degree of success for his students will convey the impression to them that he believes they can learn, and this expectation alone will tend toward its realization.

The story is told of the new third grade teacher who was warned by the second grade teacher to keep a wary eye on Albert Erickson because he had caused trouble by his deviancy all year long. The third grade teacher took great precautions with young Erickson: she seated him in the front of the room; she kept a close eye on him; she darted accusing glances at him when the least unnecessary noise or commotion arose. At first, the teacher thought she detected hurt looks on the lad's face when she looked reprovingly at him, but she told herself that he was only pretending to look hurt as a cover-up for further deviancy. And the thought that the boy was feigning innocence made her redouble her efforts to keep him in line. Later in the school term, she and· the second grade teacher were discussing behavioral problems they had encountered.

"The Erickson boy turned out just as you told me he would," said the third grade teacher; "although at first he pretended to be ever so innocent."

"The Erickson boy?" querried the second grade teacher. "Oh, I thought you knew. Albert's family moved away just before the term began. You must be thinking of his cousin, Alfred Erickson . . . But I have never heard of his causing any trouble."

The expectation that young Erickson would cause trouble was a false definition of the situation, but as the teacher continued to act as though she believed the false definition, the prophecy fulfilled itself, and the deviancy became real.

The self-fulfilling prophecy can occur without being verbalized. A smile can say more clearly than words something about the teacher's expectations of the students. So can a frown. An example of the non-verbal self-fulfilling prophecy is that of the insecure teacher who fears that he will lose control of the classroom. He keeps a watchful eye upon his students. His glances dart all about the room. He forms the habit of suddenly directing his attention toward certain areas of the classroom, thinking perhaps he will observe some incipient deviancy. Without realizing it, he is allowing his actions to speak quite clearly to his students: "I'm expecting to find some deviancy among you. I *know* you are doing things when my back is turned. I'll keep trying until I catch you."

This teacher's prophecy will begin to fulfill itself along at least two lines. Some of the students will resent the implication that they are not trusted. They will tend to rationalize that if they are being accused of misbehavior, they had just as well misbehave. Other students will see the situation as a game, the object of which is to commit deviancy without being caught. The prophecy has now been fulfilled, and the teacher becomes convinced that these students were guilty from the beginning of all the deviancy they manifested toward the end.

The teacher with a positive expectation of student response will do things which will promote the fulfillment of the expectation. He will, for example, reinforce desired student behavior with a verbal "pat on the back" or some other symbol of approval and appreciation. The student's achievement may have been slight, but the teacher's verbal reinforcement encourages him to attempt greater things. The teacher's tone and enthusiasm as he says, "Fine," "Good," "That is good writing, Bill; keep it up," or "I'm proud of you, Jane, for the way you kept your temper," does much more for the student than give temporary feelings of satisfaction. It says something more nearly like this: "I believe in you," "You can be successful," and "I trust you."

The teacher's positive expectations help students gain a more positive self-image. Each student sees himself no longer as a failure to be criticized but rather as one worthy of trust and capable of succeeding. And such a positive self-image for the student contributes a great deal to the fulfilling of the teacher's positive expectation.

Rosenthal and Jacobson [2] found that teachers' expectations of children's high potential for achievement have a definite effect upon the performance of the children. The SRA Test of General Ability (TOGA) was administered to the students of Spruce elementary school in San Francisco. Later, and ostensibly as a result of the test, twenty percent of each class was identified to each teacher as showing great academic promise, even though the pupils had actually been selected at random. Toward the end of the school term all children in the school were retested. Over the entire school the children who had been designated as intellectual "spurters" showed a gain in I.Q. score of 12.2, while the control children gained only 8.4 points. Significantly, the greatest gains were found in the first three grades, perhaps *before* both teachers and pupils had convinced themselves that no more than average achievement was expected of average pupils. The second grade showed the most spectacular gain, with experimental children gaining 18.2 I.Q. points compared with a gain of only 4.3 points for the control children.

Palardy [3] reports an interesting study of elementary teachers' beliefs concerning the relationship of sex of the child and success in learning to read. Teachers in this study were divided into two categories according to their responses to a questionnaire: those who believed boys were less successful than girls in learning to read and those who believed boys were equally

---

[2] Rosenthal, Robert and Jacobson, Lenore, *Pygmalion in the Classroom: Teacher Expectation and Pupils' Intellectual Development.* (New York: Holt, Rinehart, and Winston) 1968.

[3] Palardy, J. Michael, "What Teachers Believe—What Children Achieve," *The Elementary School Journal,* Vol. 69, April, 1969, pp. 370–4.

as successful as girls. Later, the success of children in learning to read was analyzed, and Palardy's conclusion was that:

"The findings can also be stated in terms of the self-fulfilling prophecy: when teachers in this study reported that they believed that boys are far less successful than girls in learning to read (when they defined a situation as real), the boys in their classes were far less successful than the girls (the situation was real in its consequence). Conversely, when teachers reported that they believed that boys are as successful as girls, the boys in their classes were as successful as girls." [4]

Perhaps it is time for us to examine some of the bases for our long-held beliefs and expectations concerning our fellow man, and especially our students. We must stop being unwitting accessories to nonachievement, diminished self-concept, and alienation among our students because of our low expectations and negative beliefs. It is time for us to put negativism aside and to capitalize upon the positive aspects of the self-fulfilling prophecy.

[4] *Ibid.:* p. 374.

Section SEVEN

Social Studies and the Contemporary Challenges

There is much to be said for social studies programs that focus on those pervasive social issues that seem to endure generations on end and which man has never satisfactorily resolved, among them being war and peace, poverty, famine, equality, social justice, disease, and racism. Part of the value of the study of history is to provide perspective to these enduring problems of mankind. To some extent these problems and issues are re-interpreted and dealt with in the context of the present by each generation. Likewise, each period offers some challenges that are unique and are of especial relevance to the particular time. These, too, are essential components of social studies programs.

To be effective social studies education must be attuned to these realities of present-day life. The United States today is a nation quite obviously facing different problems from those that confronted it in the days of Washington, Lincoln, Wilson, or even Franklin Roosevelt. For nearly 150 years this nation could correctly be described as rural and agricultural, although there were several large cities during that early period. But the basic style of life—whether one was a city dweller or lived in the country—was rural in outlook. Today the prevailing style of life—again, whether one lives in the city or in the country—is urban. This is reflected in food preferences, travel, entertainment, mode of dress, television programs, advertising, and, indeed, in practically all facets of modern life. A very high percentage of our people today are city dwellers, and even those who are not come under the influence of urban life.

Similarly, in international affairs the position of the United States has changed from what it was in earlier times. Today the United States is a powerful and influential nation in world affairs. The decisions it makes relative to international issues directly affect the lives of the people of many nations. With power and influence, of course, come increased responsibility, greater international visibility, and criticism. To a great extent, what the United States chooses to do or not to do in international affairs is governed by world opinion.

In this final section the authors discuss a few of the contemporary challenges facing elementary schoolteachers in the context of the social studies.

The Environment and the Teacher

PAULINE GRATZ

The health and welfare of man, both as an individual and as a society, are rooted, not only in air, water, food, etc., but in a complex system composed of all facets of the environment including man himself, interacting with and on each other. No study of man's physical environment makes sense if it focuses on one without the others. It is impossible to understand and deal with air pollution, for example, without considering its relationship to waste disposal, electric power generation, public transportation, human and animal health, or the chemistry of agriculture, to name just a few parts of an intricate interrelationship. Whether it is called an ecological community or an ecosystem, this interrelated complex governs the life of man and his biological and physical associations.

Hippocrates wrote of the uniformity of man's environment twenty-five hundred years ago in a book called *Airs, Waters and Places*. Ancient Romans complained of the sooty smoke that covered their city. Pliny, in the first century, described the loss of crops from climate changes due to the draining of lakes and the alteration of rivers' courses. In that past, however, man could leave his own waste behind and move on to some part of the planet still unspoiled. Today there is no escape. For the first time in history, man's future is in serious question. This fact is hard to believe, or even think about, yet it is the message which a growing number of scientists are trying almost frantically to get across to us. It is this fact which has implications for educating our young people toward the realization of the need for maintaining a viable environment.

Environmental Pollution

The level of oxygen in the atmosphere today is slightly over 20%. This is similar to the atmosphere 400 million years ago. This is probably due to the efficiency of the combined efforts of green plants and organisms, including animals, which use oxygen. The green plants provide the oxygen to the atmosphere at approximately the same rate as organisms use the oxygen

Pauline Gratz is a Professor of Human Ecology at Duke University, Durham, North Carolina.

Reprinted from *Social Education* 35(1):58–62 ff., 1971, with permission of the National Council for the Social Studies and Pauline Gratz.

available in the atmosphere. This fortunate state of circumstances is primarily due to the presence of marine microorganisms suspended near the surface of the ocean's water. It has been estimated that these organisms produce 70% or more of the world's oxygen. Thus, even though there is an interruption of the oxygen-carbon dioxide cycle, known as photosynthesis, during darkness and partially during winter seasons, man has been fortunate that the circulation patterns in the atmosphere move the air about the earth in such a way that he has not yet had to be concerned that he would run out of oxygen to breathe. Some scientists believe, however, there is a possibility that today we are pushing our luck.

In photosynthesis, plants such as the marine microorganisms use carbon dioxide to build their organic compounds. Animals in turn combine the organic compounds with oxygen to obtain energy for their activities. The carbon dioxide-oxygen relationship essential to photosynthesis is thus essential to the maintenance of all life; and should the relationship be altered, that is, should the balance between the plants and animals be upset, life as it is known today would be impossible.

Just as oxygen is primarily produced by marine microorganisms in the sea, the carbon dioxide in the atmosphere is created in large measure by the process of combustion. The carbon dioxide in the atmosphere before man's appearance on earth was probably due to the spontaneous combustion that occurred in the forests covering the earth. Later Primitive man burned forests for warmth and protection. As time progressed, man went on to find other uses for combustion and to find new combustible materials such as coal, oil and natural gas which provided him with heat and power.

It was the exploration of these fossil fuels which made it possible for more people to exist on earth than had ever been possible before. It brought with it, however, our serious problem of environmental pollution.

The oceans take carbon dioxide from the atmosphere producing limestone. There is danger, however, in that the amount of carbon dioxide now being added to the atmosphere is far too rapid for the oceans to completely absorb. Just consider the huge consumers of fossil fuels, the industrial facilities, automobiles, jet airplanes and private homes. In addition, the increase in the use of automobiles and jet airplanes has added to the problem. A ton of petroleum hydrocarbon when burned produces about one and one-third tons of water and about twice this amount of carbon dioxide. With the increased use of fossil fuels the amount of carbon dioxide spewed into the atmosphere is increasing tremendously. Concomitantly, vast tracts of land are being removed from the cycle of photosynthesis. In the United States alone, a million acres of green plants are paved under each year. The loss of these plants is reducing the rate at which oxygen enters the atmosphere. In addition, consider that scientists do not even know to what extent photosynthesis is being inhibited through pollution of ocean and fresh waters.

For this reason many scientists believe that the carbon dioxide-oxygen balance may be in danger. Should a point be reached at which the rate of combustion exceeds the rate of photosynthesis, the atmosphere shall begin to run out of oxygen. If this occurs gradually, the effect would be approximately the same as moving to high altitudes, such as in the Andes Mountains. Lamont Cole believes this might help to alleviate the population crisis by raising death rates. The late Lloyd Berkner, however, believed that atmospheric depletion of oxygen might occur suddenly rather than gradually.

It is quite possible to cut down on some of the carbon dioxide pollution by installing control systems in automobiles. Yet many individuals doubt whether this is truly a practical solution to the pollution problem without inordinate costs to the automobile user. If this opinion is to be followed to its logical conclusion then, as John McAnally suggests, there is no solution to the problem except to allow pollution to rise to such a level that one-half of the car operators succumb to the effects of their free use of the highways. Then, with the number of automobiles reduced to the pre-smog level, air pollution will once again become insignificant until, of course, the car operators reproduce and the population increases again. Obviously, this is madness, but it may come to this.

Again, consider another important aspect of the environment. The nitrogen cycle provides all organisms nitrogen for the building of protein. Nitrogen is released into the atmosphere, along with ammonia, as a gas when plants and animals decay. Live plants use both substances to build their proteins, but they cannot use nitrogen in gaseous form. Certain bacteria and algae in the soil and roots of some plants use the nitrogen and ammonia gas to produce nitrates with which plants build their proteins. Animals in turn build their proteins from the constituents of plant proteins. As was indicated in the discussion of oxygen, the rate of use and return of nitrogen has reached a balance so that the percentage of nitrogen in the atmosphere remains constant. It is not difficult to envision what might occur if any one of the numerous steps in the nitrogen cycle were to be disturbed. The atmospheric nitrogen might disappear. It might be replaced by ammonia which, unused in the atmosphere, would become poisonous—or, plants could not make proteins because bacteria would no longer be available to use the gas in the atmosphere. In any case, it might mean disaster for the earth.

There is some evidence that eventually man will run out of fossil fuels and consequently is now turning to atomic energy as a source of power. With this comes the probability of a different breed of environmental pollution. Atomic reactors are already in use for the production of electricity. A fear arises, however, based on what is known of the present reactors and those proposed for the future.

The uranium fuel used in current reactors has to be reprocessed periodically in order to insure a continuous chain reaction. The reprocessing yields

Strontium[90] and Cesium[137] which have long half-lives and are biologically hazardous isotopes. They need to be stored where they cannot contaminate the environment for at least 1000 years. On the other hand, it is known that a large number of the storage tanks employed for this purpose are already leaking. This problem can be taken care of because these two products can be chemically trapped and restored. Unfortunately, another product called Krypton [85] cannot be trapped and is consequently sent into the earth's atmosphere to add to the radiation exposure of the earth. At the present time, scientists and engineers have no practicable way to prevent this.

To soothe these concerns, some scientists suggest the use of "clean" fusion reactors to replace the "dirty" reactors now polluting the environment. They say that, in this way, Strontium, Cesium and Krypton Isotopes would not be produced. No one, however, knows how these generators are to be built. Even if engineers.were successful in building a fusion generator, new contaminants will be produced. One of these is tritium or Hydrogen[3] which would become a constituent of water and that water with its long-lived radioactivity would contaminate the environment. So once again, where can the solution to the problem be found? If we want to avoid ground water contamination it might be better to use fission (i.e. "dirty") devices rather than fusion (i.e. "clean") devices. But fission devices if used irresponsibly could cause a tremendous increase in the permissible exposure level of radioactive dosage. Perhaps the solution lies in an altered educational system. Prevention has always been cheaper than the cure, although as people we are loathe to face the obvious. Prediction of future problems is important in order to create effective programs of prevention. The escalation in present problem intensities is far too expensive in terms of life.

In addition, we are dumping vast quantities of pollutants into the oceans. These include pesticides, radioisotopes, nerve gas detergents and other biologically active materials. No more than a fraction of these substances have been tested for toxicity to the marine microorganisms that produce most of the earth's oxygen, or to the bacteria and microorganisms involved in the nitrogen cycle.

World Food Crisis

Our interference with these delicately balanced cycles is not, however, the entire picture. Man also faces a food crisis. The problem of feeding the people of the world is as old as civilization itself. Scientists have been predicting the crisis between population growth and food supply for the past 200 years. The only new feature of the problem is its dimensions, and the fact that there is a disproportionality in the economic development, population density and food supply throughout the world. Our nation is in a much more fortunate position as compared to the less developed countries, even though some legislators are not willing to acknowledge that starvation and malnutrition is a way of life for a large number of people who live in this country. There is no doubt that people are more knowledgeable and have greater interest than ever before in solutions to problems of poverty, hunger, and malnutrition of the less fortunate. But, whether the concern is one of genuine interest in a better life for all mankind or whether it is based on fear is not known. What is known is that unless effective steps are taken to improve conditions, general chaos may envelop the world.

Optimists dismiss the prediction of widespread famine, but more cautious individuals have considered evidence which prompted Paddock and Paddock to write a book entitled, *Famine 1975! America's Decision! Who Will Survive?* They have also considered the three-volume report issued by the President's Science Advisory Committee called "The World Food Problem," published in 1966. This 1200 page report in essence found that the requirements for solution of the world food crisis would involve astute management.

In seeking the food that is required to meet present deficiencies and provide for the population growth of the future, consideration must be given to all known sources. This includes the food from the sea, bacteria, petroleum, as well as synthetic and traditional sources.

The PSAC emphasizes the point that what we need to do is to improve the agricultural production of the developing countries. One way to do this is to send them seeds, stock and fertilizers. The problem is, ironically, that many strains of plant and animal foods which grow well in Iowa, New York State, Texas, California, and other parts of the United States may fail to grow in other climates and other soils or grow poorly.

It has also been suggested that we harvest the sea. Again it may not be as practical a solution as it seems on the surface. Another publication in 1966 by the PSAC, entitled "The Effective Use of the Sea," indicates how little we know of the sea. We understand little of the turbulence of the sea which cyclically controls the natural food chains. We have only begun to develop the technology to enable us to study the microclimate of the seas.

Efforts have begun to use bacteria, fungi or yeasts to convert petroleum directly into food for man. This is wonderful on the surface because it appears more efficient than feeding petroleum to a refinery to make gasoline, feeding gasoline to tractors and other machines which will eventually deliver the food. It is an unhappy fact, however, that the metabolism of bacteria, fungi and yeasts does not generate oxygen as do green plants.

One last remark. A few years ago this country was troubled with crop surpluses. You do not hear of these surpluses now because they no longer exist. We used to be concerned with the cost of storing our surplus crops.

The government now finds that we could ship one-fourth of each year's production to India alone and that would not be enough.

The Population Explosion

What is most disturbing is that man does not recognize that no matter what he does, it is impossible to provide enough food for a world population that is growing at an unparalleled rate of 2% per year. Translated into people, this means that 132 individuals are added to the present population per minute. This current 2% may not sound like an unusual rate of growth. However, Marker has shown that if this rate had existed from the time of Christ until the present time, the increase would result in over 20 million individuals in place of each person now alive or 100 persons for each square foot. At our present rate of 2% per year, within two centuries, there would be over 150 billion people on earth.

When we speak of the population explosion, we usually imply some other country's problem. The population of the United States has increased from 130 million in 1930 to over 200 million in 1967. This is an increase of over 70 million in less than 37 years. It is this enormous growth that has polluted our air and water; that is consuming our material resources faster than they can be replaced and has placed impossible pressures on our living conditions.

McElroy points out that we are on the logarithmic phase of a typical growth curve after a long lag period. In nature no animal, plant or bacterial population has ever maintained a logarithmic phase of growth for very long. The major factors that slow this rate of growth are exhaustion of food supply, accumulation of toxic products, decimation through disease, or the effects of some outside lethal agent which kills a high proportion of the population. Your imagination can play with which of these factors might apply to the human populations. Thus, there appears to be no way for us to survive unless man begins to identify ways and means of solving the growth of world population and increasing the world food supply.

The Role of the Teacher

Perhaps the most basic reason for our ecological crisis is ignorance. For two generations we have been almost completely ignorant of the concepts and principles of ecology. The paradox of the situation lies in the fact that we are fully capable of rooting out the underlying causes of pollution. The human, technological and financial resources are at hand. What is needed, however, is the education of young people who will be future voters and practical decision makers. The task of restoring the stability of the ecosystem is vast, complex and deeply rooted in economic, social and political issues. The responsibility for preparing people to make judgments relating to the vast restorative program lies with teachers who will need to teach young people relevant facts in understandable terms. As the custodians of knowledge teachers have the responsibility to help inform students about the crisis in the environment. It is the teacher who must help students discover why man has done so badly in his efforts to manage his affairs in this century.

What should be the philosophy of this education of the public, especially the young, concerning their environment? First of all, information is not enough. The student's way of thinking must also be developed to make it readily apparent to him that an extremely serious threat is involved—a threat that calls for action and sacrifice on his part. Secondly, the basic approach to ecology is not hard to teach. What is hard to teach is the analysis of controversy. The environmental crisis is controversial from a social, political and economic point of view. In every one of the environmental areas, legislation has its proponents as well as opponents. Students will need to learn how to weigh information that is controversial if education for survival is to be accomplished. Lastly, the stress in teaching must be on the interrelationship that exists between the various components in the environment. We have to help students understand that millions of years of a slow gradual process were needed for these delicate interrelationships to be established. We cannot disturb these relationships without causing havoc. We also have to impress students with the fact that we are not divorced from our environment but are an integral part of it. Every time another species of plant or animal becomes extinct, every time a lake dies, we lose a part of our lives.

The study of the relationships between man and his environment, both natural and technological, will help us to understand the consequences of our actions. A student who comprehends man's relationship to the environment will be equipped to do something about the environmental problems that beset the world. If we can reach enough students it is quite possible that man and his environment may survive against all the odds a while longer.

Land-Use Patterns in the City

FRED A. LAMPE AND ORVAL C. SCHAEFER, JR.

Land use and *land-use* distributions can be studied in elementary school social studies. This article presents a method for teaching these geographic concepts and describes (1) a scheme for classifying city land uses, (2) construction of land-use maps, and (3) interpretation of land-use distributions in terms of gross patterns.

Classifying Land Uses

When beginning the study of the geography of land uses in a city, one is immediately faced with the problem of dealing with the plethora of city land uses. To make such a study manageable, it is necessary to either group or classify the specific uses or work with some specific land uses, particularly, but not exclusively, those that occur in great numbers, such as grocery stores or gas stations.

In any classification system, the categories should be mutually exclusive so that a specific use can fit in only one category. (The categories should account for all of the uses.) Two examples of classification systems will be given. However, it would be most valuable for the teacher to have the class devise its own system, since the ability to group and classify like kinds of things is an important learning behavior.

When developing their own classification system, the pupils should be certain the list contains only specific land uses such as a drug store, a movie theater, a park, a residence, a bakery, or a cemetery. When a list has been completed, the teacher should ask the class: "How are we going to handle all of these?" or "What can we do to simplify the list?" With a little guidance the class will see quickly that many of the specific uses are similar, thus permitting grouping. The number of categories should be neither too numerous to be unwieldly nor too few to prevent analysis.

The United States Urban Renewal Administration and the Bureau of

Fred A. Lampe is an Associate Professor of Geography at South Illinois University, Edwardsville; Orval C. Schaefer, Jr., is an elementary school teacher in the Renton, Washington School District.

Reprinted from *The Journal of Geography* 68(5):301–306, 1969, with permission of the National Council for Geographic Education and Fred A. Lampe and Orval C. Schaefer, Jr.

Public Roads have developed a classification system to standardize the coding and classifying of all land uses, both rural and urban.* This system has nine major categories (two for manufacturing, with three lower levels of subcategories). The nine major categories are listed below with examples of some of the more common activities that make up the category:

1. *Residential:* household units, group quarters, residential hotels, and mobile parks and courts.
2. *Manufacturing:* food processing, textiles, lumber, wood and furniture products, paper, printing, publishing, chemicals, and petroleum refining.
3. *Manufacturing:* rubber and miscellaneous plastic products, stone, clay and glass, the primary metal industries, and fabricated metal products.
4. *Transportation, communication, and utilities:* railroads, rapid rail transit, streets and right of ways, airports, canals, and parking.
5. *Trade:* both wholesale and retail trade, as well as eating and drinking establishments.
6. *Services:* financial, insurance, personal and business, repair, governmental, and educational services.
7. *Cultural, entertainment, and recreation:* cultural activities, amusements, recreational activities, resorts, camps, and parks.
8. *Resource production and extraction:* agriculture, forestry, fishing, and mining.
9. *Underdeveloped land and water areas:* unused and vacant land in addition to land on which structures are under construction.

Listed below is a system, developed by the authors, that is concerned exclusively with city land uses:

1. *Single family residences.*
2. *Multiple family dwellings or apartments.*
3. *Commercial or business: retail, wholesale, and service.*
4. *Industrial, manufacturing, and railroads.*
5. *Public: schools, government functions, parks, and churches.*
6. *Streets.*
7. *Vacant and unused lands.*

An advantage of the government scheme is that it lists and places almost all of the conceivable uses so that there is very little ambiguity. In the second scheme there will inevitably be problems concerning the placement of specific uses into categories. For example, where should a dormitory be placed? Is a bakery a business or a manufacturing activity? Is a mobile home court a residence or a business? The class must determine where the

---

* *Standard Land Use Coding Manual,* First edition (Washington, D.C.: U.S. Government Printing Office, 1965).

specific uses are put in their classification system by defining the criteria of each category.

Land-Use Maps

Describing the gross patterns of land uses in a city from a land-use map is a useful starting point for gaining understanding about the geography of city land uses. Teachers have three alternatives: they can obtain a published map of land uses; have the class make a land-use map; or use a hypothetical map or model.

If a teacher could obtain a published map of city land uses, it would be unnecessary to go through the process of devising a classification system. These maps, however, are usually difficult to obtain. Most cities with planning departments have land-use maps, but frequently these are not readily available to the public. But more importantly, relying on published maps prevents pupils from classifying and grouping, an important learning behavior.

It is unrealistic to expect the class to construct a detailed, comprehensive land-use map. There are, however, two kinds of relatively simple land-use maps that can be constructed: a map of most or all of the land uses in one part of the city (probably the local area) and a map of a few selected functions for the whole city. To make either of these two maps, a base map showing the streets and the street system is needed.

The following comments are pertinent to a land-use map of the local area where most or all of the functions are to be mapped. Most of the base maps will probably be of too small a scale to be used conveniently. If the maps are too small, the class or the teacher will have to copy the street pattern of the local area at a larger scale. One way of enlarging a map is to use

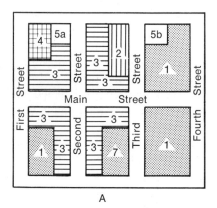

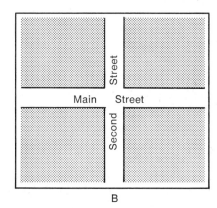

A   B

Figure 1   Data Recording Forms

an opaque projector. Project the relevant portion of the small map onto a large sheet of paper on the wall and then copy the enlarged street pattern. If the whole class works on one large map, tracing paper or transparent plastic can be placed over the base map so that corrections do not necessitate making a new base map.

Pupils should be asked what they already know about land uses in the local area. One pupil might say: "On Main Street there are businesses along two whole blocks." The teacher or the pupil can then mark the extent of this use on the map. Colors or symbols can be used to identify different land uses. Other pupils will undoubtedly be able to tell what uses are occurring at other places. Once the pupils' information has been exhausted and if there are many blank spots on the map (or if there have been disagreements), the teacher can ask how the land uses can be determined. The answer, of course, is that someone has to go to the unknown area or someone who knows will have to be asked.

If the pupils visit the area, a system of data recording is required. Figure 1 shows two examples of data recording forms. These forms are simple to construct. All that is necessary is that the streets be identified and the uses be recorded as to type and extent. This recording can be done by writing the name of the land-use type or coding the uses with colors or with some other symbol.

Using the authors' land-use scheme, various general uses are noted in Figure 1A as an example of how the data might be recorded on a field trip. This method could also be used for the master map. Figure 1B is an enlargement of a portion of Figure 1A, focusing on only one intersection, without the uses identified. This form permits a detailed description. Later, in the classroom, the pupils can generalize the specific land uses into major categories.

The second kind of land-use map is one where only a few selected specific functions within a general category are mapped for the whole city. Here again a base map is necessary, but, in this instance, a small-scale map can be used. It is desirable to have multiple copies of the same base map, possibly the type of city maps available from gas stations. The yellow pages section of the telephone book can serve as the basic source of information for the location of the specific functions. The pupils can go down the list in the yellow pages and locate all occurrences of the specific function for the whole city on one tracing paper overlay. Each pupil could be assigned a different function, or the class could be divided into small groups with each group working on a specific function.

Locate the places with a symbol on a sheet of tracing paper that has been placed over the base map. This will allow comparison of the distributional pattern of one specific function with others by placing one sheet of tracing paper over another. To do this kind of comparing, it is essential that all pupils have the same base map. The result is several maps, on tracing paper overlays, each map showing all of the locations of one specific land use. These individual maps can then be used to describe and interpret patterns. Also, the individual tracing paper maps could be grouped together, according to the general land-use categories, placed on top of each other, and the resulting patterns of the general categories described and interpreted. It is important, obviously, to use a different symbol for each specific land use to allow for discrimination between the different uses.

What functions should be selected for mapping? This will depend, to a large extent, on the size of the city. The functions that would best exemplify patterns are those that occur in large numbers, and for a large city, this fact may make it unrealistic to map such a function. Restaurants and gas stations are examples of this type of land use. Perhaps these two functions would be reasonable items for smaller cities. On the other hand, apartment houses would seem reasonable, as would department stores and shoe stores.

A third type of map is a hypothetical one, or a model. If a published map is unavailable and time is limited for constructing a map, the teacher can create a hypothetical distribution. Figure 2 shows such a distribution of a phenomena that exhibits different patterns. In using this approach the teacher would first ask the pupils to describe the pattern or patterns. After a description has been made, the teacher would go on to a discussion of possible reasons for these kinds of patterns. An advantage of using a hypothetical map is that the data can be purposefully manipulated and exaggerated. The teacher can ask: "Is the cluster of businesses in area A on the model (Figure 2) like any place that you know of in our city?" or "How is the linear pattern of businesses in area B on the model similar to the businesses along the highway that runs near here?" Area C on the model represents a dispersed pattern typical of the distribution of corner grocery stores in the older areas of the city.

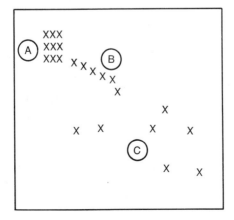

Figure 2   Land-Use Distribution Models

Patterns and Associations

When studying the distributions of phenomena and before interpretation begins, the pattern of the phenomena should be described. At one extreme the phenomena may all be in one place, or at the other extreme the phenomena may completely cover the whole area. Between these two extremes there are many possible patterns. Phenomena may be *evenly spaced;* they may be arranged in a *linear* pattern; they may tend to cluster in *nodes;* or they may be *dispersed,* or *irregular.* There are also different levels of generalizations concerning patterns. For example, if specific phenomena are arranged in a nodal pattern, the nodes themselves may form various kinds of patterns: linear; star shaped; or dispersed. By perceiving and describing the patterns formed by urban land-use functions, pupils can gain clues as to the relationships of these functions to other functions and hints as to possible causal factors.

There are two types of patterns that are useful in describing the land-use patterns in cities. These are the nodal, or cluster, and the linear, or string. They are probably best exemplified by the general category of trade or business, as well as many of the specific commercial activities that make up this general category. Nodes and linear patterns are also appropriate when studying certain aspects of residential, manufacturing, and service categories. Several different kinds of land uses persistently occur together, and these groupings of specific kinds of land uses also form patterns. A particular land-use type may also exhibit characteristics of two or more different kinds of patterns. For example, gas stations may form nodal as well as linear patterns. Linear patterns are usually related to transportation facilities: streets, highways, railroads, and canals. Clusters are usually related to some point that is strategic or accessible or both.

The term *accessibility* describes a most cogent relationship between phenomena in a city. In order for a business to survive, its customers must be able to reach it; consequently, major street or highway intersections become strategic because they are more accessible than other places. The nodes formed by the cluster of businesses in a shopping center are usually at some major intersection. The shopping center nodes themselves are frequently arranged in a disconnected linear pattern at the access points on a controlled access expressway.

In the following discussion, some examples are given of patterns formed by various land-use functions and the interrelationships among these patterns and other factors. The discussion is by no means exhaustive, rather it is intended as a sample to stimulate the interest and imagination of the teacher and pupils. These ideas have general applicability to all cities; however, in individual cities specific forces may be at work that will cause refinements in the explanations. The two key questions that are constantly asked in the approach are: "What is the pattern formed by this activity and what word can be used to describe it?" and "Why does the activity form this kind of pattern?" The idea of using the gross patterns formed by land uses is a convenient point of departure for trying to understand the forces at work controlling the location of activities.

TRANSPORTATION FUNCTIONS

Streets and highways form the circulation system of a city and are linear by their very nature. The gross patterns formed by the streets and highways can and do vary from city to city. The major thoroughfares may form one kind of pattern, whereas all of the streets together may form quite a different pattern. The checkerboard pattern is probably the most common, but in the newly developed suburban housing developments the street pattern frequently looks chaotic with its loops, curves, and *cul-de-sacs*. These suburban patterns are usually for the purpose of ensuring a measure of isolation and to break the monotony of a checkerboard pattern. Frequently, the street pattern is dictated by the terrain.

RESIDENTIAL USES

The residential land-use function accounts for the largest percentage of land in a city, and this function comes the closest to being the kind of pattern that covers the whole area. Consequently, it is difficult to apply the notion of a kind of pattern for this whole category, except for the new residential areas being built around the edge of the built-up city and for certain subcategories of residential use such as apartments. New residential areas on the edge of the built-up area do not spread out evenly, rather, they form nodal and linear patterns. A cluster will form around an access to an expressway and then frequently will spread out string-like along the feeder roads, forming a star or cross-like pattern. It is possible that nodes will form a detached linear pattern along an unlimited access thoroughfare, each node representing a residential area being built by a housing development or real estate company.

Apartments and multifamily units usually form one major node or arc near the center of the city with smaller scattered nodes near accessible intersections. Usually there are some linear aspects to the apartment function. The individual parcels of land near the center of the city are valuable because they are more accessible to the center of the city. Hence, they usually are too expensive for only one family, and it takes the combined rent of several families to pay the cost of the land. The strings of apartments are frequently oriented toward the streets where there is some sort of public transportation.

TRADE FUNCTIONS

The trade or business land-use category includes both retail and whole-sale activities. In the older parts of the city outside of the central business district there are usually single businesses scattered about individually. The pattern of corner grocery stores and drug stores can best be described as a dispersed pattern. Usually these businesses were there before zoning ordinances were enacted and were, and still are, oriented toward a market that essentially is accessible by walking. A dispersed pattern of business is usually not characteristic of the newer areas of the city because zoning ordinances prohibit it. Zoning ordinances typically require that businesses all be in one place. This, of course, dictates a nodal pattern. Businesses also form linear patterns along major streets with unlimited access and usually form a star or cross-shaped pattern along the streets of a strategic intersection. The major trade node is, of course, the central business district, which represents, theoretically, the most accessible place for the whole city. From this node there are lines of businesses extending out along major streets.

MANUFACTURING

Newer industries are frequently found together in planned industrial parks. These nodes are often related to some form of transportation. Light industries that depend upon trucks for their raw materials are near an access to a major highway. Heavy industries, such as the primary metals industry, are oriented toward either rail transportation or some form of water transportation. They may be in nodes along the railroad or they may form a linear pattern along the transportation route. Industries frequently are located on flat land, which may be along a river or in some other kind of valley, and therefore a linear pattern results. Small industries and older industries usually form a cluster or an arc or a circle around the central business district. These activities are partly explained by historical and accessibility factors. Some single industries are scattered around the edges of a city. Some of these are explained by the desire of the industry for adequate, relatively cheap space for expansion and parking.

A slightly different kind of question logically flows from some of the preceding discussion. After the class has identified the nodal patterns formed by the land-use category of trade functions as represented in shopping centers, the question could be raised as to why specific functions reoccur in all of the shopping centers. This question, however, goes beyond the purpose of this article. It does suggest, however, that a meaningful start can be made toward a better understanding of the geography of cities by learning to identify and to describe the gross patterns formed by various land-use functions and by trying to associate these patterns with other factors in the physical and cultural environment of the home community.

Introducing Cities to Elementary School Children

GARY A. MANSON AND CAROL J. PRICE

City is a perplexing word. It names an important feature of man's environment, specifying a unique settlement pattern. It implies activities such as manufacturing and commuting and precludes others such as hunting and farming. Congestion, culture, pollution, opportunity, and civilization are terms frequently attached to urban life. In spite of these apparently obvious characteristics, the fundamental meaning of city is probably vague in the minds of most pupils as well as many adults.

Scholars are hard-pressed to provide a comprehensive definition for an urban settlement. This difficulty is reflected in the questions that remain unanswered: What are the minimal requisites necessary to qualify a particular community as a city? What characteristics are shared by all cities throughout the world? Where are the boundaries between urban and non-urban in societies where communication and transportation technology has blurred the traditional distinctions? Is urban life a state of mind as well as a form of human habitat? These and similar questions make the task of defining a city in a few words or understanding a city from a few lessons almost impossible. The presence of uncertainty, however, may be fortunate; the search for knowledge of a complex world is a good definition of learning.

While it is true that cities are complicated phenomena, children can learn some dimensions of the urban concept that will enable them to develop a sharper and more powerful understanding of what a city is. This article is especially concerned with introducing elementary school children to a geographical view of the city. To provide a manageable unit of study, only two general features of cities will be considered: the people who live in the city (*population*) and the territory occupied by the city (*areal extent*).

Each lesson to follow concerning number, occupational diversity, metropolitan area, and land use begins by discussing the concept or the generalization that is to be the focus, *i.e.,* the objective, of the instruction. Next, one class activity that should lead pupils to that generalization is described. Finally, each lesson concludes by suggesting one way of expanding or evaluating the learning outcomes. The lessons are intended only to introduce

Gary A. Manson is an Assistant Professor of Geography at Michigan State University, East Lansing; Carol J. Price Chargin is a teacher at the N.B. Houge Intermediate School, San Jose, California.

Reprinted from *The Journal of Geography* 68(5):295–300, 1969, with permission of the National Council for Geographic Education and Gary Manson and Carol J. Price Chargin.

pupils to cities and may be modified and developed to suit the various conditions found in different classrooms.

Population

"A city means a lot of people live there," said one second-grader and certainly he was correct. But sheer numbers of people do not make a city. A football stadium may contain 100,000 people, but for only a few hours. Ski towns often attract thousands for a winter weekend, but can be virtually deserted in the summer. In both cases the population lacks stability. Elsewhere, large numbers of people may have inhabited a small area for hundreds of years, but all are engaged in the same activity, farming; one classic example is the Hwang Ho valley of China. An urban population is occupationally diverse. Thus, these instances cannot be regarded as cities for each fails to fulfill the basic conditions for designating a particular population as urban. An accurate conception must include:

1. A substantial number of people (number)
2. Living in close proximity (density)
3. Over an extended period of time (stability)
4. Engaging in a variety of economic activities (occupational diversity).

The proposed lessons will include only number and occupational diversity; the teacher may wish to develop his own activities concerning density and stability.

NUMBER

The number of people in a community implies a good deal about it. Population number indicates the variety of services that is available; *e.g.,* libraries are not usually found in villages. Moreover, larger populations permit an increasing degree of specialization. For example, in small communities shoes may be sold in general merchandise stores while cities can support shops specializing in shoes and sometimes only in one brand. Although the relationships between urban population size and the number and complexity of economic functions is intricate, children can be introduced to the elementary idea that the number of people in a city indicates the quantity and kind of economic activities to be found there.

Initially, the class should be given a list of familiar communities whose populations range from very small (250) to very large (one million). Because the communities are disparate in size, the class should be asked to group them into three or four categories according to population similarities. This may be done individually or as a small group activity. When the communities have been classified, several of the schemes used by the pupils should be presented to the class and any reasons for the grouping should be stated. For example, one group of pupils may decide to have three categories —villages, towns, and cities—and determine that the maximum population for a village is 500, for a town 10,000, and for a city any community over 10,000. The actual categories used and the particular population included in each category are less important than the idea that there are communities of distinctly different sizes.

The second step is to determine what, in addition to population, distinguishes one type of community from another. The question might be phrased, "Are there differences between villages, towns, and cities besides the number of people who live there?" Typical pupil responses may include:

1. "Villages don't have big buildings and cities do."
2. "Towns and villages don't have professional sports teams while cities do."
3. "Towns and cities have automobile dealers while villages don't."
4. "Villages can have hunting and fishing almost in their backyards, but this isn't true in cities."

Pupils can record the reasons suggested by the class in notebooks. They may wish to add to or modify the list as the study of cities progresses.

When the class has exhausted its ideas about the ways of distinguishing between types of communities, the lesson may be concluded by asking the pupils if they wish to reconsider any of the community classifications they made earlier. It is possible that some class members may wish to place one of the original communities in a different category after hearing the discussion. This will also provide an opportunity to determine if the class understands that the services, functions, and activities found in communities are directly related to the number of people living there.

OCCUPATIONAL DIVERSITY

The people who live in cities are more diverse than the populations of rural areas or villages. Physical appearance, religious beliefs, political views, and living standards differ widely in urban communities. For purposes of urban geography, one of the more useful ways of viewing a city's population is analyzing the various occupations found there. This method is especially useful because the number and type of occupational categories bears a direct relationship to the population size of the city. In general, the larger the city, the greater the variety of occupations. Put another way, a large city will contain not only most of those occupations found in smaller communities but also additional ones as well.

First, pupils should be given copies of a chart similar to Figure 1. In the left-hand column, the pupils should list a variety of occupations, paying

Occupation	Town	City	Both	Neither
Grocer			X	
Factory Worker		X		
Scientist		X		
Rancher				X
Lumberjack	X			
Doctor			X	

Figure 1   Classification of Occupations by Community Size

special attention to those they believe to be associated with community size. As the occupations are listed, each pupil should indicate whether he would expect to find that worker in a town, a city, in both, or in neither. This decision should be made on a basis of what is commonly the case rather than allowing an exception to determine the choice; e.g., one scientist in a small town would not alter the example in Figure 1. Because the experiences of the pupils will vary, lengthier lists and better decisions might be developed if class members worked together, either in pairs or small groups.

The next step is comparing the lists compiled by the pupils. This can be done by recording the data provided by the pupils on a master list placed on an overhead projector or the chalkboard. A list of twenty or twenty-five occupations will allow generalizations to be made without complicating the question. Disagreements about the proper locations for a particular occupation, in the town, in the city, in both, or in neither, may be resolved by having the reasons for the choices presented and allowing the class to discuss their validity. Again, it should be emphasized that exceptions to the general practice should not deter the selection of an appropriate location; geography can deal only in patterns for which there will always be exceptions, often explained in other ways. When the data have been recorded on the master list, the class should be asked what conclusions they would be willing to make about occupations and city size. Listed below are some possible statements:

1. Cities contain most of the occupations found in towns.
2. Cities contain occupations not found in towns.
3. Some occupations are not suited to living in towns or cities.
4. There are few occupations that are commonly associated with towns alone.

From these and similar statements, the pupils should be able to infer that the number and type of occupations in a community are related to the number of people living there.

Individual pupils may be asked to speculate about why certain occupations are found in towns and cities and other occupations are found only in cities. They may enjoy presenting their ideas to the class for criticism and discussion. However, while these questions make up an essential part of urban geography and thus may merit some preliminary consideration in the classroom, they are beyond the scope of this article.

Areal Extent

Areal extent refers to the actual space occupied by the city. Many kinds of boundaries can be used to outline the borders of urban communities. The most widely known is the political boundary, usually referred to as the city limits. However, given the dispersal of homes and industries beyond the city limits and the extensive movement between the suburbs and the central city, political boundaries do not reflect the real extent of a city's geographical area. Any meaningful definition of an urban area should include the population's place of employment as well as their residences. In practice, this consists of the central city itself together with the adjoining densely populated territory. It can also include nearby towns if those towns are recognized as integral parts of the central city. The geographic term for this unit is *metropolitan area*.

METROPOLITAN AREA

An understanding of the metropolitan area concept can be achieved through mapping the extent of the pupils' community as illustrated in the provided Sylvan model. For larger cities, pupils may use highway maps with insets of the metropolitan area or city street maps as sources of information. Large-scale maps of smaller communities might be obtained from libraries, city or county officials, local chambers of commerce, federal agencies such as the United States Forest Service or Geological Survey, bookstores, or the local school district, which may use such maps for school census accounting or bus-route planning. Maps and information about the local community similar to the data that follow should also be available to each pupil.

Figure 2 is a map of Sylvan, a hypothetical community, used to illustrate an appropriate teaching strategy. (If local maps are unavailable, this map and data may be substituted for use in the classroom. The teacher may also wish to present the Sylvan model, which is relatively uncomplicated, prior to studying the local community.)

The Sylvan region includes Sylvan proper, population 25,000, bounded by 8th Avenue on the north, Pine Street on the east, the Central Railroad on the south, and Spruce Street on the west. Beyond Sylvan proper lie

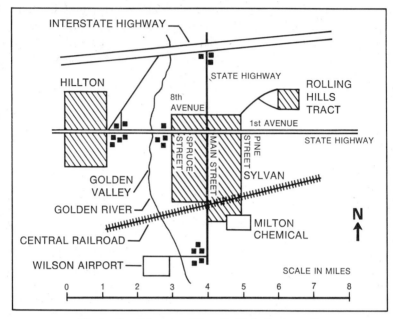

Figure 2   Sylvan, a Hypothetical Community

Hillton, population 8,500; the Golden Valley suburban area, population 3,000; and the Rolling Hills housing tract, population 1,500. Other notable features include the Milton Chemical Company, the principal employer in the area; Wilson Airport; and several residential clusters around the periphery of the above communities.

The basic question to be presented to the class is: What constitutes the Sylvan metropolitan area? Is it to be defined as Sylvan proper; *i.e.,* the Sylvan city limits? Should Milton Chemical be included, because, although it is beyond the city limits, many people who live in Sylvan work there? Should Golden Valley or Rolling Hills be included, since many of the residents work in Sylvan? Should Hillton be considered a part of the Sylvan urban area since many residents of Hillton work in Sylvan or at Milton Chemical? Because the movement between place of residence and place of employment occurs without regard for political boundaries, a class discussion of defining metropolitan areas can arrive at the possibility of establishing boundaries to include both.

As the class begins to understand the idea of defining a city to include place of work as well as place of residence, the mapping can begin. The general task is to outline the boundaries marking the outer limits of Sylvan's metropolitan area. Certain questions should be posed as guides for the mapping:

1. Should an area such as Golden Valley be included? Why?
2. Is Milton Chemical a part of Sylvan's metropolitan area? Why?
3. Can a smaller community such as Hillton be included? Why?
4. What other areas might be included? Why?

The answers to these questions can be worked out individually, in pairs, or by small groups. As decisions are made about which parts should be included, lines may be drawn by the pupils on their maps indicating the boundaries they have chosen. At the conclusion of the activity, each child or group will have outlined the Sylvan metropolitan area. Decisions should then be reported to the class along with the reasons for those decisions. It is not necessary that all pupils concur on the precise boundaries, but it is likely that there will be a high degree of consensus. (The class may inquire about why it is necessary to define a city in some way other than political. One way to answer this question is to suggest that transportation planning requires knowledge of the commuting habits; *i.e.,* residence/place of employment patterns, to develop better roads and highways throughout the metropolitan area.)

If time and facilities permit, some pupils may also enjoy selecting different cities and applying the mapping method in attempting to define the metropolitan area. They should be informed that the Sylvan example is quite simple and that much needed information about these other cities will not be available. Nevertheless, by considering probable arrangements of living and working locations and by examining the extent of the contiguous "built-up" area, they will be able to make some valid inferences about the size of the metropolitan area of virtually any city.

LAND USE

In an urban area land is used in a variety of ways. Homes, businesses, churches, cemeteries, and dairies are only a few of the city's occupants. Classifying these occupants according to the function they perform allows the geographer to map and generalize about the land-use patterns of cities. Although the number of classification categories employed by professional geographers is large, elementary school children should probably use no more than four or five categories at the introductory stage. By plotting the locations of these activities, the pupils may then be able to identify some of the significant reasons why certain activities tend to be found in certain parts of the cities.

The class should begin by listing the different ways land is used in their community. An abbreviated example of such a pupil listing is given in the left-hand column of Figure 3. Pupils should be encouraged to include a wide variety of land uses from throughout the metropolitan area and not

Original Pupil Listing	Residential	Business/ Commercial	Industrial	Public
Stores Parks Houses Banks Factories Airports Restaurants College Streets Apartments	Houses Apartments	Stores Banks Restaurants	Factories	Parks College Airport Streets

Figure 3   Classifying Urban Activities by Land Uses

to limit themselves to businesses and homes. Approximately thirty land uses are sufficient to develop the second part of the lesson, the classification of the uses into a small number of categories to facilitate mapping. The classification can be initiated by asking the class to group those activities on their lists that are alike. One classification scheme is given in Figure 3. It is important that the pupils participate in devising their own method of categorizing the various land uses; a method should not be imposed by the teacher. Pupils, however, might proceed from the suggestion to classify the land uses according to what is done there and will probably develop a system similar to the one shown in Figure 3. All land uses may not be classified easily; for example, railroads could be placed in one of several categories. Difficult instances will not be frequent and may remain unclassified without disrupting the classification process.

When the classification has been completed the pupils may undertake the final part of the activity: a mapping of the locations of these land-use types. Actual field mapping would be the ideal geographic technique. However, it may be unnecessary at this introductory stage. Instead, pupils can rely upon their knowledge of the locations, which is probably sufficient for the mapping of large clusters of each activity.

Each pupil should be given a map of his own community. If these are unavailable, copies of the Sylvan map, Figure 2, may be used. If the Sylvan model is used, the pupils would be asked to speculate about the probable locations for each of the several land-use categories. (If the pupils' community is used, the question should be changed to: "Where are these activities found?" One possible variation would be to do both the Sylvan model and the local community and compare them.) In Sylvan one likely location for a business/commercial district is the vicinity around 1st Avenue and Main Street. If the land use is industrial, one likely location is the area around Milton Chemical. However, these by no means exhaust the probable locations. The pupils should be able to suggest several possible locations for each category. By shading each land-use area with colored pencils or crayons, the pupils can designate where they believe each of these activities is likely to be found; *i.e.,* the residential districts, public lands, etc. Some public services such as streets are probably evenly distributed and need not be mapped.

Subsequently, as the pupils discuss their location choices, they should be asked to state their reasons for these activities being located where they are. Among the more common explanations will be the availability of customers (business/commercial), access to transportation (Milton Chemical), availability of open land (Wilson Airport), and recreation (Golden Valley). As these ideas are presented, the distinction between speculation and verification should be pointed out to the class. The pupils are offering educated guesses or hypotheses; they do not know why that land use is where it is. One interesting question that might be posed is how a geographer, or a pupil, might find out if his hypothesis is correct. However, the purpose of this lesson has been to suggest to pupils that certain land-use activities occur in clusters and that there are logical reasons for this occurrence.

Social Issues, Social Action, and the Social Studies

ANNA OCHOA AND GARY A. MANSON

Social studies curriculum materials that have been developed during the past decade pay scant attention to such issues as racism, war, poverty, and pollution. Where such issues are considered, personal values, public policy, and social action are ignored. A prominent social studies educator said of this silence:

"At this critical time, when society is being torn apart by some of the most profound social problems ever to confront this nation, it would seem that social scientists and social studies educators would address themselves to the development of programs that have something to say about these matters. . . . We cannot go about teaching 'social science education' on a more or less business-as-usual basis as though there is no black-white conflict, no generation conflict, no conflict over participation in decision-

Anna Ochoa is an Associate Professor of Social Studies Education at The Florida State University, Tallahassee; Gary A. Manson is an Assistant Professor of Geography at Michigan State University, East Lansing.

Reprinted from *The Elementary School Journal* 72(5):230–237, 1972, with permission of The University of Chicago Press and Anna Ochoa and Gary A. Manson. Copyright © 1972.

making in our institutions, no self-destruction problems through narcotics and alcohol use, no environmental pollution and so on. . . . . Student involvement in social action based on the social studies curriculum and growing out of it are practically nonexistent" (1: 388–89).

In some social studies classrooms current events discussions based on local or student newspapers have given superficial attention to social issues. There is some evidence that social issues are finding their way into social studies education in a more penetrating and systematic manner. Some of the newer curriculum projects are centered on social issues. The widely known Harvard Social Studies Project generated the Curriculum Focused on Thinking Reflectively about Public Issues. The Diablo Valley Education Project produced units titled "On Conflict" and "An Introduction to War and Peace." The Washington University Elementary Social Science Project was designed to develop analytical strategies for dealing with social and political controversy (2: 9, 29, 103).

Jerome Bruner has pleaded for greater attention to social issues:

"Cannot early instruction in government, economics, sociology, urban studies, public health, etc. be organized in the form of policy sciences? Cannot students work from the start like members of policy planning staffs, or members of 'think-tank' groups? Let the problems be ones *not* yet solved. . . . I believe that we must explore *first* the problems, the deep troubles, the goals for action. Then let there be an exploration in terms of the structure of knowledge—but with the issues already encountered, however dimly understood" (3: 55–56).

Explanations for social studies programs that omit social issues and social action range from the academic to the political. Some educators argue that curriculums which emphasize social issues distort man's positive accomplishments. Other educators argue that social action is an inefficient mode of learning. Still other educators warn that social action projects run the risk of violating the political and the social norms of the school community.

Social action that leads to social change is a logical outgrowth of analysis of social issues. The failure of social studies education to confront this fact demands closer examination. Let us consider an example of this failure.

On April 22, this nation celebrates Earth Day. On that day pupils from schools throughout the country try to alleviate the environmental disaster that has befallen their portion of our planet. Children collect trash, they build mountain trails, they beautify, they scrub, they march, and they protest. Many schools aid and support these activities. But what happens on Earth Day plus one—on April 23? Does everyone settle back to business as usual? By any criterion—changes in personal habits, improvements in the air and water, or an increase in the probability of human survival— little really changes.

The issues surrounding the deterioration of the human habitat are many.

No one advocates pollution, overpopulation, destruction of resources, and urban congestion, but the problems continue. Part of the difficulty lies in our unwillingness to believe what environmentalists and ecologists have been telling us: the earth can be rescued only if we turn away from continued population increases, from a growth-oriented economy, and from an anthropocentric view of the universe. Appropriate responses to the environmental problem may extend far beyond picking up paper, making anti-pollution posters, and planting trees. Other options are practicing birth control, picketing offensive industries, and eliminating private automobiles. The ecological problem—like other problems such as racism, war, and poverty—carries with it demands for altering the basic fabric of our society through social action.

Social Issues and Social Action

Social issues arise when the goals, the structures, and the processes of communities or societies combine or conflict in ways that threaten the survival, the well-being, or the progress of the group or its members. To warrant inclusion in the social studies curriculum, a social issue must be enduring: it must persistently recur in human experience. Or the issue must be pervasive: it must exist in a range of cultural settings. Or the issue must be threatening: it must challenge human survival.

In the school setting, social action is any behavior, consistent with the norms of rationality and human dignity, directed toward resolving a social issue. Ideally, social action is direct involvement by pupils of all ages in public affairs as a consequence of careful analysis of an issue and with thoughtful acceptance of the consequences of involvement.

Social action may occur in a variety of situations, ranging from spontaneous reactions to carefully planned learning experiences. Spontaneous social action projects usually arise from a situation that pupils perceive as critical. "Let's do something about that!" they cry. The social action that results usually seeks to alleviate the symptoms rather than to eliminate the causes of a social issue.

Consider the sixth-grade class that, after reading about the need for medical supplies in a foreign country wracked by civil war, donated more than a hundred pounds of medicine and bandages. Or consider the group of high-school students who vigorously campaigned for passage of a school levy. Or consider the third-graders who helped clean their neighborhood after a riot.

These actions are obviously commendable, and one would hope for an increasing number of such activities in the schools. But these are spontaneous actions originating in an immediate set of circumstances and leading to little beyond the learner's personal satisfaction. None of these actions grew out of careful study. None was designed to grapple with the roots of the problem and thus reduce the probability of recurrence; and none was intended to develop a more sophisticated understanding of the problem. This kind of social action is a by-product rather than an integral part of the social studies curriculum.

Let us consider two scenarios that provide for social action based on a careful study of social problems. These scenarios provide examples of classroom instruction that results in social action.

Scenario One

An elementary-school class has been considering problems that arise when society's need for order conflicts with the individual's desire for freedom. The framework for the study is the rule-making process in the school. While systematically observing peers' behavior outside the classroom, the class establishes the fact that the school rule against running in the halls is frequently and flagrantly violated. The class members discuss the likely causes and consequences of running in the halls. They analyze the behavior, listing times and places of frequent occurrence; they review ways of dealing with the problem; they determine the probable consequences of each solution and finally settle on a series of actions.

Each pupil selects his own method of dealing with the problem, and pupils who have similar ideas organize into action teams. One group seeks out the more prominent violators and attempts to dissuade them from breaking the rule. Another group has a similar objective but settles on an advertising campaign and designs posters to be placed in problem areas. A third group, believing the rule to be superfluous, seeks out the principal, the perceived rule-maker, and discusses with him the possibility of changing or even discarding the rule. Finally, a number of pupils conclude that the situation does not warrant their attention and choose to do nothing about it.

As the project unfolds, each pupil continues to record the frequency and the intensity of hall running; each also keeps a log describing what he did, why he did it, and how others reacted to him. Securing this information sharpens pupils' skills of data collection and social observation. The class evaluates various action strategies, expresses frustration with the difficulties of initiating social change, and raises some new questions. The pupils ask what besides rules constrains behavior and conclude that social order and human freedom are inextricably intertwined. One may suggest that these pupils are becoming more apt students of human behavior as well as more sophisticated participants in their society.

Scenario Two

In a city torn by dissension over community control of the schools, a high-school class studies a proposed redistricting plan to integrate black schools and white schools, and to delegate much decision-making authority to neighborhood school boards. Using concepts, theories, and techniques from political science, sociology, and geography, the students analyze and evaluate the proposed redistricting plan. They discover that the unannounced purpose of the plan is to add more white students to predominantly black schools. Some members of the class find this purpose objectionable. The students also discover that through gerrymandering almost all neighborhood school boards will be controlled by whites, who constitute the voting majority in most of the proposed districts.

A number of black students, incensed by these findings, immediately report them to leaders of the black community. Other students develop alternate plans, some designed to increase integration and some designed to maximize black control of black schools. Two students, believing that the proposed plan is a reasonable compromise, wage a campaign urging voter support and testify at school board hearings. During the hearings other students man picket lines protesting the plan and distribute copies of their own proposals.

As the students work, they increase and verify their knowledge of political and social realities. Of necessity, they develop skills in mapping social data, in constructing questionnaires, in organizing groups, and in evaluating information. Students find themselves testing, and sometimes changing, their own beliefs and preferences.

Opportunities for further inquiry arise. The class receives a letter that reads: "Students have no business tampering with issues they don't understand. The business of the school is teaching, not reforming. Spending precious class time on a matter that is trivial when compared with studying the history of our country is irresponsible and unjustifiable. We parents believe your teacher is not meeting his obligations to us and to you, the students."

The class decides that the letter has opened a new and significant area of interest. Students examine socialization theory and consider the roles and the goals of public education. The children choose their own school for a case study.

Each scenario focuses on a social issue. Each scenario applies relevant knowledge from the social sciences. In each scenario values are clarified. Each includes an analysis of alternatives for action. Each defines and effects a course of action, and provides for examination of the outcomes of social action, a process that augments knowledge. In such learning experiences, social action can serve as a nucleus for a social studies program.

Goals for Social Action

To resolve social issues is only one reason, and indeed not the major reason, for incorporating social action into the social studies curriculum. The other reasons have to do with learning—with acquiring knowledge, developing skills, and modifying values.

Knowledge about society is necessary for human survival and therefore should be a primary consideration in any educational program. The vehicle through which knowledge is applied to solving social issues is social action. Engaging in social action permits pupils to learn more about an issue, to determine the validity and the usefulness of their knowledge, and to ascertain where more information is required.

Bruner has written about knowledge in the context of social problems:

"Let knowledge as it appears in our schooling be put into the context of action and commitment. The lawyer's brief, a parliamentary strategy, or a town planner's subtle balancings are as humanely important a way of knowing as a physicist's theorem. Gathering together the data for the indictment of a society that tolerates, in the United States, the ninth rank in infant mortality when it ranks first in gross national product—this is not an exercise in radical invective but in the mobilizing of knowledge in the interest of conviction that change is imperative" (4: 53, 67).

Skills are properly regarded as significant educational goals. A curriculum based on the resolution of social issues through social action enhances opportunities for the social studies program to develop a broad range of intellectual and social competencies. A curriculum that is targeted on resolving social issues through social action logically includes skills in making decisions, managing authority, implementing policy, communicating effectively, and participating in groups. Social action gives pupils an opportunity to develop and use these skills in the real world. Learning is not limited to the artificial confines of the classroom. As John S. Gibson has put it:

"If knowledge is to be put to effective use in society, the individual must be equipped with certain skills he can learn and apply as a result of education in the social studies. Skills provide the indispensable linkage between knowledge and behavior" (5: 22).

Values and social action appear to have a mutually supportive relationship. Commitment to certain values can trigger social action; in turn, the consequences of social action can provide a basis for examining and testing the soundness of one's beliefs. After an experience in social action, the pupil should be able to deal more effectively with questions such as: "Were the consequences of my action consistent with my values?" "Did anything happen that should cause me to re-examine my values?"

If the social studies classroom is to develop rational social actors, the teaching-learning process cannot be confined to the accumulation of knowledge and the intellectualization of beliefs. Only by acting on his values can the individual come to understand the social and the personal consequences of active participation in the affairs of society. Through social action, teachers can provide ample opportunities for the examination, the testing, the creation, and the modification of pupils' values as well as social norms.

We argue that:

1. A powerful relationship appears to exist between knowledge, skills, values, and social action.
2. Resolving social issues through social action is basic to social studies education.
3. Social action can serve as a nucleus for the integration of the social sciences and social issues in a social studies program.
4. The education of rational social actors is the purpose of social studies education.

It is not our intent to suggest that these ideas are final and definitive; rather we regard them as forays into new territory. It may not be time for a full-scale implementation of our proposal, but it is clearly time for a discussion and an investigation of the relationship between social issues, social action, and the social studies.

References

1. John Jarolimek. "Some Reflections on a Decade of Reform in Social Studies Education," *Journal of Geography, 69* (October, 1970), 388–89.
2. *A Directory of Research and Curriculum Projects in Social Studies Education.* Corte Madera, California: Marin County Social Studies Project, 1969.
3. Jerome S. Bruner. "Notes on Divisive Dichotomies," *The Alternative of Radicalism: Radical and Conservative Possibilities for Teaching the Teachers of America's Young Children.* Edited by Thomas R. Holland and Catherine M. Lee. Washington, D.C.: United States Office of Education, Tri-University Project in Elementary Education, 1969.
4. Jerome Bruner. "The Skill of Relevance or the Relevance of Skills," *Saturday Review, 53* (April 18, 1970), 66–68.
5. John S. Gibson. *New Frontiers in the Social Studies: Goals for Teachers, Means for Students.* New York: Citation Press, 1967.

Social Interaction and Urban Space

JAMES O. WHEELER

Man has organized his cities for particular social objectives. Viewed in this sense, his cities exist to facilitate social communications or interaction. At the same time, however, diverse social goals and group frictions create barriers to the smooth flow of information among urban dwellers, as communications take place within a spatially and socially restrictive network of interpersonal contact. This paper (1) introduces the theme of urban social interaction, (2) outlines the structure of social ties in cities, and (3) examines two major urban problems relating explicitly to social interaction: the urban freeway and the ghetto. As such, this paper seeks more to provide a broad geographical perspective of social interaction and its role in urban problems than to present hard analytic data based on empirical case study. The ideas put forth here are intended to give an increased insight into one way in which the geographer may usefully view the city and its social problems.

Spatial Structure of Social Connections

Many definitions have been advanced to explain what constitutes a city. Perhaps too many of these have given emphasis to the visible features of the urban landscape, such as land use, housing density, or the extent of sewerage lines. Too often it is overlooked that these are only the more obvious manifestations of a simple desire of man to live with other men for mutual benefits. People increasingly live in cities to achieve social and economic objectives which cannot as easily be obtained in a nonurban environment. Economists and others have viewed the city as a magnet attracting rural to urban migrants wishing to improve their economic level by living near desired employment opportunities. Implicit in such migration are the benefits accruing from accessibility to job locations. Concomitant with this increased economic interaction is a whole set of social interactions necessitated by the urban life style. The tremendous variety and opportunities for social contact within the city have given rise to a social structure

James O. Wheeler is a Professor in the Department of Geography at the University of Georgia, Athens.

Reprinted from *The Journal of Geography* 70(4):200–203, 1971, with permission of the National Council for Geographic Education and James O. Wheeler.

that sets the urban area apart from the rapidly contracting traditional agrarian social system.[1] In this context, one writer describes urbanity "as a property of the amount and the variety of one's participation in the cultural life of a world of creative specialists, of the amount and the variety of information received."[2] Since such participation and information receipt are maximized in the urban area via social interaction, one meaningful conceptualization of the city involves the nature, intensity, and extent of social interactions.

Although the city may be seen as a mechanism for facilitating information exchange through social communications, it is an imperfect mechanism when compared to some hypothetically optimal system of exchange. There are two principal limitations to the present-day city as it involves social interaction. Both are geographically based. The first is the inescapable and oppressive burden of space itself. Urban space imposes barriers between all its residents, but these are unequal barriers. The transportation route system itself is confined to specified portions of the city, creating spatial irregularity via circuity. The expense in time and money of crossing urban space is weighted against the anticipated advantages to be obtained at the trip's end. Much of the mobility differential between individuals or groups in the city relates to their evaluation of the trade-off between travel cost and the extra utility or satisfaction to be achieved at a more distant location. Many of the basic problems of the city as a social environment can be traced to an inequality among its residents in their ability to overcome urban space.

A second restraint on urban social interaction is status, especially as manifest among the social neighbohoods of the urban area. Numerous studies have documented the higher probability of social contact among those of similar socioeconomic level compared to individuals of unlike status. For example, a professional worker will have a decreasing probability of social contact as one goes down the socioeconomic scale. Because of the tendency of residential clustering of similar socioeconomic groups, neighborhood barriers are created, maintained, and intensified by intervening distance. The chance of a resident from a high income neighborhood having social contact with an individual living in a low income area is even less than the distance between such households would suggest. Thus differentiated by the diversity of human activities and the inequalities of man, urban space itself is rendered unequal.[3]

Many powerful social forces exist to maintain a cohesive and functional urban environment. Fundamental among these is the complementarity of

---

[1] Charles P. Loomis and J. Allan Beegle, *Rural Social Systems* (New York: Prentice-Hall, 1950), pp. 133–203.

[2] Melvin M. Webber, *et al., Explorations into Urban Structure* (Philadelphia: University of Pennsylvania Press, 1964), p. 88.

[3] Jean Canaux, "Social Aspects of the City," *Ekistics,* XXVII (March 1969), 178–180.

social roles. The basic social unit remains the family, in which the need for privacy, safety, and security underlies its preferences for individual dwellings. In addition to the family unit, with its desire for freedom to selectively pursue interpersonal contacts, are institutional units created to facilitate societal operation through formalized organization. These institutions are administered in large measure through a hierarchy of interpersonal contact, in part social and in part impersonal. The geographical concentration within cities of these organizations imposes a spatial clustering of interpersonal ties in which the participants normally have relatively little choice in selecting each other. Furthermore, these organizations have taken a dominant position in society relative to the family, now very small in relation to the institutional unit.[4] The net result is a pattern of interpersonal relations in which professional or job contacts, both personal and neutral, have come in part to replace emotional and intimate social ties. Social ties are thus often transitory and diffused among a large number of individuals.

In the typical small agrarian community of the past, by contrast, the probability that any individual would have contact with any other individual was fairly high, and under conditions of random connections it would not be too long until contact would be made with virtually all individuals in the small community. Everyone knew what everyone else was doing. However, social relations in the agrarian society were highly biased toward members of the extended family, and the intensity of social interaction was greatest with relatives. Due to the frequency of social contact, social barriers were erected when hostilities developed between individuals; because of the intense network of social ties, or clique development, individual antagonisms often would have group ramifications.

The spatial structure of social connections in the city may be summarized as frequent, both intimate and impersonal, and areally diffused. The role of the neighborhood remains strong, reflecting both the drop-off in contacts with distance and the status preference of its inhabitants. However, as the social network becomes more conditioned by institutional factors, the neighborhood role in social ties weakens. With increased mobility, it is possible to maintain friendships over greater distances. Status, promoted by institutional organization, is a paramount factor in social contact. The role of personality attributes, though little studied, is of particular interest within the urban context. Since the diversity of human activity in cities leads to the potential for numerous interpersonal contacts, the probability of personality complementarity occurring over a period of time between participants is relatively high, thus helping to explain the basis of intimate contact within a system of substantial impersonal ties. The large *quantity* of transitory and perfunctory contacts assists the selection process for developing *quality* social relations within cities.

[4] C. A. Doxiadis, "Social Synthesis in Human Settlement," *Ekistics,* XXVII (October 1969), 236–240.

Spatial Problems in Social Interaction

It is widely recognized in the literature of transportation geography that location and transportation are two sides of the same coin. For example, in selecting a residence one obtains both a site and a location. Just as no two sites are identical in amenities, no two locations will have the same accessibility because of the spatial structure of the physical city. Social interaction, dependent on the accessibility and connectivity of the social communications network, is associated with the spatial arrangement of both the physical and social structure of the metropolitan area. How does the physical and social structure of the city affect one's actual choices of social contact?

One of the most striking illustrations of the impact of changing physical arrangements on social ties is the urban freeway, at once an impetus and a barrier to movement. The urban freeway system to a considerable extent is built in response to the desire for individual accessibility to the major institutional units and activity nodes of the city. Only secondarily does it connect households to facilitate social contact. The freeway has been accused of primarily serving the mobility needs of surburban residents and thereby maintaining their neighborhood stability at the expense of destroying the stability of inner city neighborhoods, which are either physically displaced or fragmented by freeway location.[5] Moreover, since inner city areas tend to have the lowest per capita ownership of automobiles, the residents of the "old" city are least likely to effectively utilize the freeway, whether to gain access to the growing job potential in the suburbs or to move about the urban area for social travel. The transit system in most cities has been similarly criticized, as it makes accessible only restricted parts of the metropolitan area.

The urban freeway system clearly serves the mobility needs of various social groups in the city differently. Higher income suburban residents not only have access to jobs and entertainment in the central business district but they also have ready connections to most other suburban areas, especially via circumferential freeway links. In contrast, inner city residents undertaking social travel must rely largely on the traditional street pattern in their multi-directional travel needs. The result is a more restricted area for carrying out social interaction. Even though the frequency of interpersonal contact might be similar for the high versus low status individual, the latter is more geographically confined in his choice of contacts to like social status groups. For the high status resident, his social contacts are more biased by status preferences than limited by urban space.

[5] Alan Altshuler, "The Values of Urban Transportation Policy," in *Transportation and Community Values,* Special Report 105, Highway Research Board (Washington, D.C.: Government Printing Office, 1969), pp. 75–86.

There has been increasing criticism and opposition in the United States to the construction of the urban freeway system, of which nearly 6,000 miles are yet to be built through urban areas. A large part of the opposition comes from minority and other inner city groups whose value system appears to be less oriented to access to activities than to access to people. Those with whom social ties are most desired live nearby in the same general part of the city and may be members of the same minority groups. Hence a proposed freeway is a threat both to one's precarious economic resources and to his valued sense of community and territorial control. Members of minority groups, such as blacks, achieve personal identity and recognition not so much through the powerful institutional units controlled by the white majority as they do through the social network within their own neighborhood. Residential displacement necessitated by freeway construction may be adversely perceived not only because of the economic gain or loss but also because of rending apart the social fabric of a neighborhood. In short, the freeway serves the important social and economic needs of the suburban resident, who strives for personal identity and recognition within an institutional framework spatially linked by the freeway system. For an inner city resident, especially if a member of a minority group, the freeway is a threat imposed by an "establishment" that does not understand his spatial needs for achieving personal satisfaction through social identity.

In addition to the role of the physical structure of the city in affecting social contact, the social structure of urban space exerts a fundamental influence. Members of a social group, because of intra-group communication and access to common channels of information, tend to hold similar values which may be manifest in like behavior patterns. Such information flow through social interaction is basic to group formation and maintenance. Common problems and pressures of a racial or socioeconomic status group affect its receptivity to certain kinds of information. Whereas different social status groups may generate disparate value systems, other mechanisms maintain broad patterns of similarities among groups. For example, to the extent that one participates in a variety of roles, he will have multiple channels of information through different kinds of interpersonal contact. Thus people are basically the same, except that they are members of different social, racial, or ethnic groups, perform varied roles, live in different parts of the metropolitan area, are at various stages of the family life cycle, and therefore tend to hold values consistent with the social communication network of which they are a part.

The role of social structure in interpersonal contact and information receipt is best described by the problem of racial discrimination, which results in the spatial segregation of residence and other activities. Most of all in this case, the social interaction of the racial minority is directed inward and largely blocked from outside influences. A geographically closed system of social interaction operates. Likewise, the suburban majority may have virtually no contact with members of the minority. Not only may values between these groups become divergent, but there is little mechanism for mutual understanding to develop. Although the racial minority has a spatial awareness of a large portion of the city, the group is significantly limited in its normal area of contact within urban space by discriminatory attitudes. A black's lack of interaction with an all-white suburb may not be because he has no information as to its existence or location.

In response to white hostility, black ghettos have also developed their own institutional structure, in which the church has played a prominent role.[6] The location of the black churches within the ghetto has fostered a further areal concentration of social interaction. The various churches, often reflecting a degree of social stratification within the black community, serve as an institution for maintaining social differentiation within a group whose preferences for residential status cannot always be achieved throughout the metropolitan area. In this context, it is a serious error to regard the black ghetto as homogeneous socially: in fact status barriers, as well as distance, impose a considerable influence on the patterns of social interaction.

Conclusions

Just as land use in the city is differentiated by economic function and dependent upon accessibility, urban social units are also spread over the city and functionally tied by patterns of social communications. The city, an agglomeration of people and organizational points, is a "derivative of the communications patterns of the individuals and groups that inhabit it." [7] The savings in communication costs resulting from population clustering are the modern city's greatest social asset; the inequality of social interaction associated with the spatially articulated network of communications is related to the basic social frictions and hostilities in the modern city. Since the city functions as a spatial complex, it is hoped that an appreciation of the geography of social communications gains insights into some of the uses and misuses of urban space.

[6] Allan H. Spear, *Black Chicago: The Making of a Negro Ghetto, 1890–1920* (Chicago: University of Chicago Press, 1967).

[7] Melvin M. Webber, "Order in Diversity: Community without Propinquity," in in Lowdon Wingo, Jr. (ed), *Cities and Space: The Future Use of Urban Land* (Baltimore: The Johns Hopkins Press, 1963), p. 31.

Social Studies in the Open Classroom

VITO PERRONE AND LOWELL THOMPSON

Interest in open education has grown enormously over the past three years. As an educational movement it has reached a state where responsible educators must examine it seriously. Reforms in the British primary schools are to some degree responsible for the interest in Open Education in the United States. But to a larger degree, interest is growing because of the belief that schools are failing children. The critique that schools are responsible for the "mutilation of the child's spirit . . . of spontaneity, of joy of learning, of pleasure in creating, of a sense of self"; as places that are too often "grim, joyless . . . oppressive and petty . . . intellectually sterile and esthetically barren . . . lacking in creativity . . . ,"[1] is finding an increasingly responsive audience.

That such a critique is gaining support must discourage many educators who have, over the past decade, devoted so much energy to curriculum reform. Excellent materials have been produced and are being used successfully in *some* schools by *some* teachers and children. But they have brought little change of significance to *most* teachers and children. Silberman noted that while there is considerable discussion about such things as the structure of the disciplines, learning how to learn, developing basic concepts and "postholing," the reality is that "the great bulk of students' time is still devoted to detail, most of it trivial . . . and almost all of it unrelated to any concept, structure, cognitive strategy . . ."[2] John Goodlad reported recently, on the basis of his rather extensive study of the elementary school, that:

> Rarely did we find small groups intensely involved in the pursuit of knowledge . . . rarely did we find individual pupils at work in self-sustaining inquiry . . . we are forced to conclude that much of the so-called educational reform movement has been blunted on the classroom door.[3]

The basis for the curriculum reform efforts—from mathematics and science to the social studies—was the sense that enormous gaps existed

Vito Perrone is Dean of the Center for Teaching and Learning, University of North Dakota, Grand Forks; Lowell Thompson is an Assistant Professor of Social Studies at the Center, University of North Dakota, Grand Forks.

Reprinted from *Social Education 36*(4):460–464, 1972, with permission of the National Council for the Social Studies and Vito Perrone and Lowell Thompson.

[1] Silberman, Charles, *Crisis in the Classroom* (New York: Random House, 1970), p. 10.

[2] *Ibid.*, p. 172.

[3] Goodlad, John, "The Schools vs. Education," *Saturday Review*, April 19, 1969.

between what was known and what was part of the existing school program. It became more than that. Inquiry (and/or discovery) became the key teaching-learning strategy in the reform movement. As Jerome Bruner said: "The ideal was clarity and self-direction of intellect in the use of modern knowledge." [4] Unfortunately, curriculum reformers assumed that children—regardless of ethnic, economic, or social background—would be motivated to learn as a result of new curricula. That the school as an institution needed significant changing was not sufficiently questioned.

As a part of the New Social Studies, concern about fostering the values of democracy increased greatly. Reading materials became relevant to contemporary issues. Minority people found their way into the curriculum. America's political and social institutions were dealt with more critically. At the same time, schools remained fundamentally authoritarian institutions. It seems abundantly clear today that such institutions do not encourage initiative and responsibility. Sensitivity and a belief in the dignity of the individual are not taught in settings where children are not treated with dignity. A sense of community is not fostered in settings where competition is paramount, where failure is expected, where alienation is encouraged. Personal value systems are not extended in settings where children do not confront situations that require judgments and decisions, where a variety of learning options are not available.

In many ways Open Education, unlike the curriculum reform of the past decade, is raising questions about the nature of childhood, learning, and the quality of personal relationships among teachers and children. It challenges many assumptions about schooling, its organization, and its purpose. Rather than develop an extended philosophic statement on Open Education,[5] we have chosen to provide here only a brief outline to establish

---

[4] Bruner, Jerome, "The Process of Education Reconsidered," Address, 26th Annual ASCD Conference, St. Louis, Missouri, March 6–10, 1971.

[5] For a more extensive background on Open Education, readers are directed to: Barth, Roland, *Open Education,* unpublished Doctoral Dissertation (Harvard Graduate School of Education, 1970); Blackie, John, *Inside the Primary School* (New York: Schocken Books, 1971); Featherstone, Joseph, *Schools Where Children Learn* (New York: Liveright, 1971); Hertzberg, Alvin and Stone, Edward F., *Schools Are for Children* (New York: Schocken Books, 1971); Hawkins, Francis, *The Logic of Action* (Boulder: University of Colorado, 1969); Marshall, Sybil, *Adventure in Creative Education* (London: Pergamon Press, 1968); Murrow, Casey and Liza, *Children Come First* (New York: American Heritage Press, 1971); Plowden, Lady Bridget, et al., *Children and Their Primary Schools: A Report of the Central Advisory Council for Education* (London: Her Majesty's Stationery Office, 1966); Richardson, Elwyn S., *In the Early World* (New York: Pantheon, 1969); Rogers, Vincent, *Teaching in the British Primary School* (New York: Macmillan, Inc., 1970); Silberman, Charles, *Crisis in the Classroom* (New York: Random House, 1970); Vermont State Department of Education, *Vermont Design for Education* (Montpelier: State Dept. of Education, 1968); Weber, Lillian, *The English Infant School* (Englewood Cliffs, New Jersey: Prentice-Hall, 1971); Yeomans, Edward, *Education for Initiative and Responsibility* (Boston: National Assoc. of Ind. Schools, 1967). An extended annotated bibliography is available from Educational Development Center, Newton, Massachusetts.

a context for our discussion of the social studies. The major curriculum concern in the open classroom is not so much the specific content of instruction as it is *the process* by which it is taught and the conditions under which children learn. In this regard, we believe that it is particularly important that:

Children be able to initiate activities, that they are self-directing and able to take responsibility for their own learning.

Children exhibit intense involvement, where their curiosity leads to concern and commitment.

Children continue to wonder and imagine.

Children are willing to face uncertainty and change in the process, be able to cope with complexities they have not specifically been taught to manage.

Children are open, honest, and respectful of themselves, adults, and other children, and are learning responsibility as an integral part of freedom.

Classrooms that are responsive to the foregoing will and should develop their own unique character. Still, they tend to have many common attributes. The following is a list of characteristics which we look upon as important:

1. An atmosphere of mutual trust and respect among teachers and children.

2. The teacher acts as guide, advisor, observer, provisioner, and catalyst, constantly seeking ways to extend children in their learning. The teacher views himself as an active learner and typically works without a predetermined, set curriculum.[6]

3. A wise assortment of materials for children to manipulate, construct, explore, etc., thus providing rich opportunities to learn from experience. Materials will have diversity and range with very little replication.[7]

4. Learning through play, games, simulations, and other autotelic activities is legitimized. Childhood is respected.

5. Activities arise often from the interests children bring with them to school.

6. Children are able to pursue an interest deeply in a setting where there is frequently a variety of activities going on simultaneously.

[6] We have found that the open classroom makes increased psychological demands on teachers. It also provides, as "compensation," enlarged opportunities for intellectual stimulation. Assuming the role of a learner with children frees the teacher from many of the traditional constraints of knower and dispenser of information. The teacher is more free to bring his interests into the classroom where they, too, can be extended.

[7] Much of what has come out of the New Social Studies efforts is especially helpful in open classrooms because of the inquiry base and open-ended character. We have seldom recommended any one program, generally encouraging small quantities of materials from several programs and assisting teachers in gaining understanding about their use—not only that intended but the possibilities for integration with other areas of learning.

7. There are few barriers between subject matter areas and a minimum of restrictions determined by the clock, thus providing a fluid schedule that permits more natural beginning and ending points for a child's learning activities.
8. Children's learning is frequently a cooperative enterprise marked by children's conversations with each other.
9. Older children frequently assist younger children in their learning.
10. Parents participate at a high level in the classroom sharing in children's learning. They also assist children outside the classroom where much of the children's learning takes place.
11. Emphasis is on communication, including the expressive and creative arts.

What must be readily apparent from a review of the foregoing classroom characteristics is that social studies, whether history, geography, political science, anthropology, or economics, is not looked upon as a discrete area separate from reading, language arts, science, mathematics, art, and music. The use of a single textbook doesn't fit. A curriculum that outlines specifically what will be studied at each grade level does not confront openly children's questions, concerns, and views of reality.

Teachers in open classrooms constantly look for starting points. In addition, they develop themes which have the potential for sustained interest and individuality. What are the possibilities around a theme of *printing?* Hertzberg and Stone described the activities they observed in an English primary school.

Some children were spending much time in school and local libraries, finding out how books are printed. Others were attempting to restore an old printing press brought by the teacher. Illuminated manuscripts were being examined; technology was being discussed; a small group decided to print its own newspaper . . .[8]

Children's interests in printing carried them to silk-screening, wood-block printing, potato printing, studies in advertising, alphabet system, Egyptian hieroglyphics, and the Gutenberg Bible. The theme had been under study for a month. The possibilities for continued extension appear limited only by the imagination of children and teacher.

Social studies activities vary from classroom-to-classroom because so much depends upon the children's interests and the enthusiasm of teachers and their knowledge of the varied resources existing in the local environment. It is common, however, to see themes develop around such topics as:

[8] Hertzberg, Alvin and Stone, Edward F. *Schools Are for Children* (New York: Schocken Books, 1971), pp. 129–130. Hertzberg and Stone have an interesting chapter related to "Steps toward Openness in Social Studies" that may be helpful to teachers in elementary schools.

what people do, how people take responsibility, what life was like in earlier days (a good base for oral history), people's beliefs about war, recreation, education. It is also common to focus on human relationships. While there may be a serious class study of another country—Mexico, for example—and the room has been provisioned with maps, posters, records, films, and filmstrips, individual children's study will tend to focus on a small aspect of life. We have worked with classrooms in which some children were involved in exchanges of audio-tapes, art work, and drafts with children in Mexico City; others were preparing dramatizations of stories they had read about Mexican children. Mexican food was prepared, games played by Mexican children were learned, music popular in Mexico was available, a variety of children were learning Mexican folk dances, and Spanish was being learned through elementary language topics. Obviously, these children were *actively* involved in their learning.

How do children organize for learning in an open classroom? Individually or in small groups, children plan, along with the teacher, what they are going to study. They attempt to raise questions they are interested in pursuing. They begin to identify the resource materials they need and consider community resources that may be helpful to them. They may also plan ways of sharing their discoveries with their classmates through activities such as a dramatization, slide and tape presentation, or by developing a game or simulation that could be played by the class. They might also plan to meet with the teacher periodically to review their progress. Equipping the classroom to extend individual children's learning becomes a crucial task for the teacher. It is not uncommon to see mathematics, science, or language arts become an integral part of a child's project. The open classroom, in essence, encourages children to become significantly involved in planning what they are going to learn and how they are going to learn it. This balance between the content to be learned and the planning by students is central to much of what happens in an open classroom, especially at the intermediate level. Gordon, in his detailed analysis of the Coleman report, indicated that:

> In addition to the *school* characteristics which were shown to be related to pupil achievement, Coleman found a *pupil* characteristic which appears to have a stronger relationship to achievement than all the school factors combined. The extent to which a pupil feels he has control over his own destiny is strongly related to achievement.[9]

If a student is told what he is to learn, how he is to learn it, when his learning will terminate, and what grade he will receive, one could expect a situation that contributes little to a child's sense of efficacy. If, on the other hand, a student is involved in the planning of his learning and, more im-

---

[9] Gordon, ·Edmund, *JACD Bulletin,* Ferkauf Graduate School, Yeshiva University (Vol. !II, No. 5, November, 1967).

portantly, in the process of evaluating his own growth, one can more readily expect to find the kind of achievement suggested by Gordon.

Meaningful Experiences

The starting points for meaningful classroom experiences may grow organically out of a particular experience the class has had; for example, a field trip, a classroom discussion, a conversation with a friend, or something as simple as an object a student brought to school to share. A group of nine- and ten-year-old-children in Fargo, North Dakota, turned a story they read together into a house-building experience. The story, about a class which built a clubhouse, prompted a similar idea—the class would build one of its own. Children greeted the idea with such enthusiasm that some visited a lumberyard and arranged to get some old plywood. They developed rather elaborate plans which involved measurement and geometry. An architect demonstrated model making, which the children then tried. They viewed a variety of films on house building. A tape-recorded lesson taught them about tools—the lever, plane, and gear. Retired carpenters in the community provided additional demonstrations. Individual children pursued many different interests in relation to the house-building project. They wrote letters telling others of their experiences. They engaged in individual projects involving Indian homes, termites, trees, creatures who live in trees, homes around the world, workers who build homes, old and modern tools, skyscrapers, doll houses, and, of course, they built the 10′ × 8′ × 6′ clubhouse. They gave a party to thank parents and others who had helped, and presented their construction to the younger children in the school for use during recess.

Students not only have chances to structure their own learning experiences through this type of approach, but they are also able to approach learning in a more unified way, without the narrow and sometimes artificial categories of mathematics, science, English, and social studies impinging on the breadth of their possible learning experience.

Another example of the breadth of experience inherent in a seemingly inconsequential experience involved a junk motor from a Renault automobile. The motor was brought into a fourth- and fifth-grade classroom, and several boys began to take it apart. Before they were through, they learned not only the principle of the internal combustion engine, but also developed a vocabulary of key words like piston, head, cylinder, carburetor, etc. (spelling); wrote several letters requesting information on the motor (language arts); had read parts of several repair manuals (reading); had learned about fractions, the metric system, and cubic measure (mathematics); had learned something about levers and gears, power, and gases (science); and had learned certain things about France, its people, and the Renault Automobile Company, which had developed a car that set an auto speed record (social studies). These boys were "turned on" to learning, and as John Lubbock has said: "The important thing is not so much that every child should be taught, as that every child should be given the wish to learn."

"Brotherhood" became the focus for a group of sixth-grade youngsters in Minot, North Dakota. The range of activities pursued by individual children included: biographical study of individuals like Martin Luther King, Ralph Bunche, and Eleanor Roosevelt; reasons for racial discrimination; simulations on race relations; the Indians in North Dakota; new towns and integration; bias in reading materials; stereotyping; television and cultural bias; ways of promoting better relations among children in the classroom, in the school, and visual montages of man's varied relations with others.

Interest in Open Education has influenced quite directly the approach being taken by the State Department of Public Instruction in rewriting the North Dakota Social Studies Curriculum Guide. The new guide will be less prescriptive than the old and its major focus will be upon teaching-learning strategies in preference to the more traditional scope and sequence orientation of state courses of study. The content of the social studies, then, will be determined by individual communities, schools, and teachers. This type of guide, it is anticipated, will encourage local communities and their teachers to think through and to organize the kind of social studies program that appears most appropriate.

The Department of Public Instruction will make available printed materials and human resources to individual communities and teachers as they forge ahead in the task of developing individual (and individualized) curricula. The task of the Department becomes one of assisting each community in developing a social studies program which capitalizes on the competence and creativity of each teacher, the interests of individual children, the richness of community resources, and the perceived needs of individual communities.

Much more could be said about social studies in the open classroom, especially with regard to the use of the local community as a base for intensive study. This, however, is another article. We have attempted here only to introduce the open classroom, some of its dimensions—starting with children's interests, the need for children to be actively involved in all aspects of their learning, from planning to evaluation—and its concerns for an integrative quality curriculum rather than the linear, formally-organized curriculum so familiar to most of us.

Understanding Others—Humanities and Art Project

EDITH W. KING

Many teachers are presently working to help their classes perceive the world as a multi-nation whole—now we must couple this with "world-mindedness" or a defined sense of global responsibility. Children need to become sensitive to the needs of others not only intellectually but emotionally, appreciating both the cultural likenesses and diversities of the world of people that surround them. Studies of the Eskimo, the Kalahari Desert people, or the Pygmy can show how these groups use their ingenuity and special talents to adapt to and express their environment, but we must not present them as strange people in faraway places, carrying out peculiar customs, eating queer foods, dressing like barbarians, covered with paint and tattoos.

Highlighting Commonalities

The arts and humanities are ideal for achieving goals for teaching world-mindedness, through both the commonalities and diversities of other cultures. The commonalities should come first, and as William Schuman, president of the Lincoln Center for the Performing Arts, New York City, has pointed out, the arts are crucial to understanding the complex world society in which we live. Writing in "Cultivating Student Taste" (*Today's Education,* November, 1968), he said, "For educators not to grasp the vitality, the spirituality, and the intellectuality of art as central to an educated man is to ignore the measure by which our civilization will be judged."

Music, art, literature, and drama know no national or cultural boundaries. The common expressions of human feeling found in these forms develop children's capacities to identify with other groups, other societies, and indeed, the totality of mankind.

Edith W. King is an Associate Professor of Education at Denver University, Colorado.

From *Instructor* 79:65–66, 1969. Reprinted from *Instructor,* © October 1969, The Instructor Publications, Inc., used by permission of the publisher and Edith W. King.

445

Awareness of Diversity

The cause of worldmindedness is also served by children's recognition of the diversities of the human condition. Aesthetic experiences can be utilized to create this awareness of cultural diversity, providing both understanding and appreciation. Doing a dance, examining a craft, hearing a fable or story —all demonstrate the logic and feeling of others even though they live thousands of miles away, or lived hundreds of years in the past.

Diversity should be thought of as adaptation rather than strangeness or queerness. It is healthy for children to ask why about any cultural expression that differs from their own, but instead of supercilious inquiries, their questions should prompt real in-depth research to find the answers.

Getting Perspective

In presenting both commonalities and diversities, we should help children realize that as the world becomes a multi-nation whole, commonalities tend to increase and diversities diminish. Cultures overlap, and art, music, and literature reflect merging influences. For this reason, communities especially try to preserve distinctive qualities of cultural patterns in dress and foods that are no longer relevant but still very characteristic. Children might look for examples of this, such as wooden shoes in the Netherlands, feather headdresses among the Indians, and perhaps, eventually, the kimono in Japan.

Development of an international set of road signs and other symbols is an example of worldmindedness or commonality being considered more important than preserving national customs. Children should also hunt other examples of this.

The more ways your class can experience the cultural expressions and patterns of living of other peoples around the world, the more likely they are to identify with them easily. In addition to sampling their art, music, and literature, they should taste their foods, play their games, and try out their customs. These activities are just as relevant as learning a country's latitude and longitude, its population, or the amount of rainfall.

Music

Music especially "opens the heart" to warm, friendly feelings and identification with all humanity. Children delight in discovering that people all over the world sing about many of the same things—love, building a home, pets, jobs, the beauty of nature around them. The bibliography "Music for Developing Cultural Pluralism" found in the appendices of *The Sociology of Early Childhood Education* by King and Kerber (American Book Co.) will help you develop a program with your class.

Music especially should lead pupils to sense the universality of human experiences. For instance, young children can be helped to enter the life space of children from other cultures through hearing and singing lullabies. Everywhere around the globe, mothers sing to their babies. In France—"Go to sleep, baby. Mama is up high baking a cake. Papa is below making chocolate" (*Fais, Do, Do*); in Nigeria, "Go to sleep, baby, like the monkey in the tree. Safe in his mother's arm" (*Sleep, My Baby*); in Spain, "Sleep, my baby, among the roses, while your mother goes to buy you flowers" (*Hala Nananita*); in Israel, "By the lake of Kinneret, all is still because the teacher is reading the Book" (*Altzvat Yam Kinneret*). Each of those lines tells children something important about the culture of the country from which it comes.

What kind of music do people dance to? march to? use to praise God? These are only a few of other areas children can explore.

Ideas for expanding the concept of worldmindedness are certainly available in museum displays. Exhibits of artifacts from a country during particular periods of its history often focus on daily activities, family life, and religious and ceremonial occasions. Appropriate films or slides of art work of certain cultures or historical periods (usually available from museums and galleries for loan or rental) can further suggest to children concrete examples of the commonalities and diversities of various world cultures, yesterday and today.

Audiovisual materials designed to present concepts in areas other than the fine arts often utilize art work to get across similar ideas. One example of such a film is *Children Who Draw Pictures* (Brandon Films, Inc.), a sensitive movie focusing on young Japanese children's drawings as an outgrowth of their daily classroom studies. The film, designed to present concepts in child psychology, supports the idea that art is a mode of communication, and that young children express their thoughts and feelings through drawing, no matter what country they are from.

A principal from North Bend, Oregon, reports using the film *Four Artists Paint a Tree* (from Walt Disney, distributed by Buena Vista Distribution Co., Inc.) to emphasize that all people, of the same or different origins, see a tree (or any experience) from their own viewpoint. He also asked pupils to illustrate the film *A Place in the Sun* (Encyclopedia Britannica Educational Corporation) with chalk and cut paper. The captions indicate what these pupils learned about human relationships from the film and even from their own experiences.

The UNICEF *1969 Wall Calendar for Children* features children's art from around the world. Pupils will see that scenes depicted are very similar to their own experiences.

Literature

Perhaps one of the most meaningful ways for children to become acquainted with the literature of another country is through listening to folk and other stories told by a person from that country. College teachers and students, high-school exchange students, and others are usually willing to help. *Stories to Tell to Children* (Carnegie Library of Pittsburgh) has a comprehensive listing, by countries, of folk tales which pupils may enjoy reading, or even telling themselves.

Looking at America as a multicultural society, with many subgroups that draw their customs from countries around the globe, may also be an entirely new idea to pupils. We are a multicultural nation and this is reflected in the practices of our daily life.

Perhaps an occasion to discuss East Indians (or Japanese or Russians or Swedes) living in this country will arise because a new family moves into the area, a child transfers to your school, or a touring company brings a performance to your vicinity. For older elementary pupils, the *In America* series (Lerner Publications) provides in-depth material for discussions on customs, foods, problems encountered by people from other countries who settle here, and so on.

Similarly, children reading and then acting out a play from and about life in a particular country can gain insights into the pluralistic nature of man's ways. They can get in-depth knowledge about life styles, traditions, and great literature.

The IQ Debate

LILLIAN ZACH

Intelligence testing, from basis to implications, continues to be the center of heated debate. Despite a history which is almost three quarters of a century long and despite the fact that the IQ is by now a household term in America, mental tests are still reeling under the impact of criticisms which term them, among other things, invalid, misleading, and based upon false assumptions of human development.

In a highly controversial article published in December 1969, Arthur Jensen, a professor at the University of California at Berkeley, proposed that compensatory education failed to raise the IQ of black children because of a biological difference in the way these children learn. The topic became incendiary; psychological, educational, political, and racist groups began interpreting the data to suit their views. Arguments and criticism continue. Yet, unquestionably, the Stanford-Binet, the Wechsler Scales, and certain group tests do provide useful information, and the tests remain the most relied-on source for sorting children according to their presumed learning ability. Is it any wonder that teachers are uncertain what to believe about intelligence testing?

Binet's original intent was to develop an instrument to determine which children in Paris were retarded and in need of special education. In 1905, he produced the first Binet scale, designed to measure a retarded child's intelligence and compare it to the intelligence of normal children the same age. There was no attempt to determine whether the child's retarded learning was genetic or curable.

In 1912, German psychologist Wilhelm Stern suggested that one could express the developmental level, or mental age, of a given child as the age at which the average child achieved equivalent ability. If mental age (MA) were used as a ratio to the child's chronological age (CA), one could arrive at a brightness index, now called the Intelligence Quotient (IQ).

Like Binet, Stern did not claim that the test measured inborn capacity. In 1914, he wrote, "No series of tests, however skillfully selected it may be, does reach the innate intellectual endowment, stripped of all complications, but rather this endowment, in conjunction with all influences to which the

Lillian Zach is an Associate Professor of Psychology and Education at the Ferkauf Graduate School of Humanities and Social Sciences, Yeshiva University, New York City.

Reprinted from *Today's Education* 61:40–43 ff., 1972, with permission of the National Education Association and Lillian Zach.

examinee has been subjected up to the moment of testing. And it is just these external influences that are different in the lower social classes. Children of higher social status are much more often in the company of adults, are stimulated in manifold ways, are busy in play and amusement with things that require thinking, acquire a totally different vocabulary, and receive better school instruction. All this must bring it about that they meet the demands of the test better than children of the uncultured classes." But H. H. Goddard, who brought the test to America in 1910, had a very different viewpoint. Dr. Goddard translated the test into English for use at the Vineland Training School for the mentally defective. Perhaps it was an act of fate that the man who brought mental testing to this country was someone who emphasized the importance of heredity on human behavior.

Goddard was working with grossly defective children, and one can speculate that he was probably not convinced they could be educated. (Further, the chances are they were biologically defective as well as mentally retarded.) Goddard became intrigued with the notion that, being able to measure innate intelligence, we had the means for a sweeping program of social reform, with every man working on his own mental level. Soon, mental testing was adopted in every training school and teachers college in the country. Few stopped to consider that perhaps the innate intelligence which Goddard postulated and the intelligence measured by the test were not the same. Shortly thereafter, in 1916, L. M. Terman revised the Binet Scale at Stanford University to give birth to the Stanford-Binet, the standard of today's intelligence test. The test was revised and updated in 1937 and 1960. The rapid growth of compulsory education in the United States required some means to identify the intellectual capacities of pupils in the schools, and the Stanford-Binet seemed to fill the bill.

When the intelligence test is evaluated solely in terms of its value to meet specifically defined, immediate situations, its usefulness has proven itself. A good case in point can be seen in its use since the start of World War I to screen men for the armed forces. In these instances, the mental test has provided the means for appraising what an individual could do, here and now, as the product of his biological inheritance and his training and background.

But as testing proliferated, some problems became apparent. Testing in America was growing along two separate paths. One was in the real world of the school, the armed forces, and the industrial plant. The other was in the halls of academe, where the basic theoretical issues of intelligence were not yet settled. This lack of a universally accepted theoretical framework led to the anomolous situation in which intelligence is defined as that which intelligence tests test.

Herein lies a dilemma: Intelligence was only vaguely defined by the test maker, but the tests were used to define intelligence. This is perhaps the greatest failure of the testing movement in the United States. The pragmatic value of the mental test is undiminished. Test scores are good indicators of functioning abilities as long as their limitations are clearly understood, but these scores should not be used outside of their immediate significance. The failure lies not in the mental tests themselves, but in the perversion of the test results by investigators and social philosophers who use numbers in support of particular far-reaching positions. It is unfair both to the person tested and to the test itself to say that the scores of any one individual represent support for broad statements concerning human development.

There is nothing inherently wrong with practical definitions as long as they are clearly understood. The tests, after all, were developed to measure those aspects of human behavior which correlate well with scholastic achievement. In order to succeed in school, an individual must demonstrate certain types of abilities. If we develop tests to measure these abilities and if they prove to be valid and reliable instruments, we are measuring some form of intellectual ability. But if we lose sight of what we are measuring and if we claim for the test qualities for which it was never intended, we can be led into invalid implications.

The IQ, like the MA, is nothing but a score. The IQ indicates a child's performance on a test in the same way that a score of 80 on an arithmetic test does, except that intelligence tests purport to measure more general learning skills. Further, the scores merely reflect the child's performance on a specific test at a given time. The difference between the IQ and other test scores is that intelligence tests are standardized. Standardization means that the same test items are developed and revised on a large group, representative of the population for whom the test is designed—U.S. elementary school students, for example. Standardization also requires that the same test be administered under the same carefully controlled conditions to all who take the test. This means that a given child's score can be compared with scores obtained by other children of the same age on whom the test was originally standardized. It also permits prediction of the chances that in later testing a given child will obtain a score which is close to the original score, and further, to what extent a given child's performance is the result of the construction of the test rather than his own ability.

In order to interpret the results of standardized tests, certain fundamental assumptions are implicit. It is assumed, for example, that test norms are fair, since they are based on a representative national sampling of children. But this does not take into consideration the fact that the national sample is weighted heavily by average white children.

Since the mental test purports to measure basic learning capacities, it is also assumed that the items which make up the test are of two types—information which for the most part all children have been exposed to or situations to which no one has been exposed.

For items based upon supposedly equal opportunities of exposure, it is possible to reason that a child who has learned what he has been exposed to is bright; one who has not done so is not bright. Observation tells us that this does not have to be true.

In my own testing experiences, I found that many black children who had just come North gave a response to the question, "Who discovered America?" the answer, "Abraham Lincoln." The response is obviously wrong and adds no points to the IQ score. But does this response mean that this child has no ability to learn or does it merely reflect the child's background? In certain ways, the answer could be considered a meaningful and pertinent response.

For items to which no one has been exposed and which therefore demand "on the spot" learning, similar problems arise. Usually, tests try to utilize nonverbal materials like blocks and puzzles as a way of minimizing factors like education and experience. But these are not equally novel experiences for all children. Many youngsters are familiar with educational toys long before they enter school. (Even more important, and less easy to identify, are factors related to "learning to learn" and test-taking abilities.)

Another assumption is that the mental test is a sampling of behaviors which directly reflect the general capacity for learning. Actually, all available intelligence tests are direct measures only of achievement in learning. We wrongly equate the inferences from scores on IQ tests to some native inherent trait. Many persons think of intelligence as a discrete dimension existing within the individual and believe that different people have different amounts of it. In a certain sense this is true, but one's intelligence is not a characteristic of a person so much as it is a characteristic of the person's behavior. We can only hope to measure or observe manifestations of it.

It is also not possible to add up the elements of someone's intelligence in the same way that you can count the number of fingers on his hand. Although two people can have the same IQ score, they may demonstrate quite different abilities by virtue of the fact that they succeeded on different parts of the test. All too often, undue weight is given to an IQ score, although numerical assignment of a child to a man-made concept, untied to real characteristics of the child, tells us very little. Even more unfortunate, parents and some teachers are led to believe that the IQ concept has deeper significance than its meaning as a score.

Unquestioning faith in descriptive concepts reaches the height of absurdity in the notion of overachievers—a word used to describe children whose classroom performance is higher than their IQ scores would predict. The concept makes no sense at all because it says, in effect, that although these children are achieving, they do not have the ability to do so. Their success is laid to other factors, such as motivation. It's like telling the child who had the highest batting average in the Little League that, on the basis of batting practice, he's really a very poor hitter. He only did it because he wanted to.

The danger in a meaningless concept like overachieving is that children so designated may not receive as positive a recommendation for college as other children with the same grades but higher IQ scores. Few stop to consider that the methods used to judge ability must have been inadequate and that terms like IQ, MA, and overachievement are man-made.

In view of all the drawbacks, one might reasonably ask, then, why do we continue using mental tests? Even though many have argued for abandoning them, most psychologists still feel that they have value. In most cases, we can describe, evaluate, and even predict certain kinds of behavior much better with tests than without them. The paradox exists that most psychologists, who were responsible for the tests, have never given them as much weight as those in schools and industries who use and misuse them.

While various practical problems were being confronted, the academic world of psychology was still trying to resolve many basic issues about intelligence testing. One of these, the focus of several decades of research, concerned the whole heredity-environment controversy—the battle over nature versus nurture.

Not all psychologists in America were convinced that the IQ was the highly predictive, hereditarily determined measure it was held to be by Goddard and his followers. It wasn't long before studies were reported which demonstrated that not only was the IQ not fixed but that it could be altered with training, experience, and changes in adjustment patterns.

Although research was reported from all over the nation to support one or the other position, two distinct battle camps could be located. One group, at the University of Iowa, came to be known as the environmentalists. The other, at Stanford University, supported the significance of heredity. After a while, it seemed as if the heredity-environment controversy had settled down into a comfortable compromise: Most people were content to accept the notion that the IQ is the result of the interaction between the gene structure and the environment.

Everyone knew that the argument was not settled, however, probably because people were asking the wrong kinds of questions. Instead of asking how *much* is contributed by heredity and environment respectively, they should have been asking *how* each makes its particular contributions.

For example, in our present state of knowledge, nothing will enable a child who is born deaf to hear. How differences in environment can affect his future development, however, is a terribly significant factor: With appropriate educational procedures he can develop into a literate, communicating adult; without them, he can remain illiterate and uncommunicative. Concentrating on heredity versus environment obscures the more important problem of determining how education can help each child best use what he has at his disposal.

In recent years, the black community has become more and more vociferous in its objections to the mental test as being biased against them.

The outcry has been especially strong against group testing because these tests depend almost entirely on the child's ability to read. Since the child has to read the questions in order to answer them, blacks question whether the test measures capacity to learn or ability to read. They also argue that IQ tests are self-fulfilling predictions. A child with a low IQ score is placed in slow learning classes, where he learns less, thereby supporting the original score. Prompted by such arguments, many major school systems abandoned group intelligence testing. Individual tests like the Stanford-Binet and the Wechsler Scales are less subject to criticism, since, hopefully, the trained psychologist ensures that the test is administered properly under an optimum testing climate, and is able to evaluate better to what extent a given child's performance is influenced by emotional, motivational, educational, and socioeconomic factors.

Some people have suggested that we discard the IQ test entirely and substitute for it a battery of achievement tests. The problem is that since the achievement test is a sampling of what a child has learned, usually in specific academic subjects, the achievement battery does not provide much information about general learning skills. Others have looked to new methods of measurement which could meet the limitations and criticisms posed by our current models.

One such method has been developed by John Ertl at the University of Ottawa. Dr. Ertl records the brain response to a flashing light by placing electrodes on the motor cortex. By averaging the responses, which are recorded on a computer so as to eliminate noise, he arrives at a score, known as the *evoked potential,* which he claims is a culture-free index of intellectual functioning.

Several drawbacks can be cited to Ertl's approach. For one thing, he has no strong theoretical rationale to support his hypothesis that more intelligent people respond faster to stimulation than do less intelligent ones. The results he reports may be explained, not by the greater (or lesser) strength of the brain, but by the fact that some people are better able to pay attention and to fixate on the light source. In addition, correlations with IQ, although significant, are low—as are correlations on retesting with the same subject. In view of all this, in my opinion, it is doubtful that Ertl's method can be of real use to the teacher, at least at this time.

Previous attempts had been made at developing culture-free scales. For example, an effort was made to remove the middle-class bias of IQ tests by changing the wording of questions and by introducing content more relevant to the lower-class child's background and life experiences.

The results were unsuccessful, and since the task of developing culture-free tests poses difficult problems, it seemed to make better sense to concentrate on improving the environment of the culturally deprived rather than on changing our tests.

As a result, many special programs were started that were designed to educate children from the lower socioeconomic strata. In too many cases, these programs were established in an atmosphere of emergency, with little planning and with limited knowledge of what should constitute suitable curriculums for such classes. Professional educators were not too surprised, therefore, when these programs failed to raise the IQ of black children.

Using the failure of these programs and an impressive array of statistical data, Dr. Jensen shocked many educators when he proposed that the reason these programs failed can be traced to an hereditary inferiority in black children. The great fear this aroused in the minds of socially oriented psychologists and educators is that it might be possible, by misinterpretation, to obtain "proof" that no matter what compensatory education the black child receives, he remains inferior in intellect. Another possible interpretation is that the schools are not to blame if black children fail to achieve academically.

The IQ Argument: Race, Intelligence, and Education (Library Press. 1971), a recent publication by Hans J. Eysenck, a British psychologist, lends support to Jensen's position. Actually, there was nothing so new about Dr. Jensen's position; it's the old nature-nurture controversy in new clothes. It is a fact that blacks as a group score lower than whites as a group on intelligence tests. It is also a fact, however, as Jensen notes, that many blacks score higher than a very large number of whites. People concentrating on the main conclusions in the article tend to forget this.

I recently received a rather touching letter from a young black boy attending an Ivy League college. He wrote: "I was interested that the specific areas in which Jensen indicated blacks were inherently inferior are precisely those areas in which I scored highest in my class. Maybe it was luck." Even he had lost sight of the fact that the Jensen data refer to averages and not to individuals.

It is unfortunate that Jensen presented his material within the context of a racial issue, since the emotional impact of this tends to negate all of what he has to say. Despite its incendiary qualities, the Jensen paper has the major merit of reminding us that we are dealing with a biological organism and that the educational environment is only one of the many influences affecting the growth and development of a given individual.

Black people as a group in America are poor, and poor people are subject to all kinds of health risks deriving from prenatal conditions and malnutrition. The relationship between poverty, health, and learning failure is now receiving the attention it deserves. It is becoming clear that not only does malnutrition play a role in retarded intellectual development but that more than one generation may have to be well-fed before all the effects of dietary deficiency are overcome.

Jensen was premature in evaluating just what portion of the black child's biological structure actually resides in the genes. It is difficult to evaluate the amount of damage caused by health hazards resulting from poverty, or to say how even slight changes in environment can produce large changes in behaviors, even where those behaviors are linked to genetics and biology.

Another criticism of the Jensen material is that the public does not have a clear appreciation of just what kinds of information can be validly drawn from hereditability data. The method used by Jensen and Eysenck can only tell what proportion heredity contributes to the variance of a specified trait in a given population under existing conditions. The data cannot tell us the reason for a given child's low intelligence, the origin of ethnic differences in test performance, or what educational intervention programs can accomplish.

Jensen's article should be credited with helping us recognize that compensatory programs of education in their beginning phases were inadequately structured. That he used these poorly planned programs as a basis for postulating hereditary inferiority in blacks is a major weakness. His reasoning could have proceeded the other way. If the programs failed to raise IQ scores, why place the onus on the black child's shoulders? Why not look at what's wrong with the programs?

A peculiar characteristic of American education is that, although we give lip service to meeting the needs of individual children, we seldom follow through with concrete actions. We meet the needs of individual children as long as they respond to the existing curriculum, but when a child fails to learn under the existing structure, we assume there is something wrong with him. If "meeting the needs of individual children" is to become meaningful, we should consider the possibility that perhaps a particular teaching method is all wrong for a particular child.

Certainly, we can't make wholesale prescriptions for black children as if they were all alike. A black child who is not doing well in school may be more like a white child who is similarly unsuccessful than he is like an achieving black child. The problem of understanding learning deficiencies and of locating appropriate pedagogy for overcoming them is not something we know too much about. The storm over the Jensen article may provide the impetus toward working for a true understanding of education and individual differences.

A first step might well be to define our aims and come to grips with why we test. Are we concerned with measuring the amount of cognitive ability an individual is born with, or do we wish to appraise, by sampling performance, the level of adaptive capacities at his disposal?

Do we seek to predict, by way of one or several tests, what an individual will do 20 years from now? Or do we seek to know how and at what stage educational circumstances might be arranged for the individual to achieve his highest level of intellectual functioning ability? Piaget, among others, has never been impressed with standard IQ tests because they do not lead to an understanding of how intelligence functions. His work is not based on predictions, but rather on assessments of the presence or absence of the essential abilities related to intellectual functioning.

Schools must decide what is the purpose of testing. If all we wish is to separate the bright child from the dull child, the brain-damaged from the neurologically intact, the retarded learner from the gifted, and to attach labels to the children in our schools, we can go on using tests the way we always have, and the argument over genes will continue. But if we mean what we say about meeting individual needs, we can put tests to better use.

The intelligence test, not the IQ score, can tell us the level of the child's functioning in a variety of tasks which measure general intelligence and which are intimately correlated with classroom learning. The goal of testing then becomes to describe the developmental level the child has attained. The next step requires that educators and psychologists together formulate the educational environment necessary to raise the child to the next developmental level.

Mental Health Aspects of the Effects of Discrimination upon Children

JOSEPH H. DOUGLASS

Scientists now are convinced that the more we know of the external forces involved in mental illness, the clearer there is an obviously complex connection between individual pathology and social pathology. The mental health practitioner and his closely allied workers are concerned with the psychological and social climate in which the individual lives in terms of the influences and impact of these factors upon the individual's emotional health and his ability to attain and maintain maximum functional ability.

In general, concepts of mental health include the ability to adapt to one's environment, to perceive reality accurately, to manage stress healthfully, to stand on one's own two feet, to learn and to experience a feeling of well-being. Ego-shattering experiences in early infancy and young childhood can produce tremendously serious and permanent individual harm, severely incapacitating the person's optimal functioning ability and im-

Joseph H. Douglass is Chief in the Office of Interagency Liaison, National Institute of Mental Health, Bethesda, Maryland.

Reprinted with permission from *Young Children* 22(5):298–305, 1967. Copyright © 1967, National Association for the Education of Young Children, 1834 Connecticut Avenue, N.W., Washington, D.C. 20009.

pairing his happiness. Furthermore, it is known now that physical health and mental health, or physical illness and mental illness, always are associated. Thus it is in the context of its harmful effects upon children that racial discrimination is of such central concern to the mental health field. Discrimination can thwart the personality development of children and can impair their characterological development. It adds an additional burden to those critically stressful circumstances with which every young child must cope—a burden which disastrously results in self-concepts of lowered self-esteem. It impairs affective states and processes, reduces cognitive functioning, distorts perceptions of reality, and even surrounds the individual with threats to the security of his person. As if these burdens were not heavy enough, discrimination in our society most often is equated with poverty—an overwhelming lack of those material and emotional resources so desperately needed by the individual to cope effectively with the viscissitudes of life.

Discrimination against children is one of society's greatest mistakes; and we continue to pay the price in broken lives, human pain and suffering, riots, violence and other forms of intergroup hostility, and in numerous other social deficits. Often in dealing with its victims, as someone has noted, "we give up, label them 'psychopathic' and expect them to commit crimes or hurt others. They often live up to our expectations."

The Crisis of Ego Development and Personal-Social Identification

Numerous manifestations of discrimination may be so displaced or otherwise disguised that only a skilled observer or trained therapist is able to identify them and note their relationship to the individual's basic character structure and personality. When children are discriminated against or otherwise deprived in any of a number of ways, their responses may not be conscious mechanisms but they are likely to be manifest in various asocial or anti-social behavior patterns. Heightened ego-defense mechanisms may be exhibited which reflect underlying feelings of insecurity or inferiority and unintegrated core-ego identities. Hostility, aggression, frustration, anxiety and self-hatred are among the reactions which may serve as ego defenses or as other reactions. For some children the experiences of discrimination are traumatic; for others, less so, depending upon the preparation and psychological support they have been given. The development of unintegrated core-identity feelings and the emergence of anxiety-producing self-concepts remain, nevertheless, as ever-present possibilities, if not present realities in the lives of most victims.

The child consciously and unconsciously learns the structure, content and attitudes which constitute his psycho-social environment. He learns from others who he is and what his life's chances are in terms of his family, class and group identification. Thus, variables such as his parent's occupation, the kind of neighborhood in which he lives and the status ascribed to his race, color and religion in comparison with other groups become major considerations and determinants of self-concepts. Doubtless, more than anything else, group membership is the most significant variable in providing the child with feelings of belonging, which in turn have such great significance for his aspirations, his social expectations, his values and allegiances and his beliefs as to what he may do or become.

In sum, it is largely within the child's family and group membership that his values and goals are defined and in which he receives his identity and self-concepts. In addition, as society has become more complex, the extrafamilial social factors have become more important to the understanding of individual personality and neurosis.

Numerous psychological studies have revealed that by four or five years of age, and possibly earlier, the Negro child in America becomes convinced that he is an inferior person. In other words, these Negro children have become prejudiced against themselves at nearly the start of their lives, by accepting the prejudices against them. They perceive themselves as socially rejected by the prestigeful elements of society, and as unworthy of help and affection. As one observer has noted, "The hearts of children can die, their minds close tight at any age, even though their bodies live out the years allotted them."

Almost needless to state, but necessary to re-emphasize, is the fact that in our society today, as a direct correlate of continuing racial discrimination, the Negro child (as one example of many minority groups)—in terms of both poverty and race—inherits an inferior caste-like status, and as a result almost inevitably acquires the negative self-esteem that is the realistic ego reflection of such status.

The content of both white and Negro children's responses shows an awareness of this situation that is marked. Mutual distrust and hostility are normative, and the groups tend to attribute language, behavioral, personality and social differences to one another. Further, children of both groups realize that they differ in life chances for economic and social rewards. Kardiner and Ovesey, among others, find a higher-than-average repressed and suppressed hostility in Negro subjects, a tendency to exaggerated self-hatred, and a white ego-ideal as a result of emulating the white culture in which they live. Goodman's and Clarke's studies of doll preferences also dramatically have shown the extent to which Negro children interiorize a white ego-ideal and negative self-feelings. Other research of this type has shown, further, that Northern Negro children experience many of the same problems found in the South.

The large problems being evidenced by Negroes, as reflected in their disproportionate concentration both in low-income circumstances and in state institutions for the mentally ill, clearly reveal that the mental health needs neither of parents nor children of this group are being met.

Social Class Subordination

Dr. Robert Coles has stated that perhaps statistics have some bit of strange and effective eloquence. If so, he states, they are to be had in profusion: During this decade more than 7,000,000 young people will leave school without graduating, and one-third of them will have an eighth-grade education or less; one-third of the young men now turning 18 would be rejected by the Selective Service System if they were examined, half of them because they could not pass the mental examinations, the remainder because of failure to qualify physically. While it is impossible to determine what the nature or role of racial discrimination may be in contributing to these conditions, this circumstance had led numerous observers to reach the conclusion that it seems probable that our society actually discovers and develops no more than perhaps half its potential intellectual talent.

It is in the sense of both alienation and social class subordination that the group in which the discriminated child belongs, or with which he is identified, takes on such mental health importance and significance in terms of not only the development of his ego structure but also his interpersonal relations. If, as Dr. Spock, among others, has observed, white children are told that they must avoid Negroes because they are undesirable or bad, they are really being taught that they must be afraid of them. This kind of fear also produces hate in addition to producing feelings of alienation. Thus, both white and Negro children know fear, apprehension and uncertainty in their orientations toward one another as a result of discrimination, and, as recently pointed out by the Center for the Study of Democratic Institutions, "the tragedy of discrimination is that it provides an excuse for failure while it erects barriers to success."

The late Dr. Charles S. Johnson, an eminent authority in human relations, indicated that the frustration accompanying the feelings of subordination encountered by Negro children may take a variety of forms—direct aggression, antisocial behavior, neurotic repressions, withdrawal from the world of reality, chronic avoidance or fantastic patterns of displacement, or deflection of aggression. Thus, as other observers also have noted, generalized feelings of inadequacy and unworthiness make discriminated-against children prone to overrespond with anxiety to any threatened situation. On the other hand, as Dr. Fritz Redl put it, "a lot of youthful 'defiant' behavior is *not* the outcropping of a corrupt or morbid personality, but the defense of a healthy one against the kind of treatment that shouldn't happen to a dog, but often does happen to children."

Racial discrimination, of course, hit Negro children with special force for their group has continued to be subordinated in our society and has been compelled to accept a measure of long-term isolation based upon the sometimes subtle and sometimes not-so-subtle premise of basic and immutable differences from the rest of the population. Not only has segregation as a function of discrimination become the norm in our society, but in addition, as Eunice Grier states, "despite the tremendous gains of the past 20 years in the educational achievements of Negroes, despite their gains in employment, and despite their increased money income, the bulk of Negroes are still inadequately educated, severely restricted in their opportunities for good jobs, and very poor."

A "Culture of Poverty"

As is being increasingly borne out in anti-poverty efforts, the known effects of these circumstances are to create and maintain a "culture of poverty," "cultural deprivation," a "poverty syndrome," or social class subordination. Under these conditions, struggle and adaptation to the severest psychic and social stresses are an everyday experience and a way of life. For example, Negroes in the Aid to Dependent Children Program represent about 44 percent of the case-load. In other aspects, admission rates to state mental hospitals continue to be considerably higher for non-white adolescents and adults than for whites.

It is hypothesized that *emotional depression* may be the prevalent life style of many lower-class members and that this depression has its origins in overwhelming anxiety associated with the powerful frustrations and threats which surround the slum-dweller from infancy to old age. Persistently, welfare data shows that there are apparently higher rates of child abuse, child neglect, delinquency, crime, vandalism and general social deviancy in the so called "lower-lower class."

Further, as Dr. Chilman has noted, the nonwhite individual has a particular source of frustration in American society in that there is no way that he can move into full membership in the majority group through his own efforts and achievement. "No matter what educational-occupational level he achieves, no matter what behavior patterns he adopts, he remains nonwhite. So long as our society maintains a 'success image' as being Caucasian, the nonwhite person must experience, in one way or another, a sense of deviancy." Thus, much of the pathological behavior which ordinarily carries a racial or nationality group label continues to be linked with lower-class status with its accompanying social, psychological and economic limitations.

Complete Insulation Unattainable

The most devastating aspects of these circumstances which both produce and support discrimination reflect the probability that no minority child can be fully insulated against the possibility of being made to feel, through inference, word or action, that he is not only "alien" to but "beneath" the normative standards of our society; and that, accordingly, he may neither aspire to the goals of, nor achieve full acceptance in, the majority society, though its models and values are constantly held up to him. "Ironically," according to Lola M. Irelan of the U.S. Welfare Administration, "it appears that the people most in need of medical services are the ones who least often procure them. The poor are simultaneously subjected to increased health hazards and insulated from sources of help."

Similarly, another person has noted that "those pockets of poverty are also pockets of many kinds of psychopathology, mostly untreated." Answering his question of what happens to the neuroses and psychoses of the millions of the poor, Dr. Coles states: "They live with them and die with them or of them. In cities, violence, vagrancy, alcoholism, addiction, apathy . . . high murder rates, high delinquency rates bespeak the hopelessness which becomes depression, the doubts which become paranoia, the confusions which become addiction, the frantic attempt to make sense of a senseless world which becomes drunkenness or sudden irrational ferocity."

In addition to their being the victims of discrimination, nonwhite families contain approximately 40 percent of all children under six in poverty. Accordingly, it is not unrealistic to expect that they would evidence disproportionate degrees of immaturity, psychopathic behavior, and retardation of growth, speech and intellect.

Social and Asocial Consequences

With generally less ego strength, the very poor individual is apt to have greater need than his middle-class counterpart for security-giving psychological defenses. Lewis Yablonsky recently observed that:

In the modern disorganized slum, the gang has been for many Negro youths their only source of identity, status and emotional satisfaction. Ill-trained to participate with any degree of success in the dominant middle-class world of rigid ideas, community centers and adult demands, they construct their own community. They set goals that are achievable; they build an empire, partly real and partly fantasy, that helps them live through the confusion of adolescence. . . . He will kill if need be to maintain his position of self-styled integrity in the gang. . . .

For the Negro youngster growing up in places like Watts or Harlem, the schools, community centers, even the modern Job Corps are foreign lands.

Many children, for example, show signs of delinquency early in life. As they mature, their offenses frequently become progressively more serious. Many show a distribution coincident with poverty, lack of education, core city residence, unemployment and minority group membership. Drs. Norris Hansell and William G. Smith have observed that one kind of offender is fully oriented in time and space with no clear alteration in cognitive functions such as perceptions, memory or ability to vision logically. He is, however, impulsive, lacks judgment in complicated decision-making involving the consequences of his actions, and often manifests little ability to tolerate frustration or postpone action. He lacks adequate emotional attachment to persons or groups, and shows little feeling of guilt for actions victimizing others and little remorse or anguish about the offense. His values often include heavy emphasis on toughness, gang memberships, risk taking, predatory skills and opposition to the values of the mainstream of society.

In a very important significant way, Drs. Gisela Konopka and Jack V. Wallinga, of the Minnesota Children's Center, have reported on some children who present primarily severe character disorders, often with delinquent, prepsychotic and psychotic symptoms. Most of these children have suffered severe emotional trauma and deprivation; and their impulse-ridden, impoverished egos and defective superegos produce aggressive, destructive, acting-out behavior. To these children the Center offers a therapeutic, group-work oriented milieu supplemented with intensive individual casework and psychiatric therapy. In the opinion of these doctors, these children have in common what appear to be manifestations of immunity to anxiety. As they state, these children do not merely *pretend* indifference, they have *acquired* it. They ward off human involvement. Since no anxiety is felt, such children may seem to lack conscience. Their anxiety is not hidden—it has vanished, and it cannot be produced, at least not through the same stimuli that normally produce anxiety. They are not only *insulated,* they are actually *immunized.*

One child reports: "You think it is hard to meet a new family? What difference does it make? It's about the tenth time in my life. I only know one thing for sure: Don't get too close to people. Otherwise, you get hurt."

Such are some of the mental health concerns with the lives of the millions of children in our Nation which is the richest that mankind has ever known.

Selected Implications

Data from the National Institute of Mental Health indicate that an adolescent may move from his intolerable family life to a delinquent gang, to a hospital for drug addicts with alarming rapidity. To respond effectively, society's mechanisms for attempting to restore the child to more normal behavior must also be mobile and continuous, varying—to follow the same example—from strengthening family life to street corner social work, to rehabilitation efforts in the hospital, and often all of these in combination. With NIMH support, a psychoanalyst is working on new means of assessing psychopathology in childhood. She and her associates at a clinic are attempting to construct, at various stages, psychological pictures of the child, utilizing psychodynamics, social, genetic and adaptive data. Since the profile includes information on both the ill and the healthy parts of the child's personality, the investigator believes such a profile can contribute to knowledge about normal variations and indicate deviations before pathologic formations occur.

A highly promising means of prevention and treatment that NIMH has helped to pioneer is the field of family therapy. Projects here aim to develop and test clinical methods for improvement of interpersonal communication within families, and to show how modification of environmental factors may serve to modify a child's behavior. In a number of states the mental health staffs of school systems are utilizing family interview techniques with parents of children having behavior or learning problems. This practice has proved helpful in focusing on the personality problem inherent in behavioral and academic lags.

The NIMH also has reported that children with hospitalized parents suffer severe disruption, particularly those from lower socioeconomic groups living in large urban centers where there is a minimum of resources, in terms of both finances and neighborliness, to support the broken family. An investigator studied 50 families of hospitalized parents from 14 small towns, and reported that over half the children were experiencing difficulties—neurotic traits, health difficulties (nearly 40 percent of the children had been hospitalized during this period), behavioral and school problems. A "community intervention" scale was devised to measure the effectiveness of the community's agencies in meeting child care needs. These and other activities are re-emphasizing the idea of comprehensive treatment, provided in the community *for all* who need it, as a new concept and challenge.

As we continue to confront the problems, let it be recalled that out-patient psychiatric clinics in the United States serve more persons in the 10- through 19-year age group than in any other decade of life. Let it also be re-emphasized over and over again that the harmful effects of discrimination are not limited to its victims alone but affect those who perpetrate it in many adverse ways as well.

Goals of prevention, early diagnosis and early treatment continue to guide the work of those in the child mental health field and in youth serving organizations. But these goals are very difficult to attain. Often the sick child is not recognized early, treatment comes too late or not at all, or it is simply not effective.

Perhaps in a most important and significant way we are too busy in our efforts to treat the symptoms and results of our psychological and social difficulties rather than their causes. Even if we were to redirect our efforts, however, improvement of conditions depends both upon advances in knowledge and upon demonstrations of how these advances can be applied. One thing seems certain—we can and should rid ourselves of many persistent absurdities which are not in keeping with our stature as a great nation or with ourselves as a great people.

Index of Contributors